Shojo Beat

Tail of the Moon

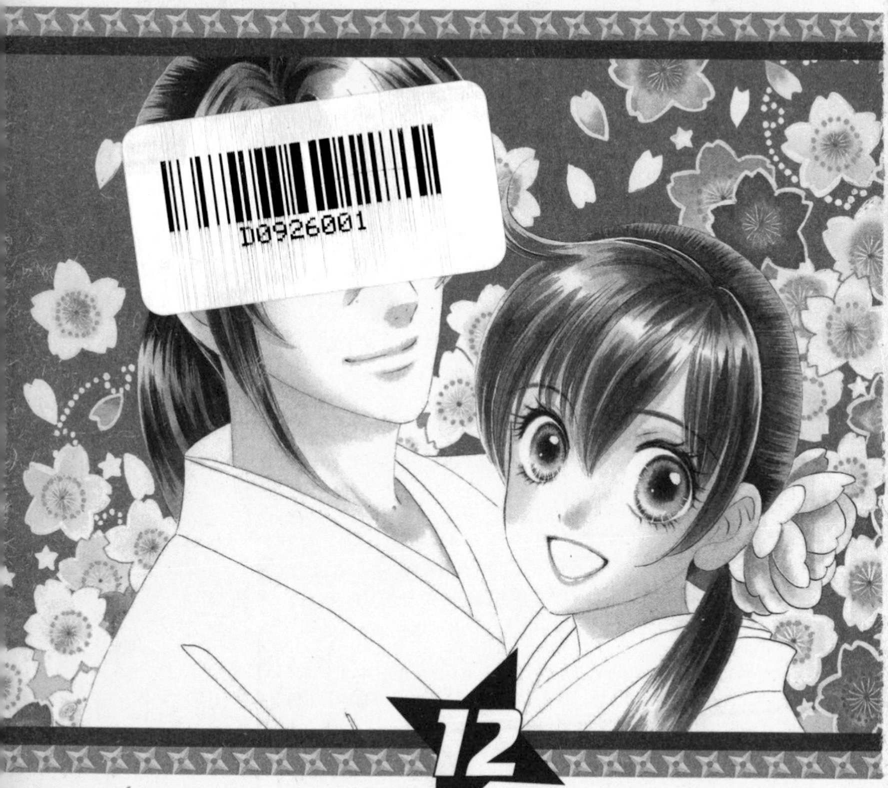

12

Story & Art by

Rinko Ueda

Tail of the Moon

Volume 12

CONTENTS

Story Thus Far...

It is the Era of the Warring States. Usagi is a failure as a ninja, but she is a skilled herbalist. She is working hard to qualify as a ninja so she can be the bride of Hattori Hanzo (aka "Shimo no Hanzo")!

Because Mamezo had gone missing in the Capital, Usagi searches for him and finally finds him inside a huge mansion. It turns out that Mamezo is actually the son of a court noble. Usagi decides to leave him, believing that he would have a better life there. Before returning to Iga, Usagi drops by to see Mamezo one last time. Mamezo clings to Usagi, claiming that he wants to go back to Iga with her. Seeing the strong bond between the two of them, Mamezo's grandfather entrusts Mamezo to Usagi.

Meanwhile, Oda Nobunaga decides to attack Iga once again and orders Mitsuhide Akechi to lead the army. Having no knowledge of this, Usagi and the others head back to Iga happily...

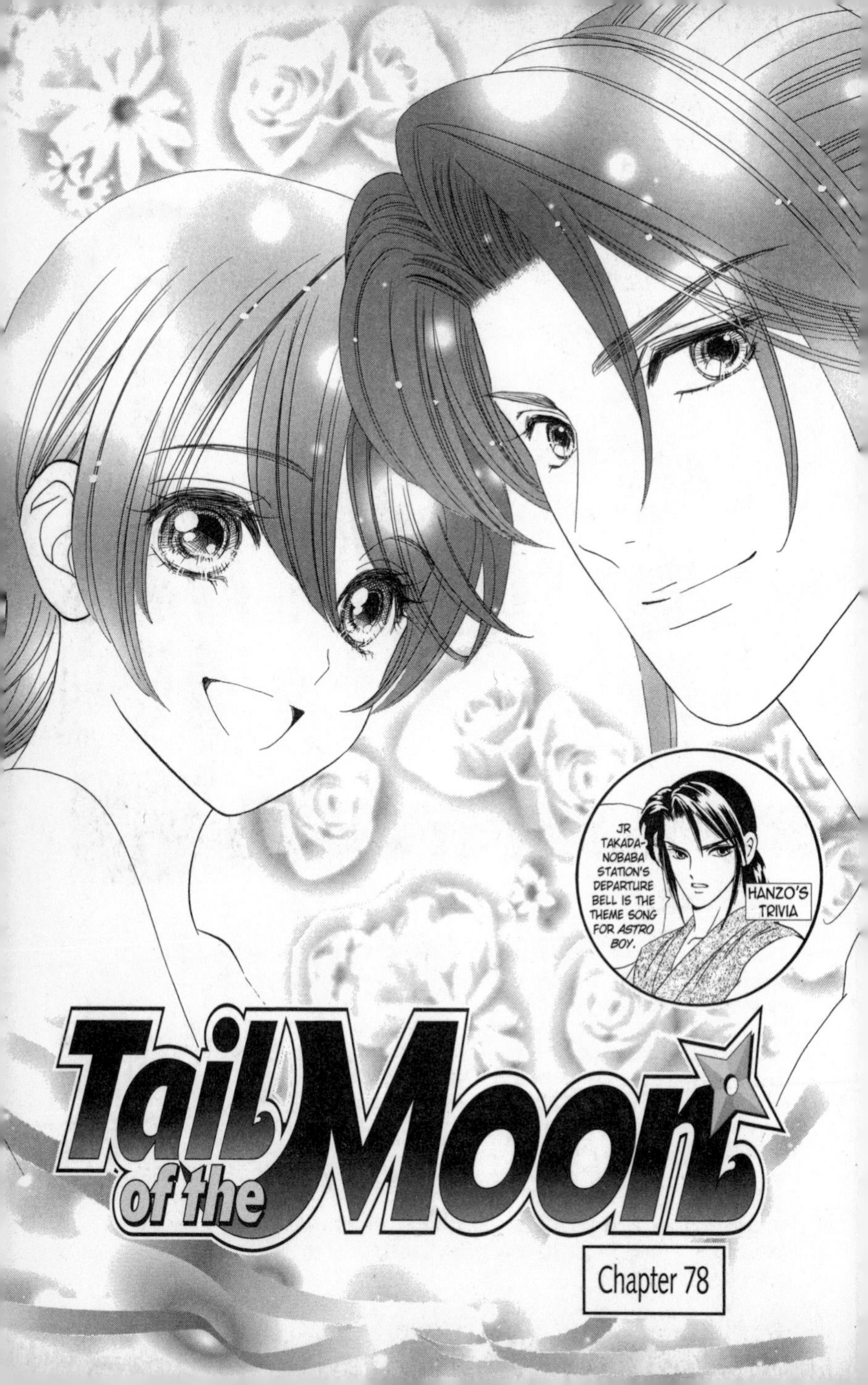
JR TAKADA-NOBABA STATION'S DEPARTURE BELL IS THE THEME SONG FOR *ASTRO BOY*.
HANZO'S TRIVIA
Tail of the Moon
Chapter 78

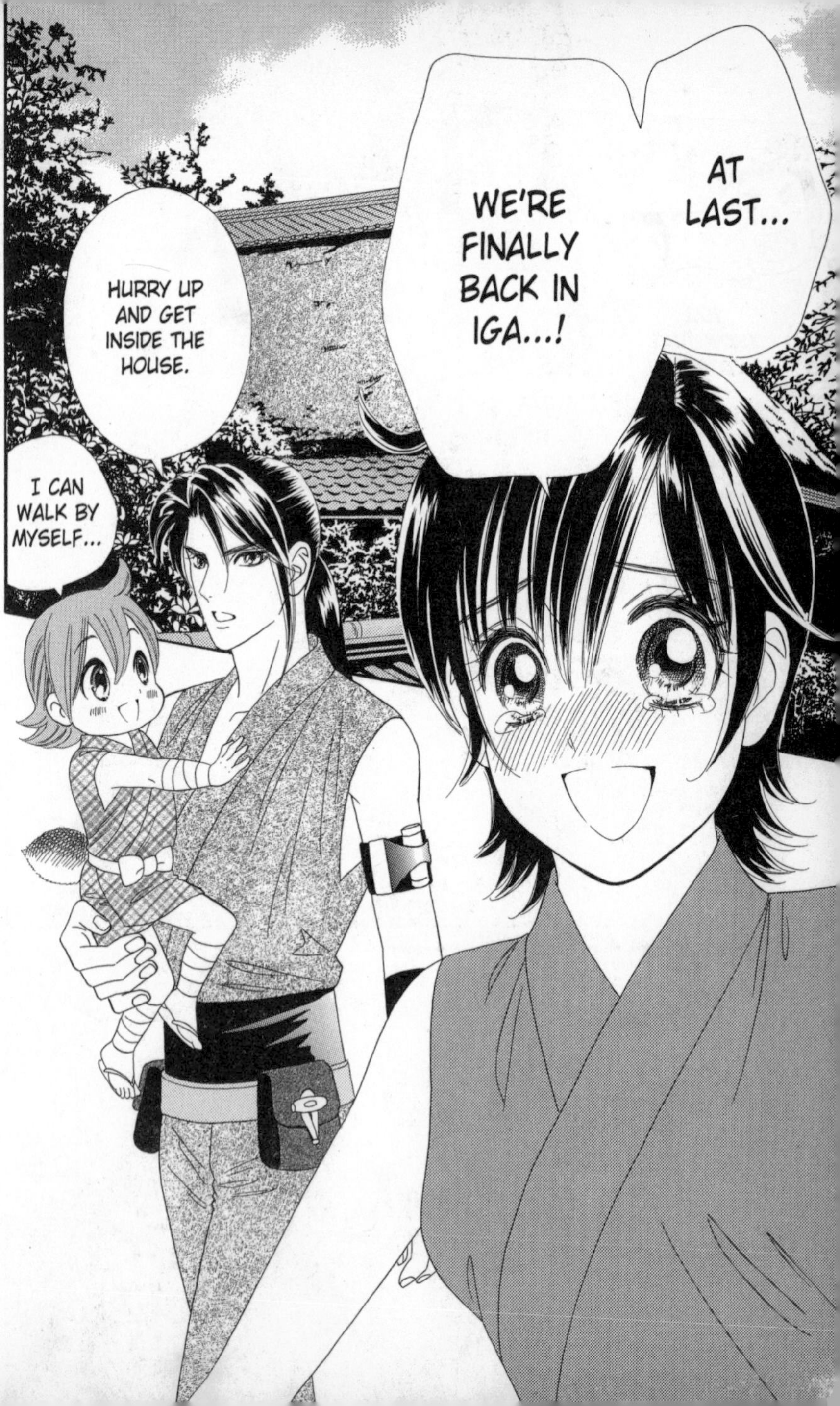
AT LAST...
WE'RE FINALLY BACK IN IGA...!
HURRY UP AND GET INSIDE THE HOUSE.
I CAN WALK BY MYSELF...

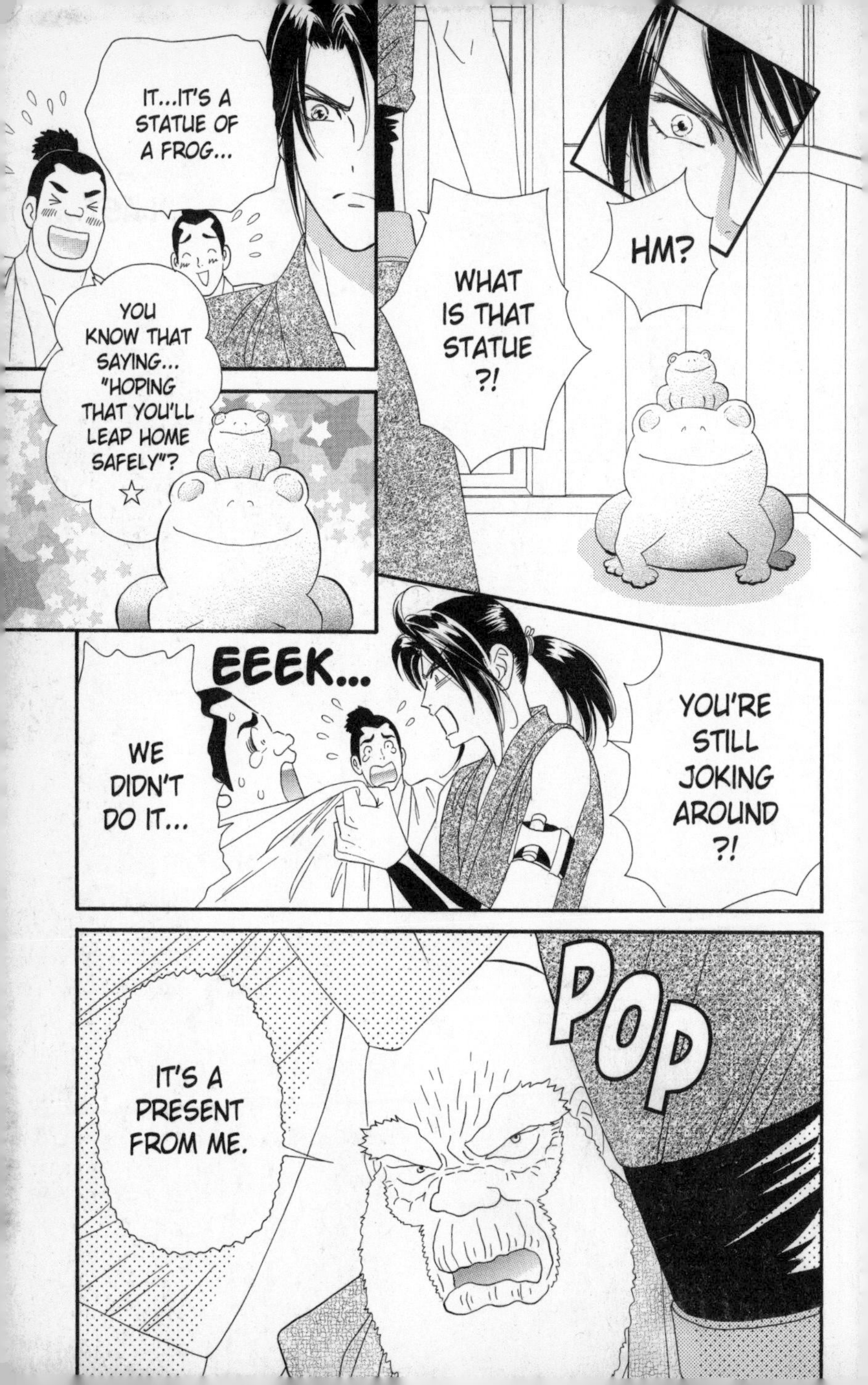
HM?
WHAT IS THAT STATUE?!
IT...IT'S A STATUE OF A FROG...
YOU KNOW THAT SAYING... "HOPING THAT YOU'LL LEAP HOME SAFELY"? ☆
YOU'RE STILL JOKING AROUND?!
EEEK...
WE DIDN'T DO IT...
POP
IT'S A PRESENT FROM ME.

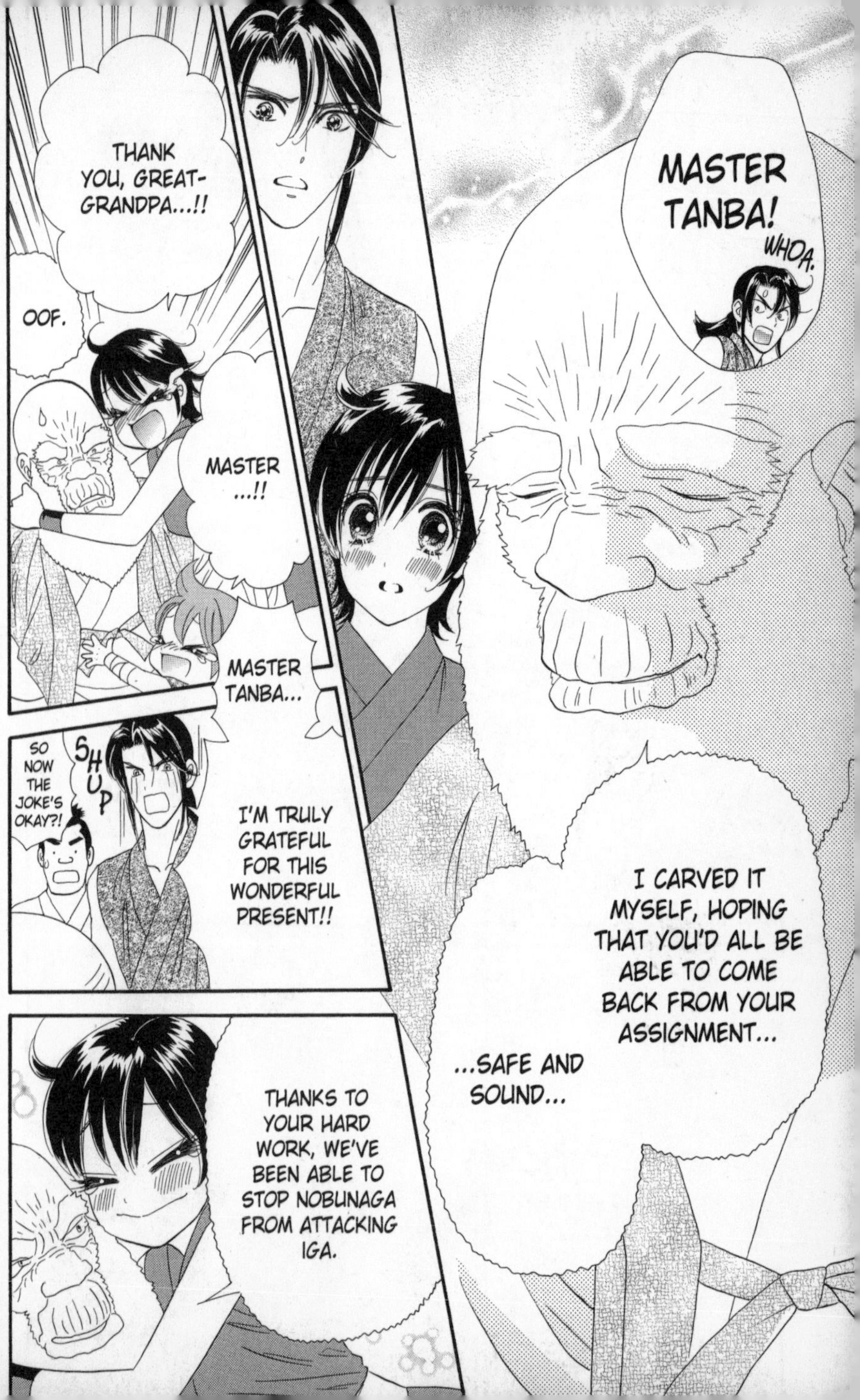
MASTER TANBA!
WHOA.
I CARVED IT MYSELF, HOPING THAT YOU'D ALL BE ABLE TO COME BACK FROM YOUR ASSIGNMENT...
...SAFE AND SOUND...
MASTER TANBA...
THANK YOU, GREAT-GRANDPA...!!
MASTER ...!!
OOF.
I'M TRULY GRATEFUL FOR THIS WONDERFUL PRESENT!!
SHUP
SO NOW THE JOKE'S OKAY?!
THANKS TO YOUR HARD WORK, WE'VE BEEN ABLE TO STOP NOBUNAGA FROM ATTACKING IGA.

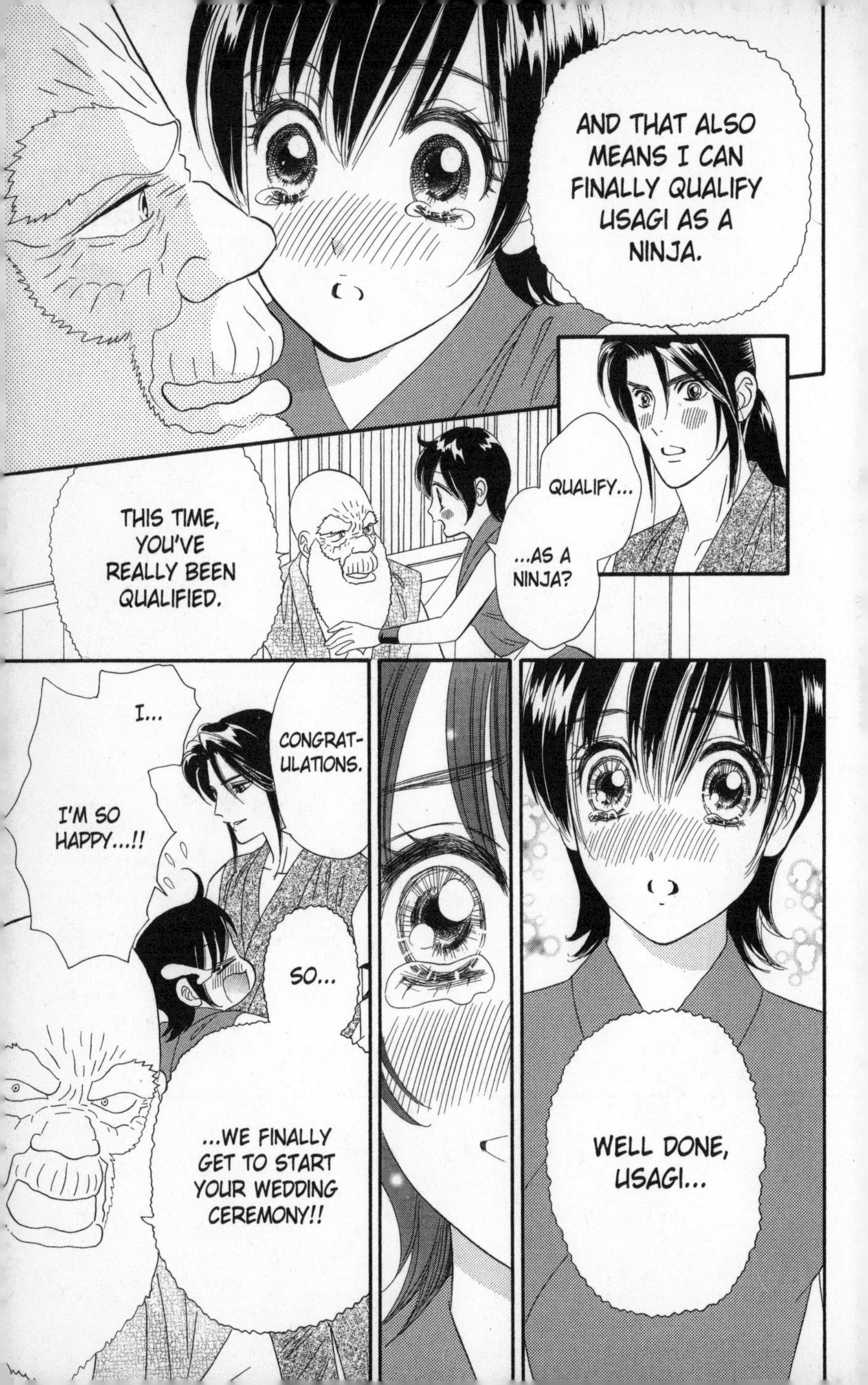
AND THAT ALSO MEANS I CAN FINALLY QUALIFY USAGI AS A NINJA.
QUALIFY...
...AS A NINJA?
THIS TIME, YOU'VE REALLY BEEN QUALIFIED.
WELL DONE, USAGI...
CONGRAT-ULATIONS.
I...
I'M SO HAPPY...!!
SO...
...WE FINALLY GET TO START YOUR WEDDING CEREMONY!!

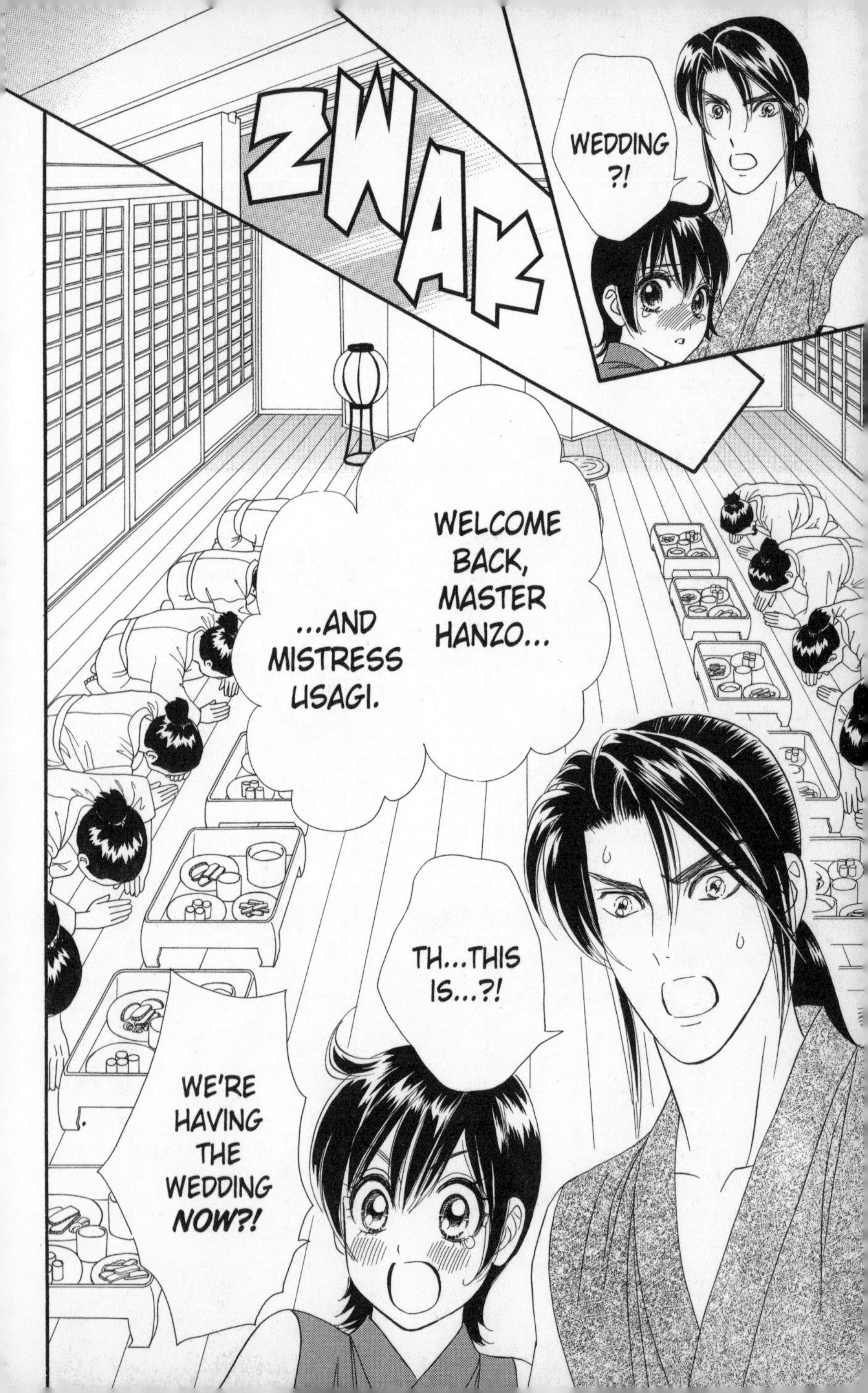
ZWAK
WEDDING ?!
WELCOME BACK, MASTER HANZO...
...AND MISTRESS USAGI.
TH...THIS IS...?!
WE'RE HAVING THE WEDDING NOW?!

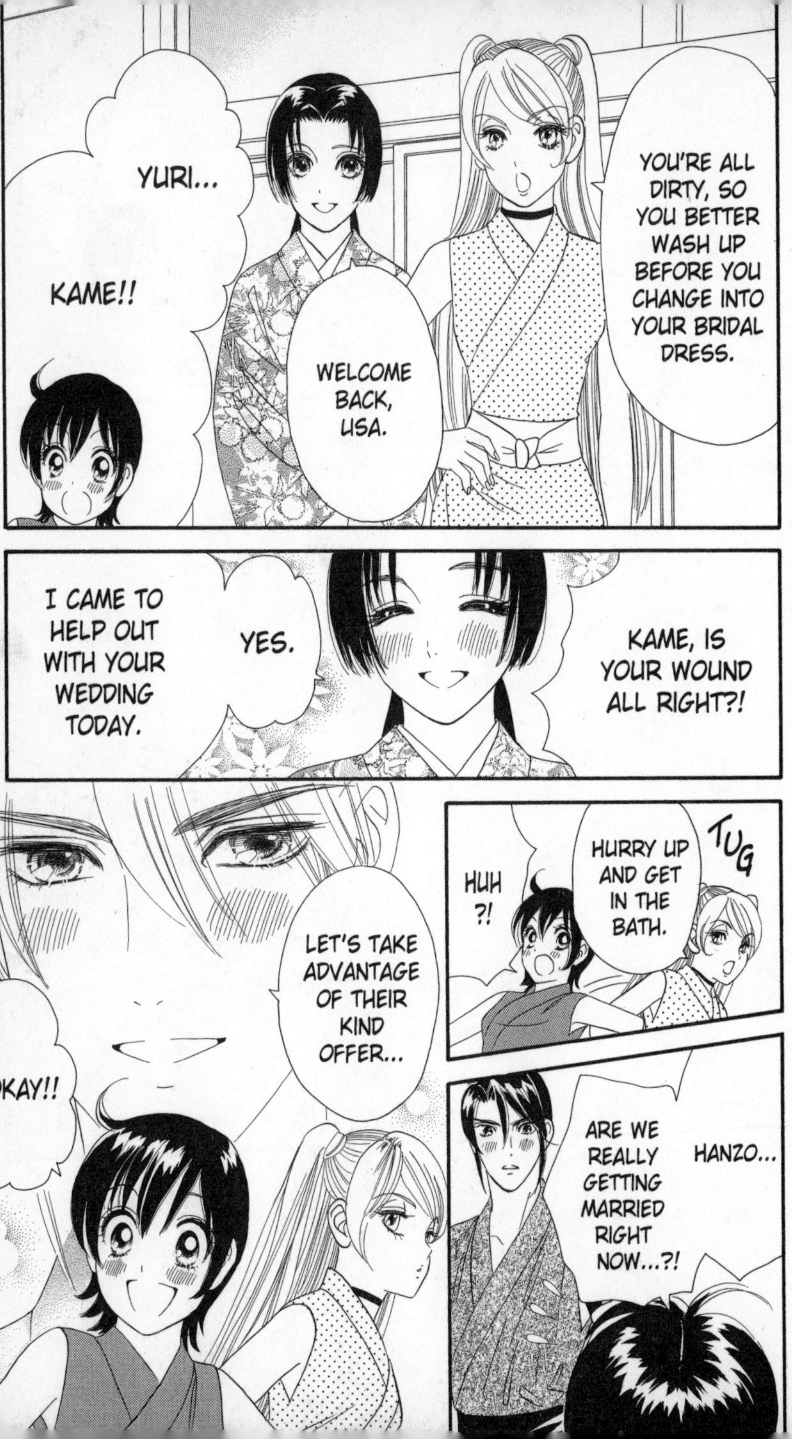
YOU'RE ALL DIRTY, SO YOU BETTER WASH UP BEFORE YOU CHANGE INTO YOUR BRIDAL DRESS.
WELCOME BACK, USA.
YURI...
KAME!!
KAME, IS YOUR WOUND ALL RIGHT?!
YES.
I CAME TO HELP OUT WITH YOUR WEDDING TODAY.
TUG
HURRY UP AND GET IN THE BATH.
HUH?!
HANZO...
ARE WE REALLY GETTING MARRIED RIGHT NOW...?!
LET'S TAKE ADVANTAGE OF THEIR KIND OFFER...
OKAY!!

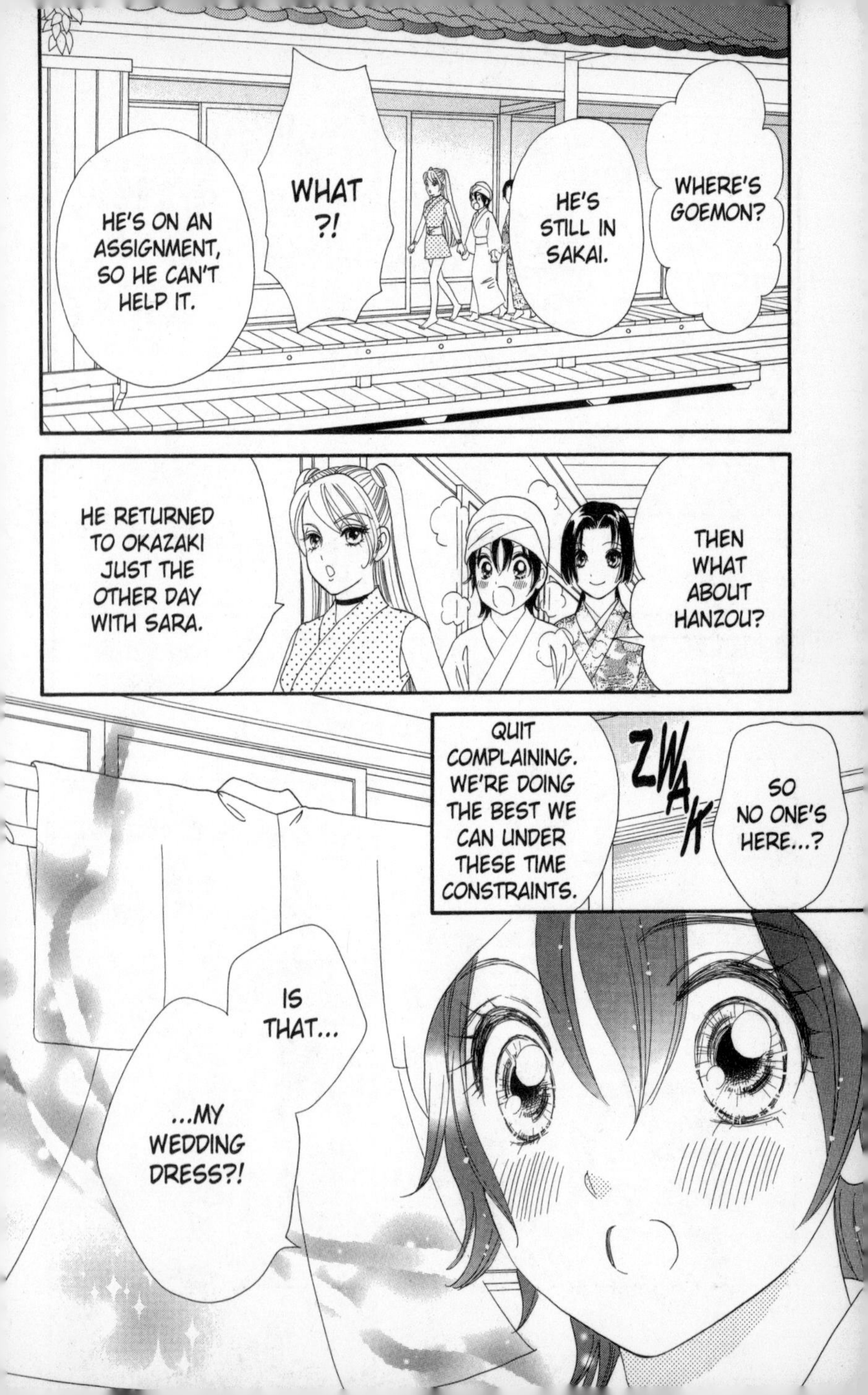
WHERE'S GOEMON?
HE'S STILL IN SAKAI.
WHAT ?!
HE'S ON AN ASSIGNMENT, SO HE CAN'T HELP IT.
THEN WHAT ABOUT HANZOU?
HE RETURNED TO OKAZAKI JUST THE OTHER DAY WITH SARA.
SO NO ONE'S HERE...?
ZWAK
QUIT COMPLAINING. WE'RE DOING THE BEST WE CAN UNDER THESE TIME CONSTRAINTS.
IS THAT...
...MY WEDDING DRESS?!

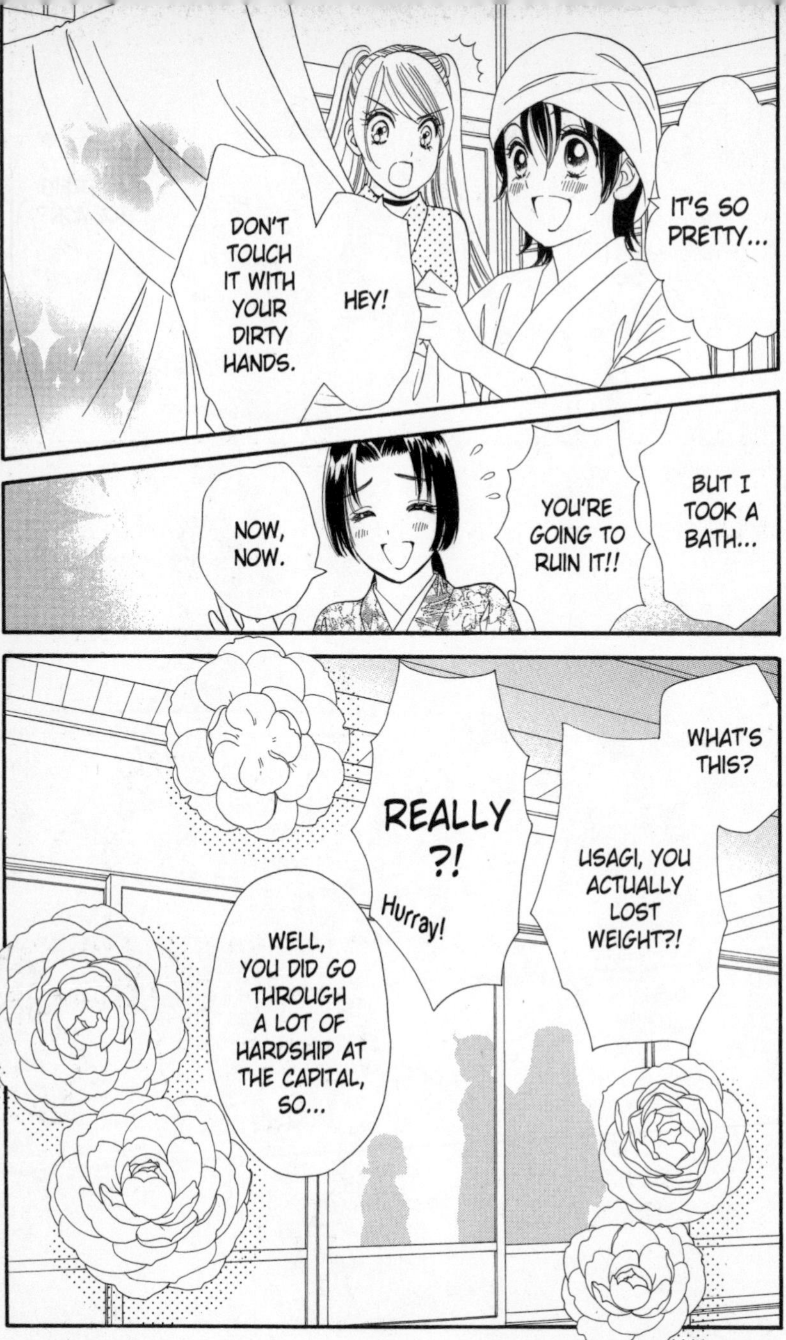
IT'S SO PRETTY...
HEY!
DON'T TOUCH IT WITH YOUR DIRTY HANDS.
BUT I TOOK A BATH...
YOU'RE GOING TO RUIN IT!!
NOW, NOW.
WHAT'S THIS?
USAGI, YOU ACTUALLY LOST WEIGHT?!
REALLY?!
Hurray!
WELL, YOU DID GO THROUGH A LOT OF HARDSHIP AT THE CAPITAL, SO...

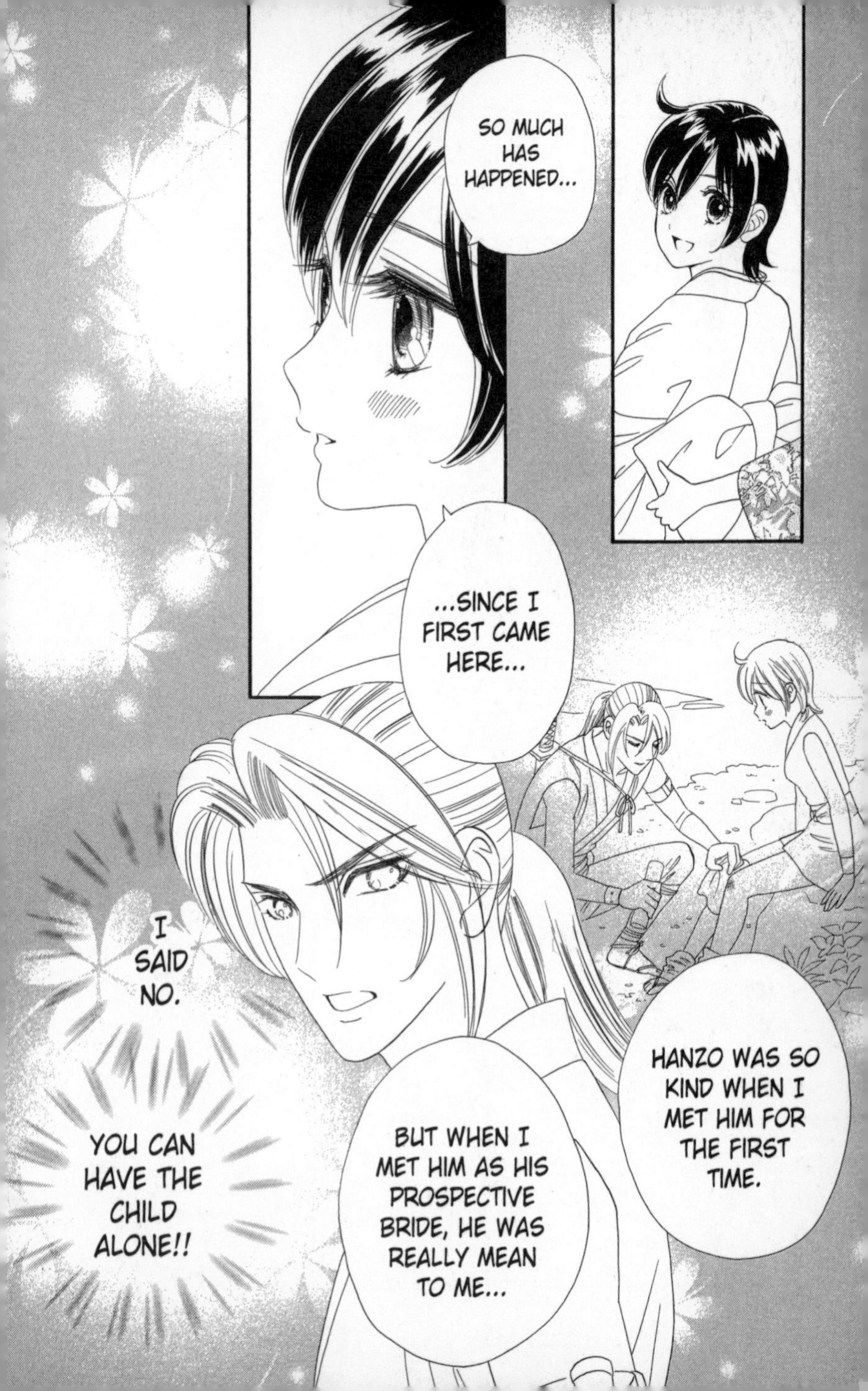
SO MUCH HAS HAPPENED...
...SINCE I FIRST CAME HERE...
HANZO WAS SO KIND WHEN I MET HIM FOR THE FIRST TIME.
BUT WHEN I MET HIM AS HIS PROSPECTIVE BRIDE, HE WAS REALLY MEAN TO ME...
I SAID NO.
YOU CAN HAVE THE CHILD ALONE!!

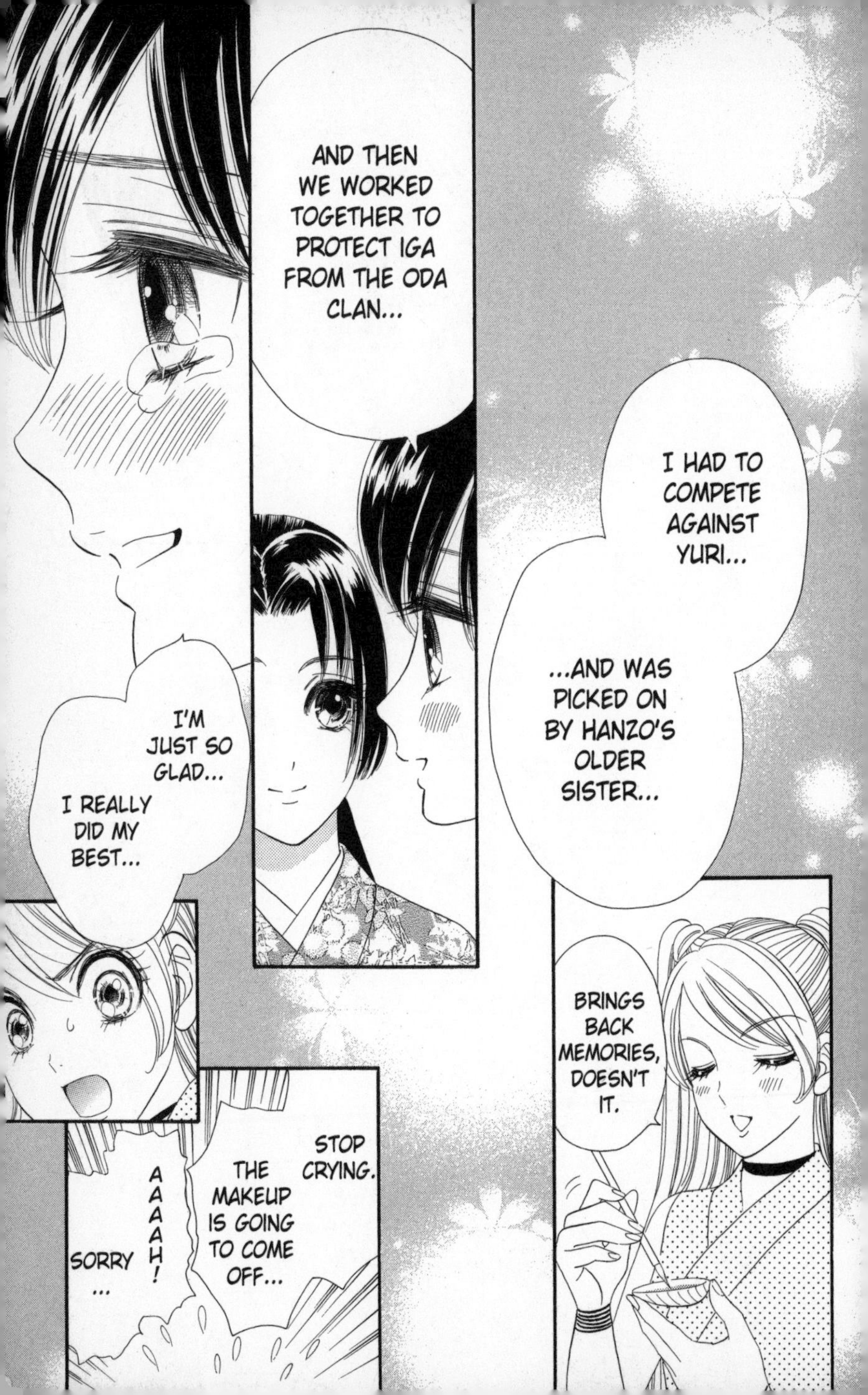
I HAD TO COMPETE AGAINST YURI...
...AND WAS PICKED ON BY HANZO'S OLDER SISTER...
AND THEN WE WORKED TOGETHER TO PROTECT IGA FROM THE ODA CLAN...
I'M JUST SO GLAD...
I REALLY DID MY BEST...
BRINGS BACK MEMORIES, DOESN'T IT.
STOP CRYING.
THE MAKEUP IS GOING TO COME OFF...
AAAAH!
SORRY ...

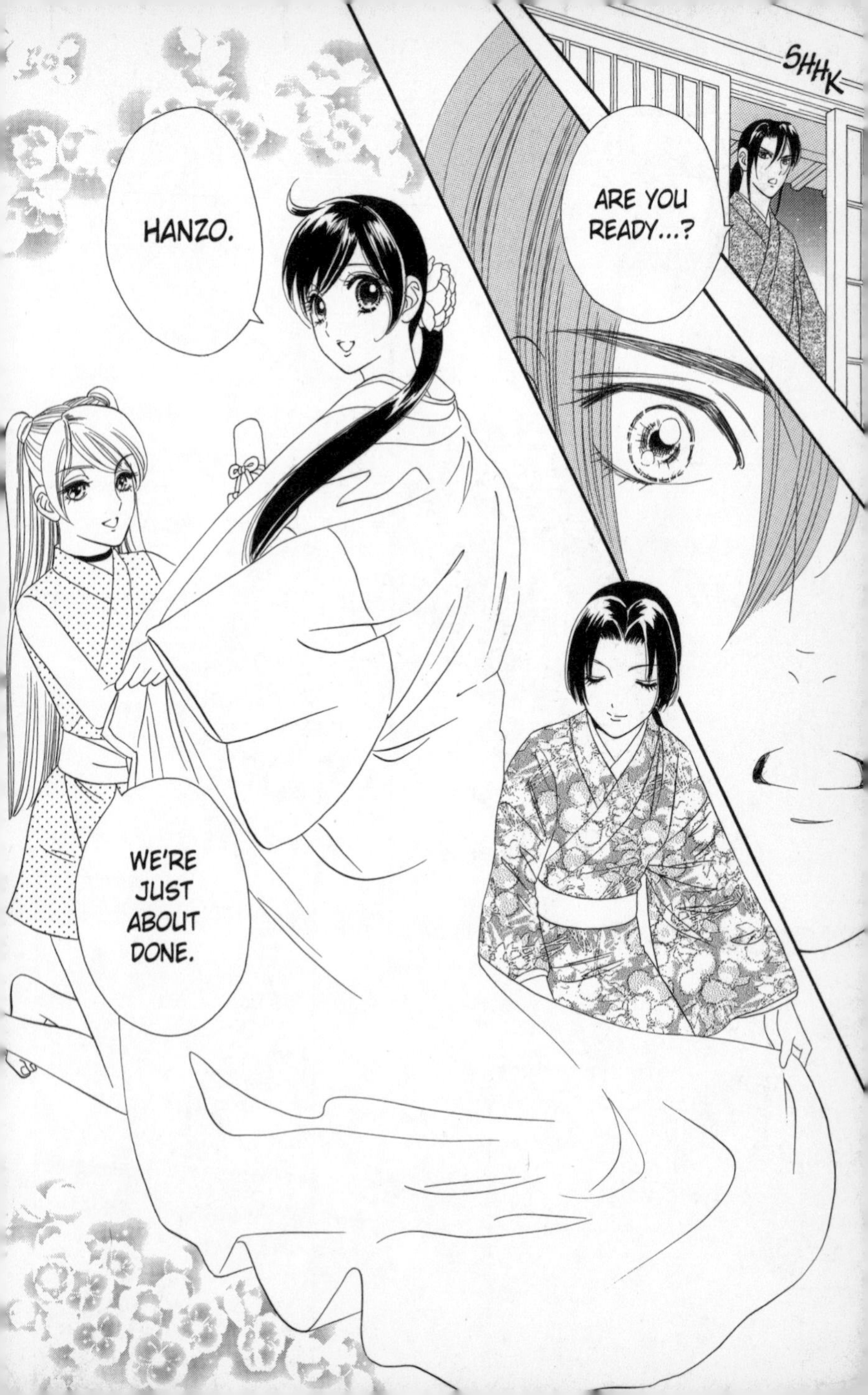
SHHK
ARE YOU READY...?
HANZO.
WE'RE JUST ABOUT DONE.

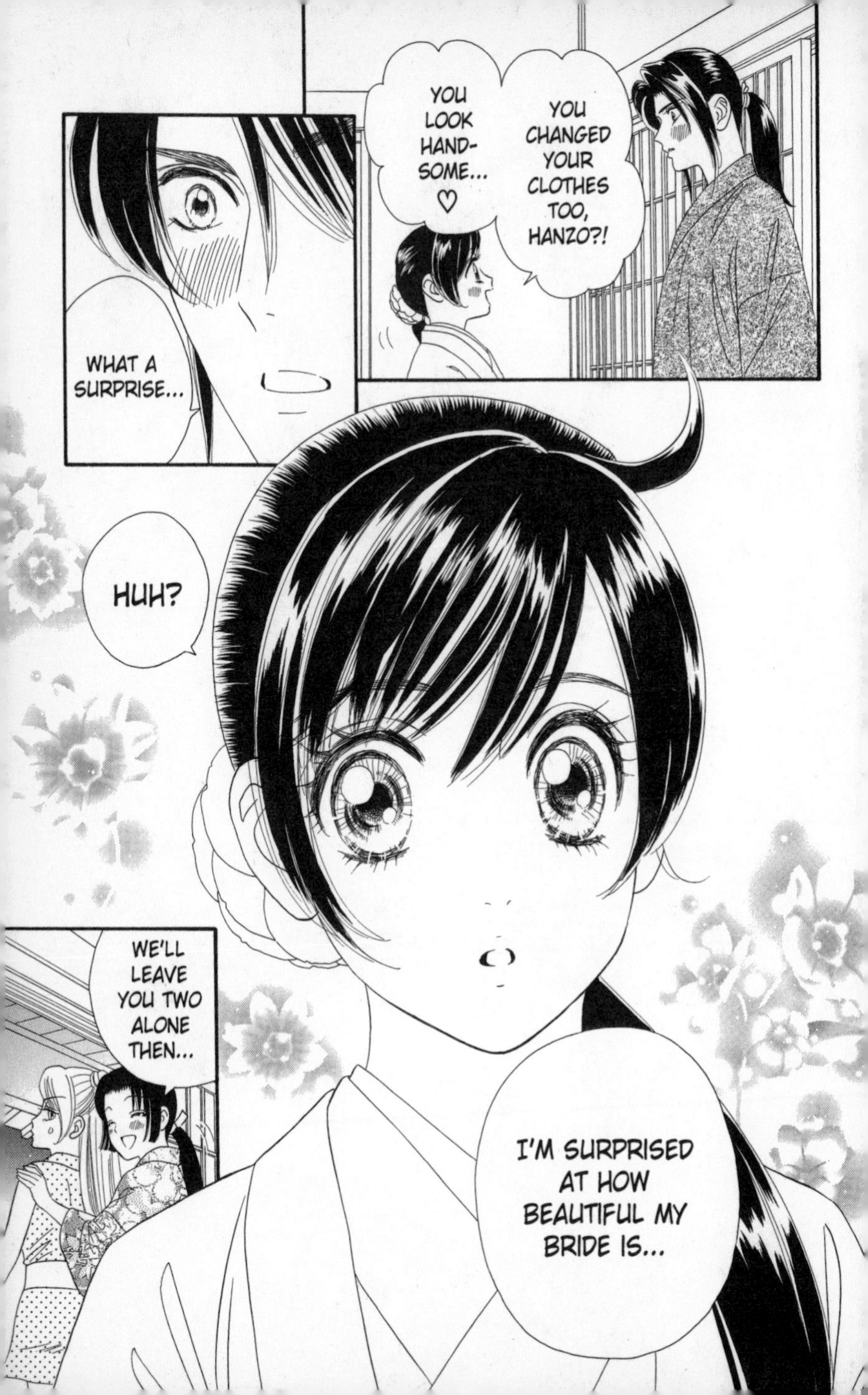
YOU CHANGED YOUR CLOTHES TOO, HANZO?!
YOU LOOK HAND-SOME... ♡
WHAT A SURPRISE...
HUH?
I'M SURPRISED AT HOW BEAUTIFUL MY BRIDE IS...
WE'LL LEAVE YOU TWO ALONE THEN...

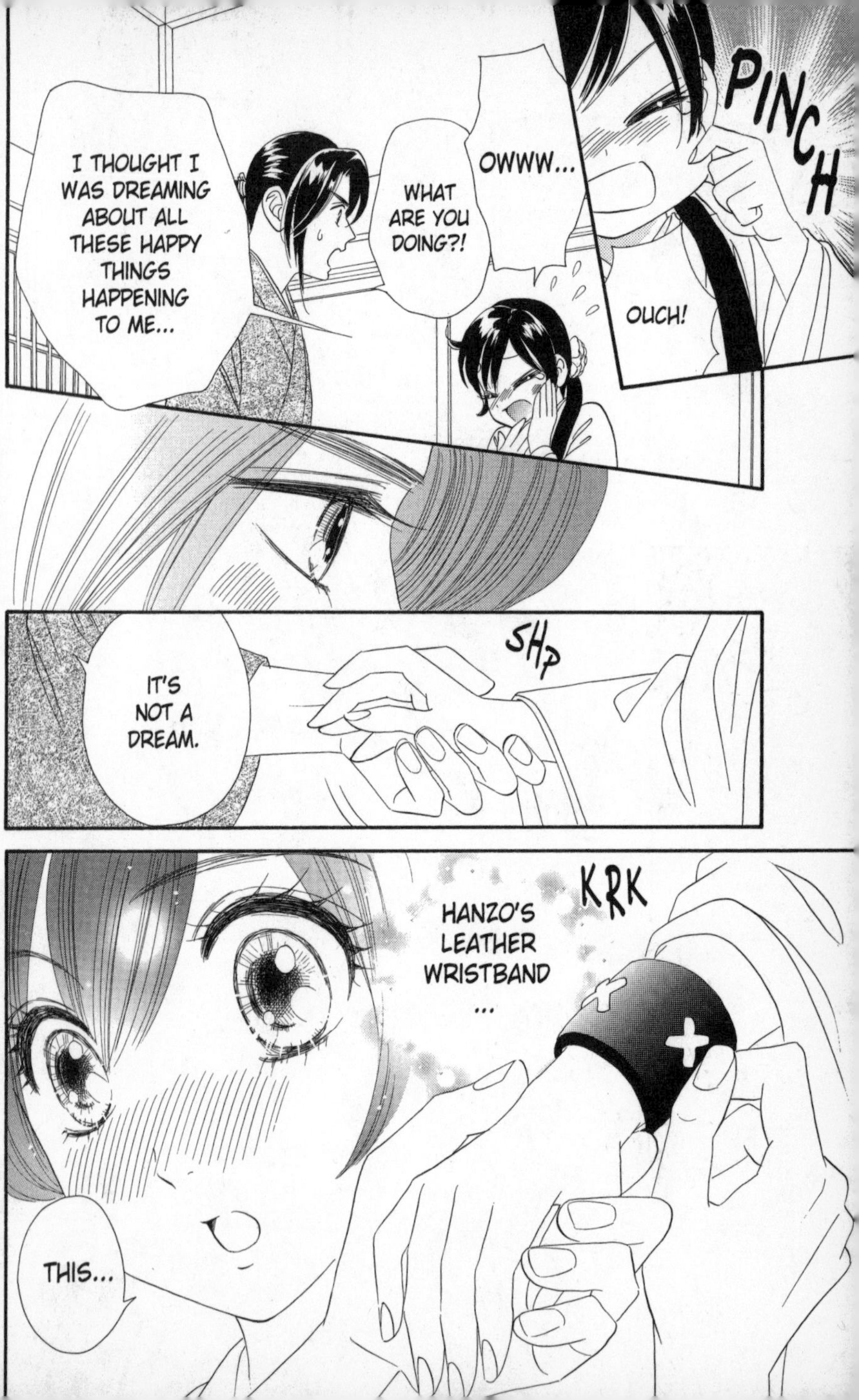
PINCH
OUCH!
OWWW...
WHAT ARE YOU DOING?!
I THOUGHT I WAS DREAMING ABOUT ALL THESE HAPPY THINGS HAPPENING TO ME...
SHP
IT'S NOT A DREAM.
KRK
HANZO'S LEATHER WRISTBAND ...
THIS...

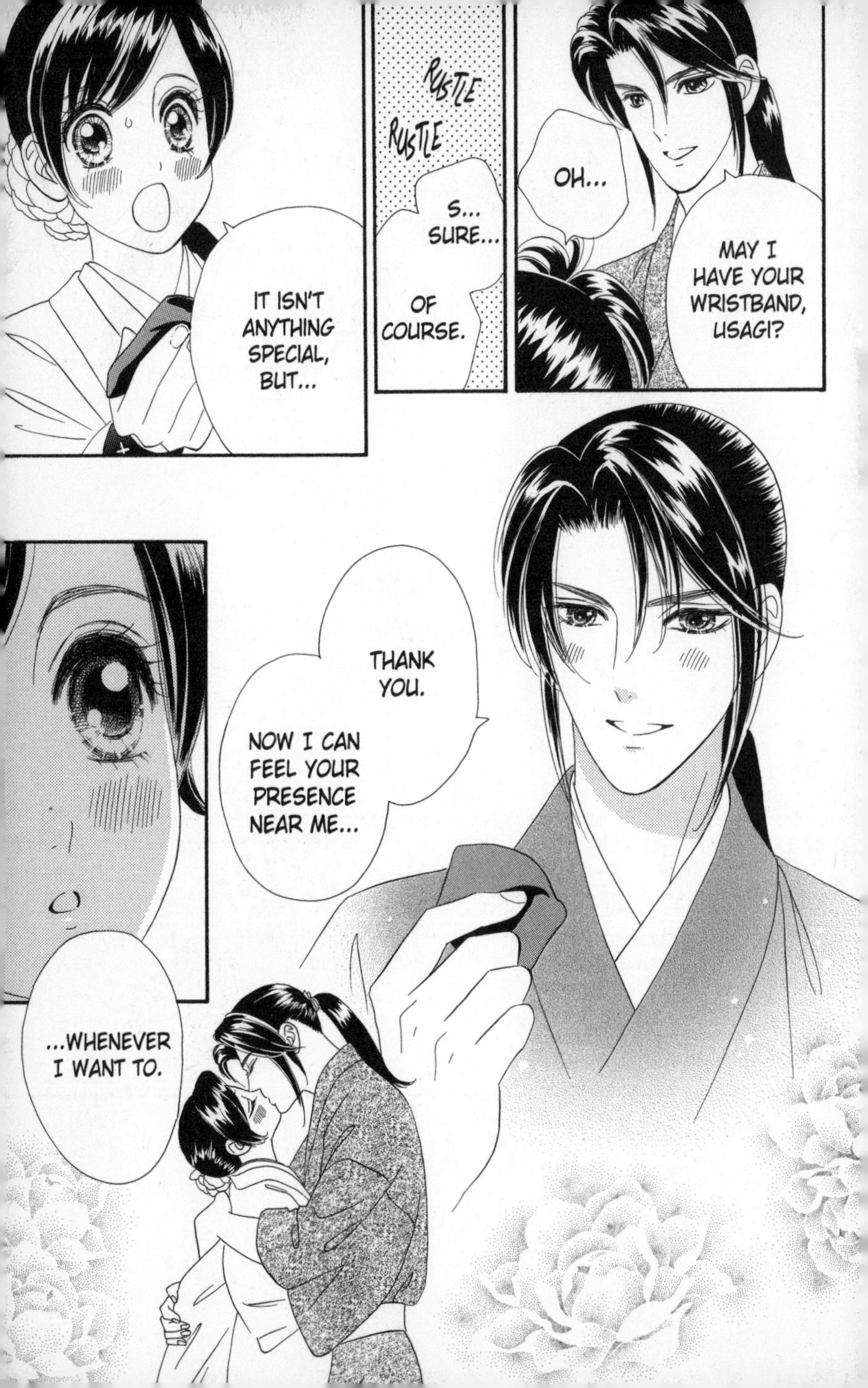
OH...
MAY I HAVE YOUR WRISTBAND, USAGI?
RUSTLE
RUSTLE
S... SURE...
OF COURSE.
IT ISN'T ANYTHING SPECIAL, BUT...
THANK YOU.
NOW I CAN FEEL YOUR PRESENCE NEAR ME...
...WHENEVER I WANT TO.

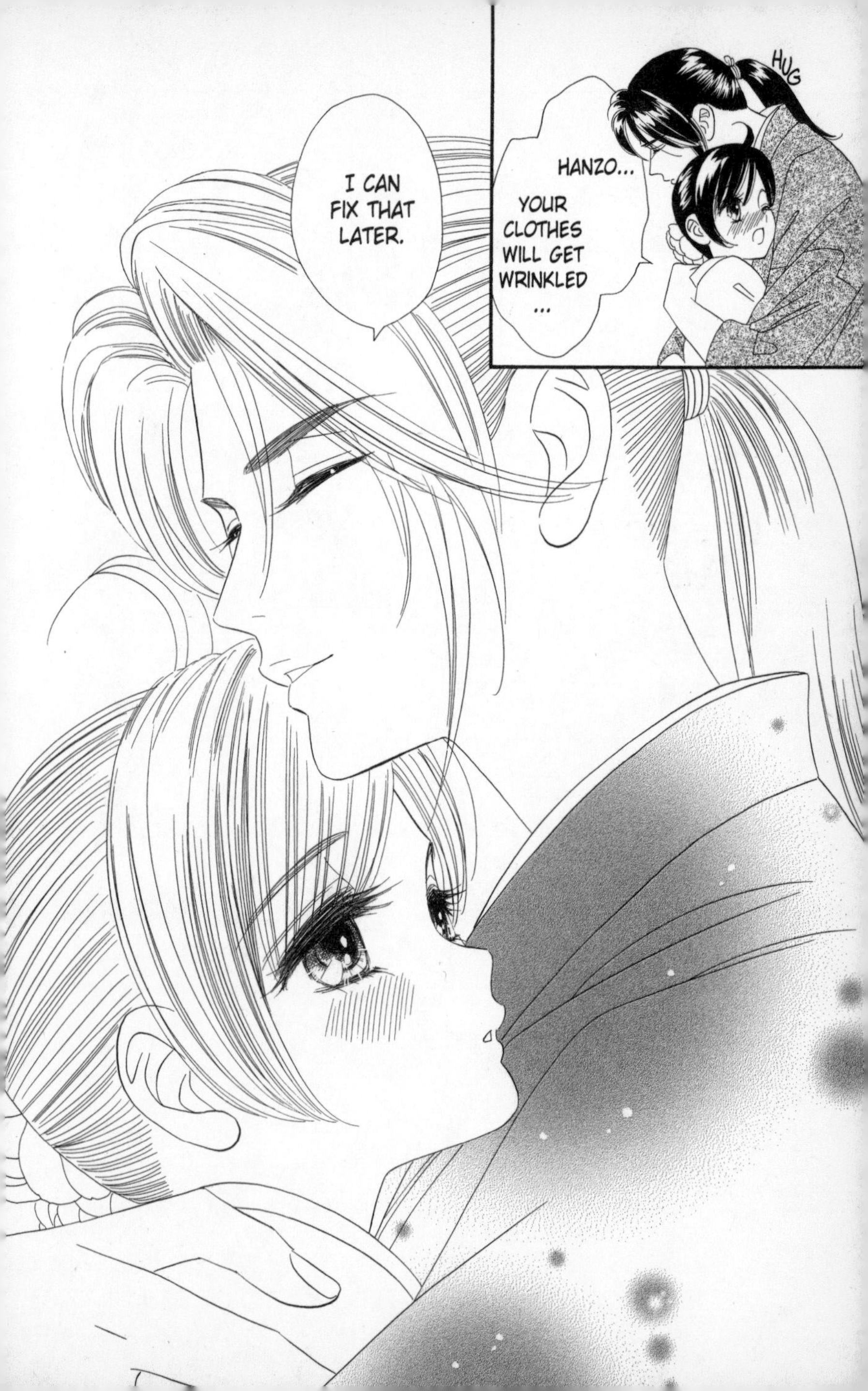
HUG
HANZO...
YOUR CLOTHES WILL GET WRINKLED ...
I CAN FIX THAT LATER.

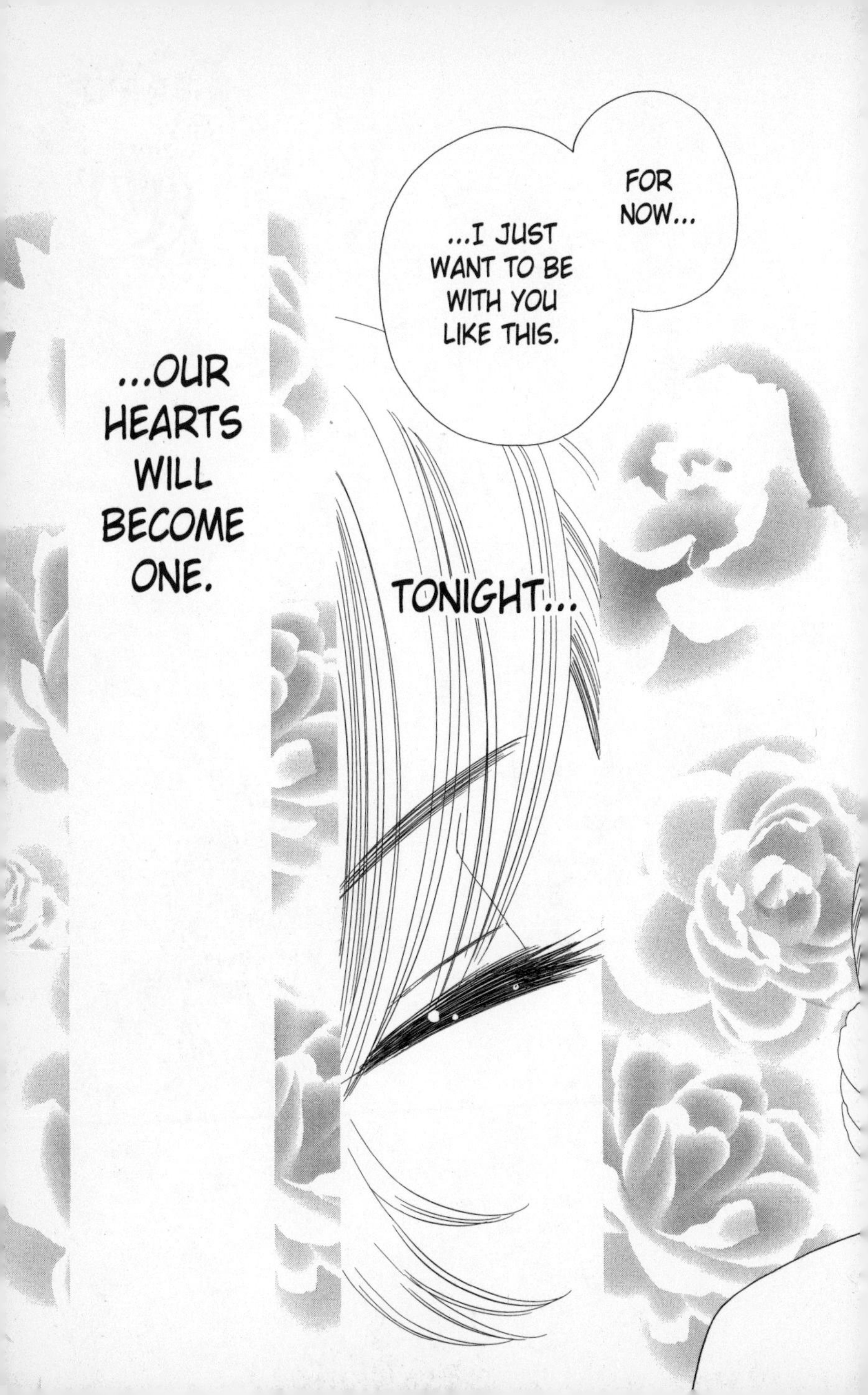
FOR NOW... ...I JUST WANT TO BE WITH YOU LIKE THIS.
TONIGHT...
...OUR HEARTS WILL BECOME ONE.

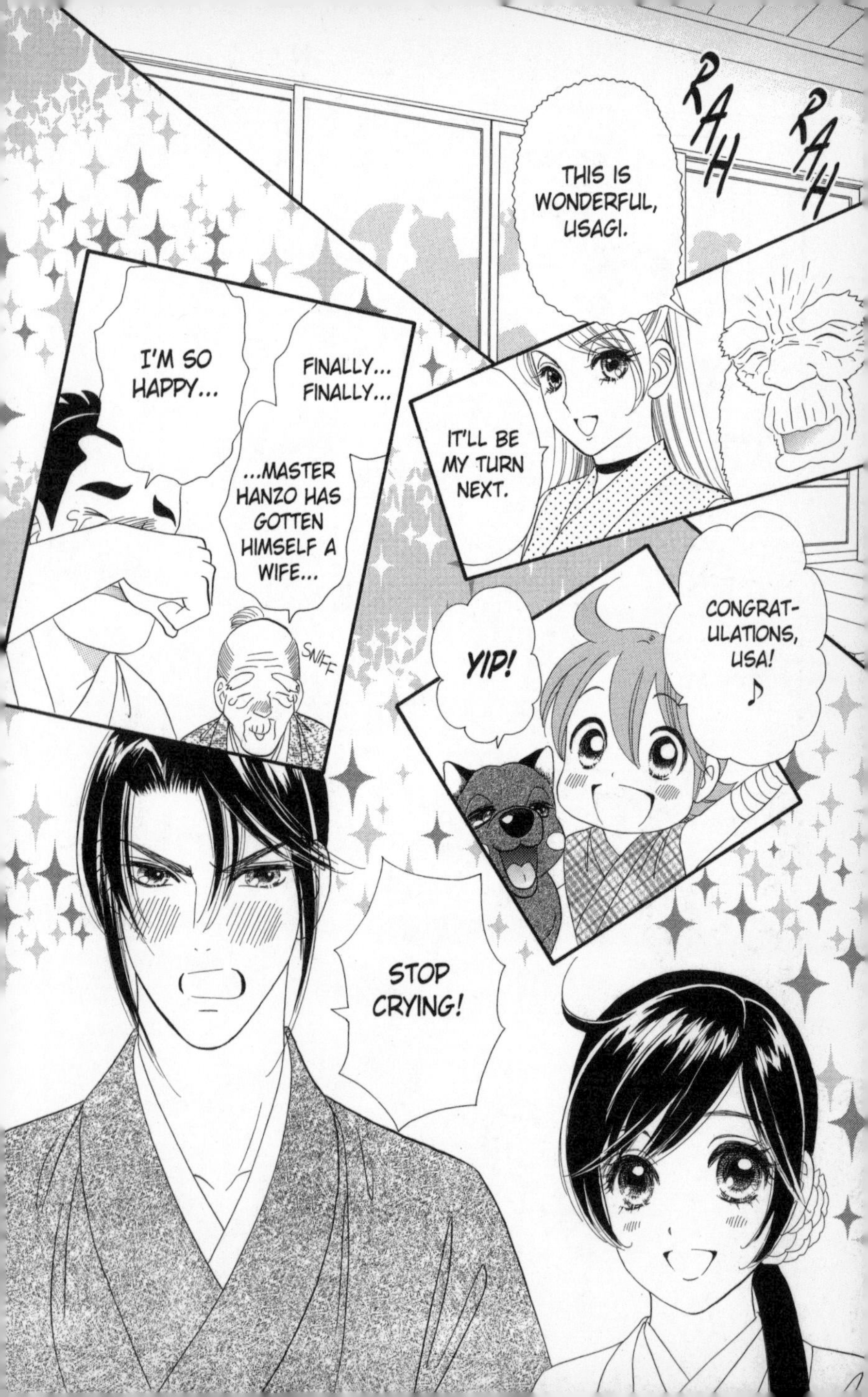
RAH RAH
THIS IS WONDERFUL, USAGI.
IT'LL BE MY TURN NEXT.
CONGRAT-ULATIONS, USA! ♪
YIP!
FINALLY... FINALLY...
I'M SO HAPPY...
...MASTER HANZO HAS GOTTEN HIMSELF A WIFE...
SNIFF
STOP CRYING!

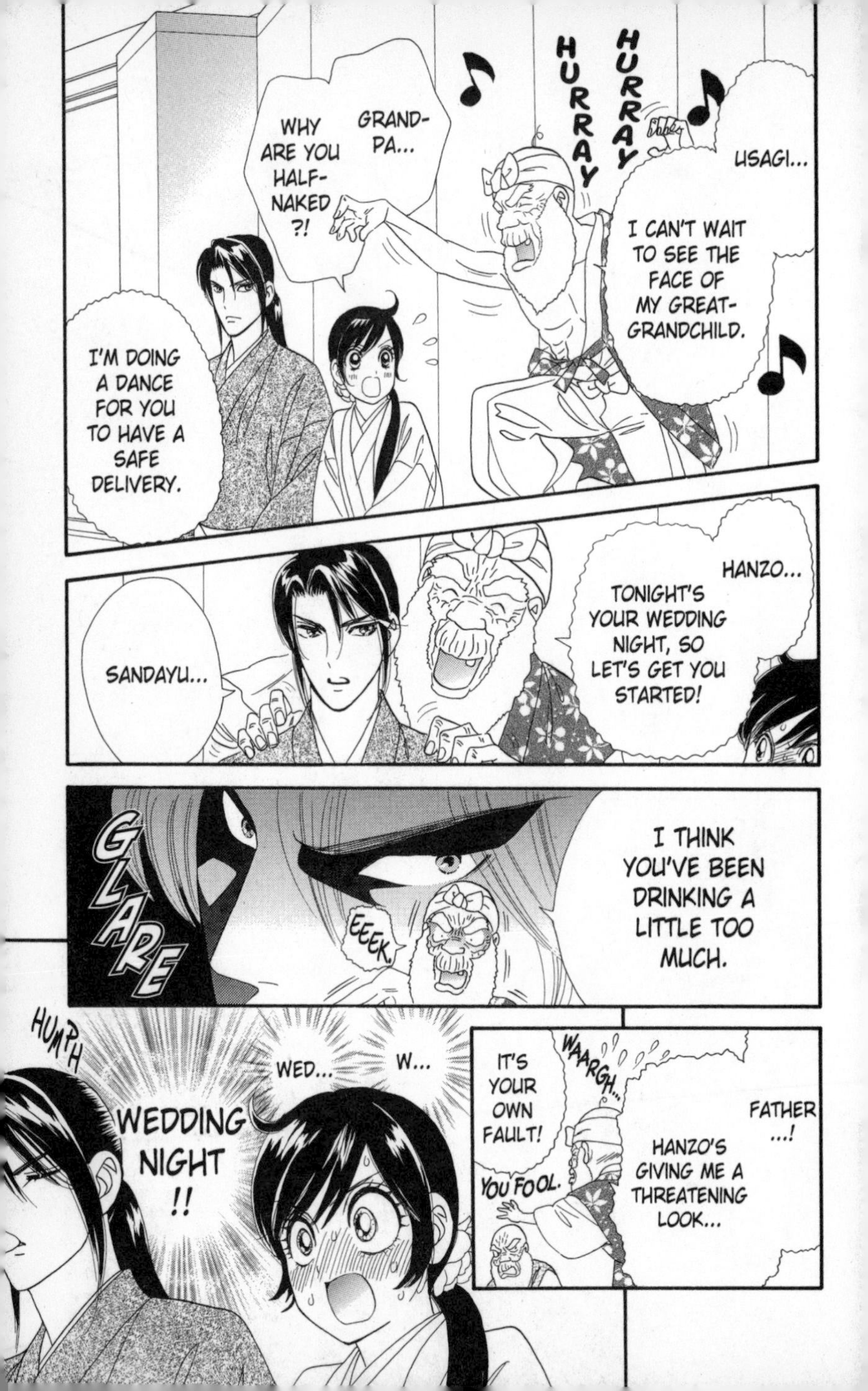
USAGI... I CAN'T WAIT TO SEE THE FACE OF MY GREAT-GRANDCHILD.
HURRAY HURRAY
GRAND-PA... WHY ARE YOU HALF-NAKED?!
I'M DOING A DANCE FOR YOU TO HAVE A SAFE DELIVERY.
HANZO... TONIGHT'S YOUR WEDDING NIGHT, SO LET'S GET YOU STARTED!
SANDAYU...
I THINK YOU'VE BEEN DRINKING A LITTLE TOO MUCH.
EEEK.
GLARE
FATHER ...!
HANZO'S GIVING ME A THREATENING LOOK...
WAARGH...
IT'S YOUR OWN FAULT!
YOU FOOL.
W...
WED...
WEDDING NIGHT !!
HUMPH

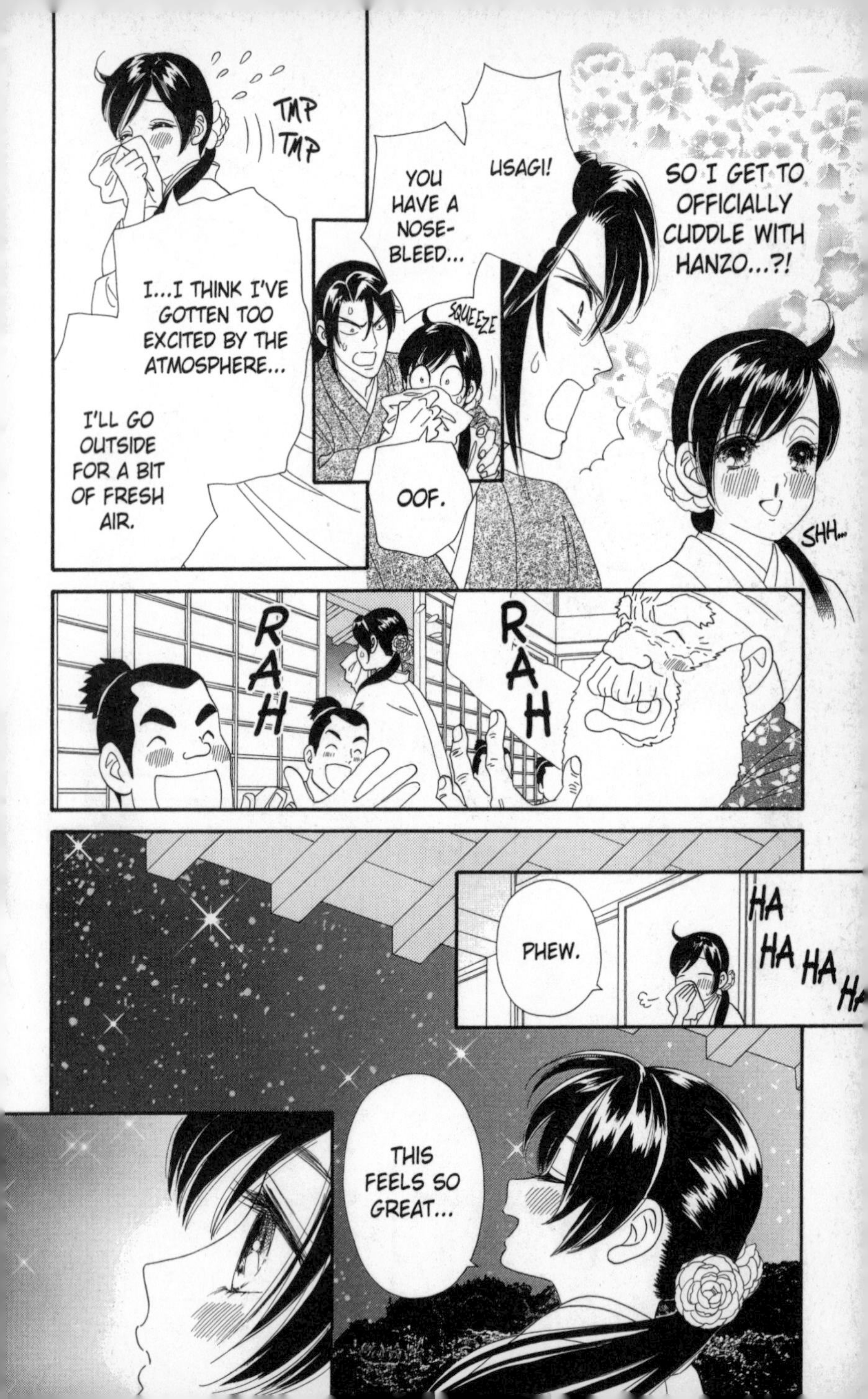
SO I GET TO OFFICIALLY CUDDLE WITH HANZO...?!
SHH...
USAGI!
YOU HAVE A NOSE-BLEED...
SQUEEZE
OOF.
TMP TMP
I...I THINK I'VE GOTTEN TOO EXCITED BY THE ATMOSPHERE...
I'LL GO OUTSIDE FOR A BIT OF FRESH AIR.
RAH
RAH
HA HA HA
PHEW.
THIS FEELS SO GREAT...

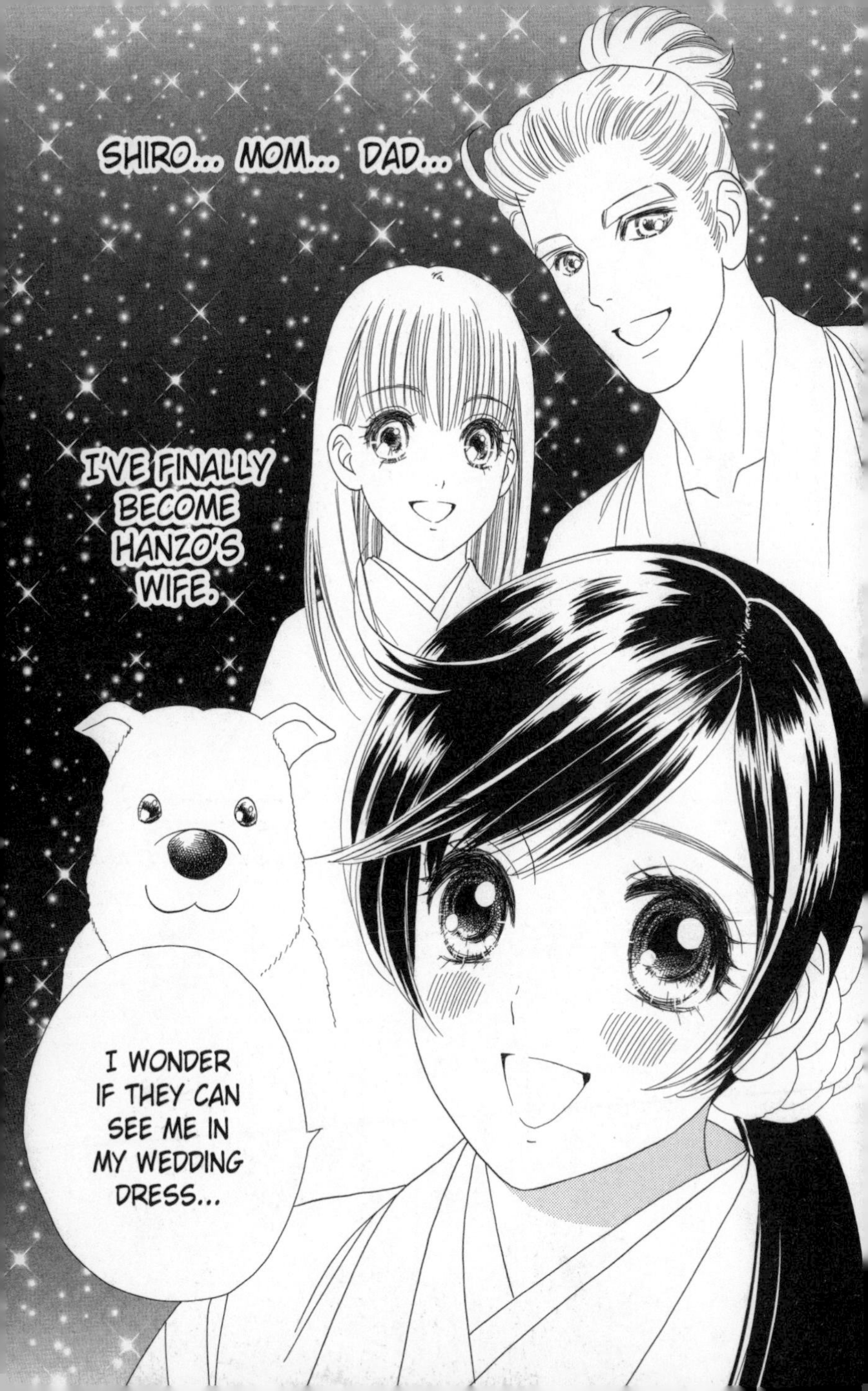
SHIRO... MOM... DAD...
I'VE FINALLY BECOME HANZO'S WIFE.
I WONDER IF THEY CAN SEE ME IN MY WEDDING DRESS...

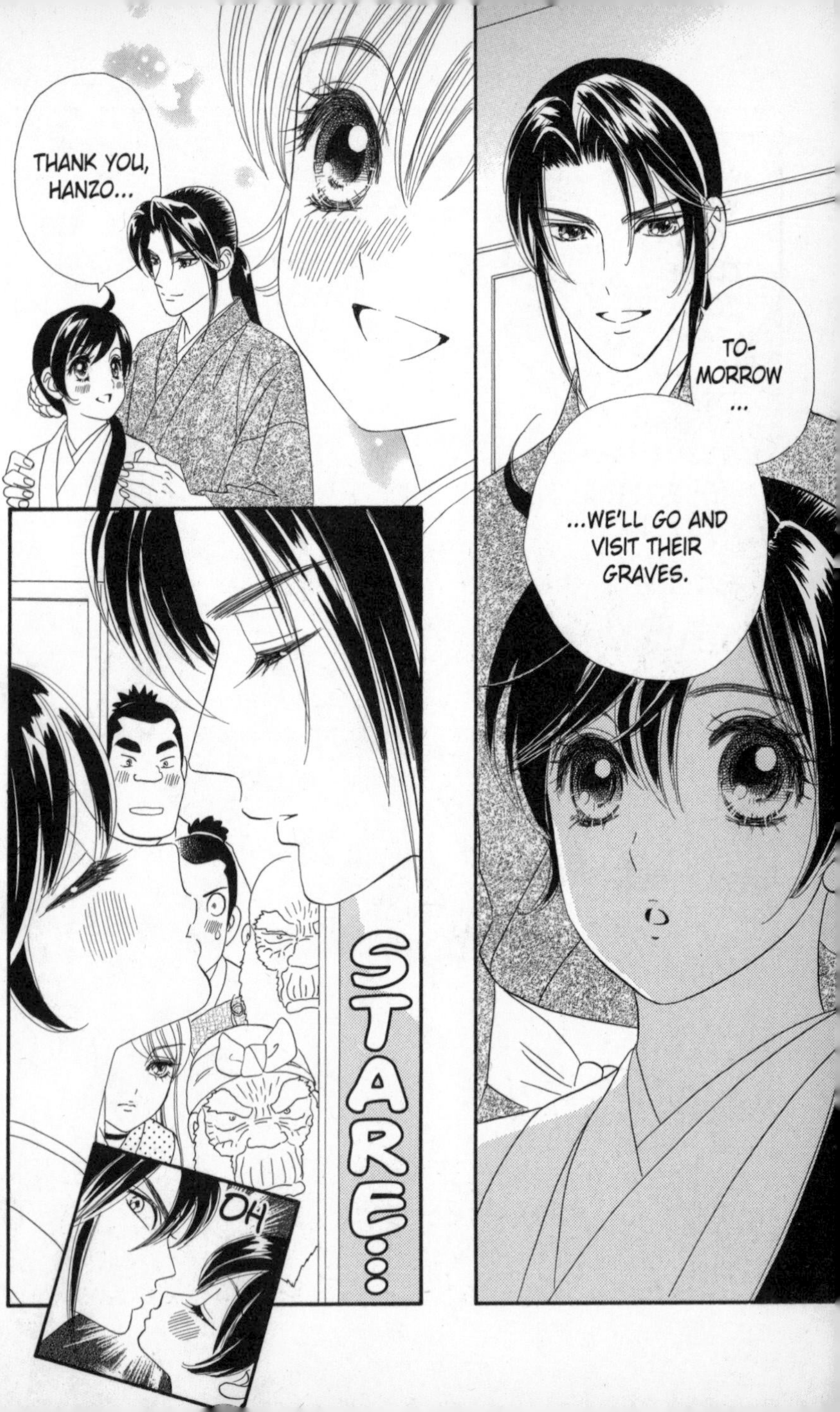
TO-MORROW ...
...WE'LL GO AND VISIT THEIR GRAVES.
THANK YOU, HANZO...
STARE...
OH

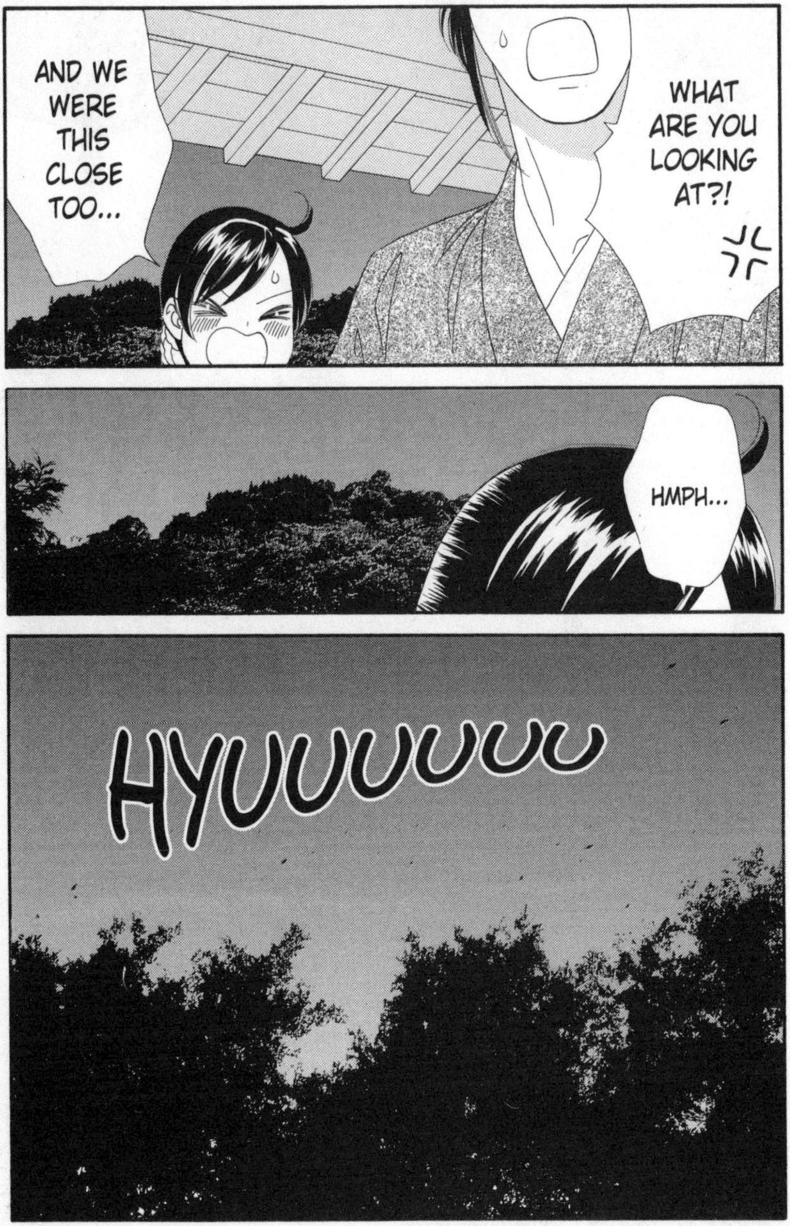
WHAT ARE YOU LOOKING AT?!
AND WE WERE THIS CLOSE TOO...
HMPH...
HYUUUUUU

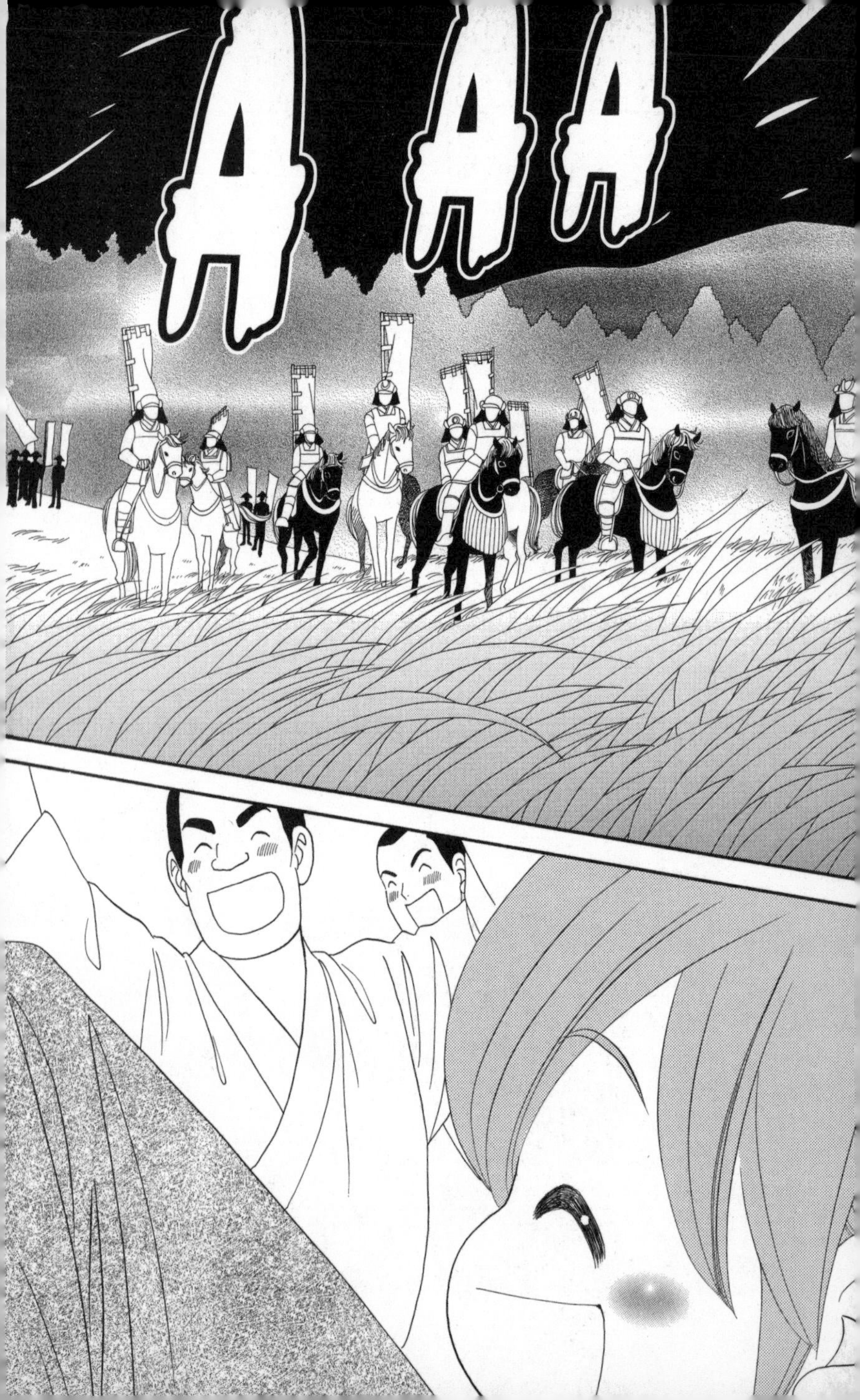
AAA

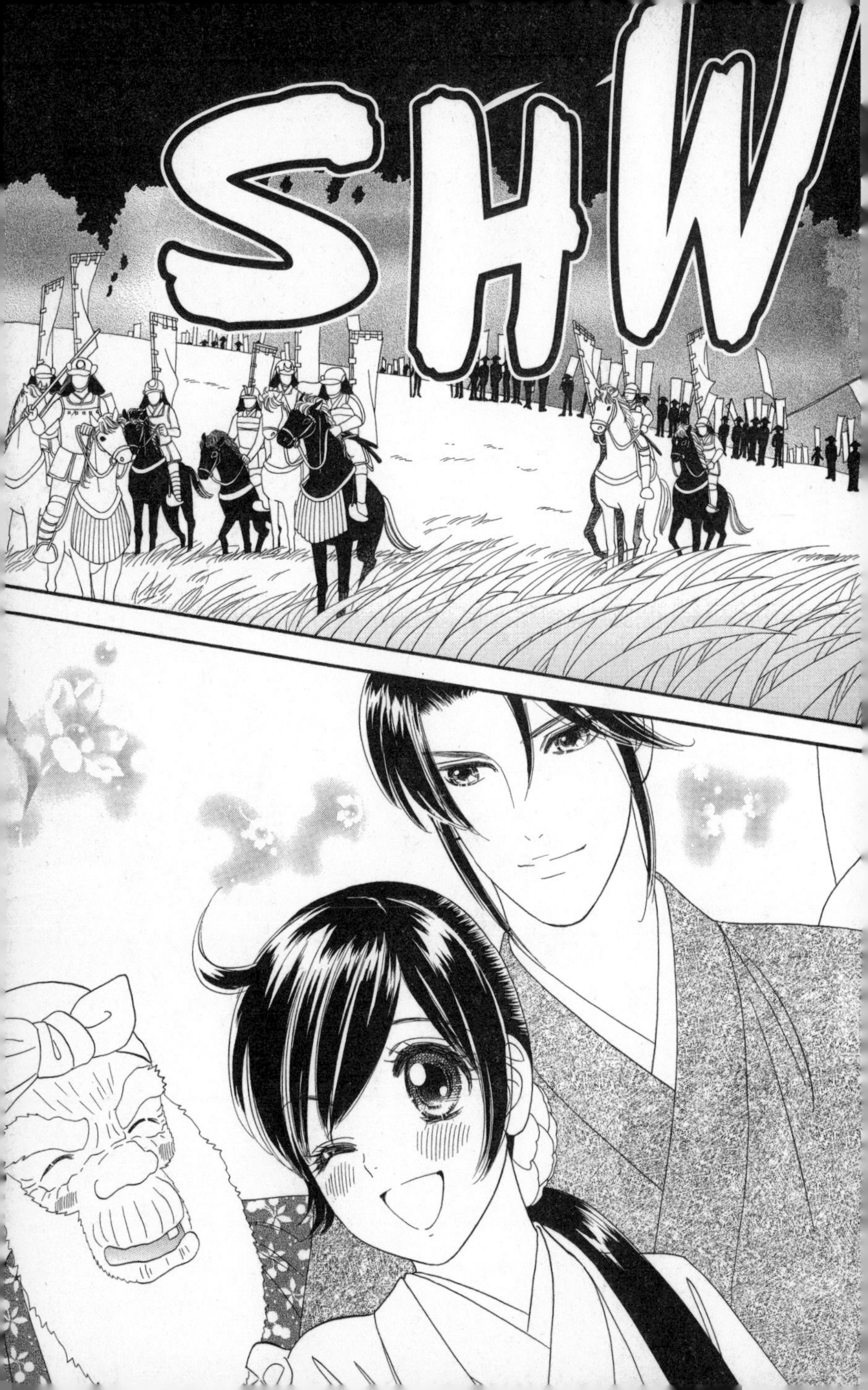
SHW

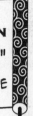

TAIL OF THE MOON EXTRA: TODAY'S MISSION

"I WANT TO SEE HANZO WITH GLASSES!"

-MISS "I LOVE BOYS WITH GLASSES", SAITAMA PREFECTURE

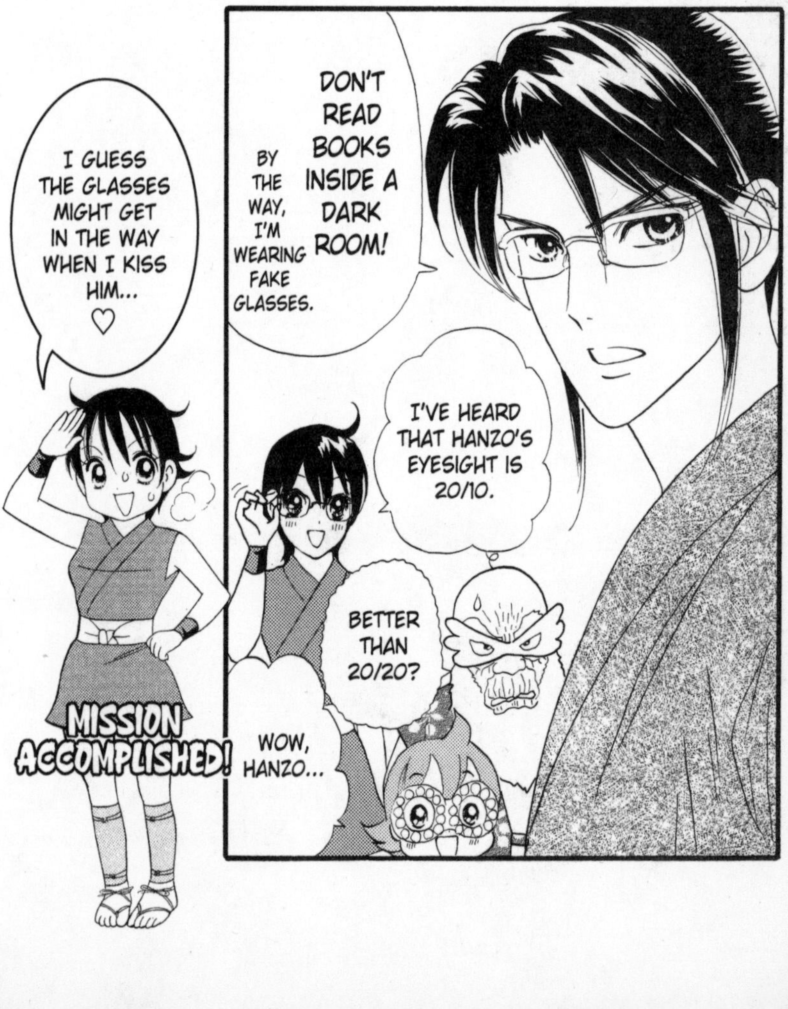
DON'T READ BOOKS INSIDE A DARK ROOM!
BY THE WAY, I'M WEARING FAKE GLASSES.
I'VE HEARD THAT HANZO'S EYESIGHT IS 20/10.
BETTER THAN 20/20?
WOW, HANZO...
I GUESS THE GLASSES MIGHT GET IN THE WAY WHEN I KISS HIM... ♡
MISSION ACCOMPLISHED!

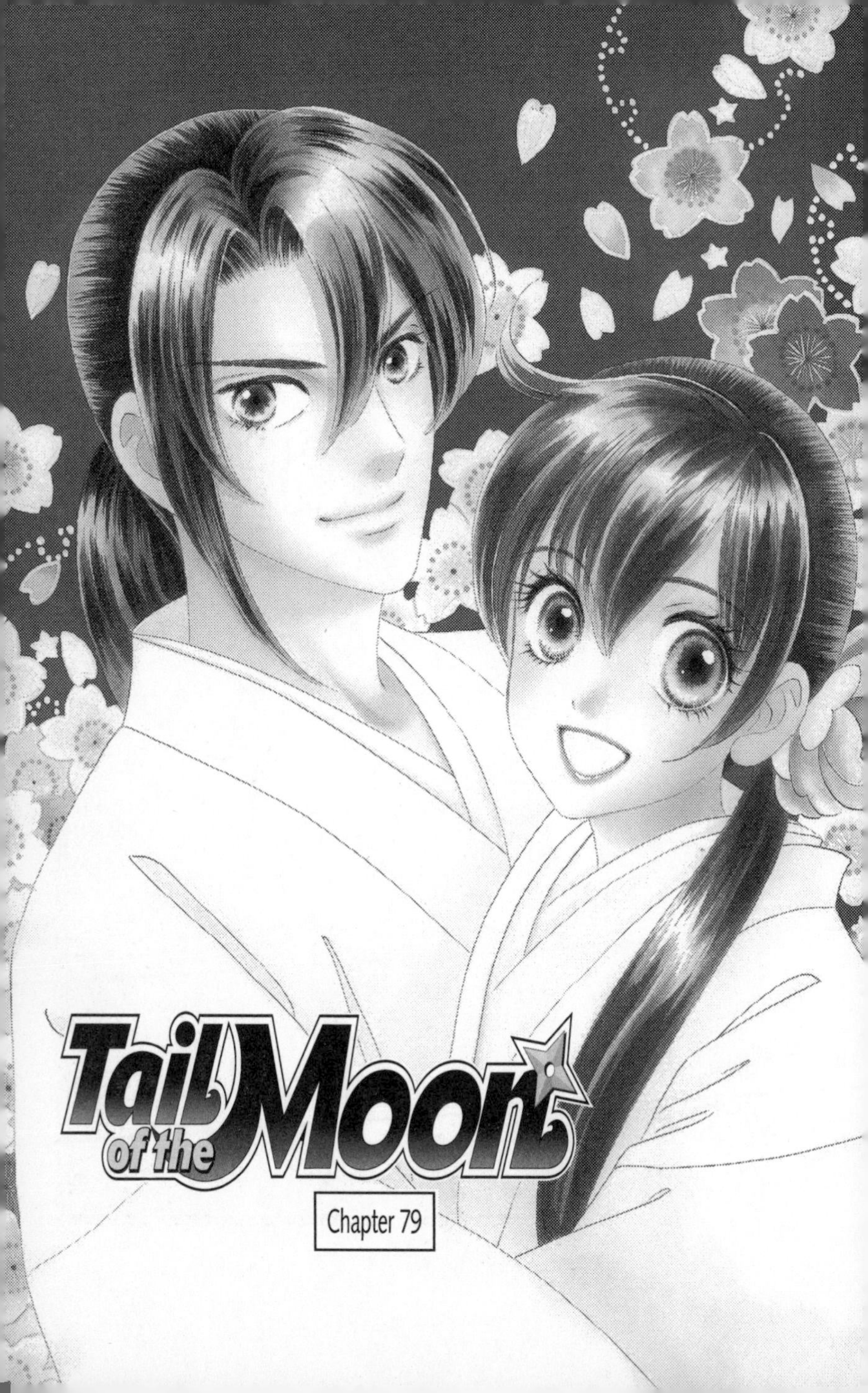
Tail of the Moon
Chapter 79

TAIL OF THE MOON EXTRA: TODAY'S MISSION
"I WANT TO SEE USAGI IN A WEDDING DRESS!"
-MIYUKING, YAMAGUCHI PREFECTURE

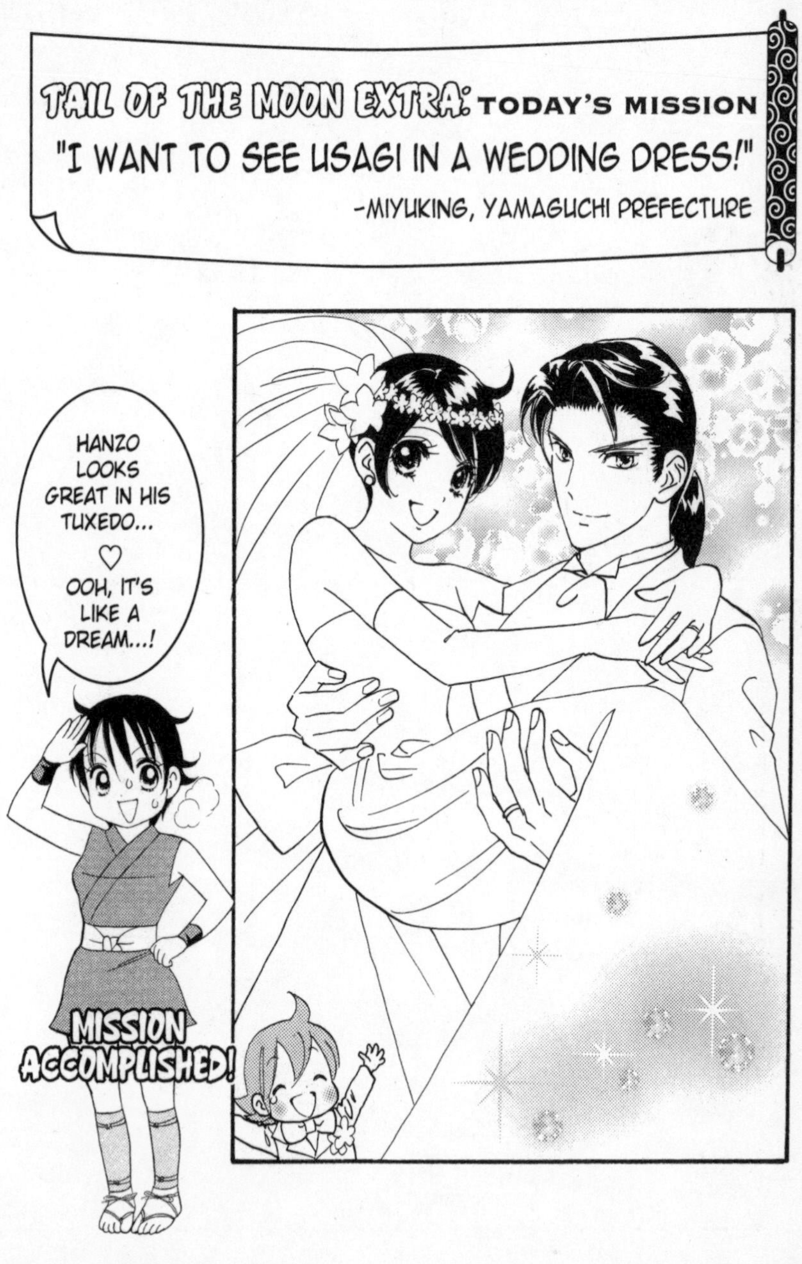
HANZO LOOKS GREAT IN HIS TUXEDO... ♡ OOH, IT'S LIKE A DREAM...!
MISSION ACCOMPLISHED!

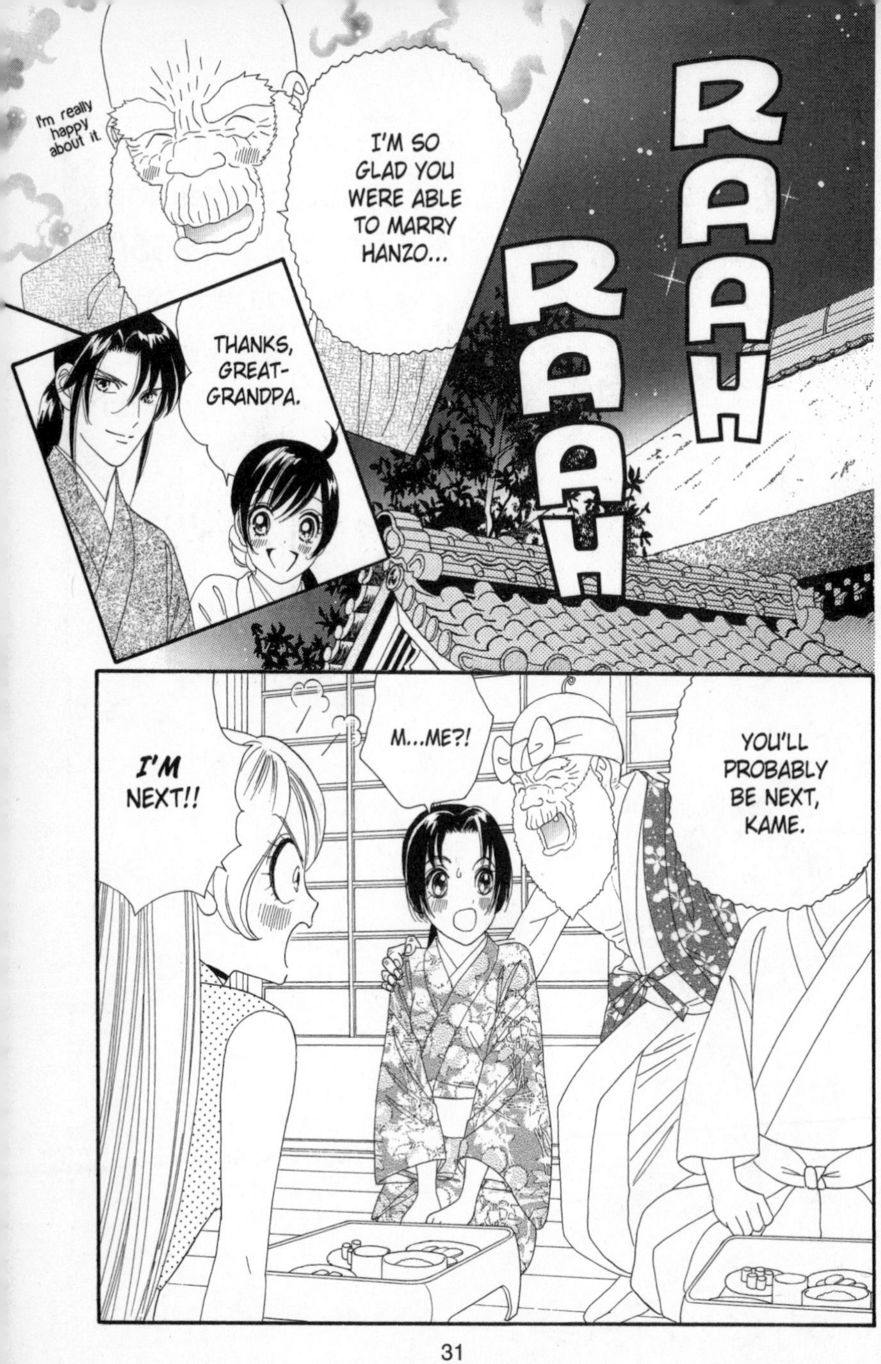
RAAAH
RAAAH
I'M SO GLAD YOU WERE ABLE TO MARRY HANZO...
I'm really happy about it.
THANKS, GREAT-GRANDPA.
YOU'LL PROBABLY BE NEXT, KAME.
M...ME?!
I'M NEXT!!

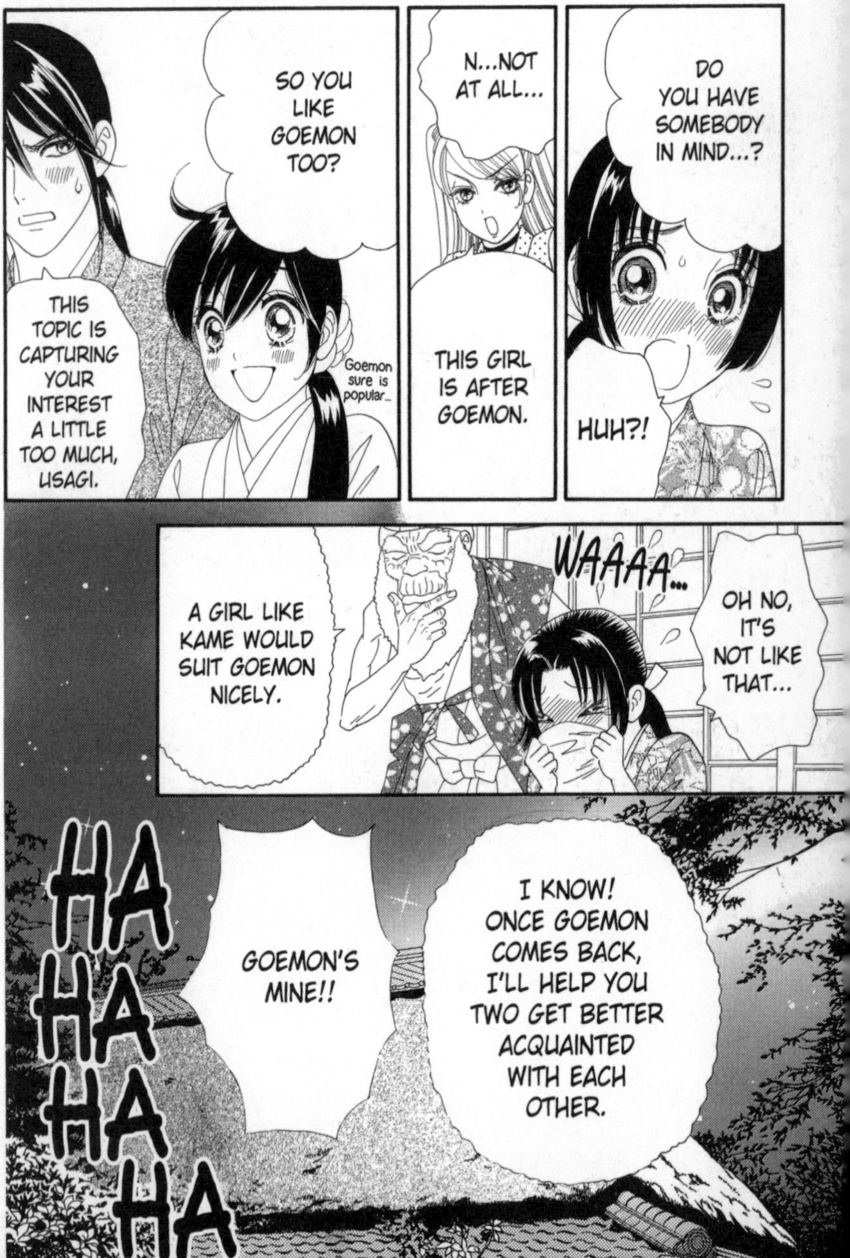
DO YOU HAVE SOMEBODY IN MIND...?
HUH?!
N...NOT AT ALL...
THIS GIRL IS AFTER GOEMON.
SO YOU LIKE GOEMON TOO?
Goemon sure is popular...
THIS TOPIC IS CAPTURING YOUR INTEREST A LITTLE TOO MUCH, USAGI.
OH NO, IT'S NOT LIKE THAT...
WAAAA...
A GIRL LIKE KAME WOULD SUIT GOEMON NICELY.
I KNOW! ONCE GOEMON COMES BACK, I'LL HELP YOU TWO GET BETTER ACQUAINTED WITH EACH OTHER.
GOEMON'S MINE!!
HA HA HA HA

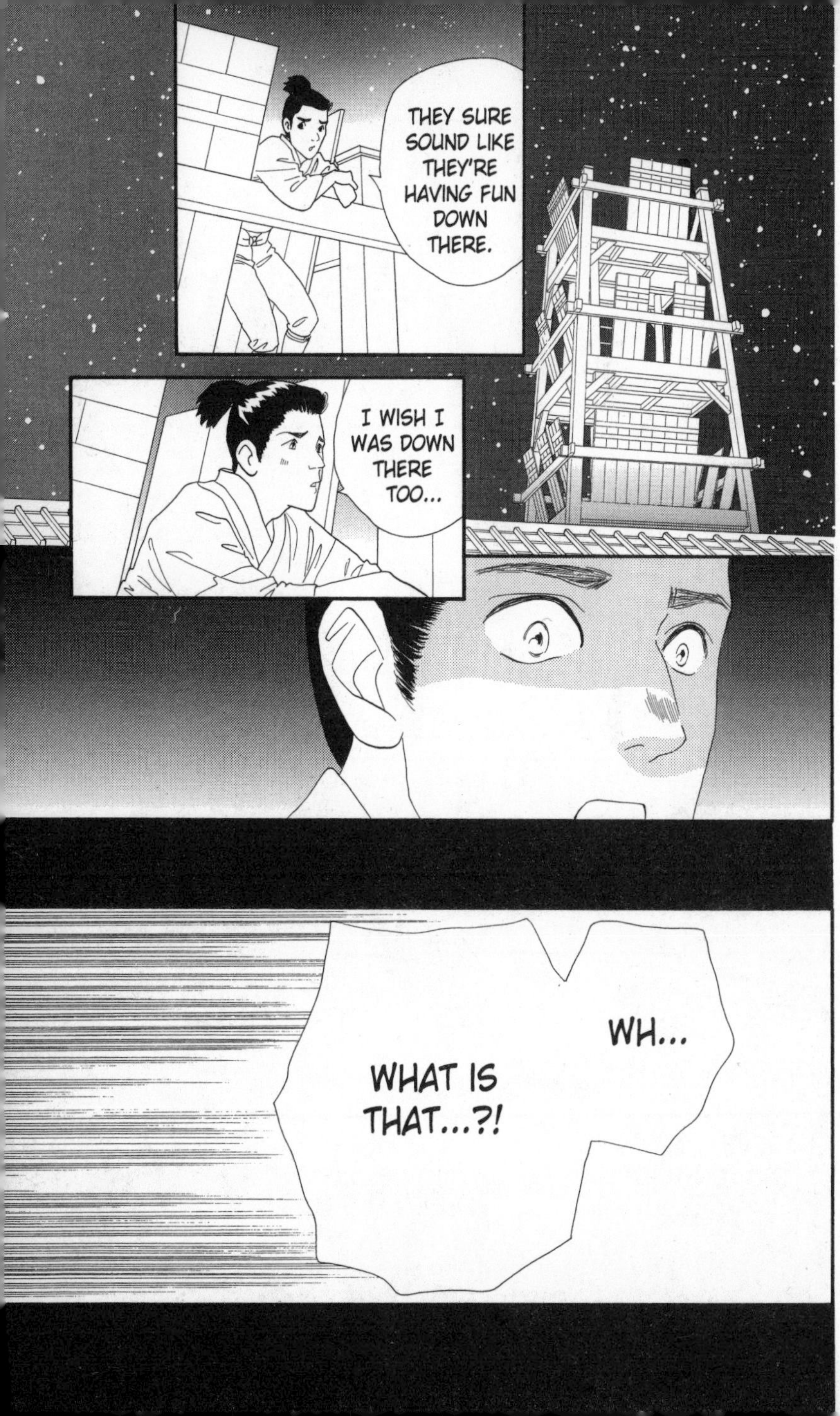
THEY SURE SOUND LIKE THEY'RE HAVING FUN DOWN THERE.
I WISH I WAS DOWN THERE TOO...
WH...
WHAT IS THAT...?!

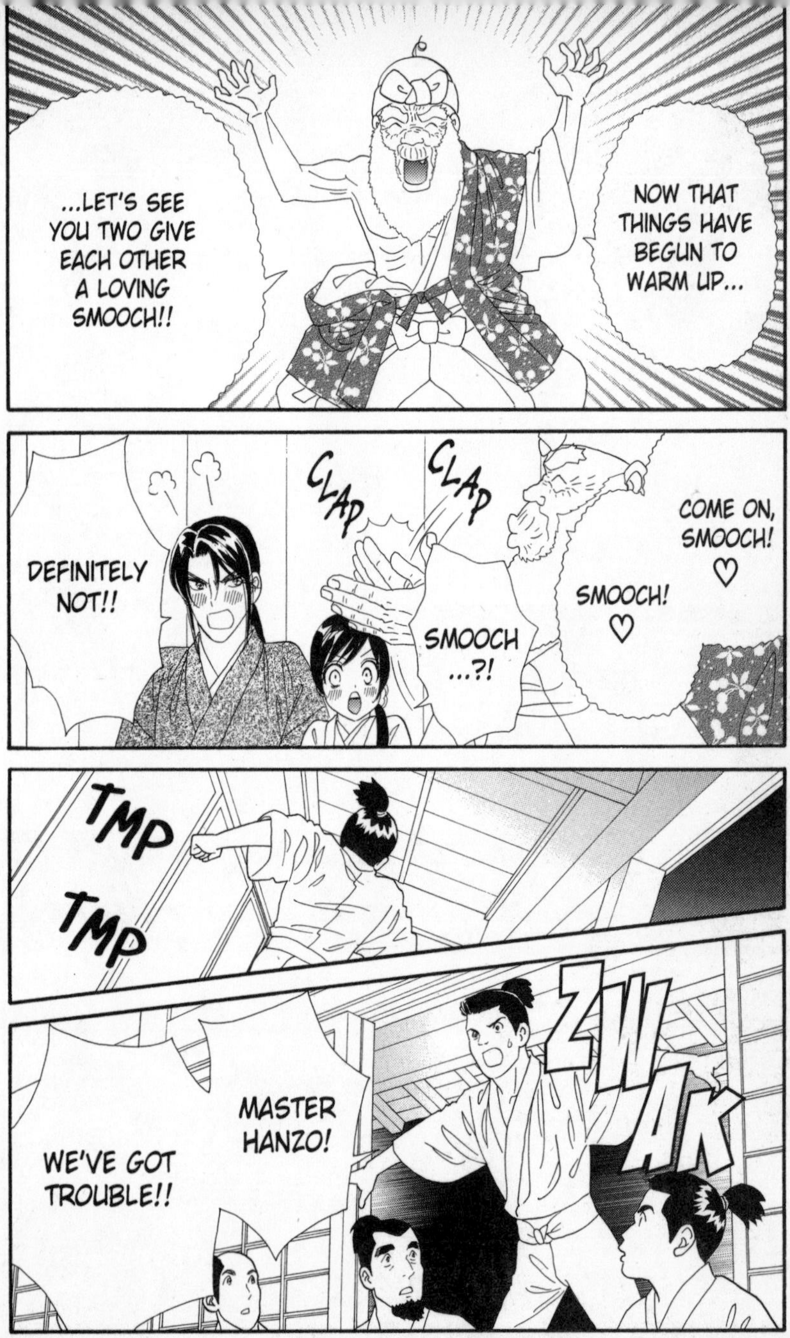
NOW THAT THINGS HAVE BEGUN TO WARM UP...
...LET'S SEE YOU TWO GIVE EACH OTHER A LOVING SMOOCH!!
COME ON, SMOOCH! ♡
SMOOCH! ♡
CLAP CLAP
SMOOCH ...?!
DEFINITELY NOT!!
TMP TMP
ZWAK
MASTER HANZO!
WE'VE GOT TROUBLE!!

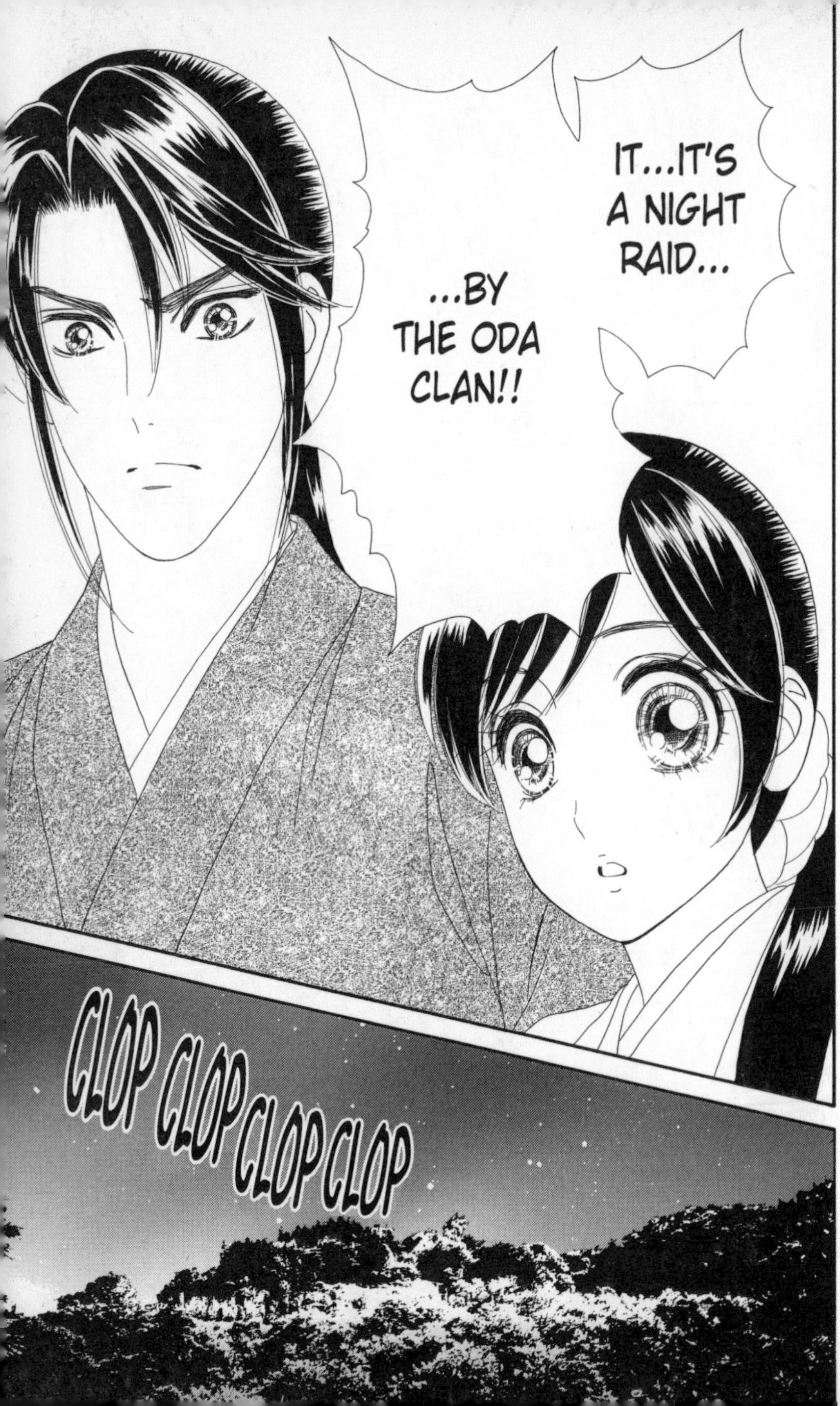
IT...IT'S A NIGHT RAID...
...BY THE ODA CLAN!!
CLOP CLOP CLOP CLOP

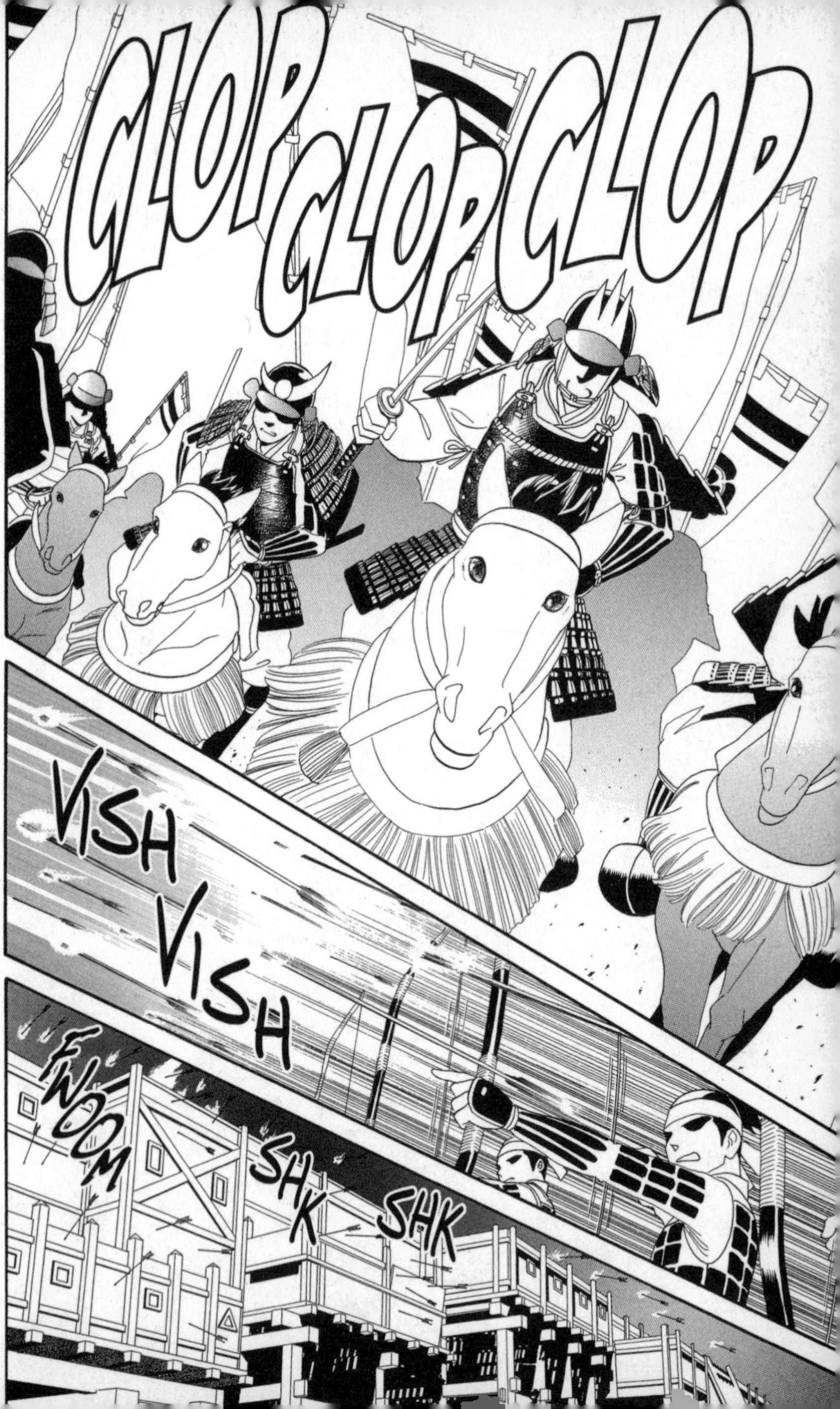
CLOP CLOP CLOP
VISH
VISH
FWOOM
SHK
SHK

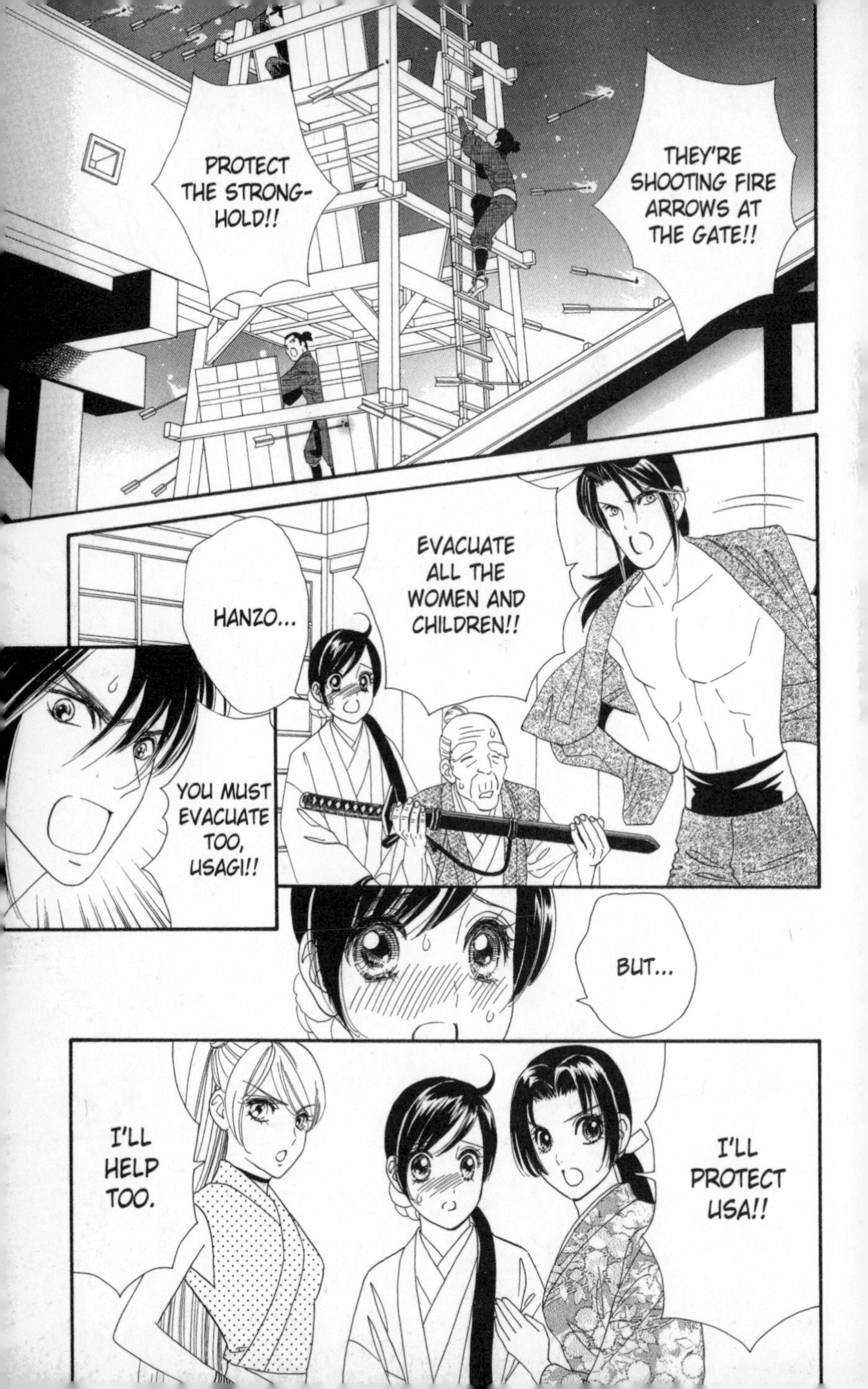
THEY'RE SHOOTING FIRE ARROWS AT THE GATE!!
PROTECT THE STRONG-HOLD!!
EVACUATE ALL THE WOMEN AND CHILDREN!!
HANZO...
YOU MUST EVACUATE TOO, USAGI!!
BUT...
I'LL PROTECT USA!!
I'LL HELP TOO.

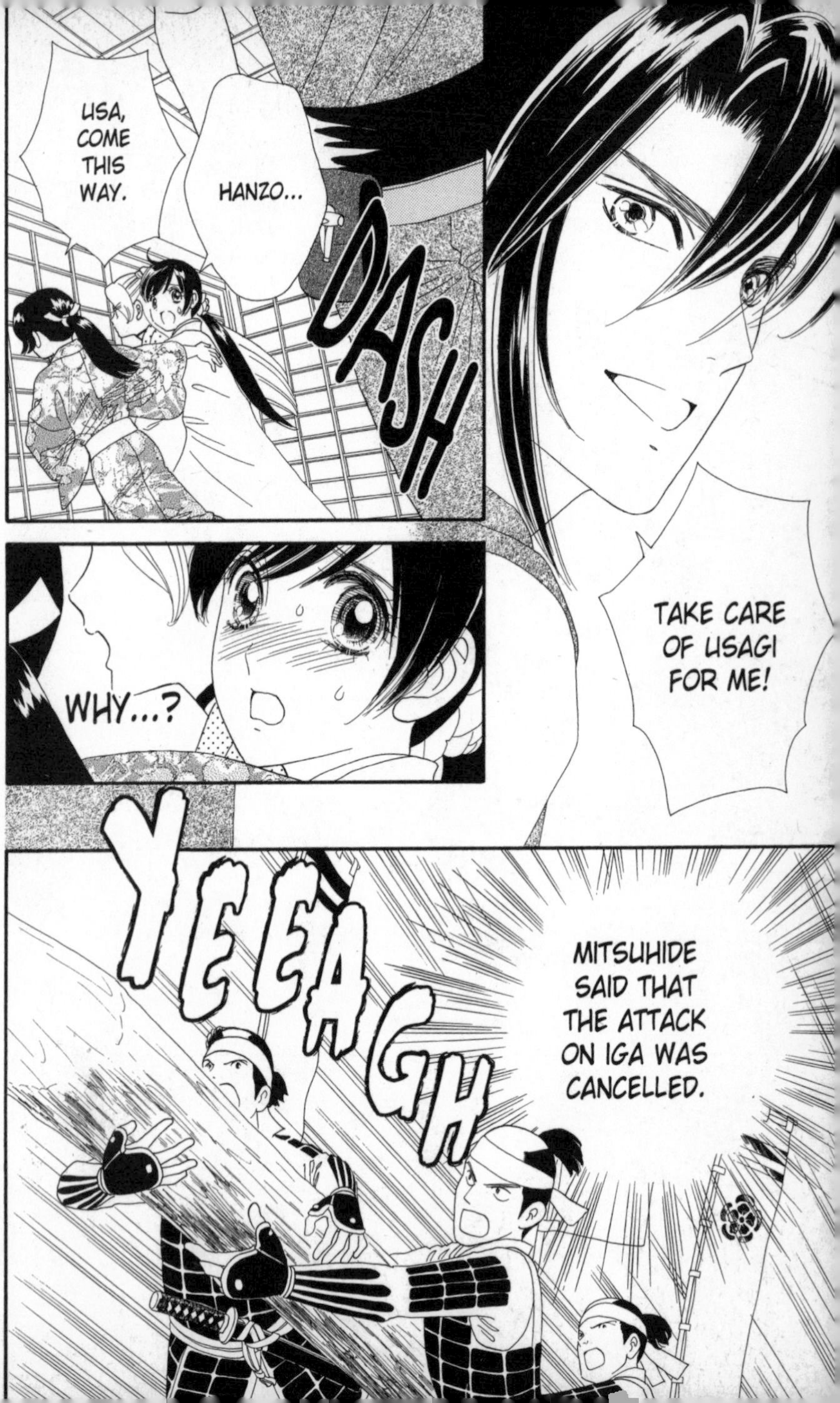
DASH
TAKE CARE OF USAGI FOR ME!
HANZO...
USA, COME THIS WAY.
WHY...?
YEEAGH
MITSUHIDE SAID THAT THE ATTACK ON IGA WAS CANCELLED.

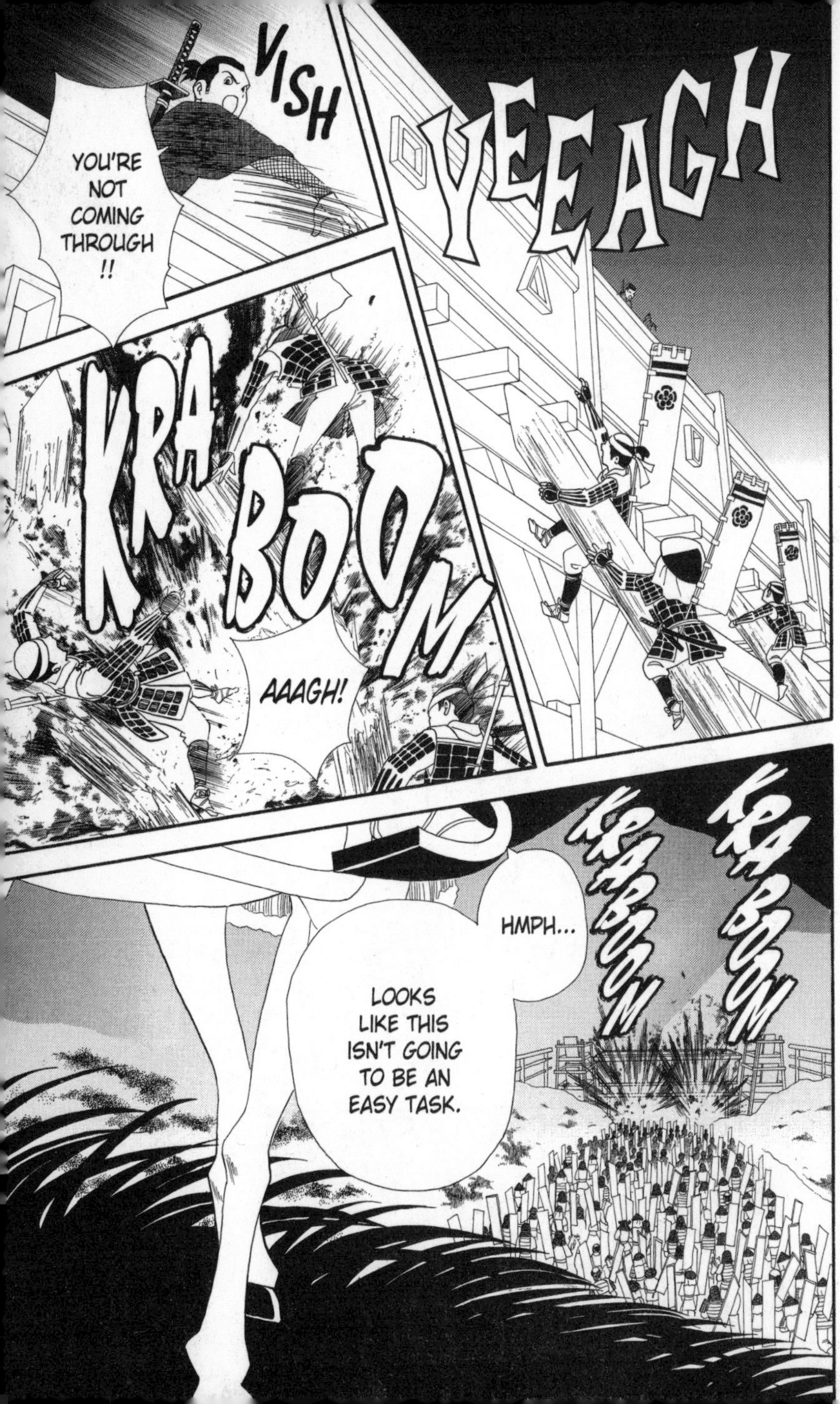
YEEAGH
VISH
YOU'RE NOT COMING THROUGH !!
KRA BOOM
AAAGH!
KRA BOOM
KRABOOOM
HMPH...
LOOKS LIKE THIS ISN'T GOING TO BE AN EASY TASK.

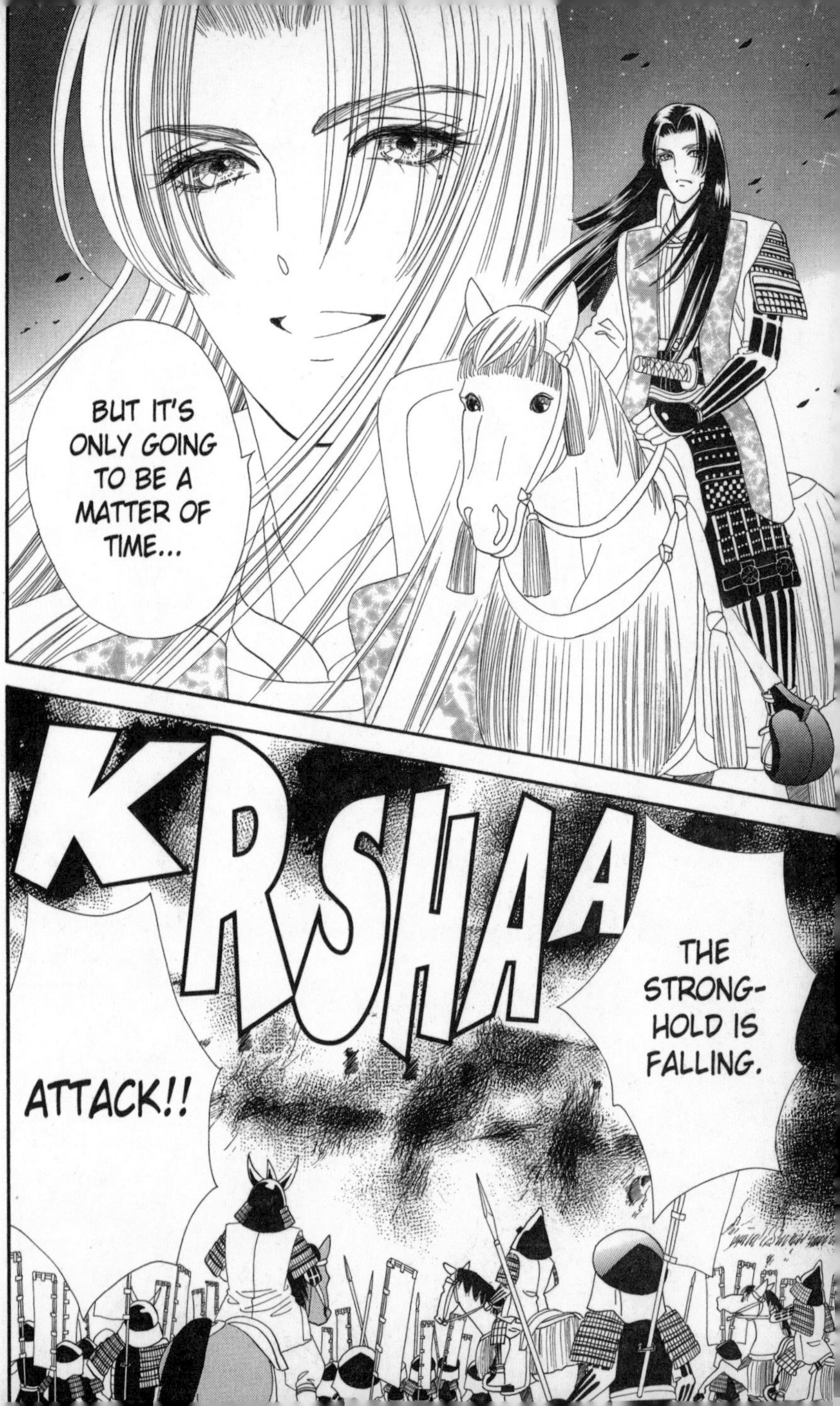
BUT IT'S ONLY GOING TO BE A MATTER OF TIME...
KRSHAA
THE STRONG-HOLD IS FALLING.
ATTACK!!

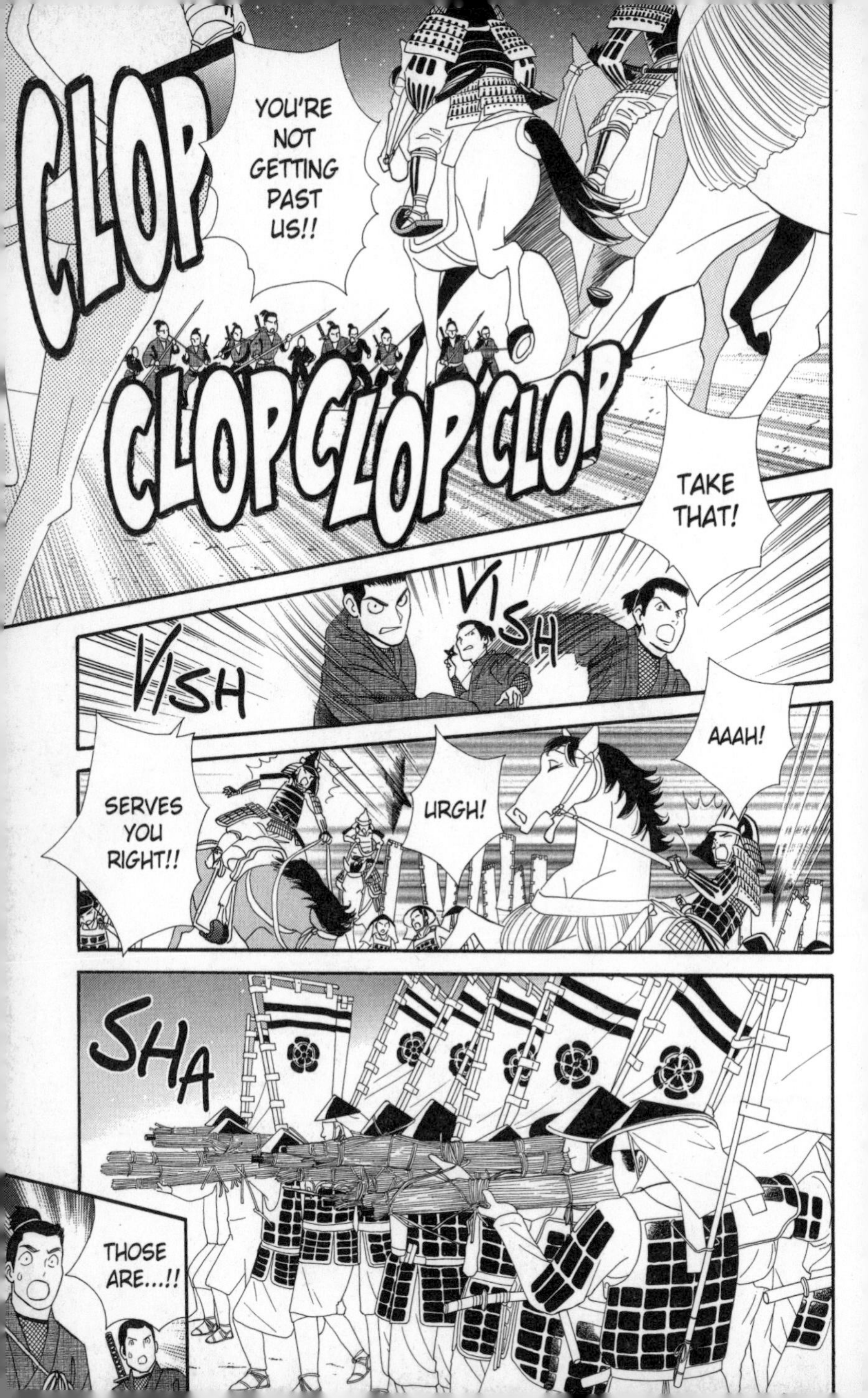
YOU'RE NOT GETTING PAST US!!
CLOP
CLOP CLOP CLOP
TAKE THAT!
VISH
VISH
AAAH!
URGH!
SERVES YOU RIGHT!!
SHA
THOSE ARE...!!

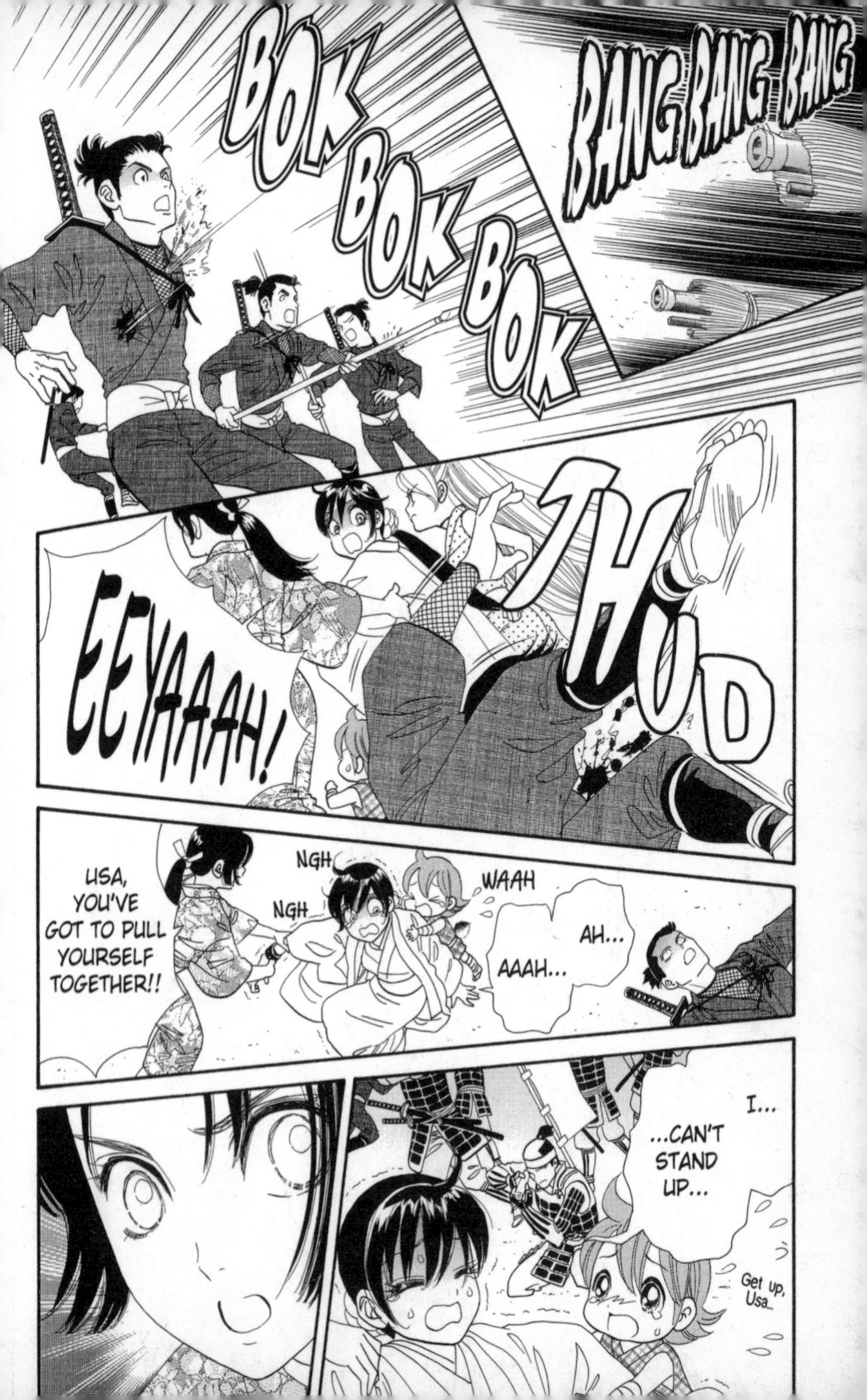
BANG BANG BANG
BOK BOK BOK BOK
THUD
EEYAAAH!
AH...
AAAH...
WAAH
NGH
NGH
USA, YOU'VE GOT TO PULL YOURSELF TOGETHER!!
I...
...CAN'T STAND UP...
Get up, Usa...

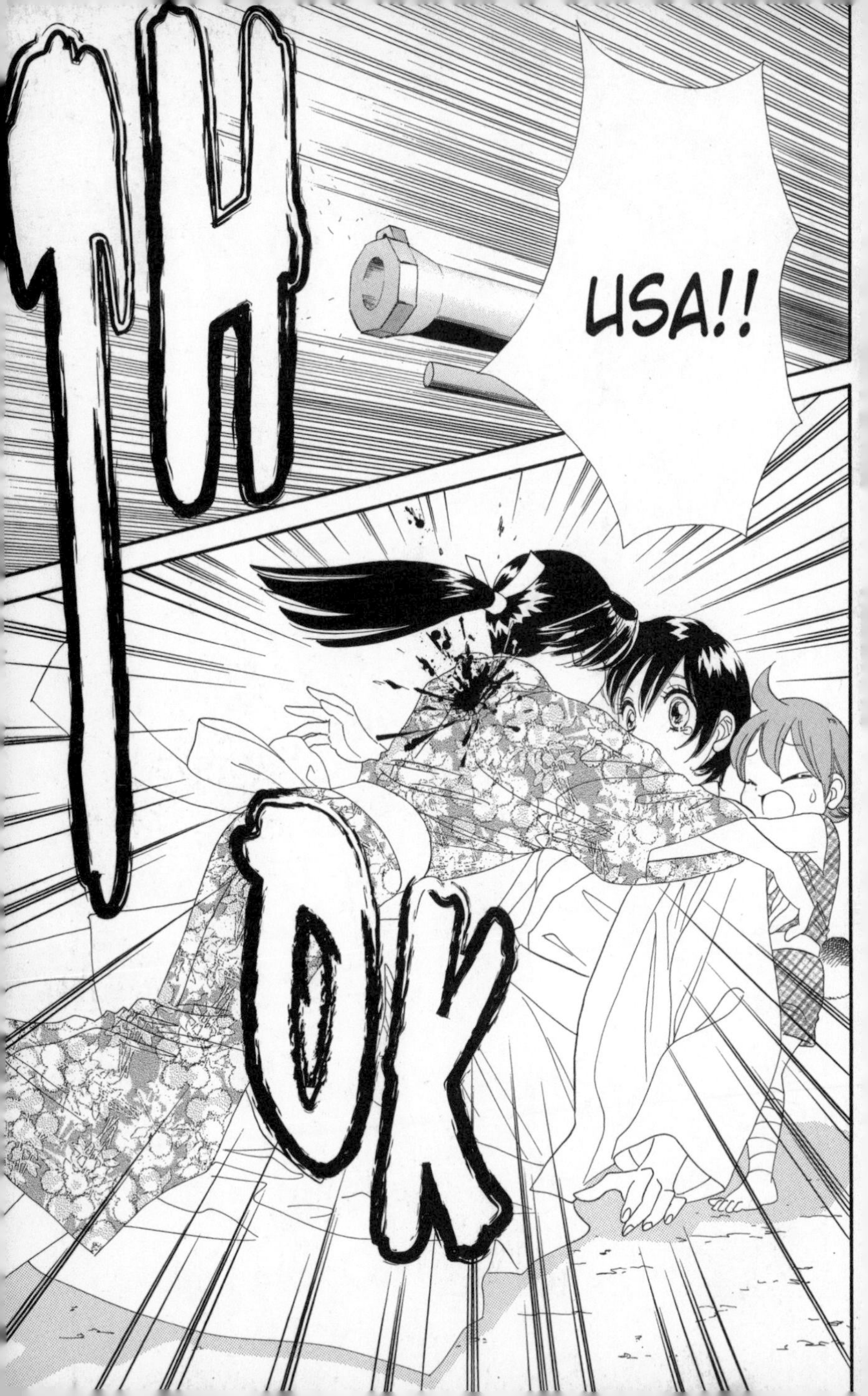
USA!!

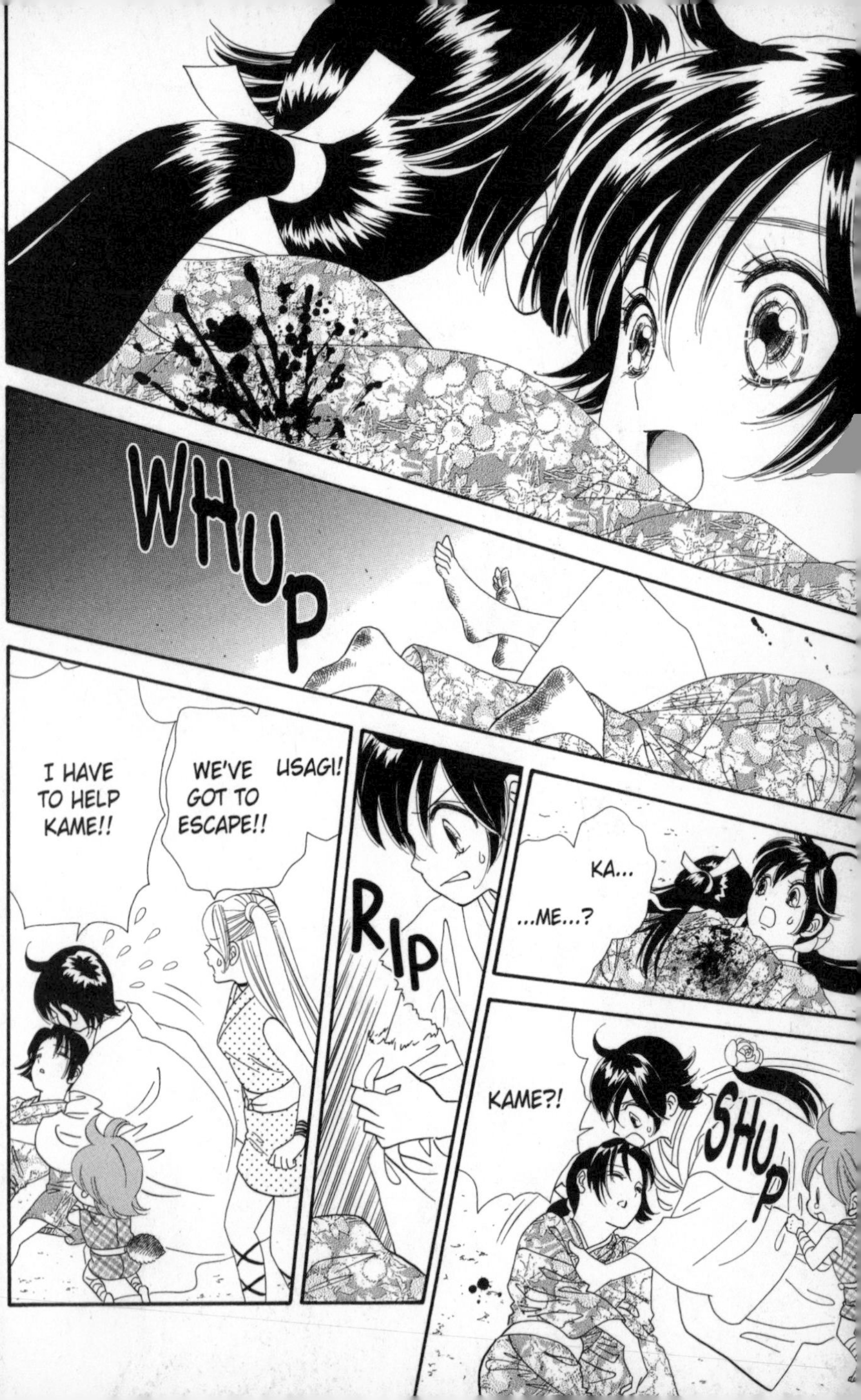
WHUP
KA...
...ME...?
KAME?!
SHUP
RIP
USAGI!
WE'VE GOT TO ESCAPE!!
I HAVE TO HELP KAME!!

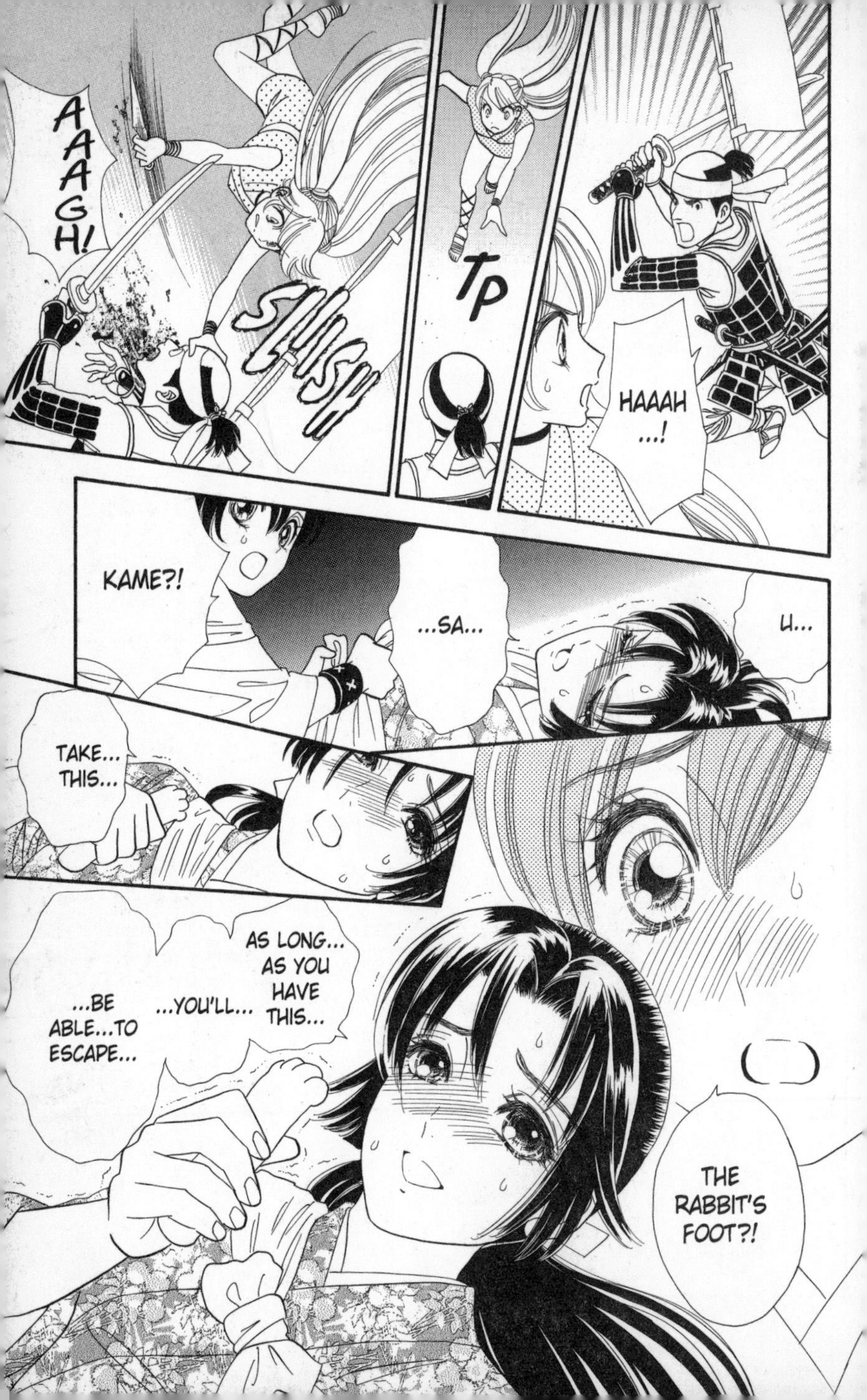
HAAAH ...!
TP
AAAAGH!
SHUSH
U...
...SA...
KAME?!
TAKE... THIS...
THE RABBIT'S FOOT?!
AS LONG... AS YOU HAVE THIS...
...YOU'LL...
...BE ABLE...TO ESCAPE...

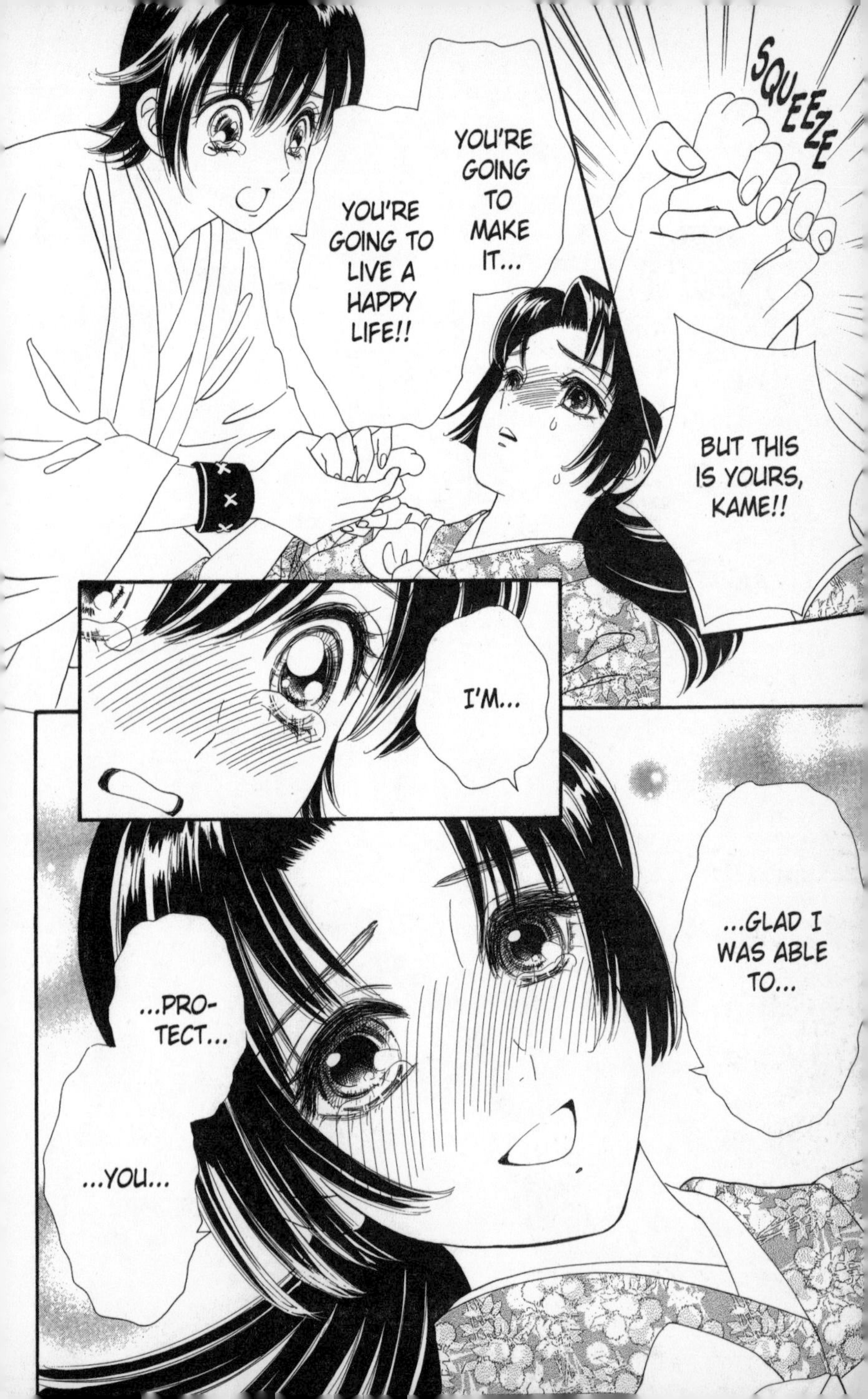
SQUEEZE
BUT THIS IS YOURS, KAME!!
YOU'RE GOING TO MAKE IT...
YOU'RE GOING TO LIVE A HAPPY LIFE!!
I'M...
...GLAD I WAS ABLE TO...
...PRO-TECT...
...YOU...

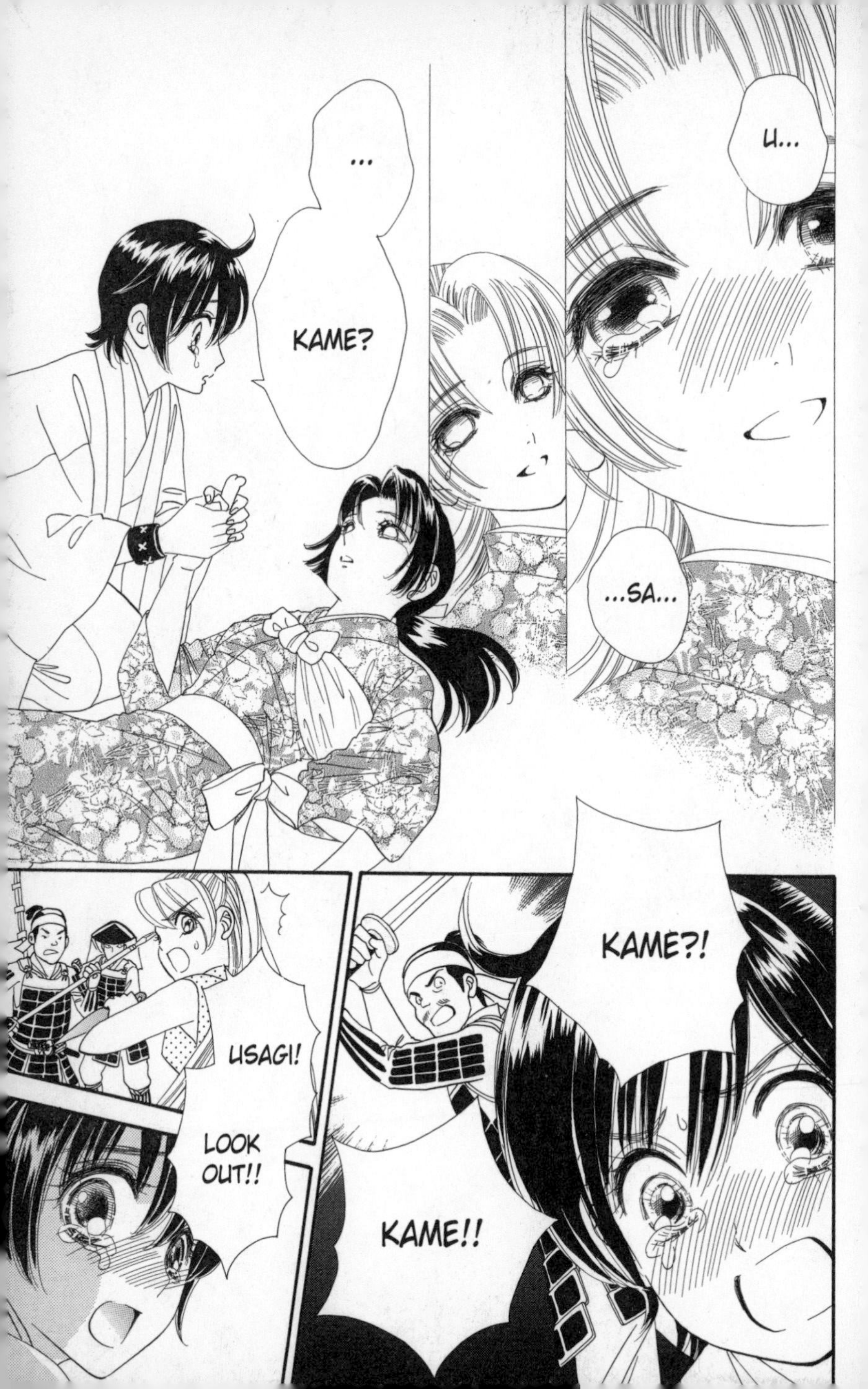
U...
...SA...
...
KAME?
KAME?!
USAGI!
LOOK OUT!!
KAME!!

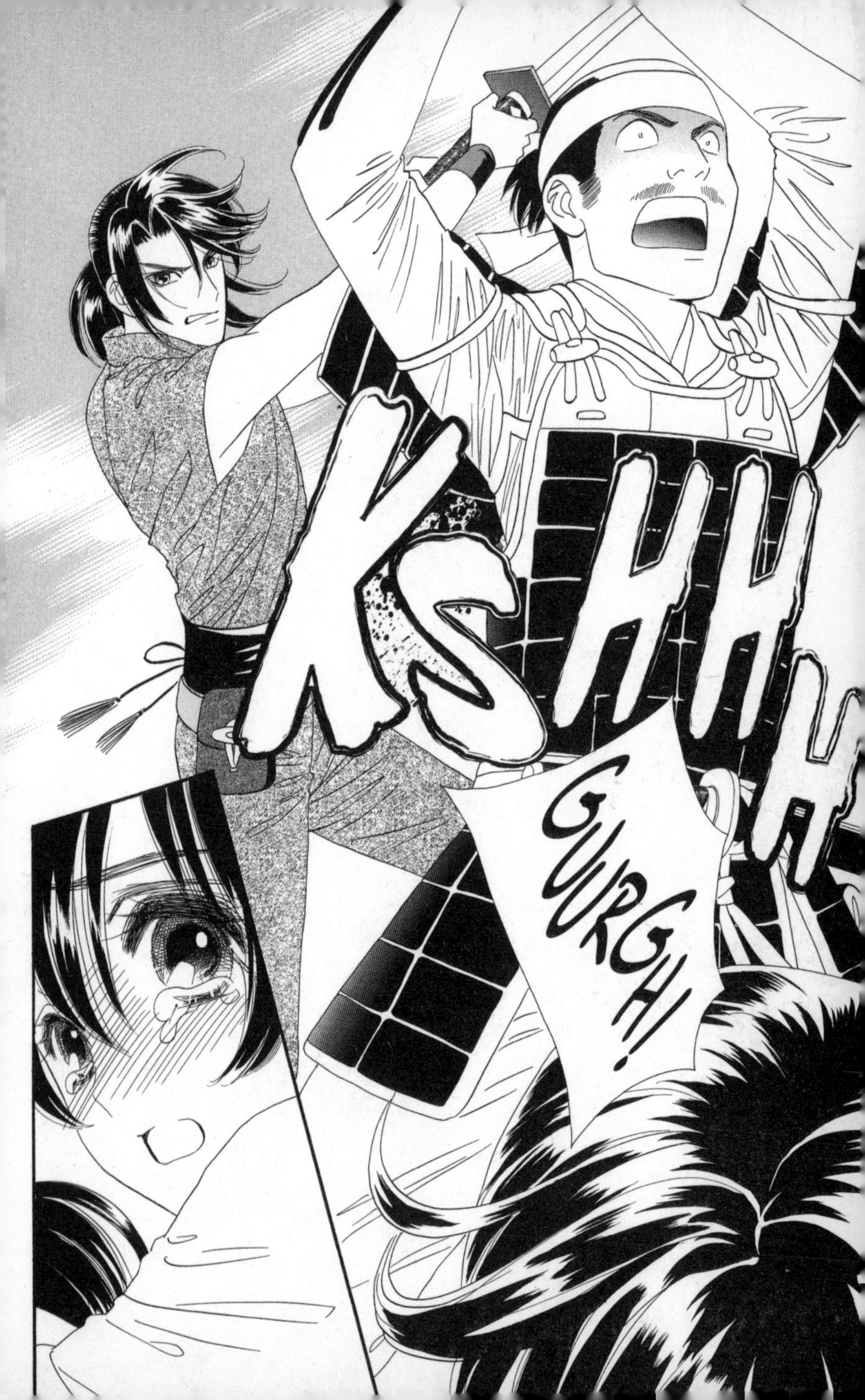
KSHHH
GUURGH!!

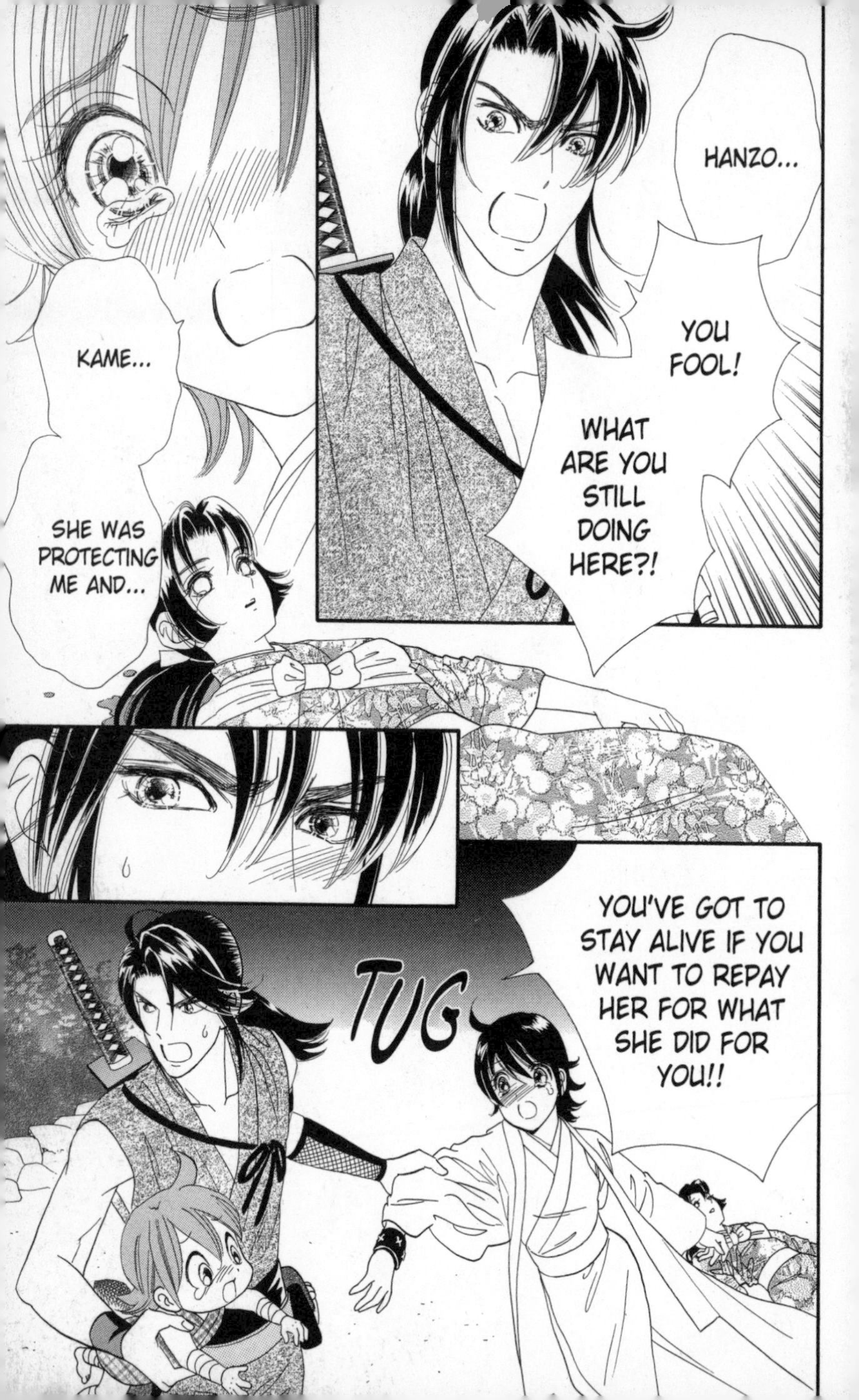
HANZO...
YOU FOOL!
WHAT ARE YOU STILL DOING HERE?!
KAME...
SHE WAS PROTECTING ME AND...
YOU'VE GOT TO STAY ALIVE IF YOU WANT TO REPAY HER FOR WHAT SHE DID FOR YOU!!
TUG

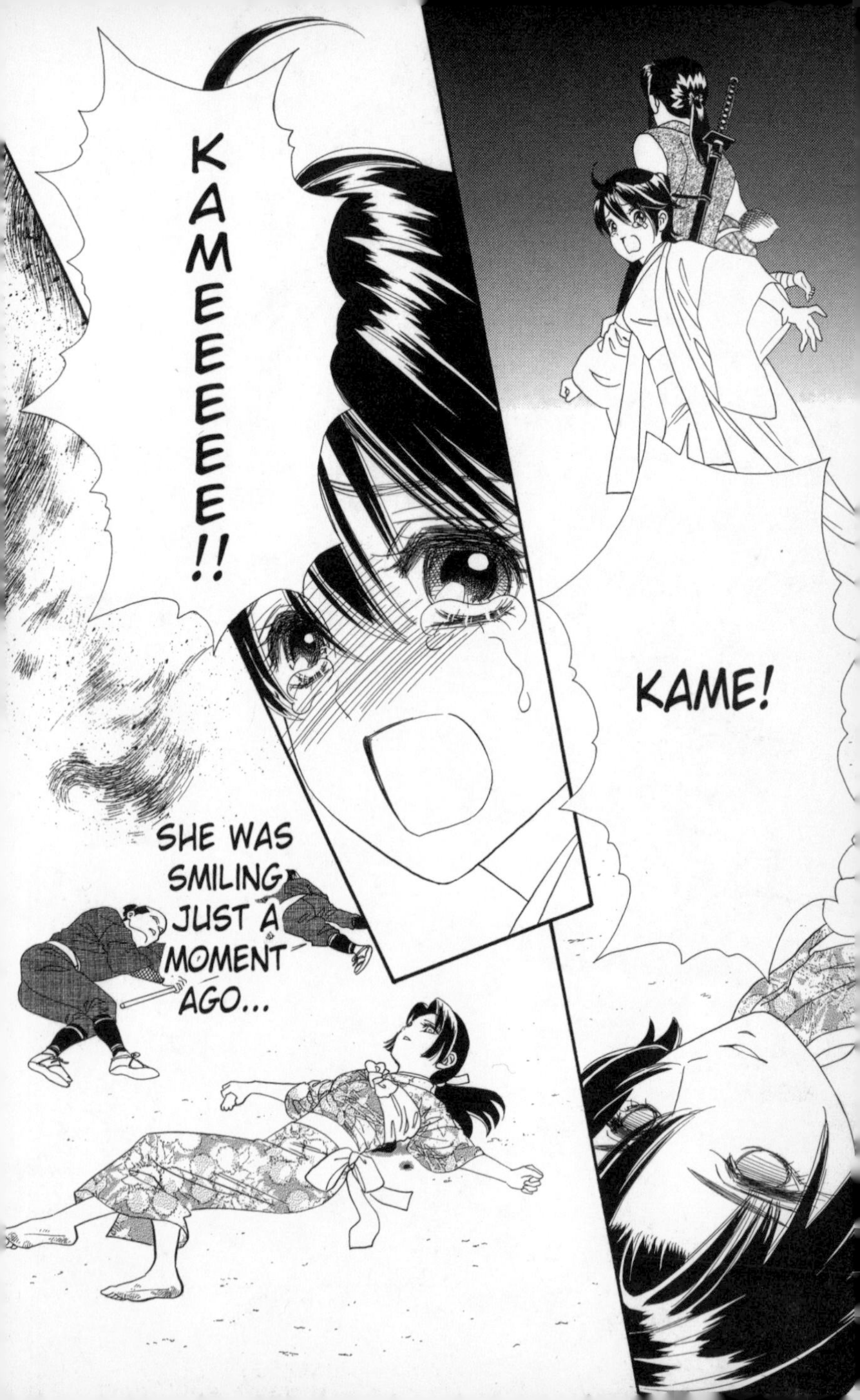
KAME!
KAMEEEEEEE!!
SHE WAS SMILING JUST A MOMENT AGO...

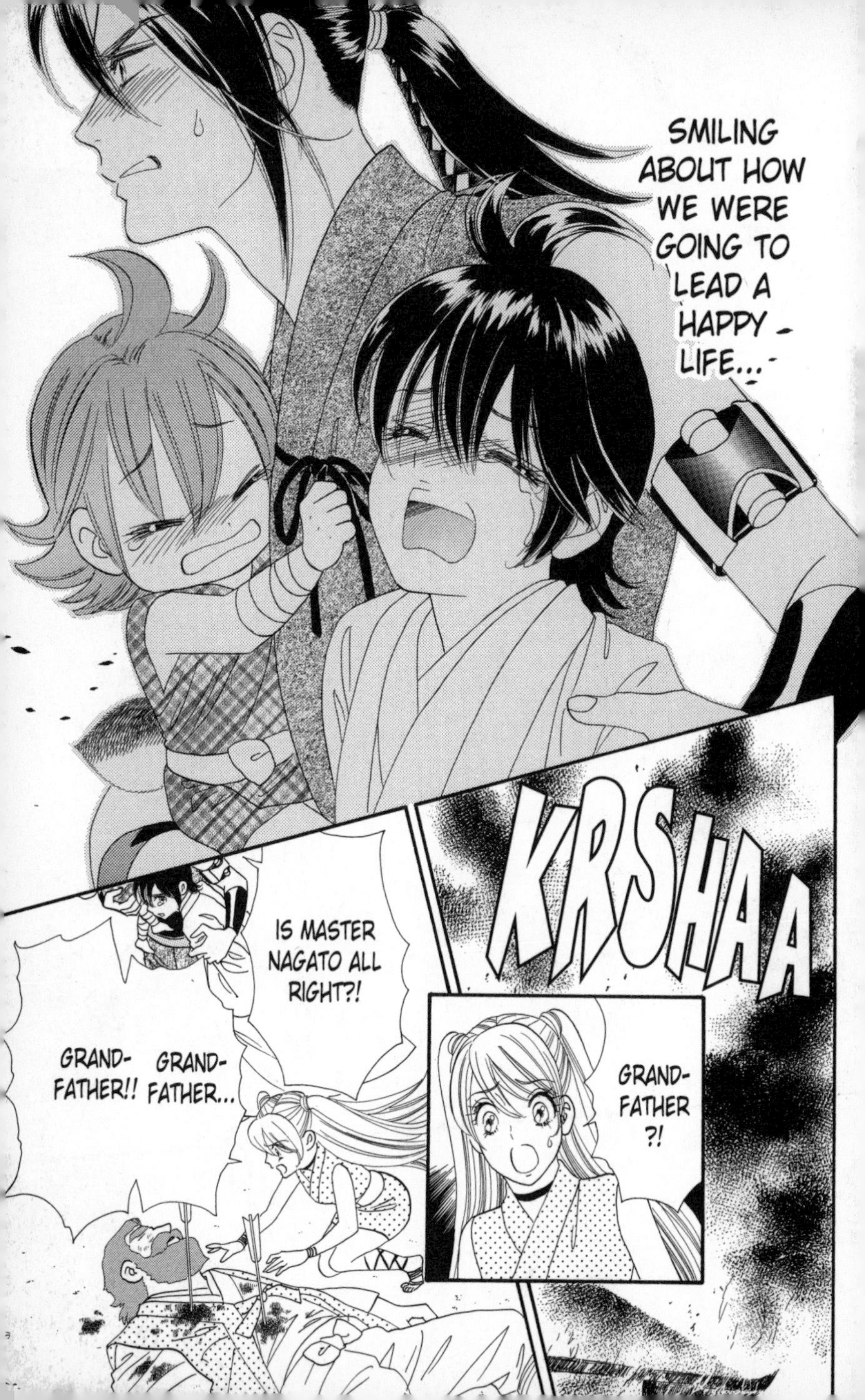
SMILING ABOUT HOW WE WERE GOING TO LEAD A HAPPY LIFE...
KRSHAA
GRAND-FATHER ?!
IS MASTER NAGATO ALL RIGHT?!
GRAND-FATHER...
GRAND-FATHER!!

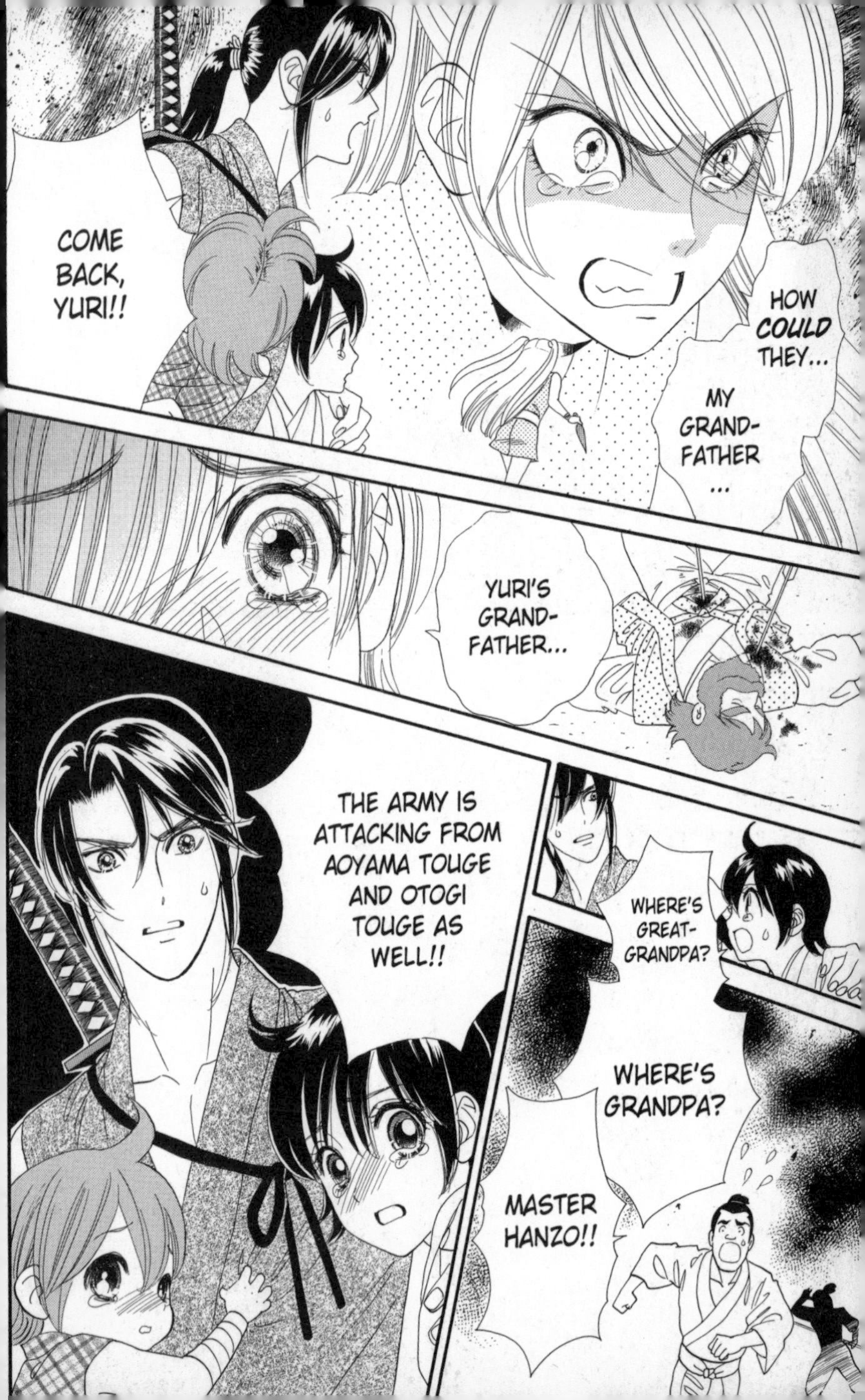
HOW COULD THEY...
MY GRAND-FATHER...
COME BACK, YURI!!
YURI'S GRAND-FATHER...
WHERE'S GREAT-GRANDPA?
WHERE'S GRANDPA?
MASTER HANZO!!
THE ARMY IS ATTACKING FROM AOYAMA TOUGE AND OTOGI TOUGE AS WELL!!

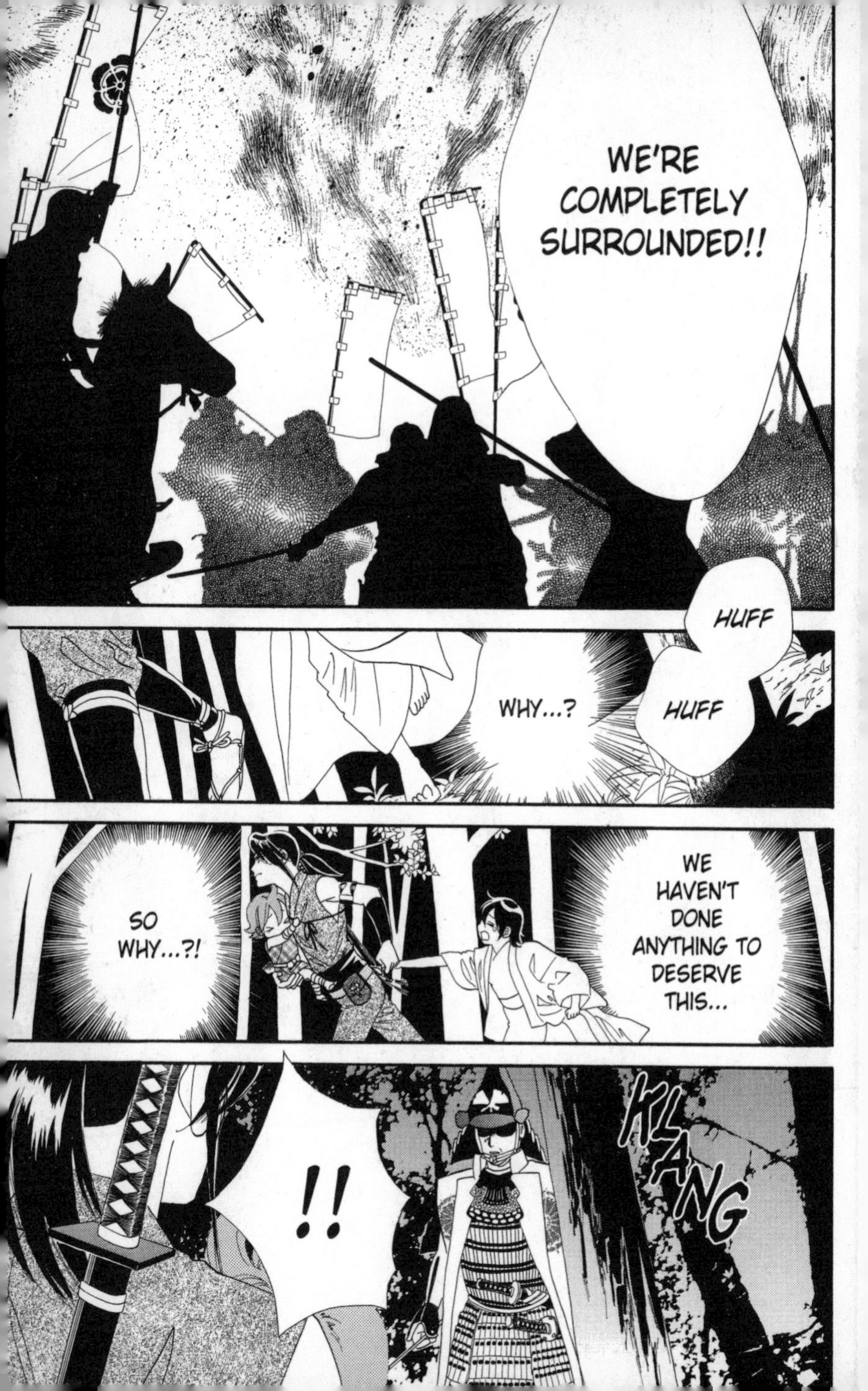

WE'RE COMPLETELY SURROUNDED!!
HUFF
HUFF
WHY...?
WE HAVEN'T DONE ANYTHING TO DESERVE THIS...
SO WHY...?!
KLANG
!!

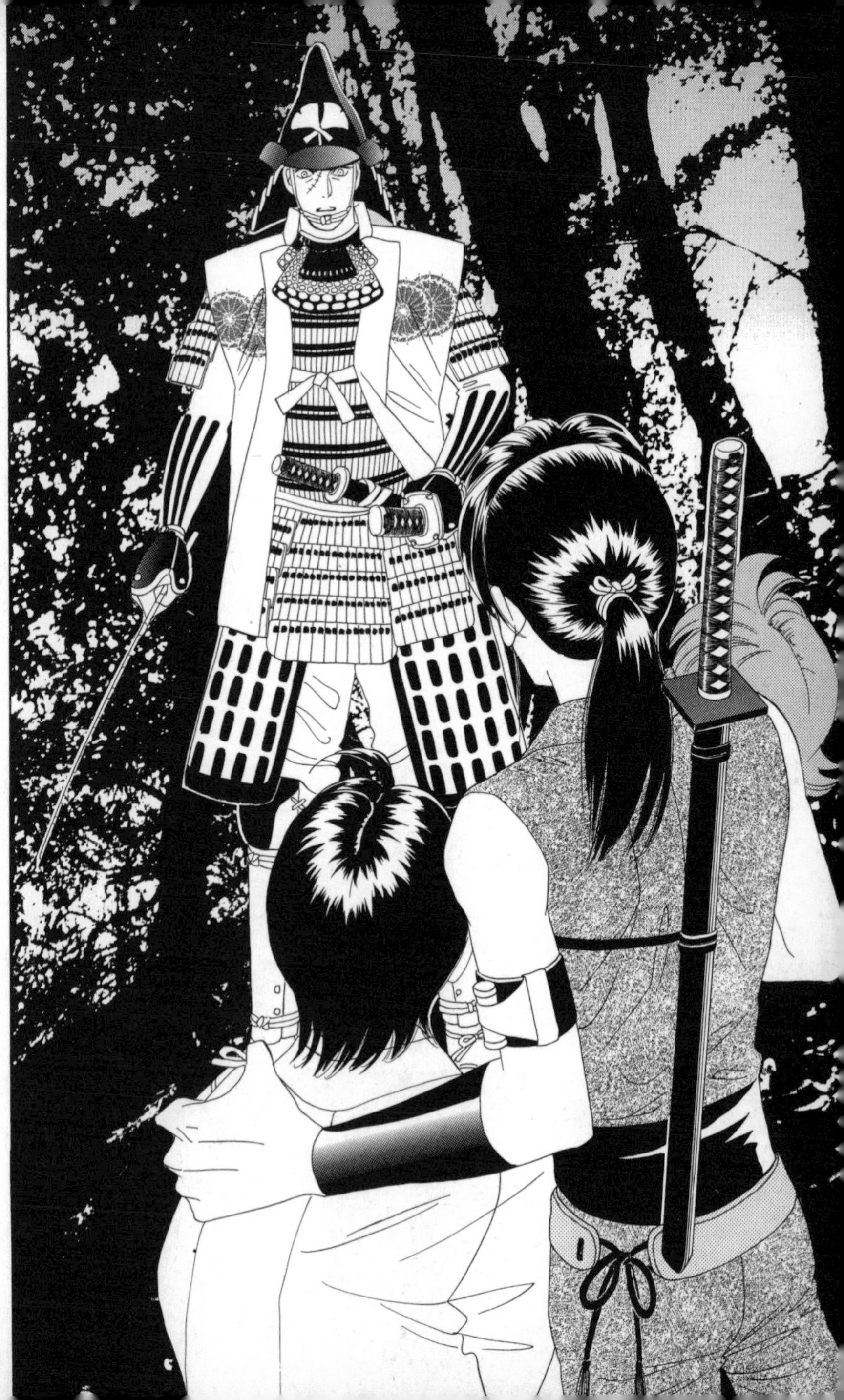

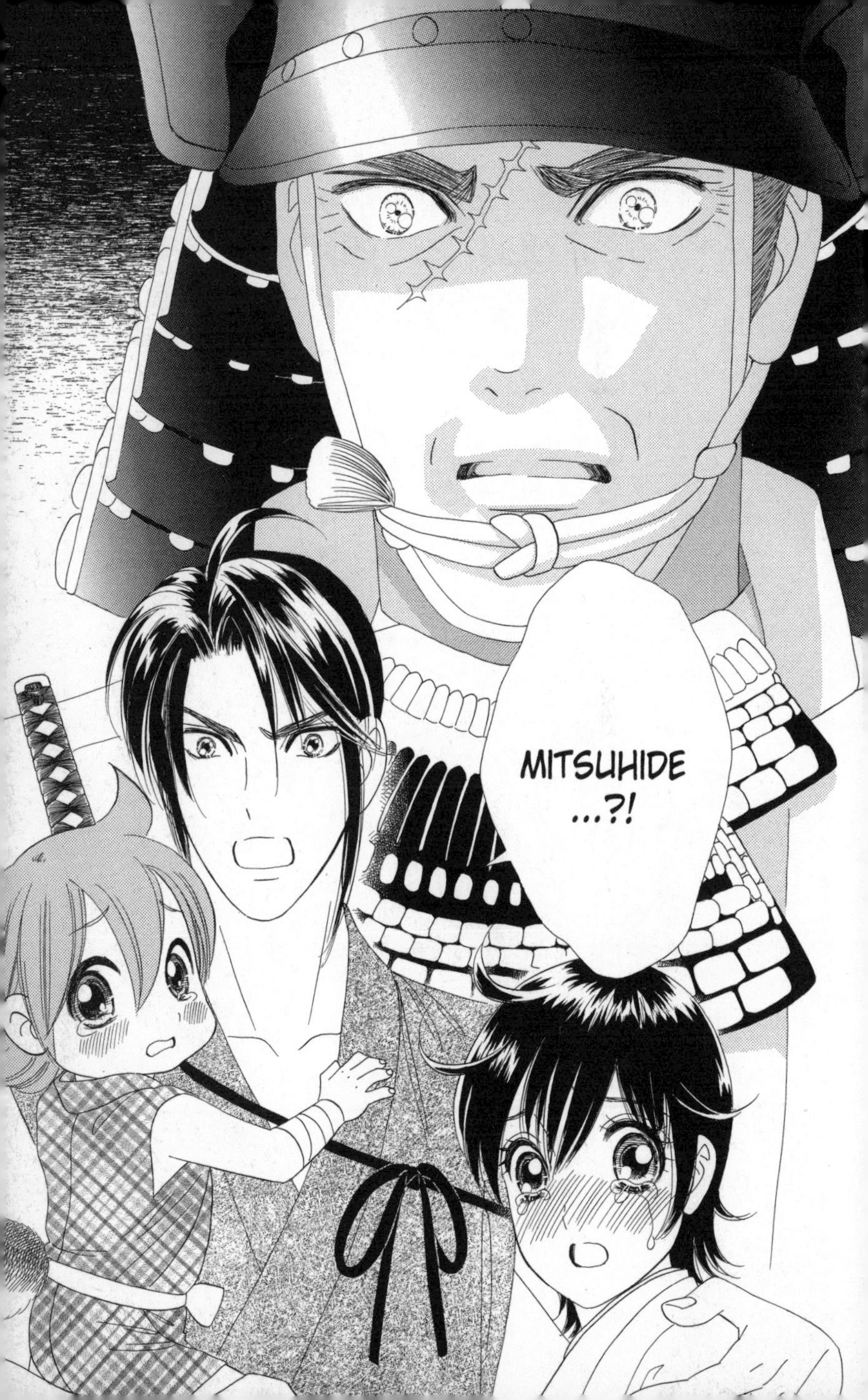
MITSUHIDE ...?!

TAIL OF THE MOON EXTRA: TODAY'S MISSION

"I WANT TO SEE USAGI AND THE OTHERS DOING HANAMI!"

-MIWA, KANAGAWA PREFECTURE

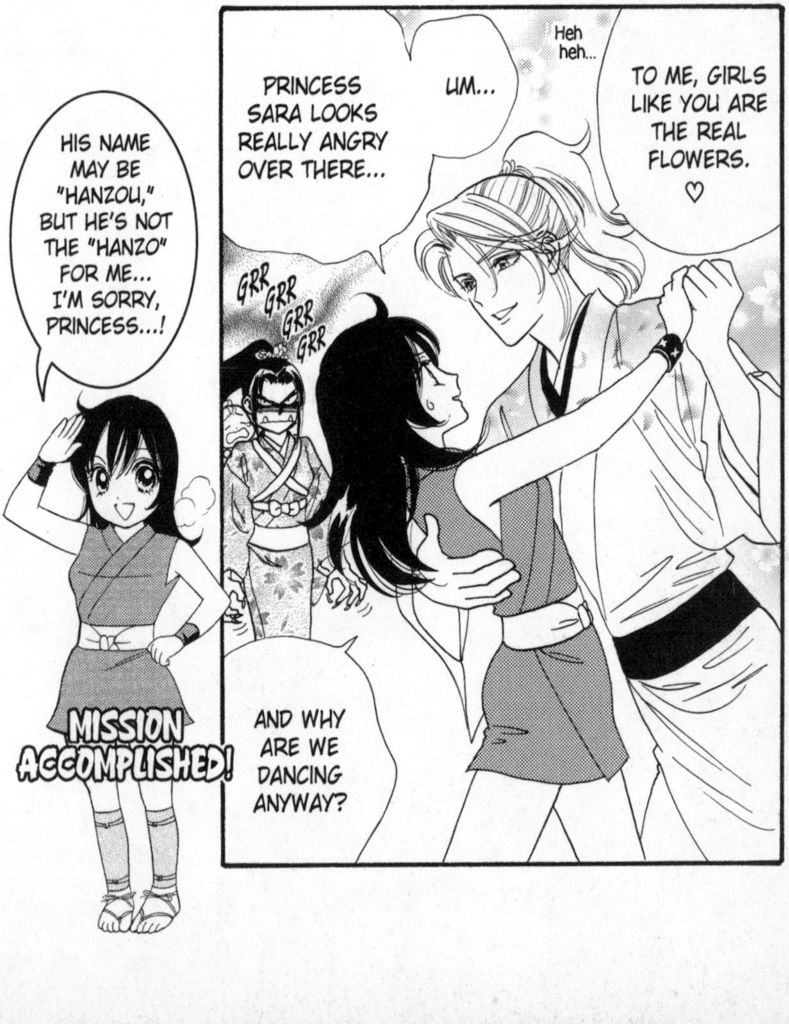
Heh heh...
TO ME, GIRLS LIKE YOU ARE THE REAL FLOWERS. ♡
UM...
PRINCESS SARA LOOKS REALLY ANGRY OVER THERE...
GRR GRR GRR GRR
AND WHY ARE WE DANCING ANYWAY?
HIS NAME MAY BE "HANZOU," BUT HE'S NOT THE "HANZO" FOR ME... I'M SORRY, PRINCESS...!
MISSION ACCOMPLISHED!

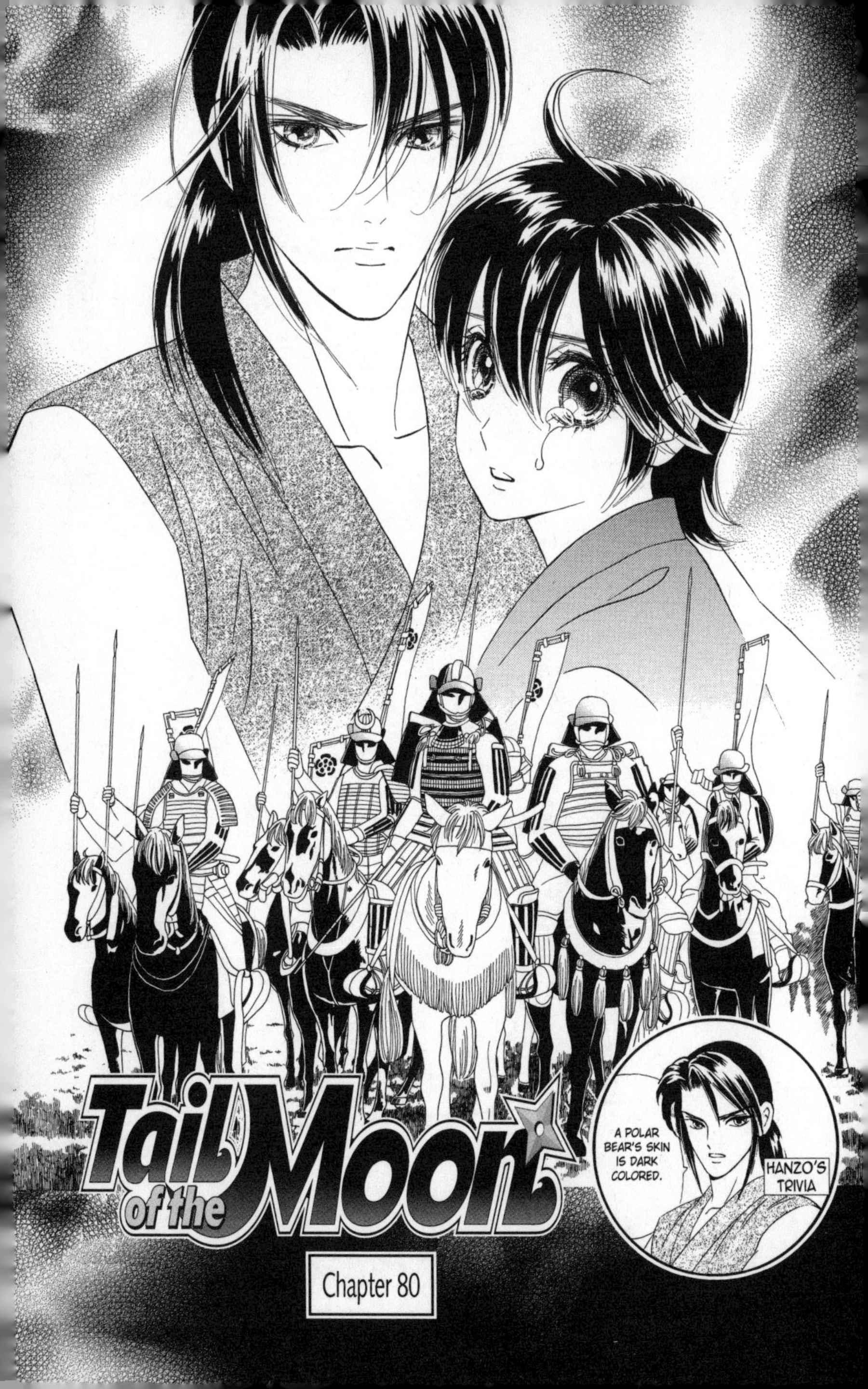
Tail of the Moon
Chapter 80
A POLAR BEAR'S SKIN IS DARK COLORED.
HANZO'S TRIVIA

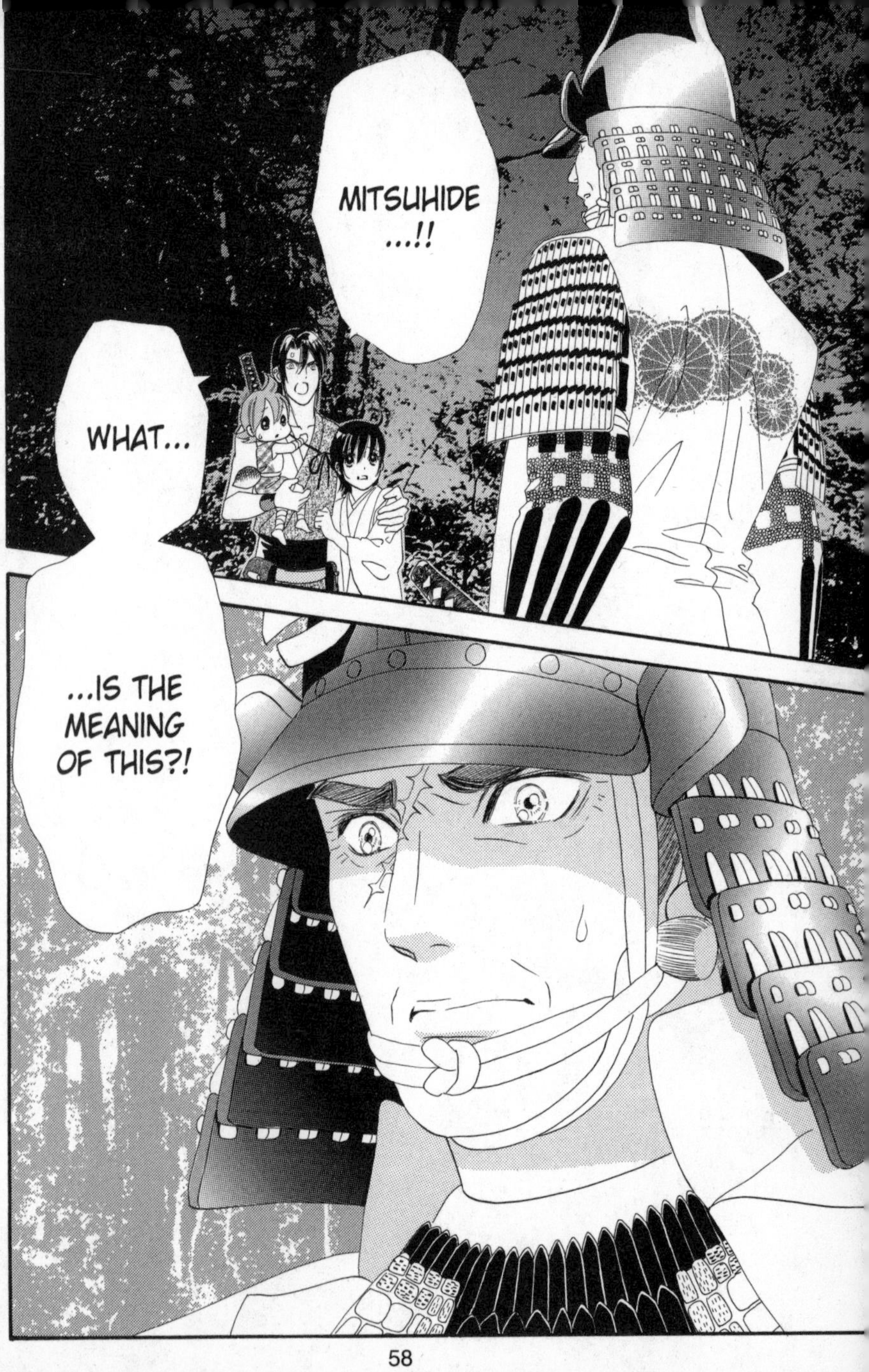
MITSUHIDE ...!!
WHAT...
...IS THE MEANING OF THIS?!

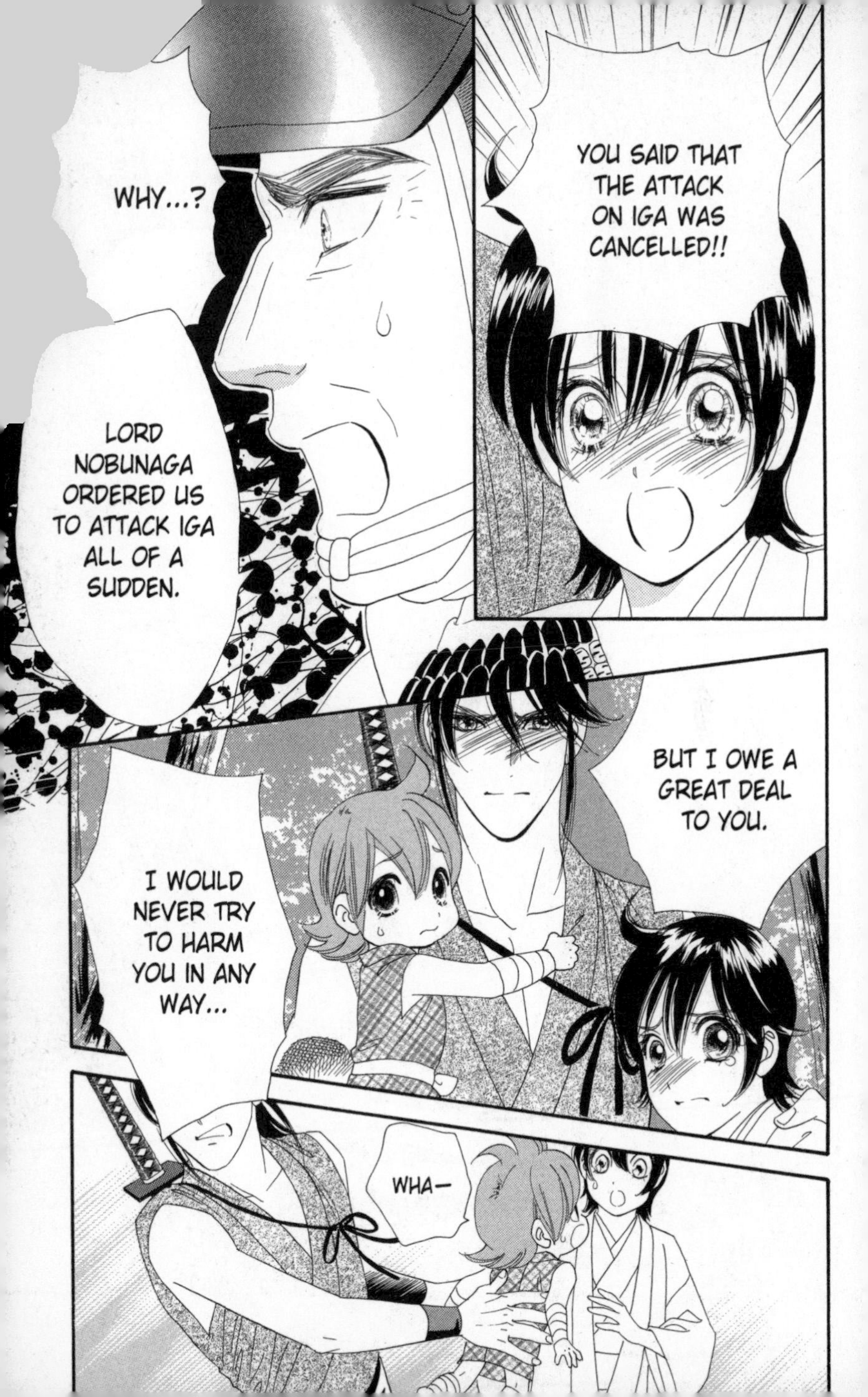
YOU SAID THAT THE ATTACK ON IGA WAS CANCELLED!!
WHY...?
LORD NOBUNAGA ORDERED US TO ATTACK IGA ALL OF A SUDDEN.
BUT I OWE A GREAT DEAL TO YOU.
I WOULD NEVER TRY TO HARM YOU IN ANY WAY...
WHA—

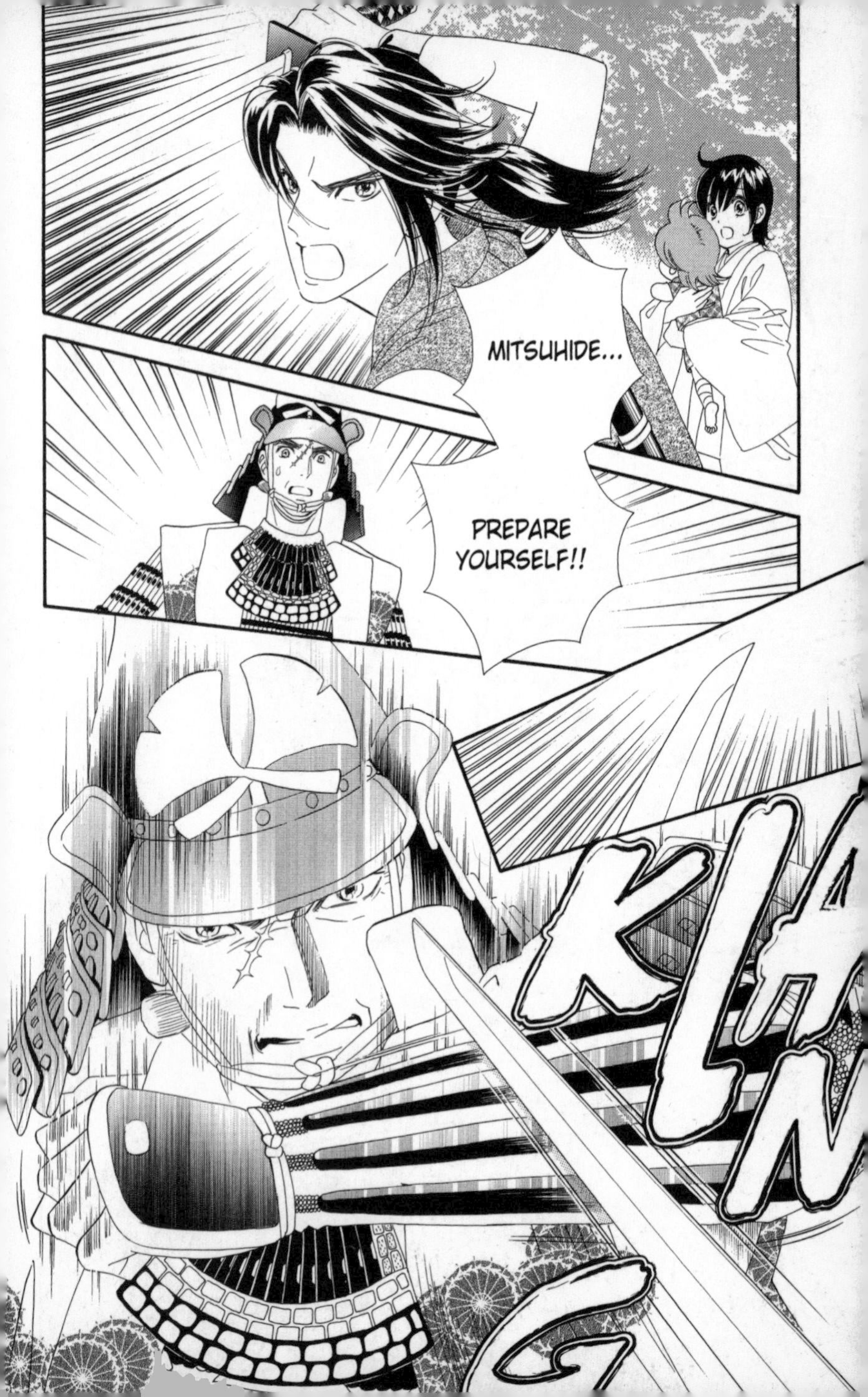
MITSUHIDE...
PREPARE YOURSELF!!

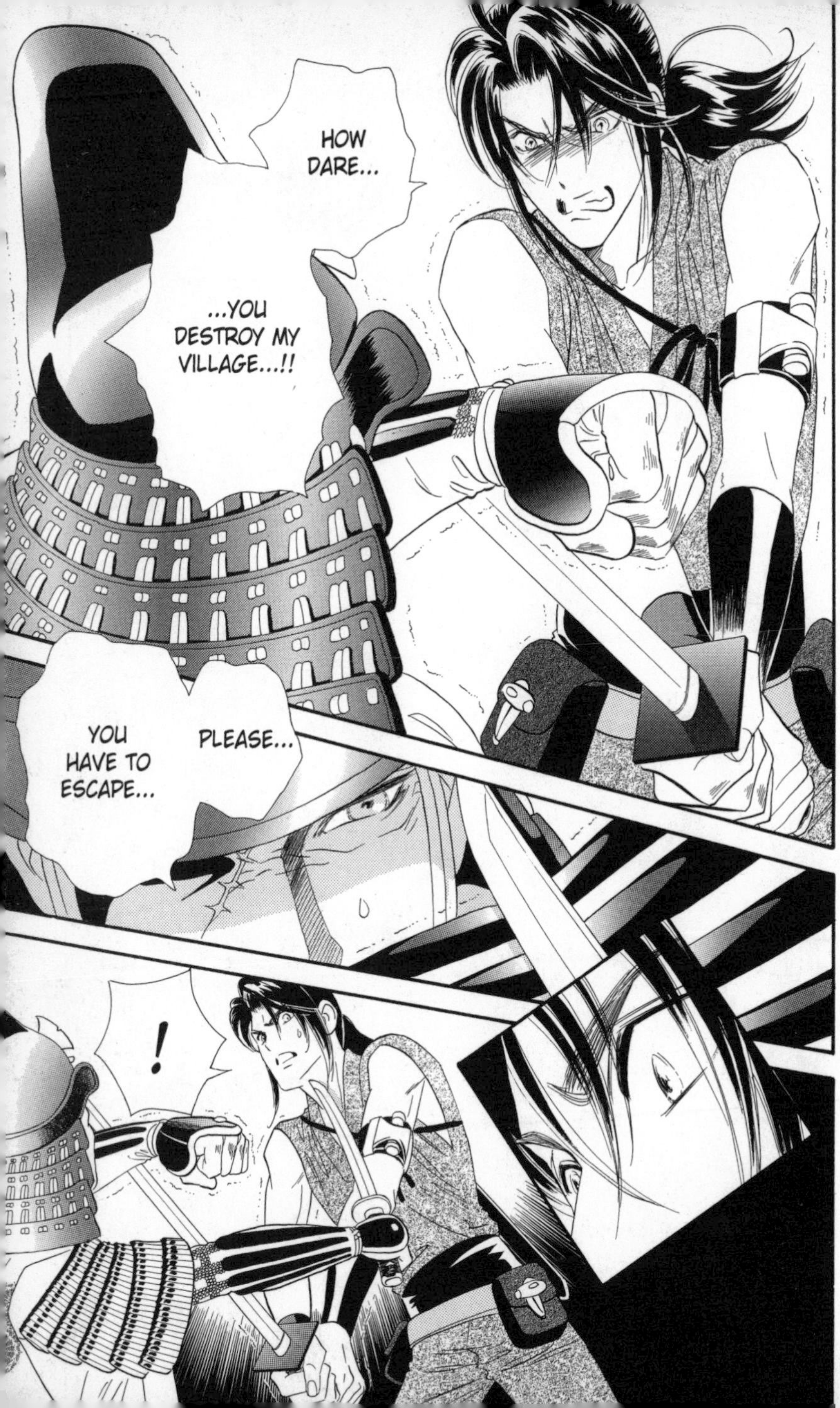
HOW DARE...
...YOU DESTROY MY VILLAGE...!!
PLEASE...
YOU HAVE TO ESCAPE...
!

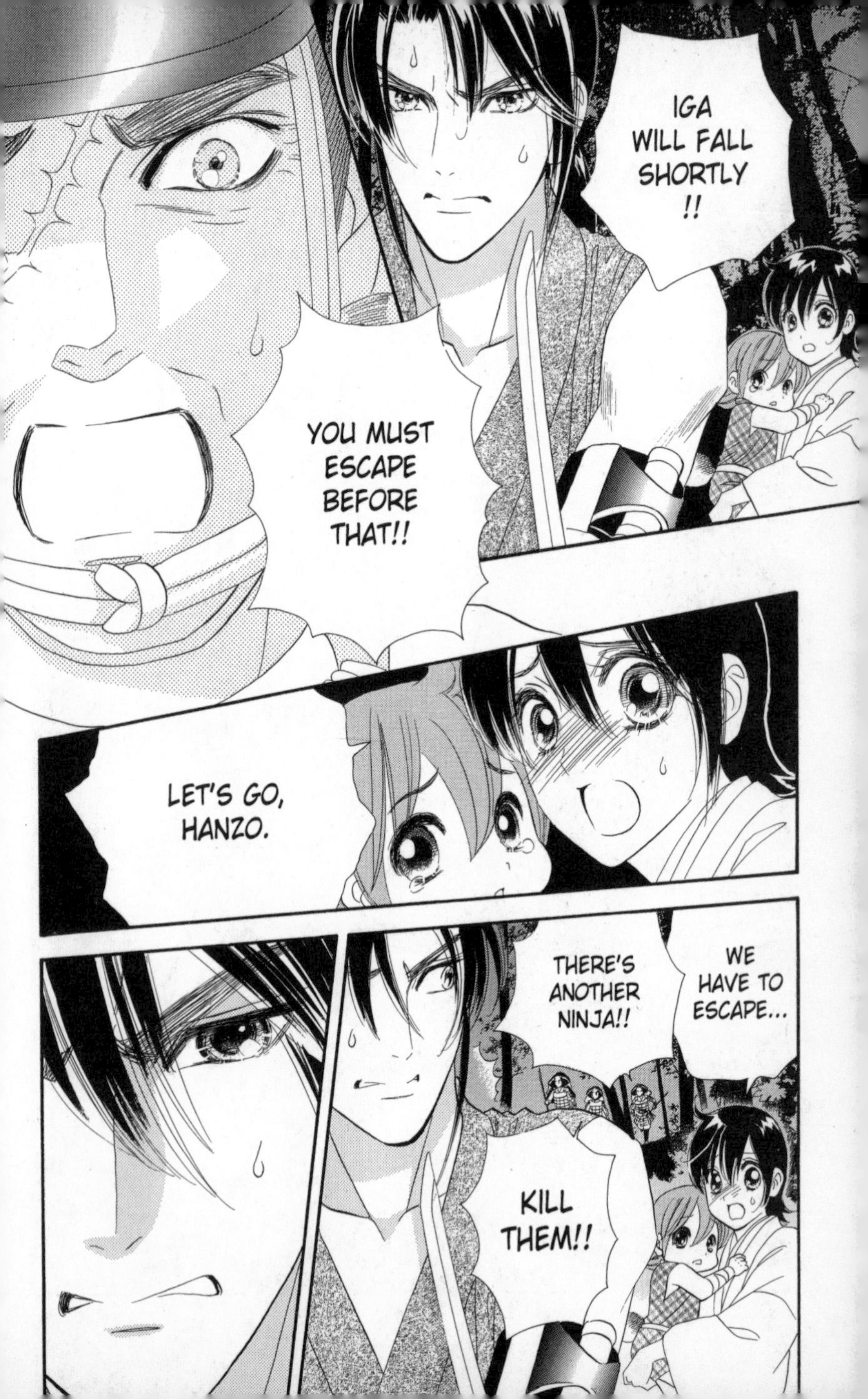
IGA WILL FALL SHORTLY!!
YOU MUST ESCAPE BEFORE THAT!!
LET'S GO, HANZO.
WE HAVE TO ESCAPE...
THERE'S ANOTHER NINJA!!
KILL THEM!!

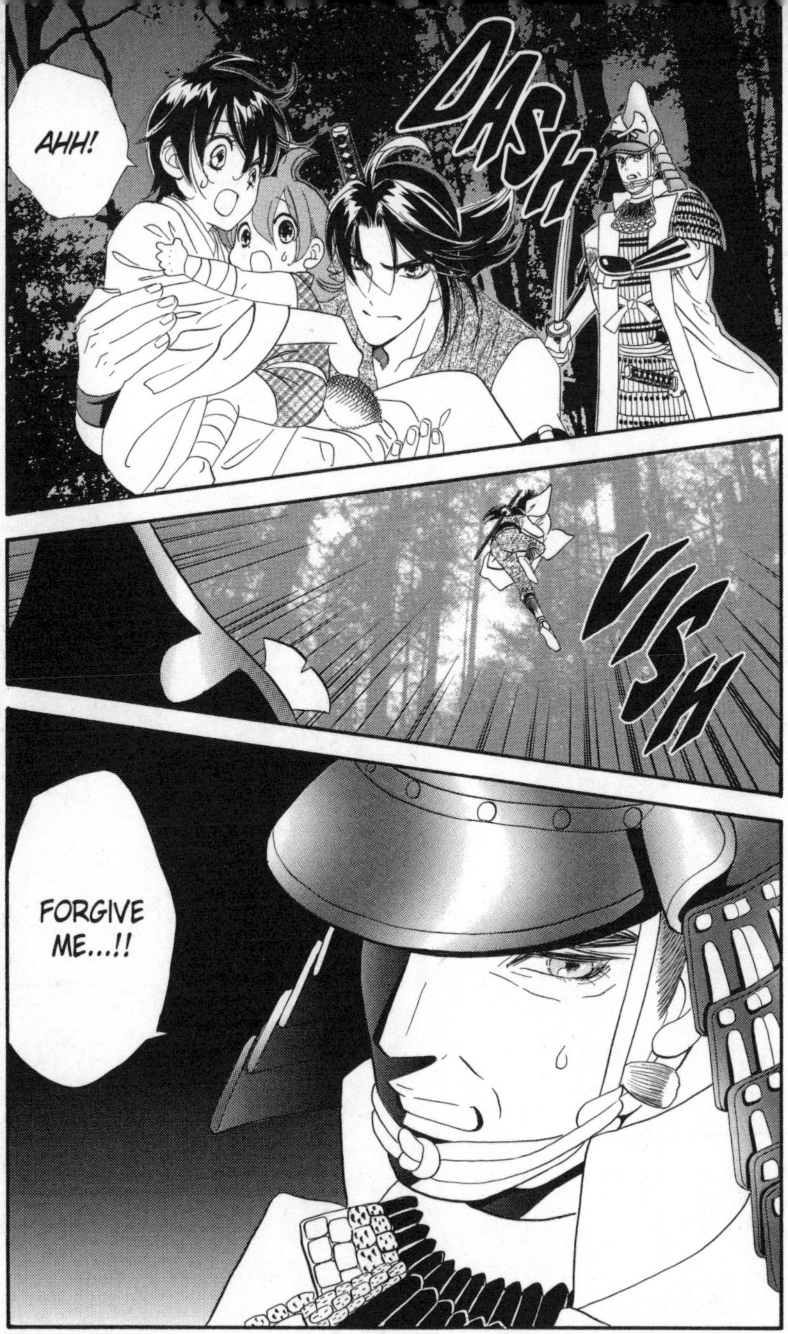
DASH
AHH!
VISH
FORGIVE ME...!!

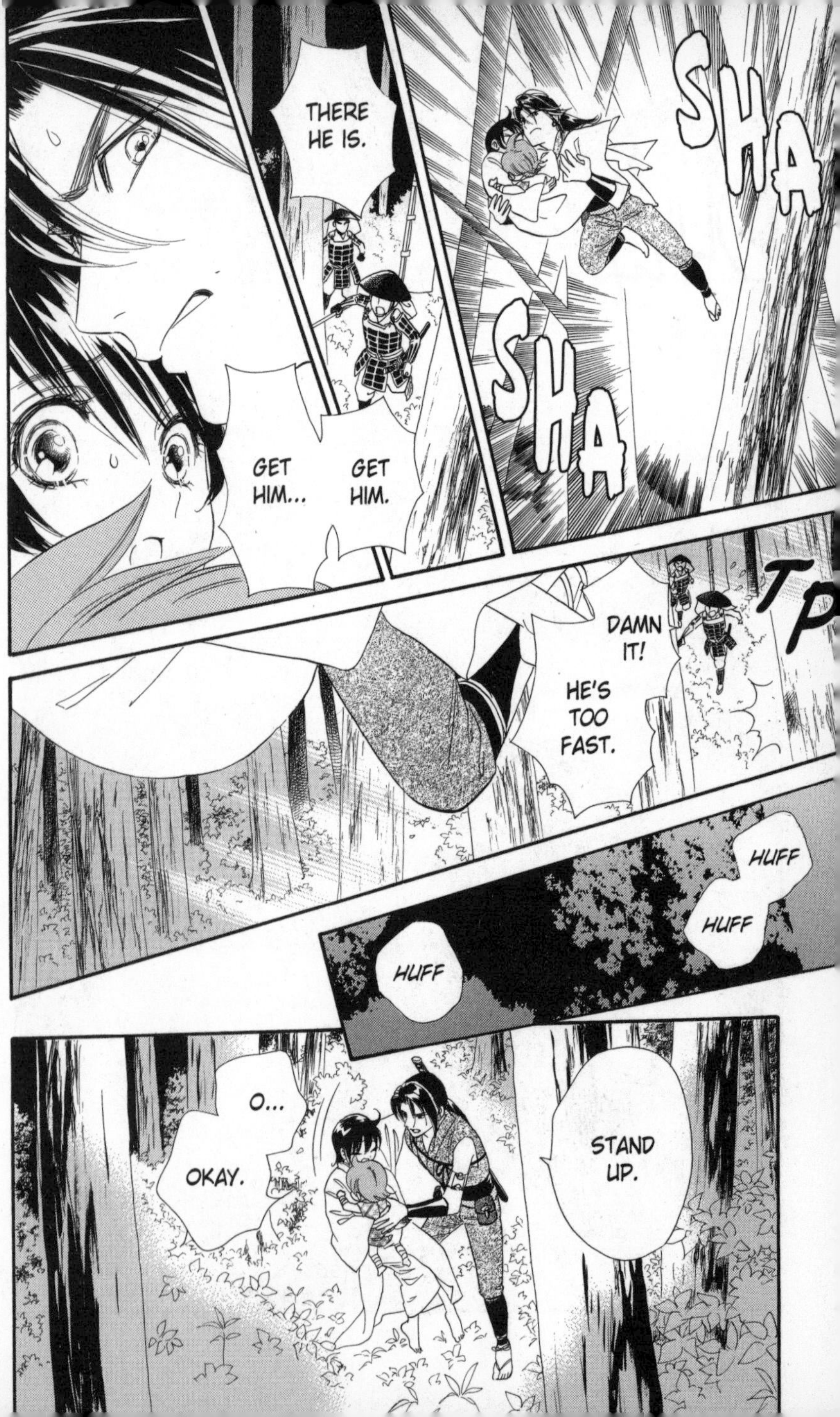
SHA
SHA
THERE HE IS.
GET HIM... GET HIM.
TP
DAMN IT!
HE'S TOO FAST.
HUFF
HUFF
HUFF
STAND UP.
O... OKAY.

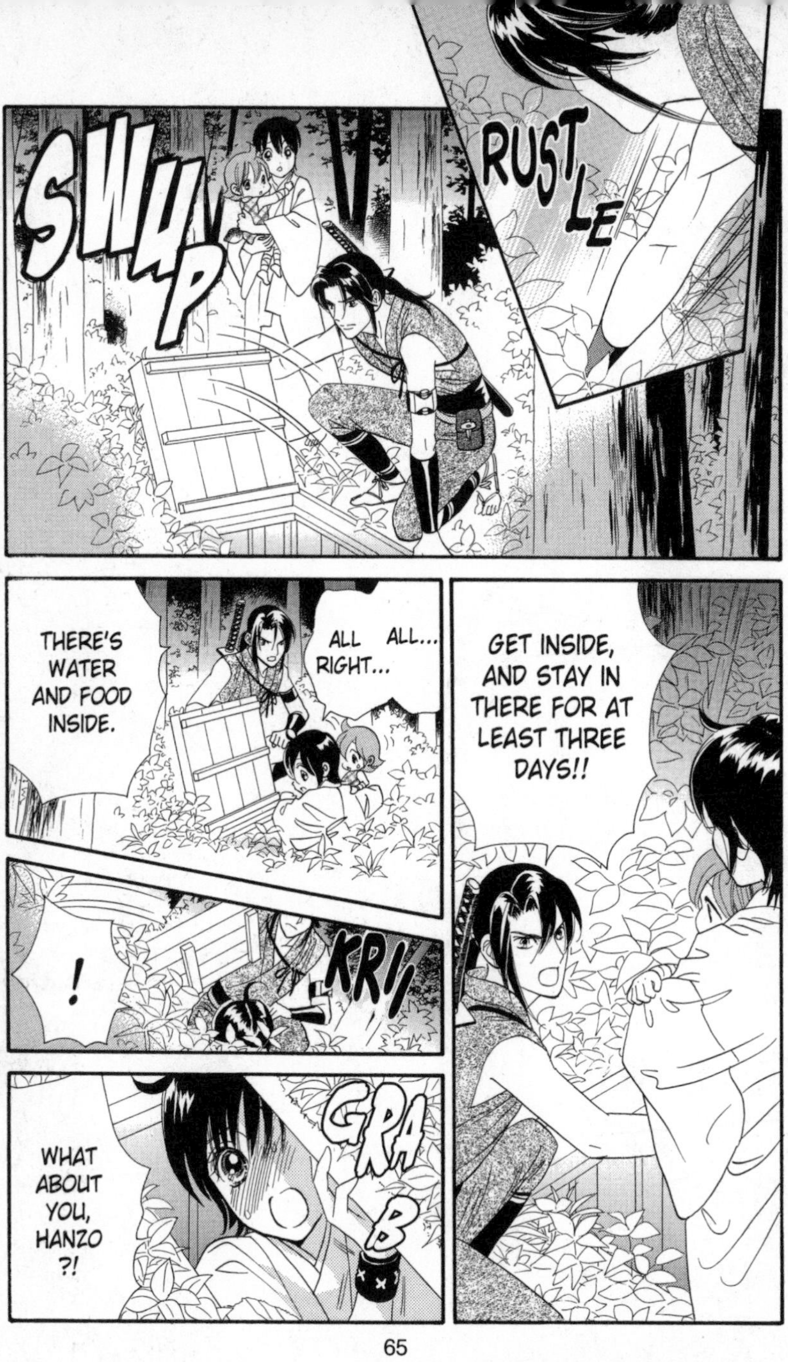

RUSTLE
SWUP
GET INSIDE, AND STAY IN THERE FOR AT LEAST THREE DAYS!!
ALL ALL... RIGHT...
THERE'S WATER AND FOOD INSIDE.
KRI
!
GRAB
WHAT ABOUT YOU, HANZO?!

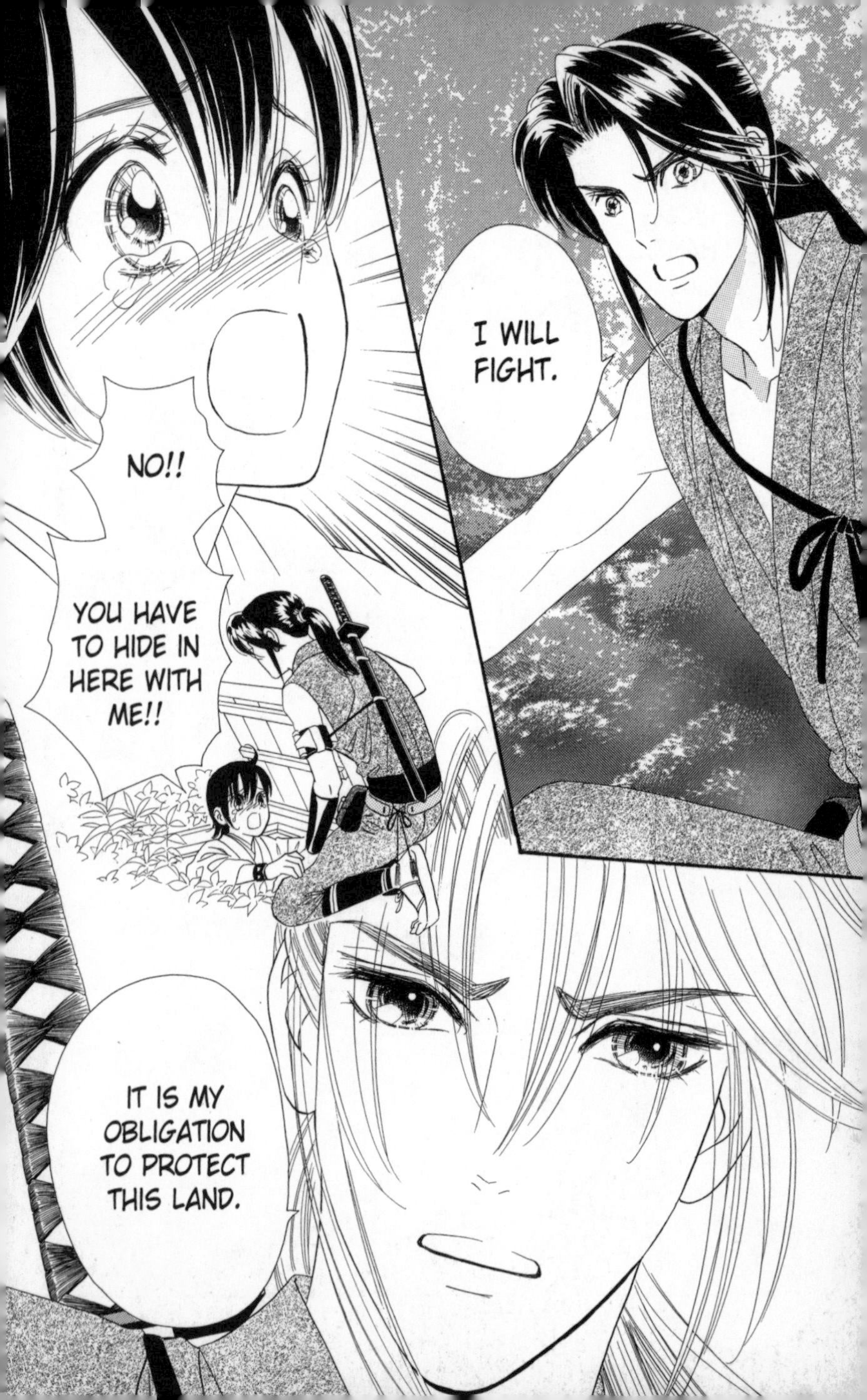
I WILL FIGHT.
NO!!
YOU HAVE TO HIDE IN HERE WITH ME!!
IT IS MY OBLIGATION TO PROTECT THIS LAND.

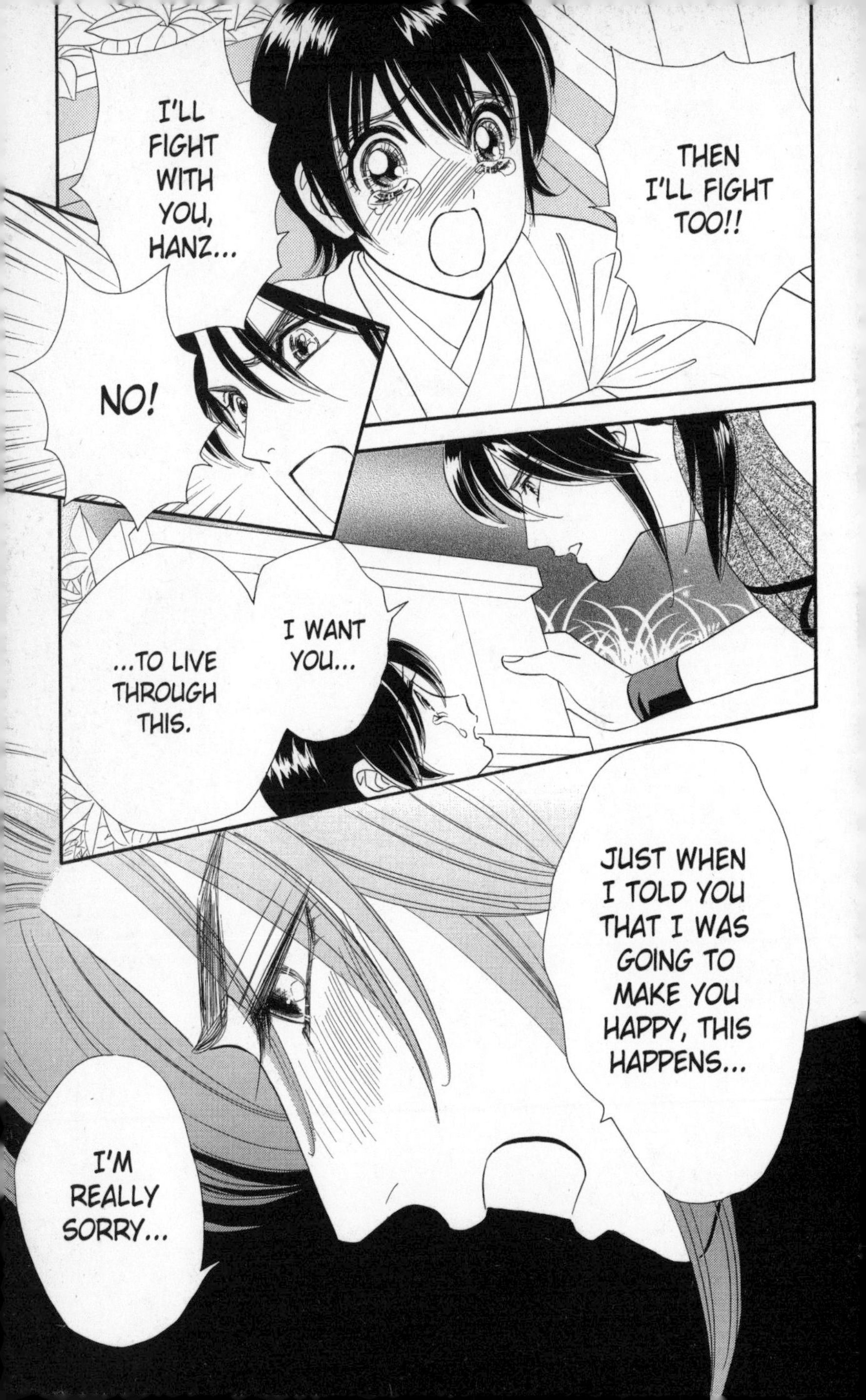
THEN I'LL FIGHT TOO!!
I'LL FIGHT WITH YOU, HANZ...
NO!
I WANT YOU...
...TO LIVE THROUGH THIS.
JUST WHEN I TOLD YOU THAT I WAS GOING TO MAKE YOU HAPPY, THIS HAPPENS...
I'M REALLY SORRY...

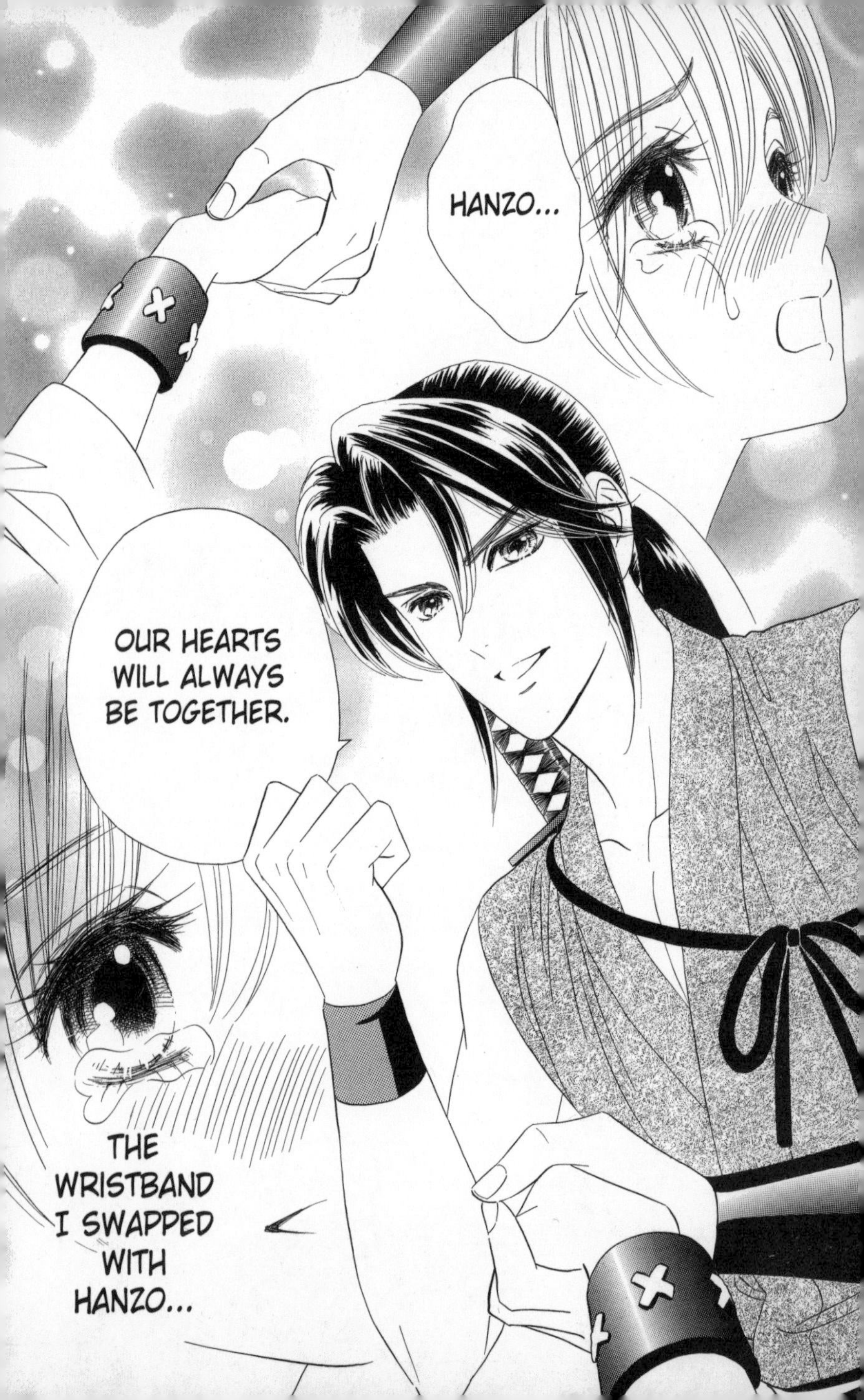
HANZO...
OUR HEARTS WILL ALWAYS BE TOGETHER.
THE WRISTBAND I SWAPPED WITH HANZO...

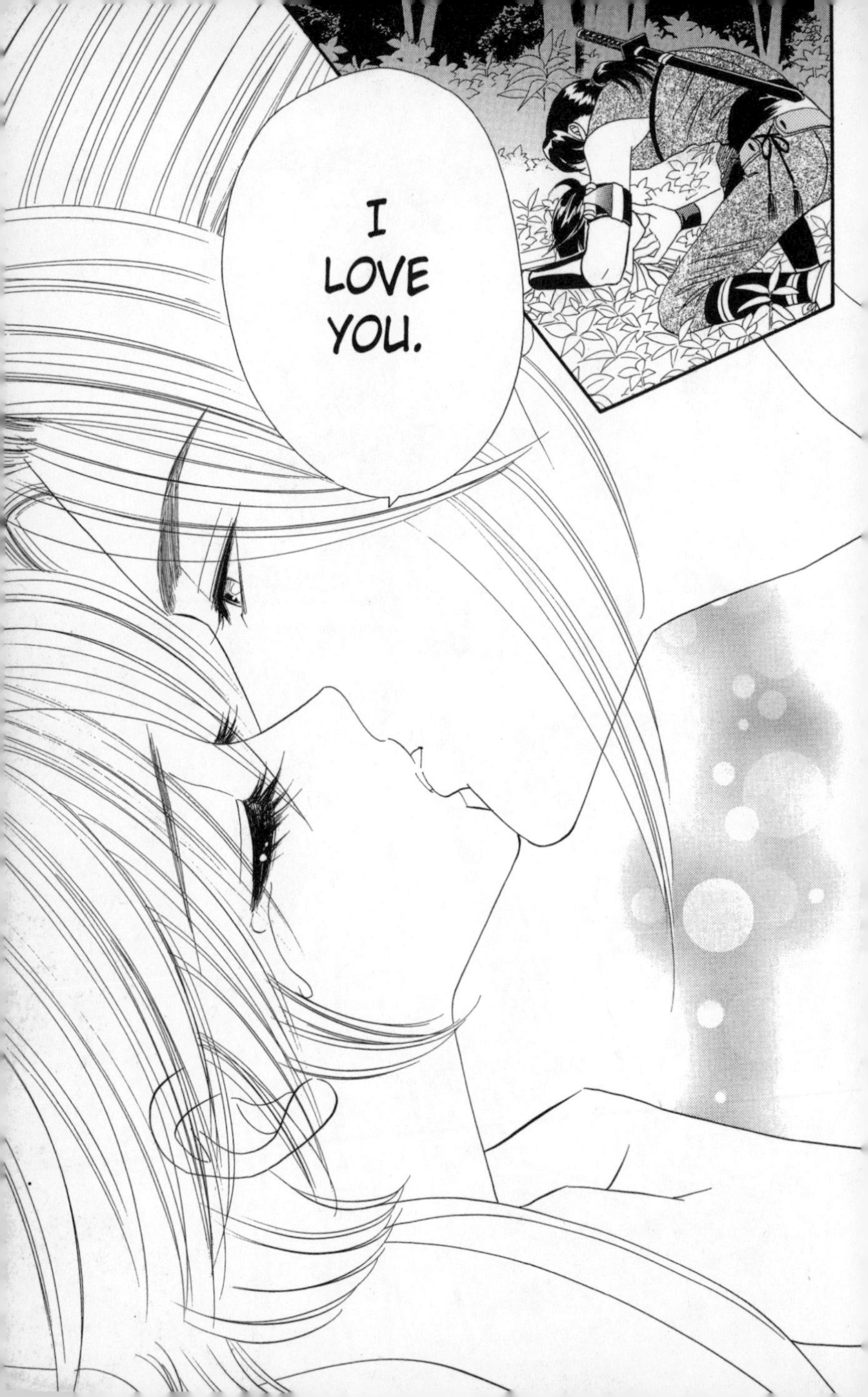
I LOVE YOU.

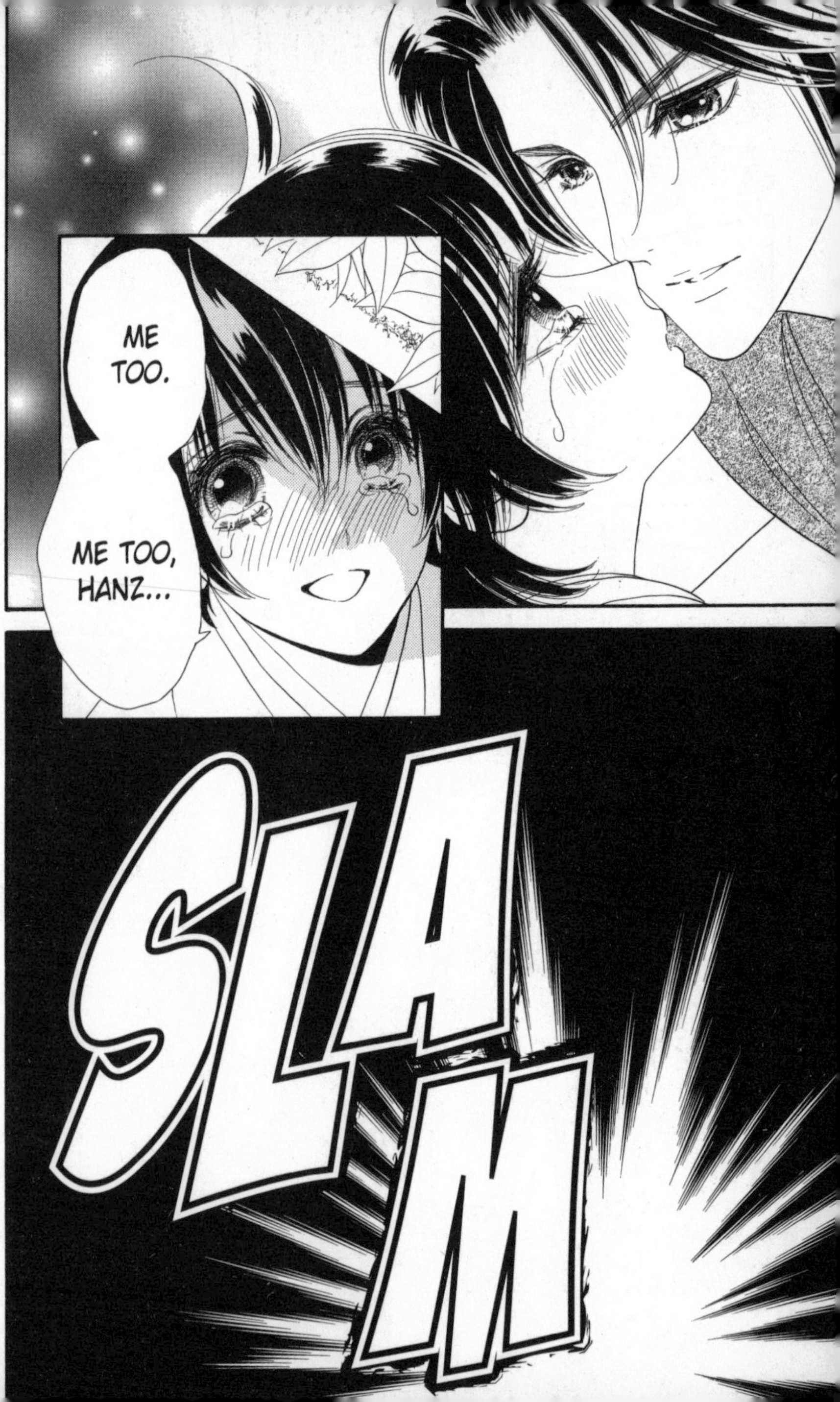
ME TOO.
ME TOO, HANZ...
SLAM

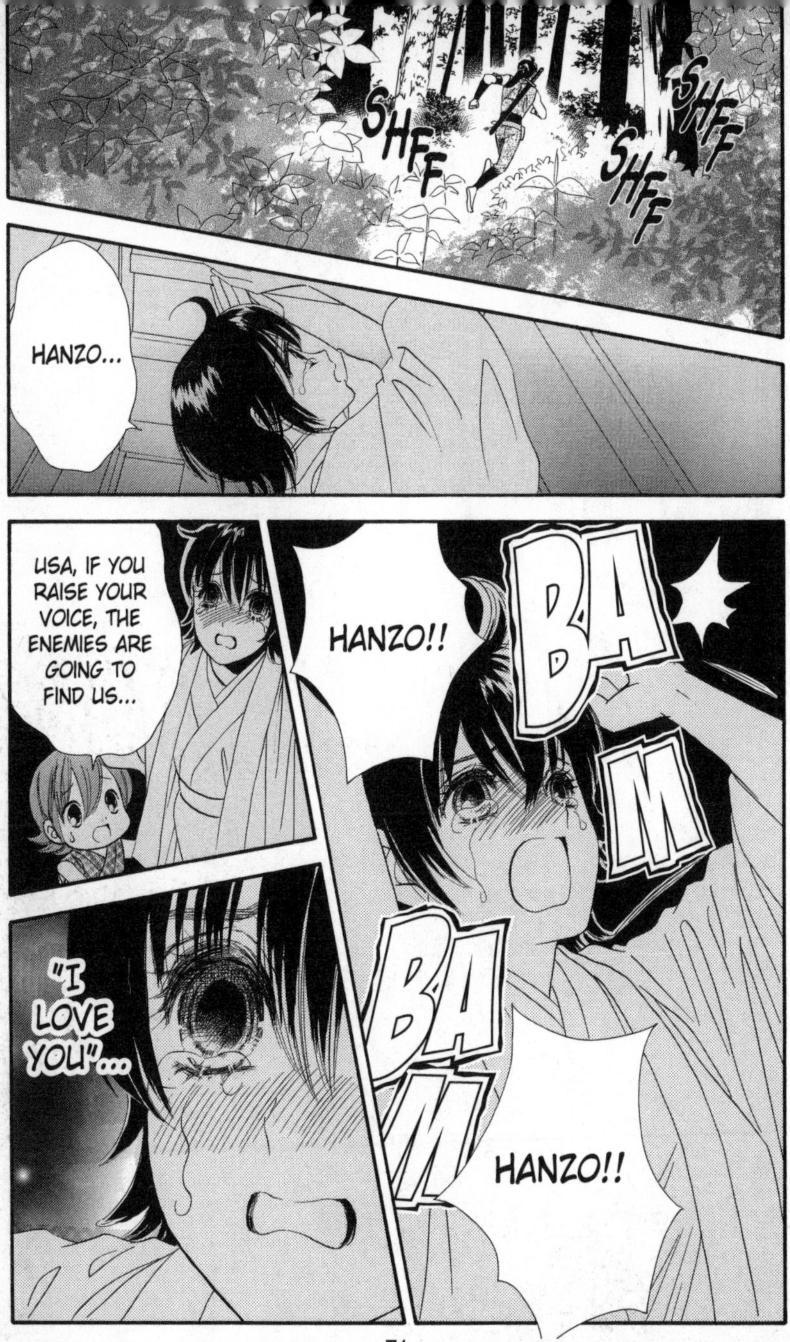
SHFF
SHFF
SHFF
HANZO...
BAM
HANZO!!
BAM
HANZO!!
USA, IF YOU RAISE YOUR VOICE, THE ENEMIES ARE GOING TO FIND US...
"I LOVE YOU"...

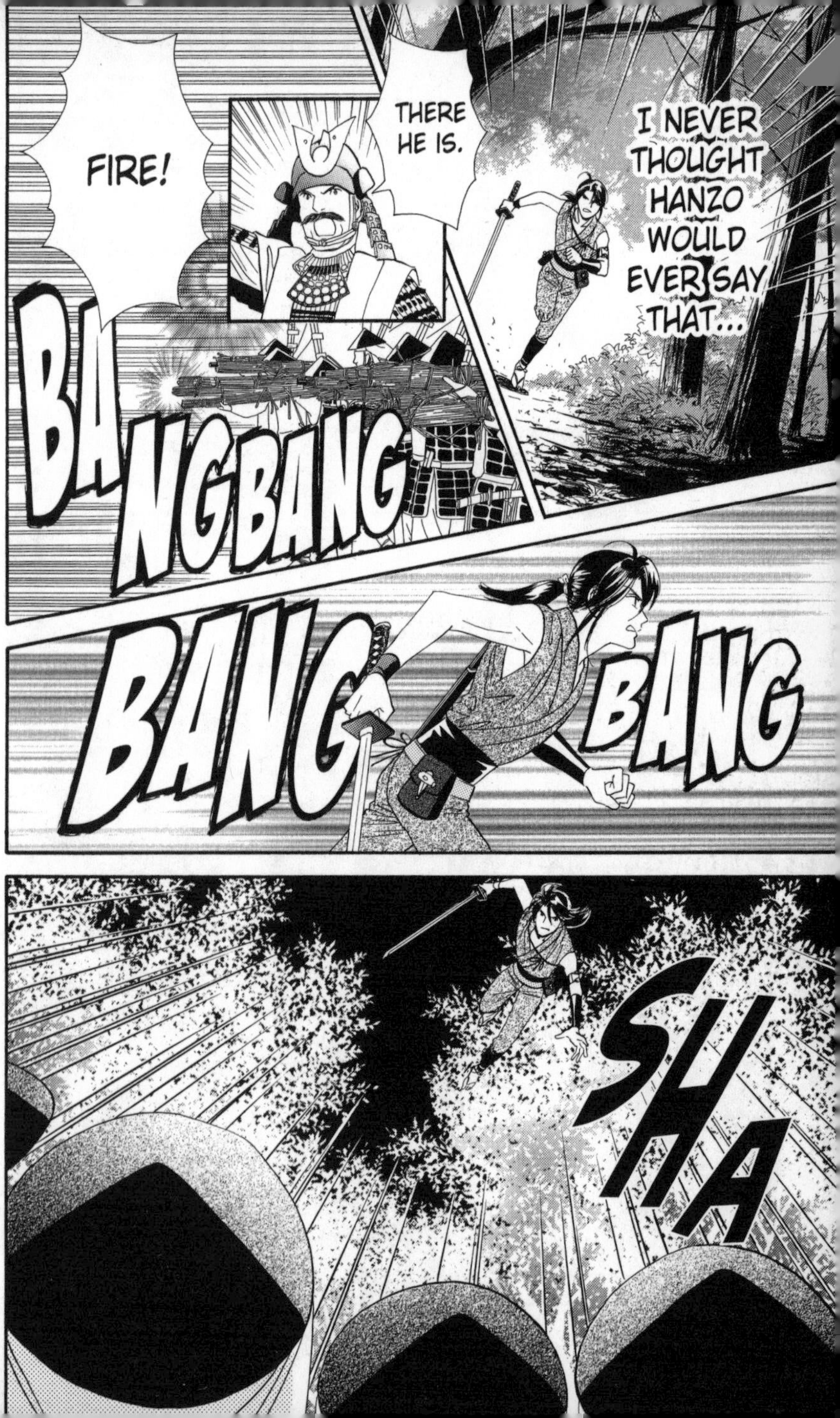
I NEVER THOUGHT HANZO WOULD EVER SAY THAT...
THERE HE IS.
FIRE!
BANGBANGBANG
BANG
BANG
SHA

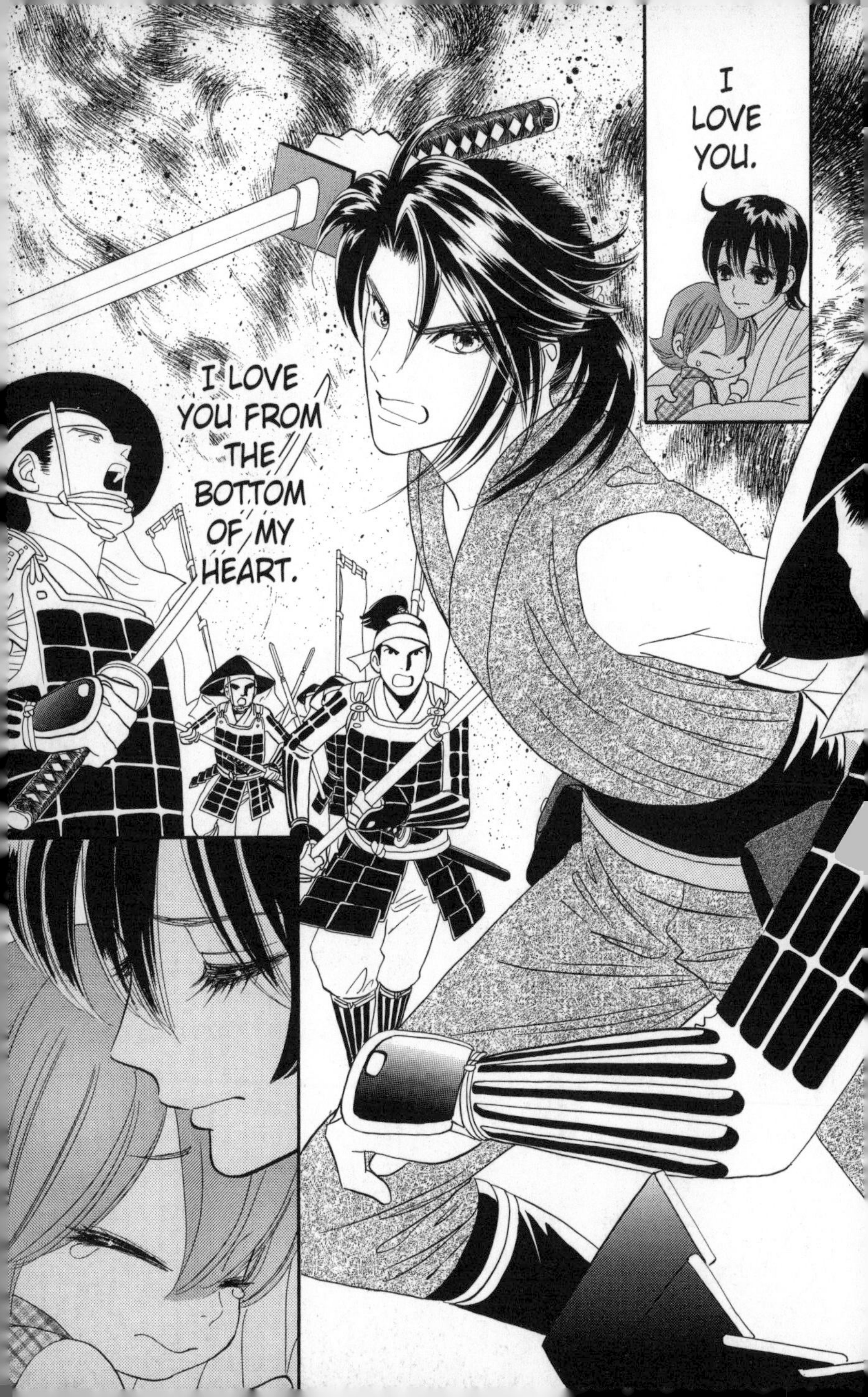
I LOVE YOU.
I LOVE YOU FROM THE BOTTOM OF MY HEART.

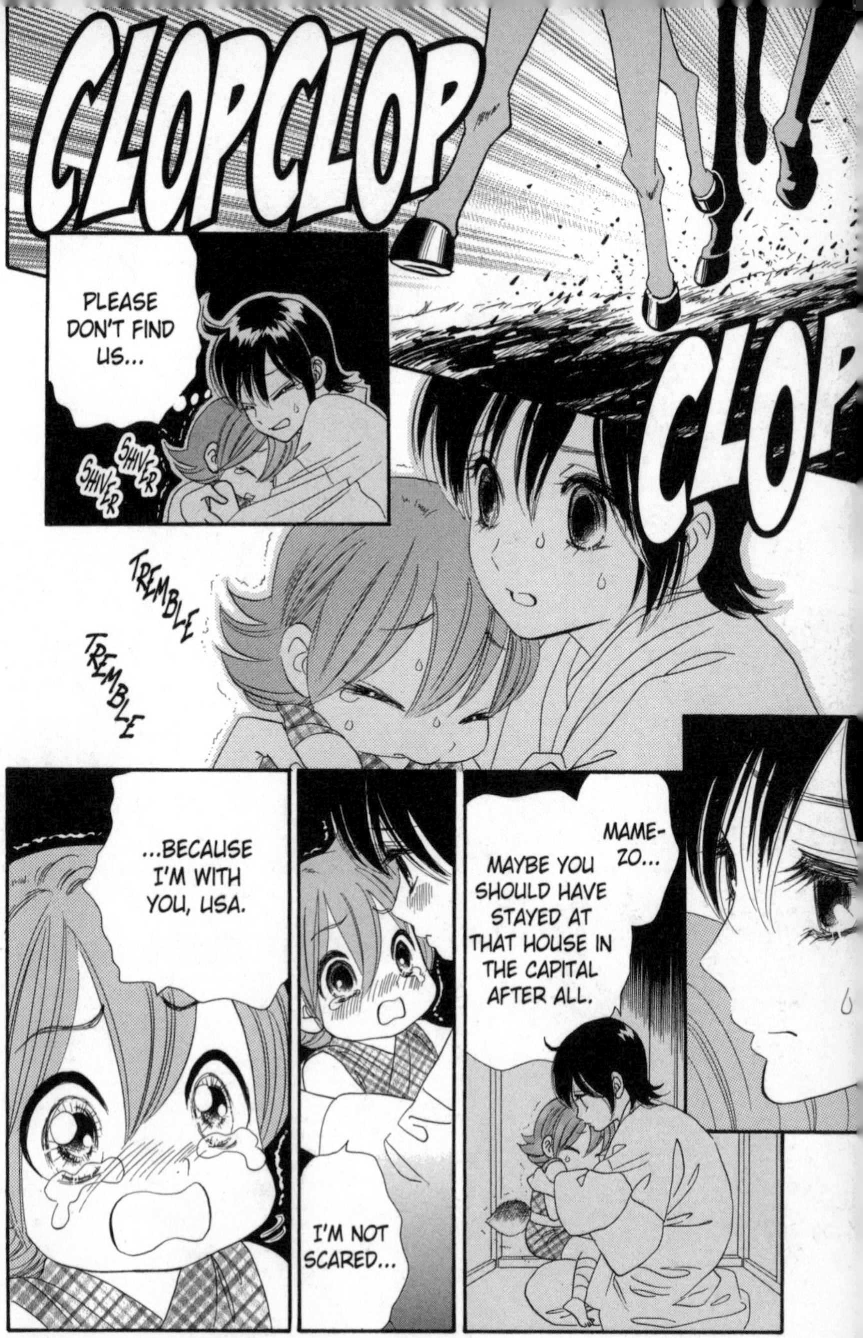
CLOPCLOP
CLOP
PLEASE DON'T FIND US...
SHIVER
SHIVER
TREMBLE
TREMBLE
MAME-ZO...
MAYBE YOU SHOULD HAVE STAYED AT THAT HOUSE IN THE CAPITAL AFTER ALL.
I'M NOT SCARED...
...BECAUSE I'M WITH YOU, USA.

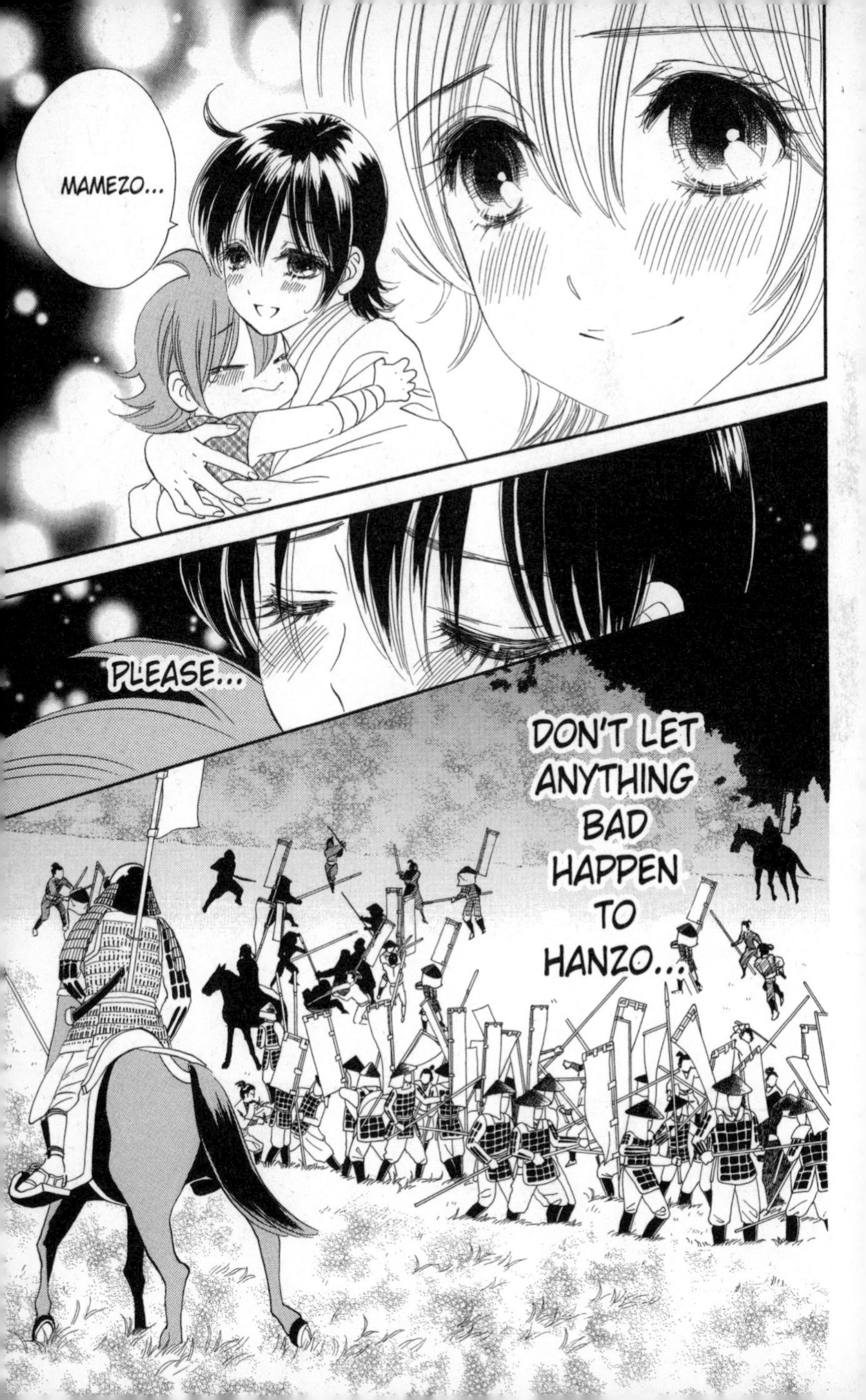
MAMEZO...
PLEASE...
DON'T LET ANYTHING BAD HAPPEN TO HANZO...

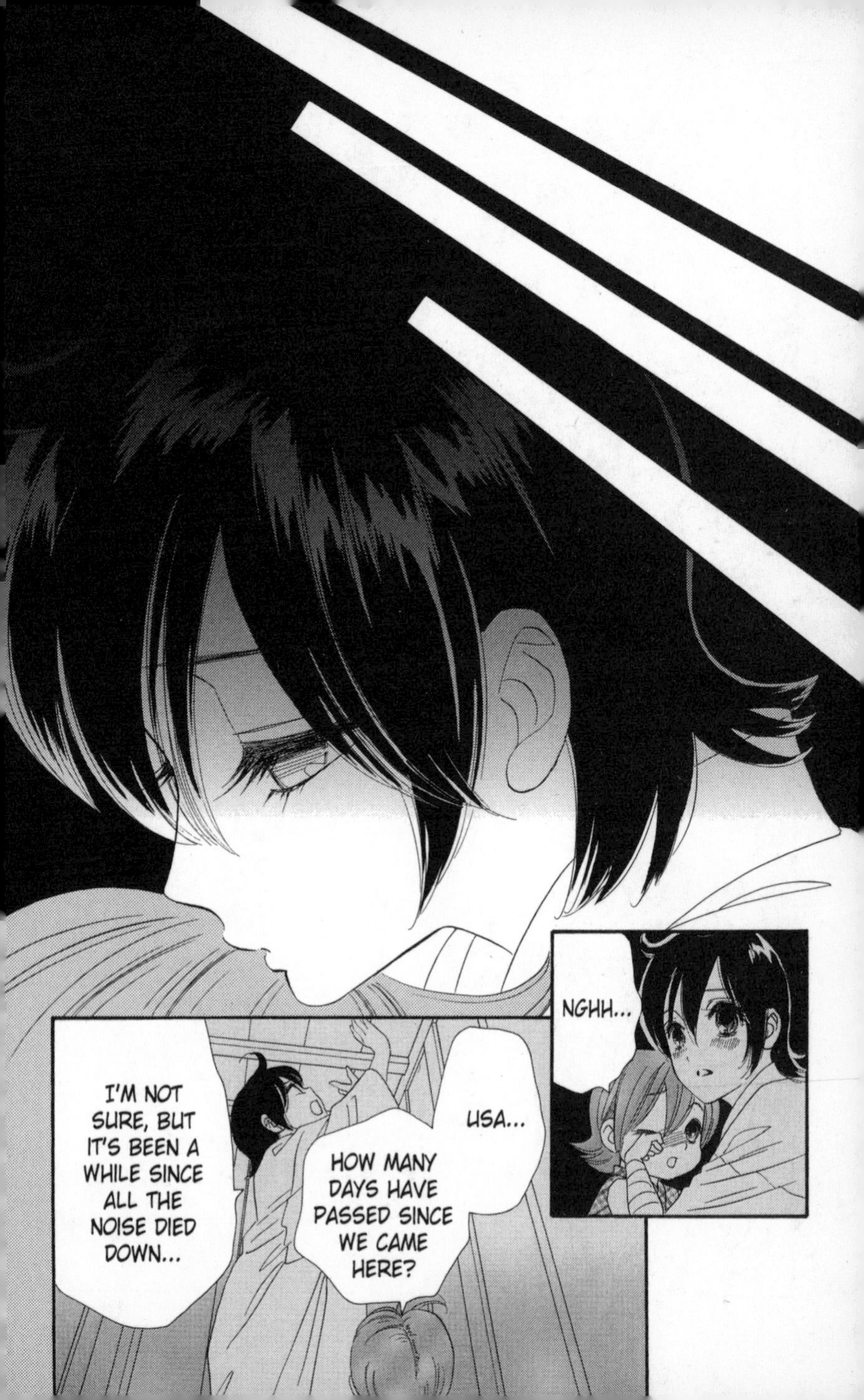
NGHH...
USA...
HOW MANY DAYS HAVE PASSED SINCE WE CAME HERE?
I'M NOT SURE, BUT IT'S BEEN A WHILE SINCE ALL THE NOISE DIED DOWN...

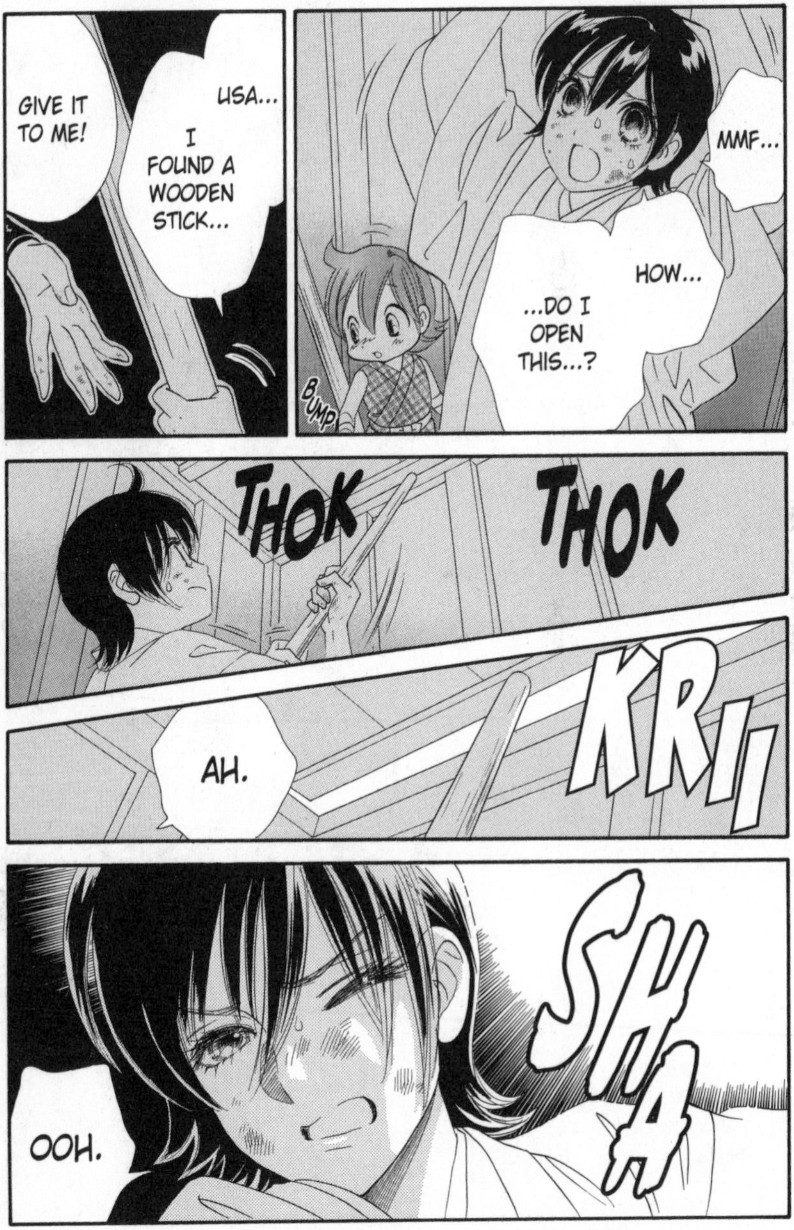
MMF...
HOW...
...DO I OPEN THIS...?
BUMP
USA...
I FOUND A WOODEN STICK...
GIVE IT TO ME!
THOK THOK
KRII
AH.
SHA
OOH.

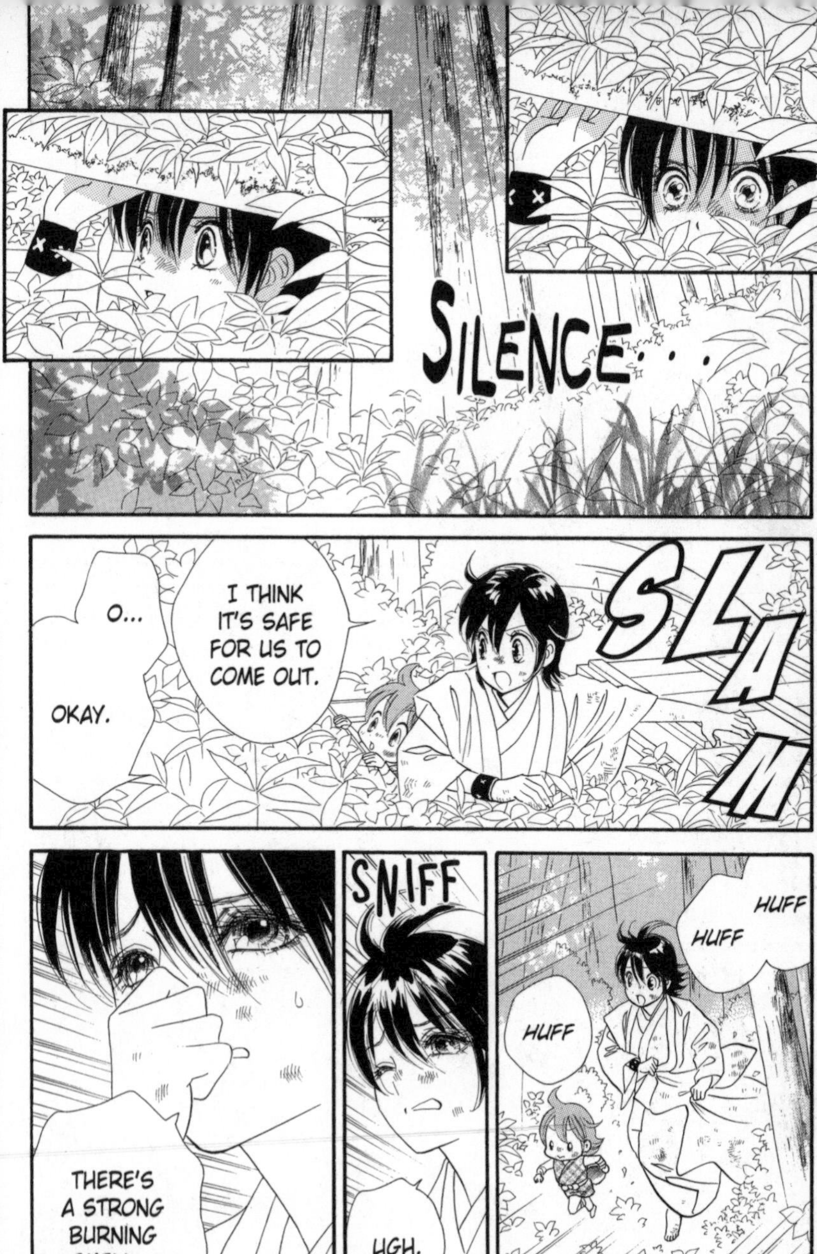
SILENCE...
SLAM
I THINK IT'S SAFE FOR US TO COME OUT.
O... OKAY.
HUFF HUFF
HUFF
SNIFF
UGH.
THERE'S A STRONG BURNING SMELL...

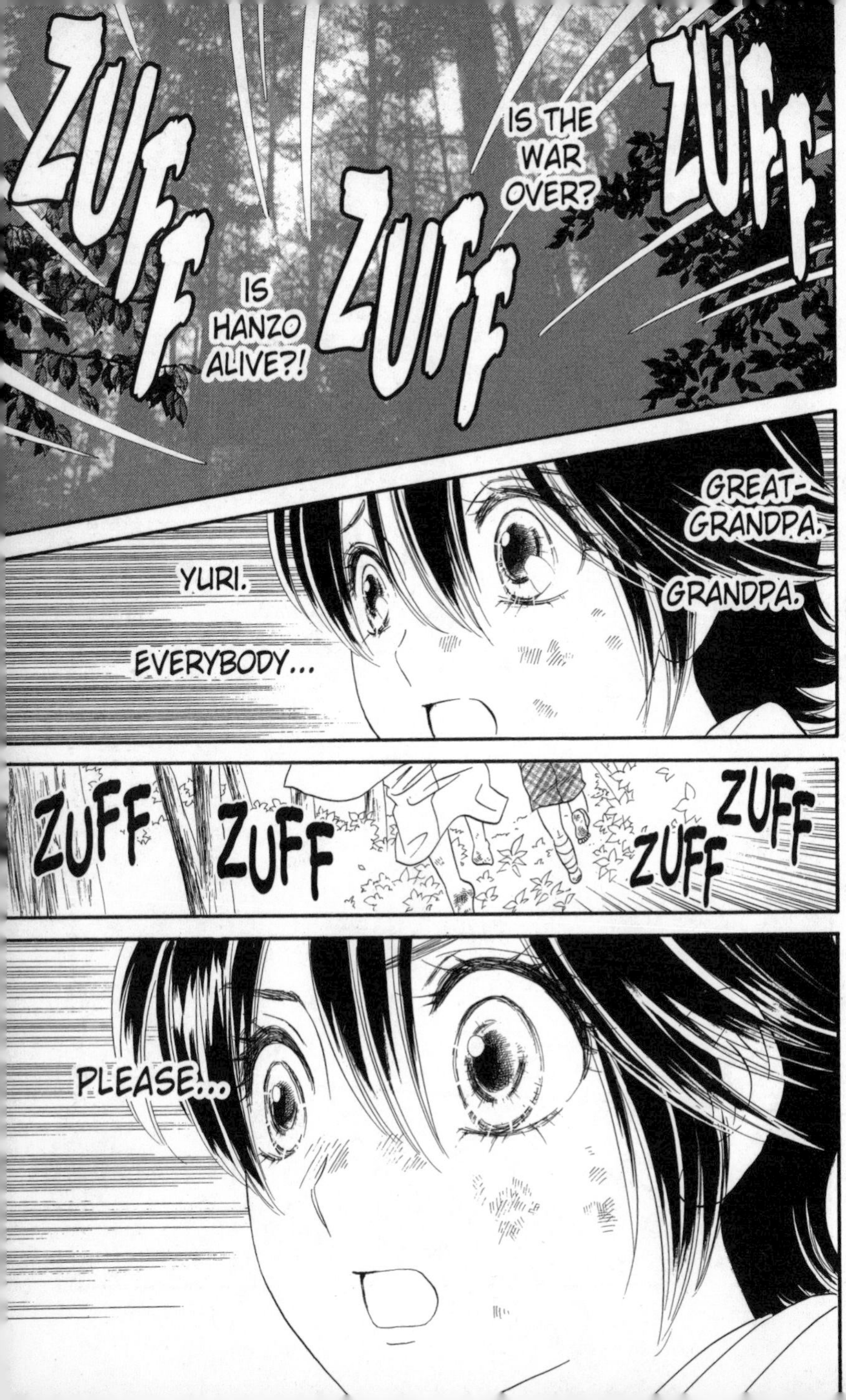
ZUFF-
IS THE WAR OVER?
ZUFF
IS HANZO ALIVE?!
ZUFF
GREAT-GRANDPA.
GRANDPA.
YURI.
EVERYBODY...
ZUFF
ZUFF
ZUFF
ZUFF
PLEASE...

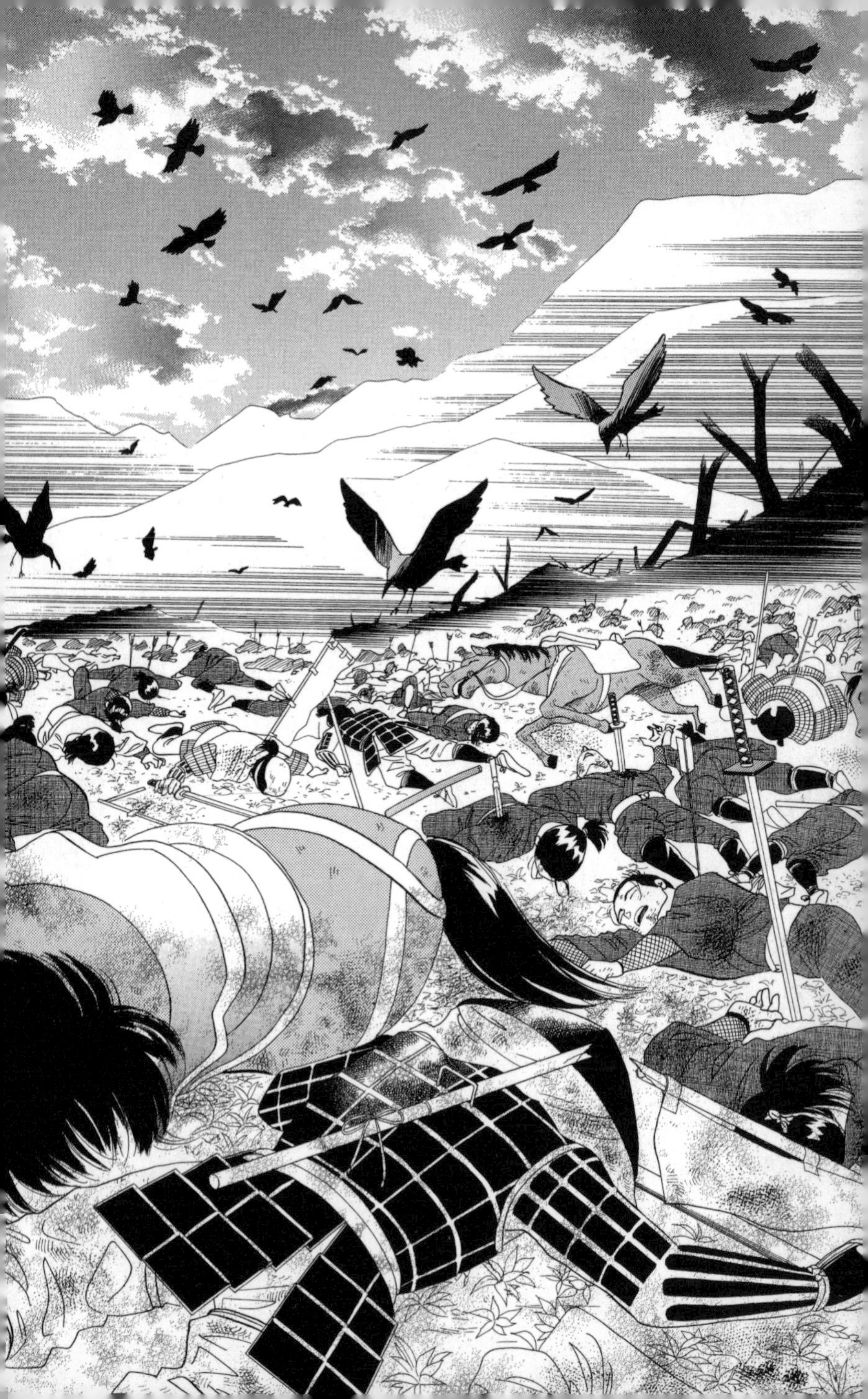

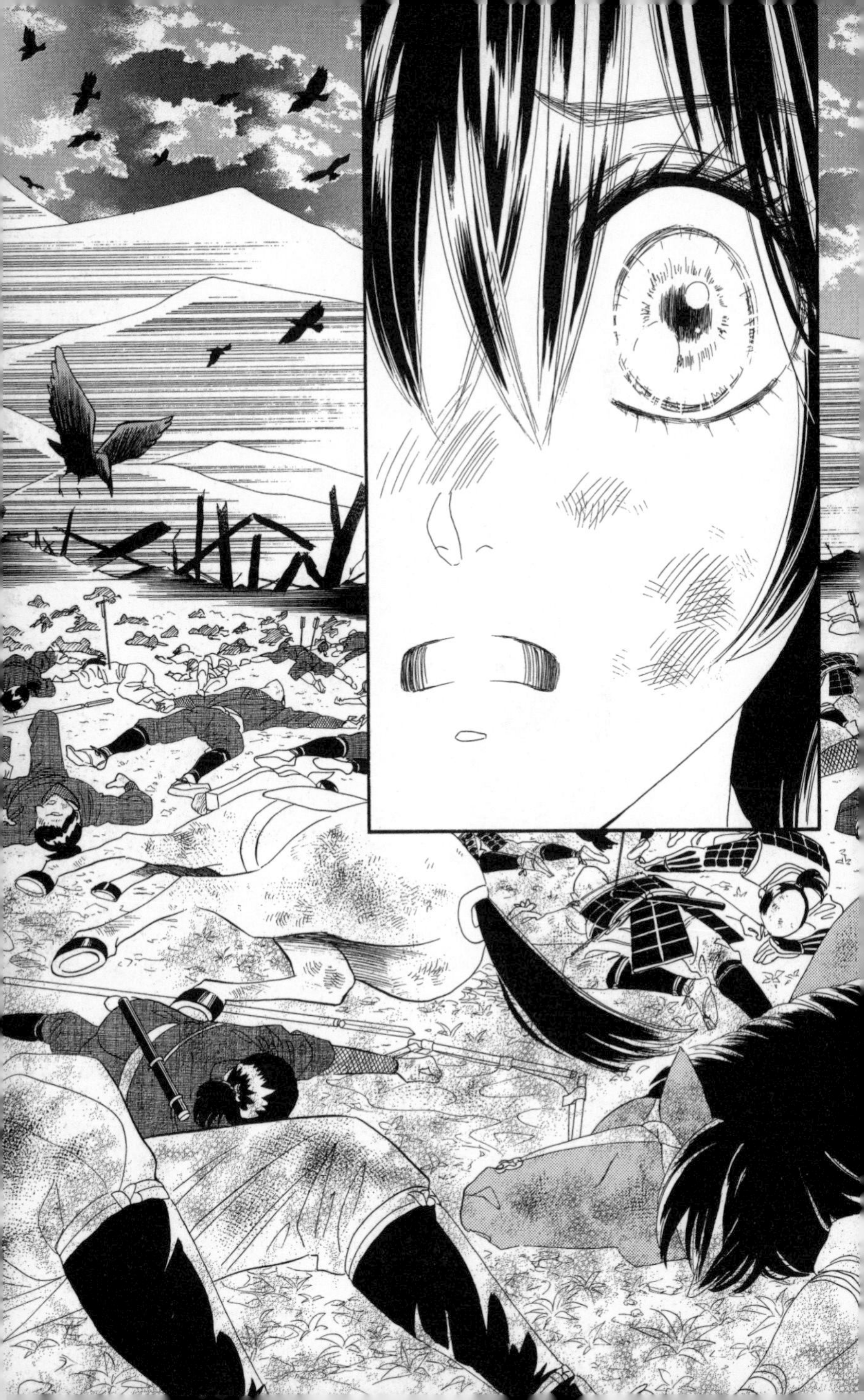

LET'S GO! LITTLE HANZO

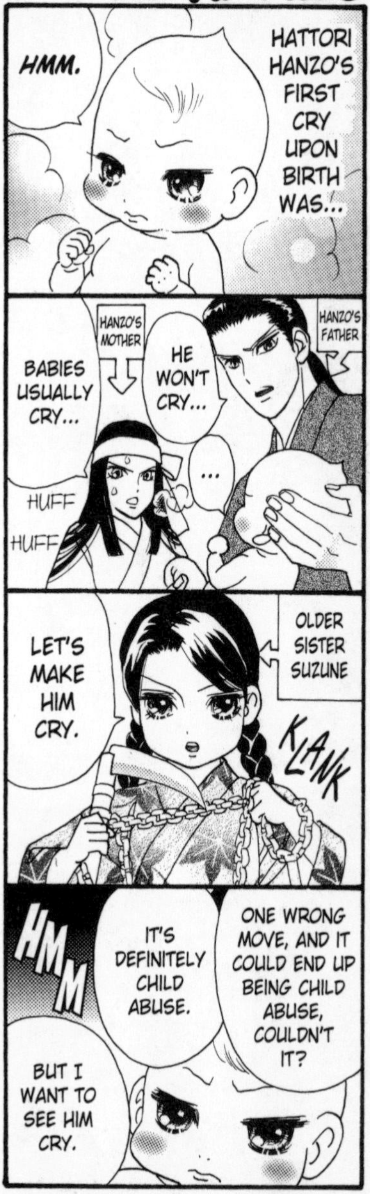
HATTORI HANZO'S FIRST CRY UPON BIRTH WAS...
HMM.
HANZO'S FATHER
HE WON'T CRY...
HANZO'S MOTHER
BABIES USUALLY CRY...
...
HUFF HUFF
OLDER SISTER SUZUNE
KLANK
LET'S MAKE HIM CRY.
ONE WRONG MOVE, AND IT COULD END UP BEING CHILD ABUSE, COULDN'T IT?
IT'S DEFINITELY CHILD ABUSE.
HMM
BUT I WANT TO SEE HIM CRY.

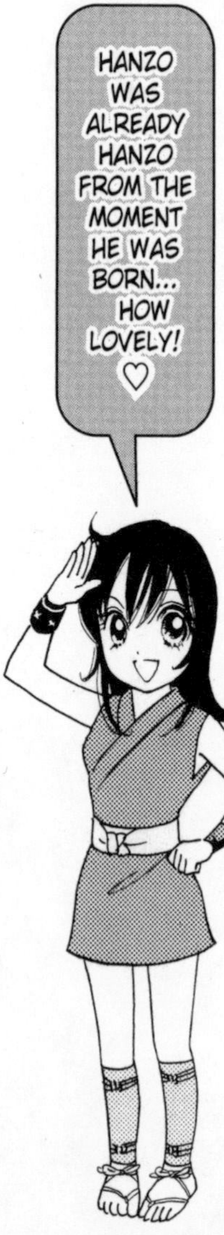
HANZO WAS ALREADY HANZO FROM THE MOMENT HE WAS BORN... HOW LOVELY! ♡

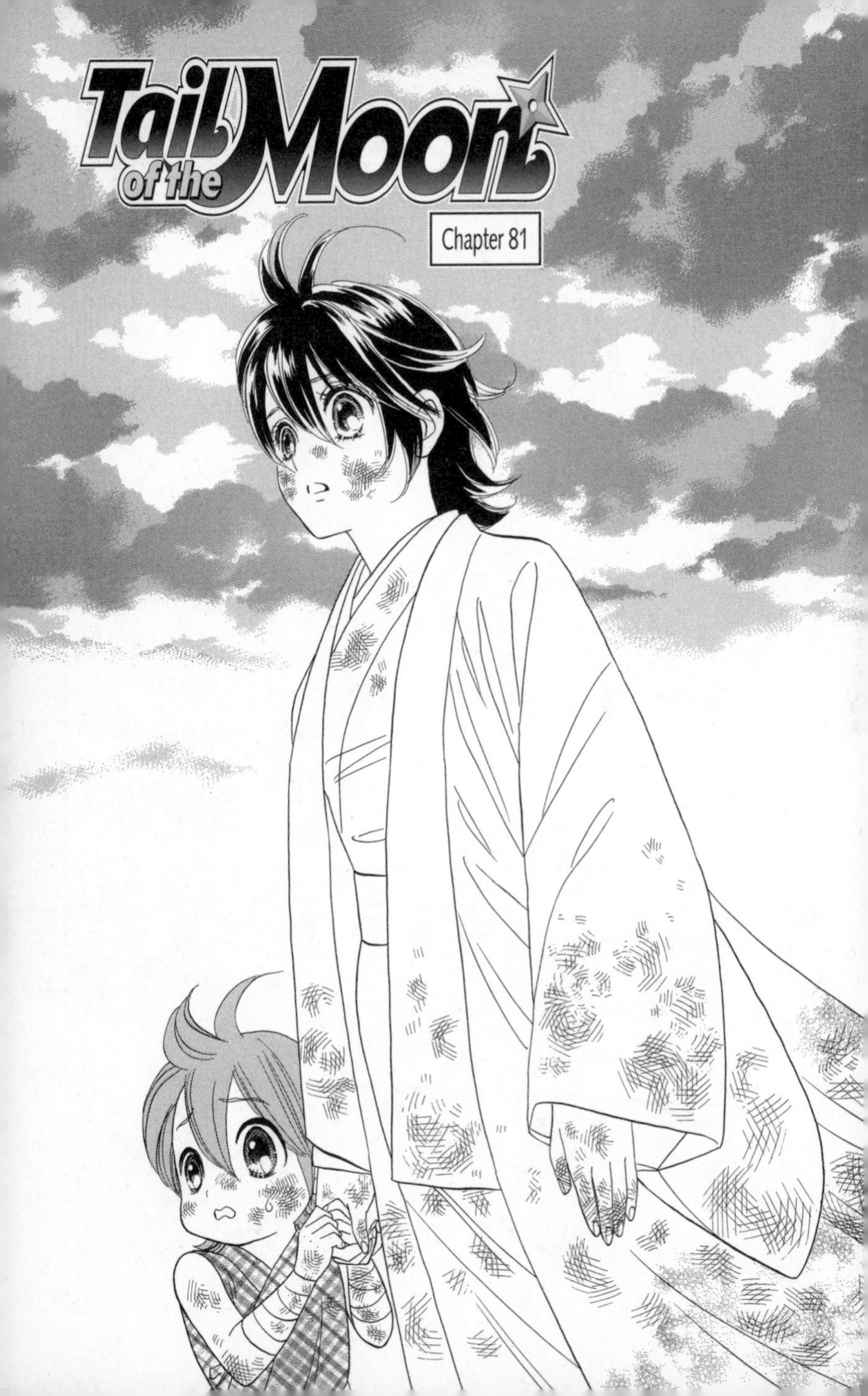
Tail of the Moon
Chapter 81

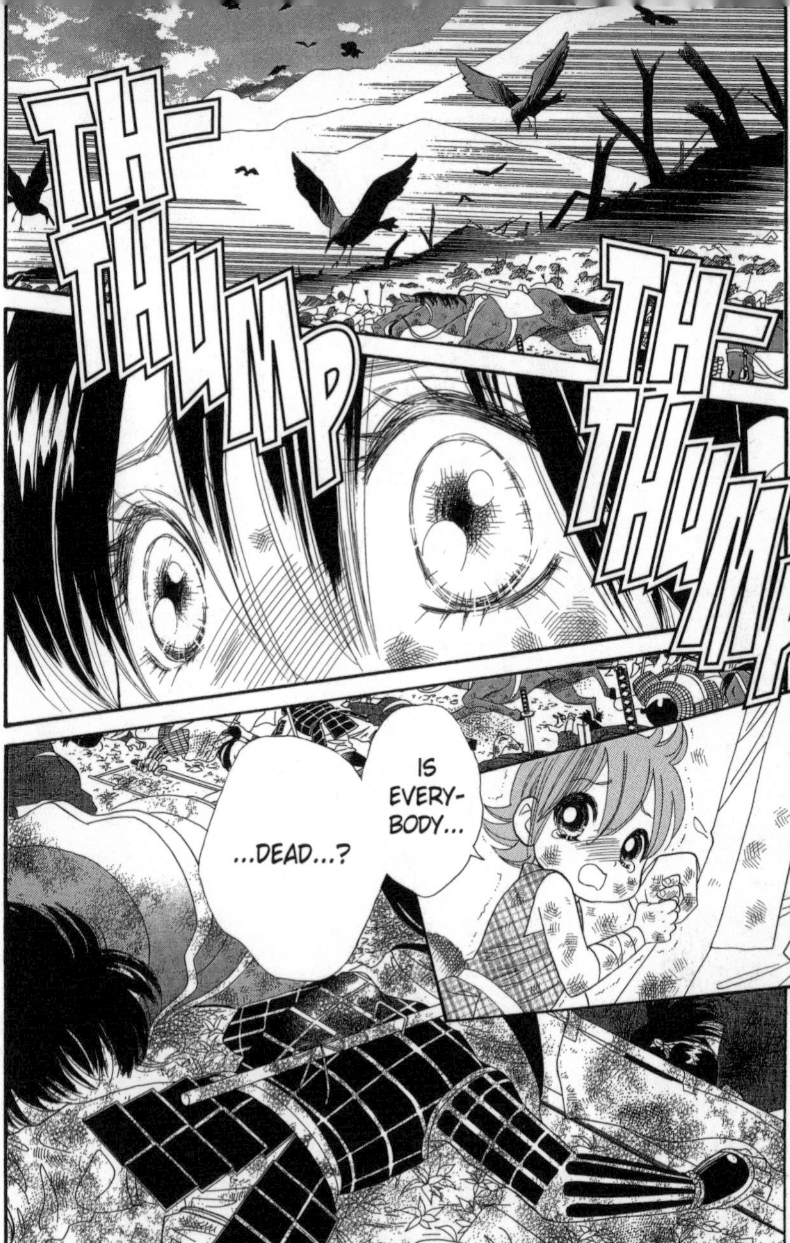
TH-THUMP
TH-THUMP
IS EVERY-BODY...
...DEAD...?

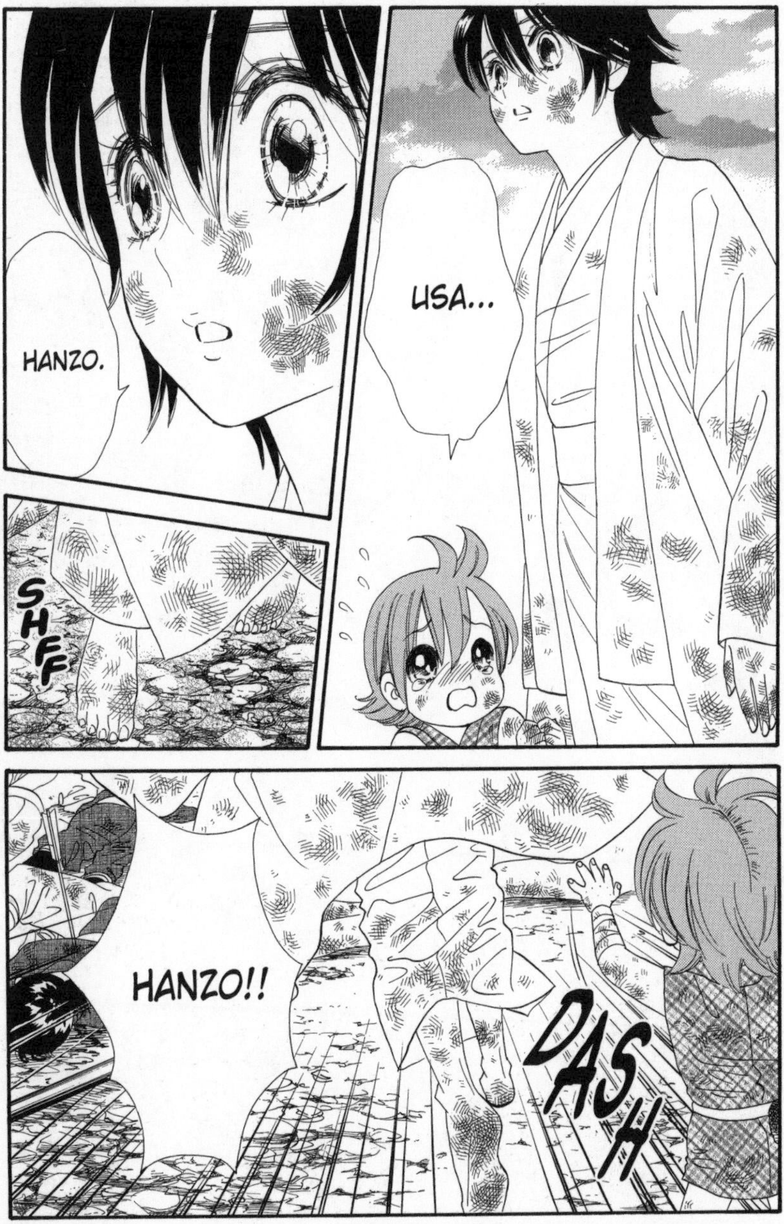
USA...
HANZO.
SHFF
DASH
HANZO!!

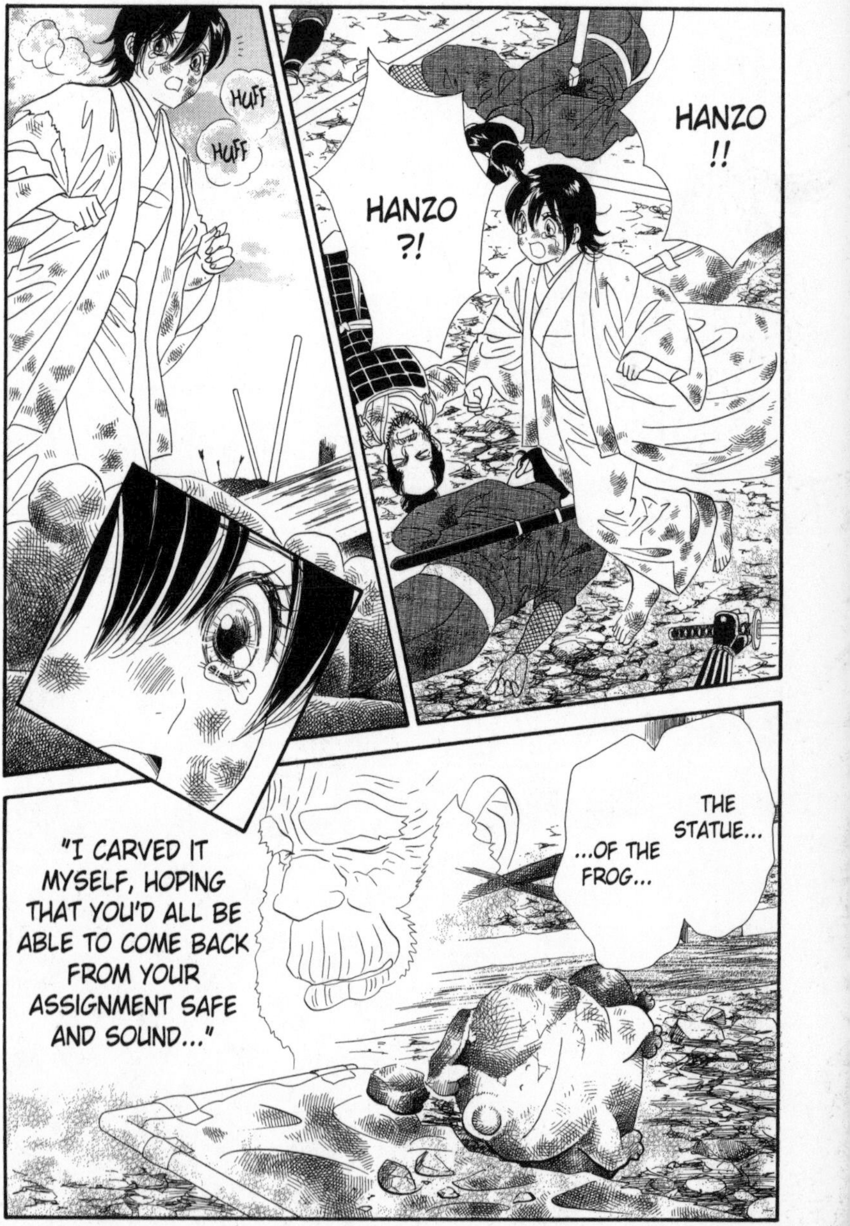
HANZO !!
HANZO ?!
HUFF
HUFF
THE STATUE...
...OF THE FROG...
"I CARVED IT MYSELF, HOPING THAT YOU'D ALL BE ABLE TO COME BACK FROM YOUR ASSIGNMENT SAFE AND SOUND..."

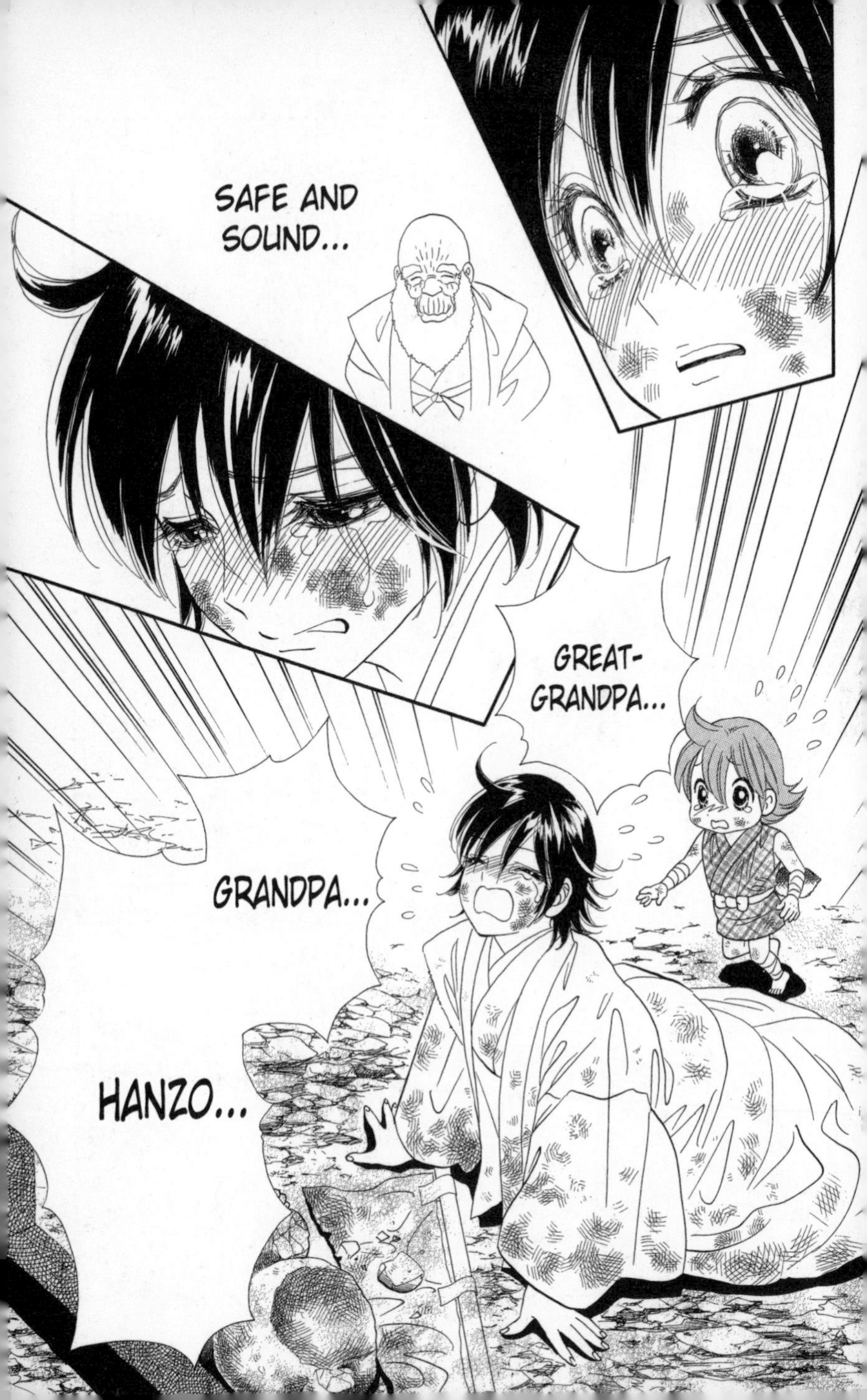
SAFE AND SOUND...
GREAT-GRANDPA...
GRANDPA...
HANZO...

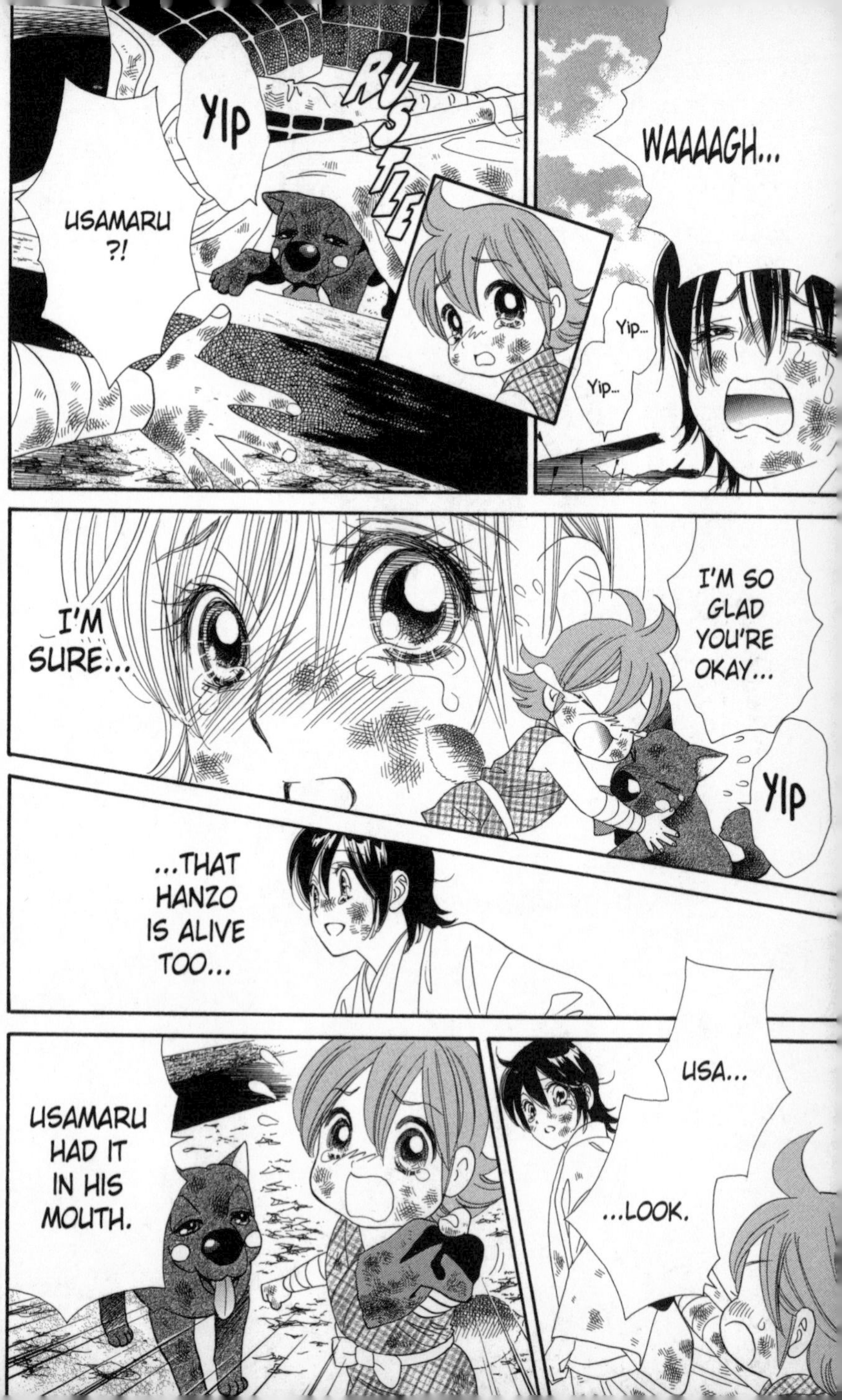
WAAAAGH...
Yip...
Yip...
RUSTLE
YIP
USAMARU ?!
I'M SO GLAD YOU'RE OKAY...
YIP
I'M SURE...
...THAT HANZO IS ALIVE TOO...
USA...
...LOOK.
USAMARU HAD IT IN HIS MOUTH.

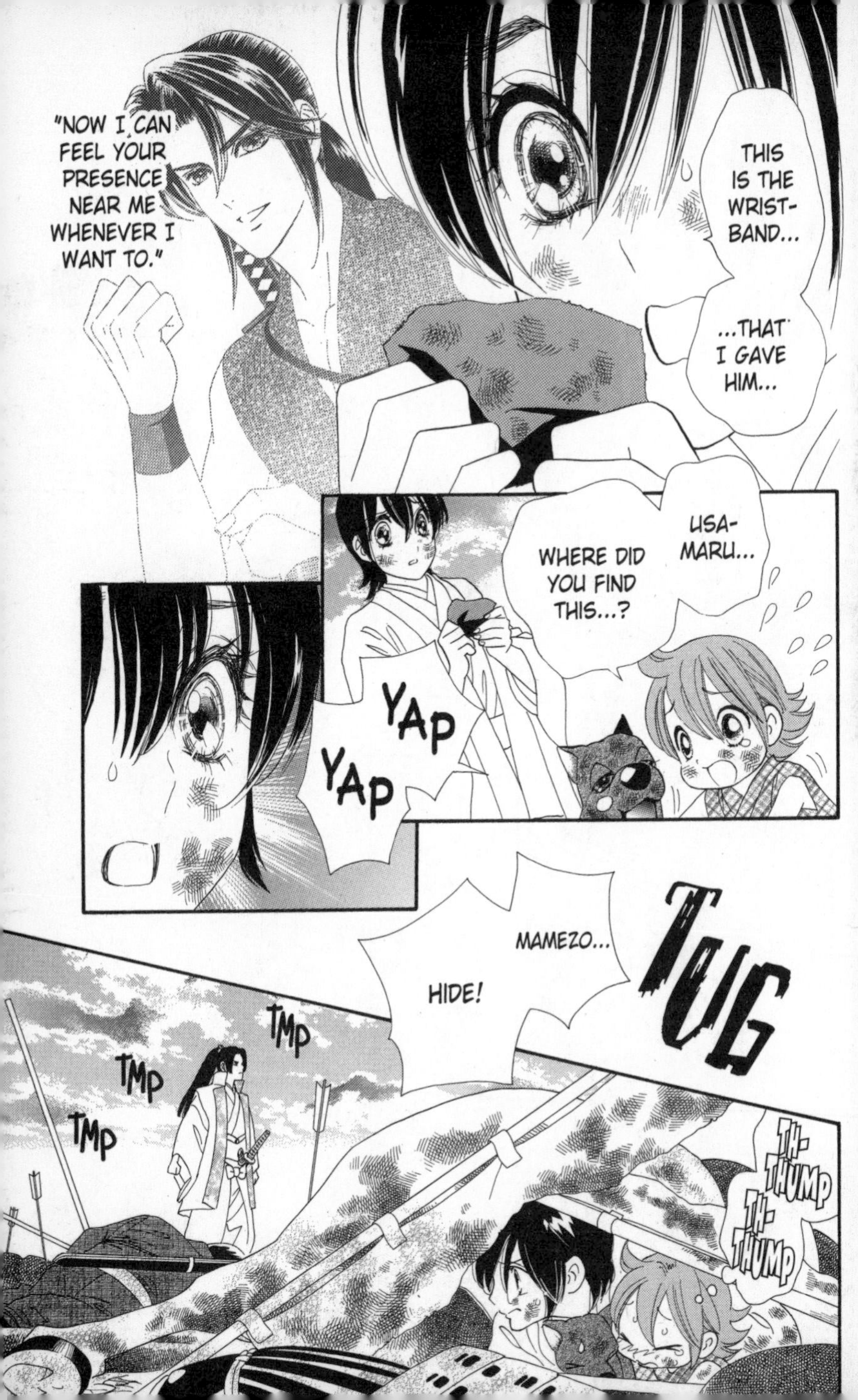
THIS IS THE WRIST-BAND...
...THAT I GAVE HIM...
"NOW I CAN FEEL YOUR PRESENCE NEAR ME WHENEVER I WANT TO."
USA-MARU...
WHERE DID YOU FIND THIS...?
YAP
YAP
TUG
MAMEZO...
HIDE!
TH-THUMP
TH-THUMP
TMP
TMP
TMP

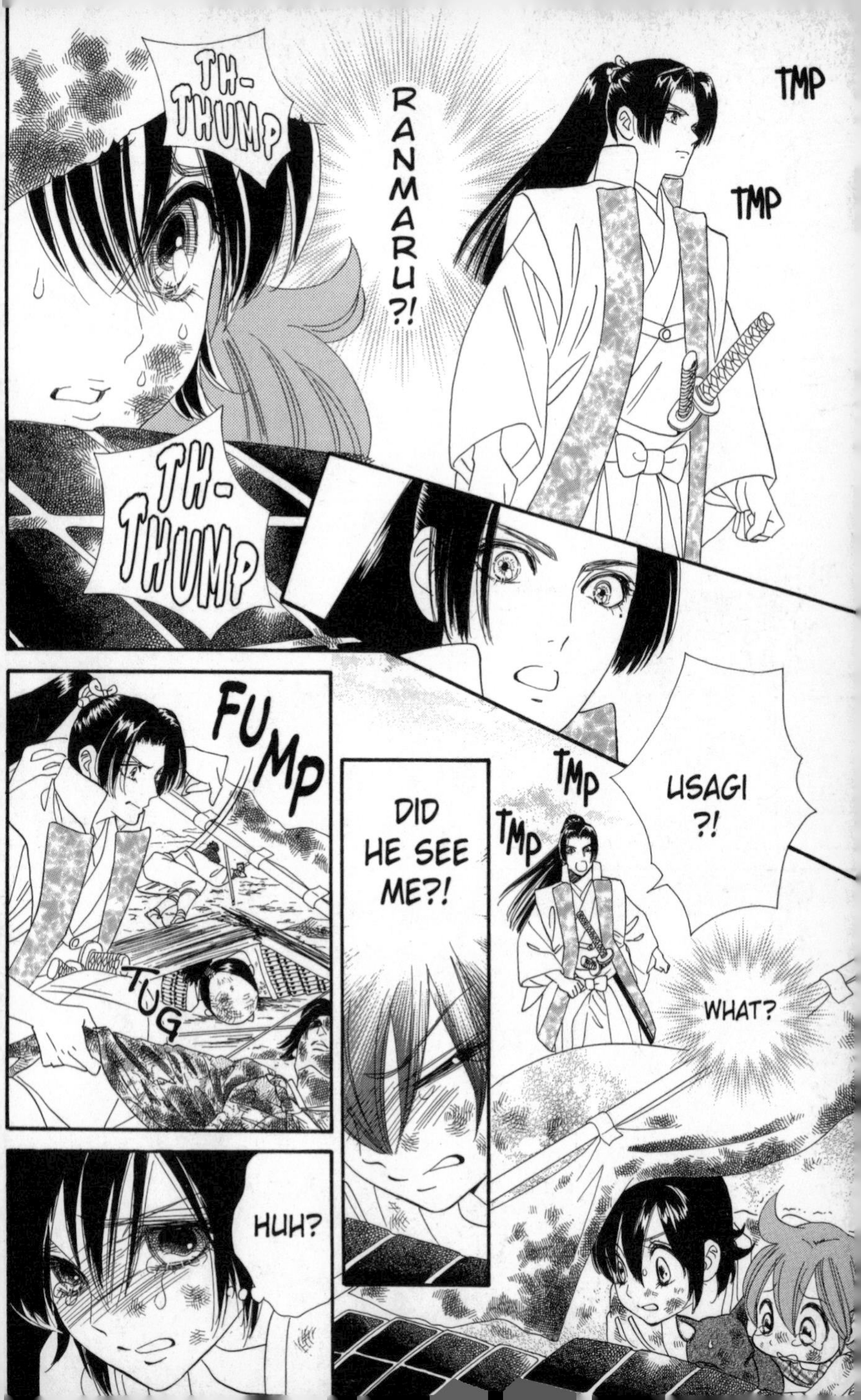
TMP
TMP
RANMARU?!
TH-THUMP
TH-THUMP
USAGI?!
TMP
TMP
WHAT?
DID HE SEE ME?!
FUMP
TUG
HUH?

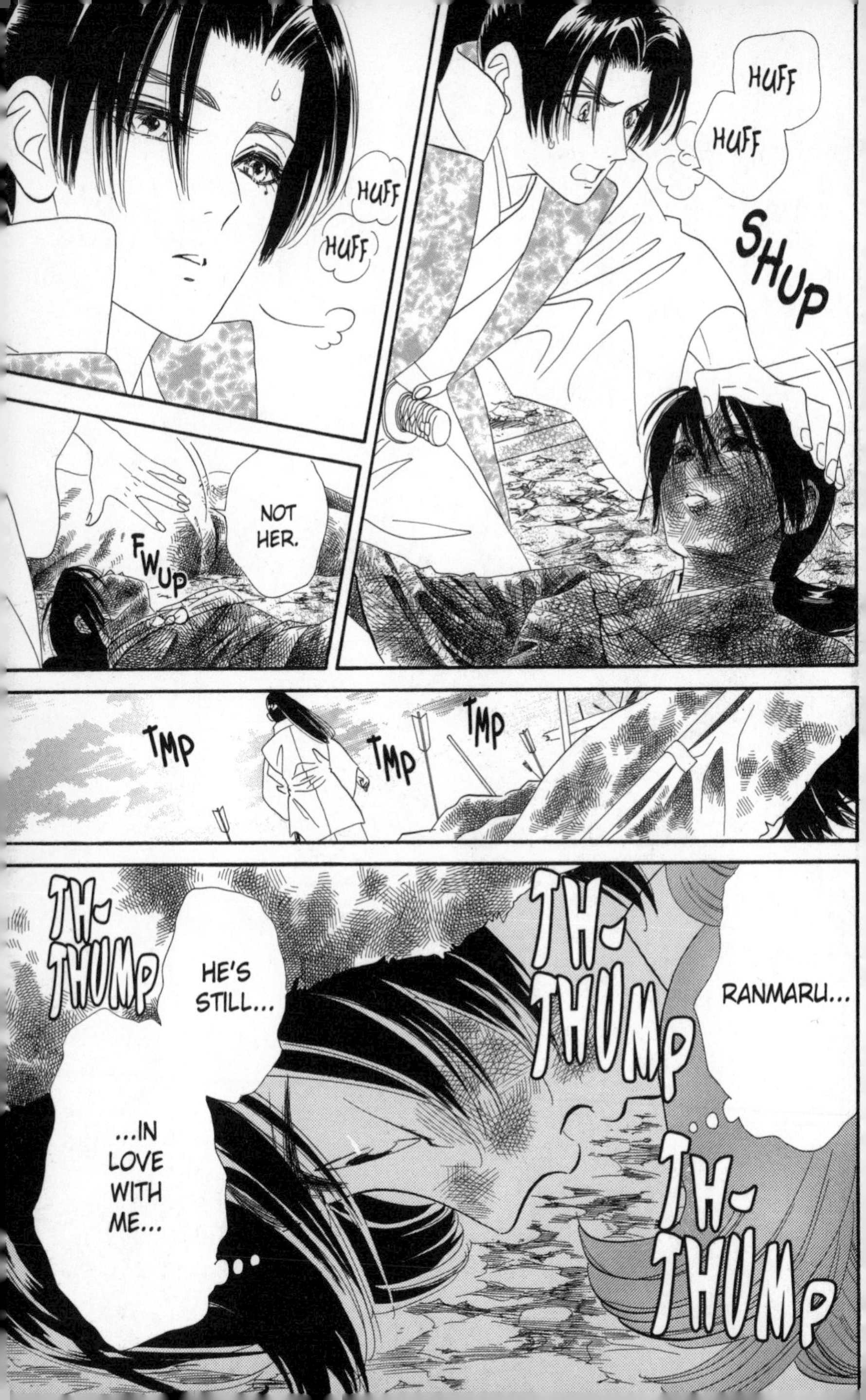
HUFF
HUFF
SHUP
HUFF
HUFF
NOT HER.
FWUP
TMP
TMP
TMP
RANMARU...
TH-THUMP
TH-THUMP
HE'S STILL...
...IN LOVE WITH ME...
TH-THUMP

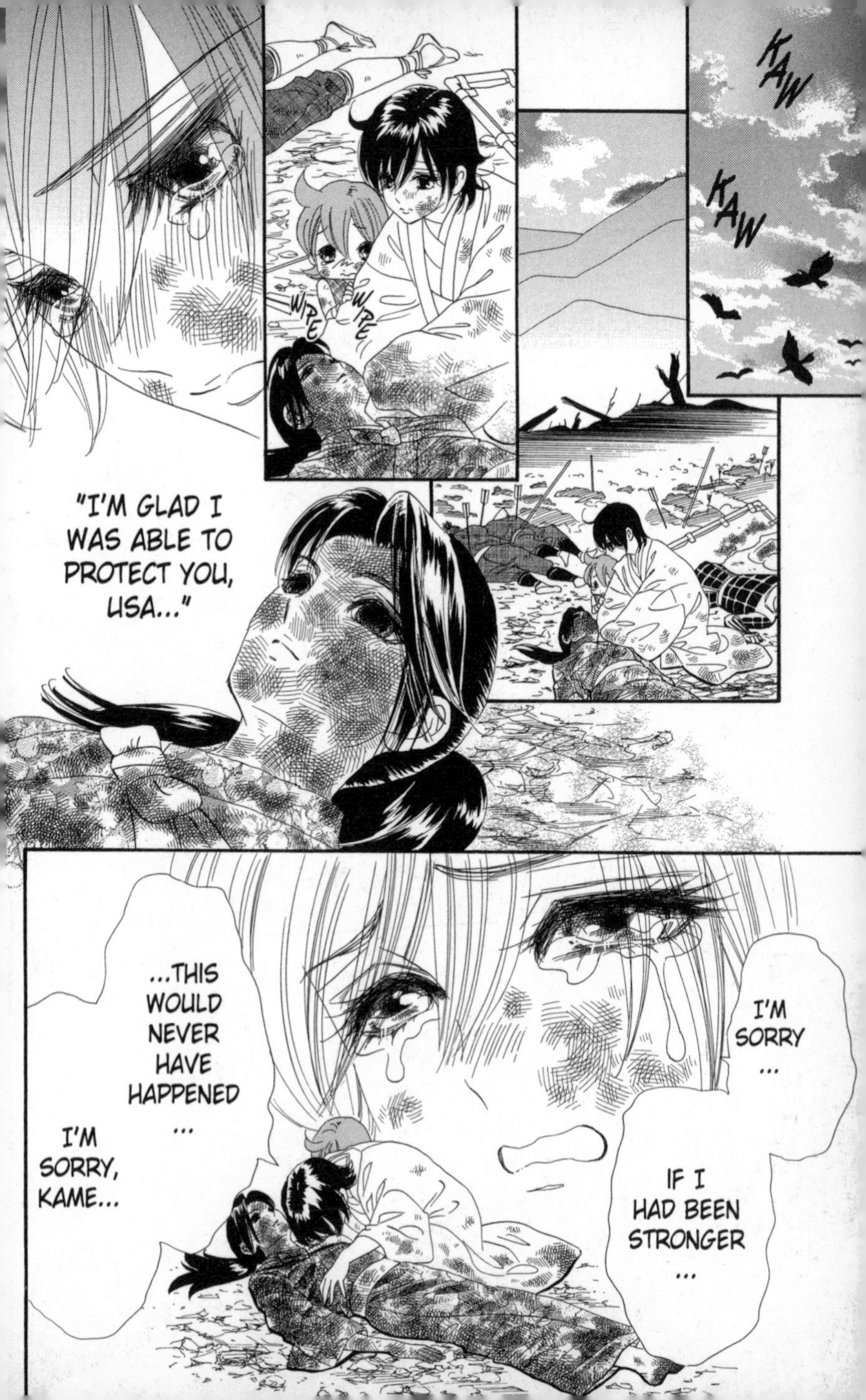
KAW
KAW
WIPE
WIPE
"I'M GLAD I WAS ABLE TO PROTECT YOU, USA..."
I'M SORRY...
IF I HAD BEEN STRONGER...
...THIS WOULD NEVER HAVE HAPPENED...
I'M SORRY, KAME...

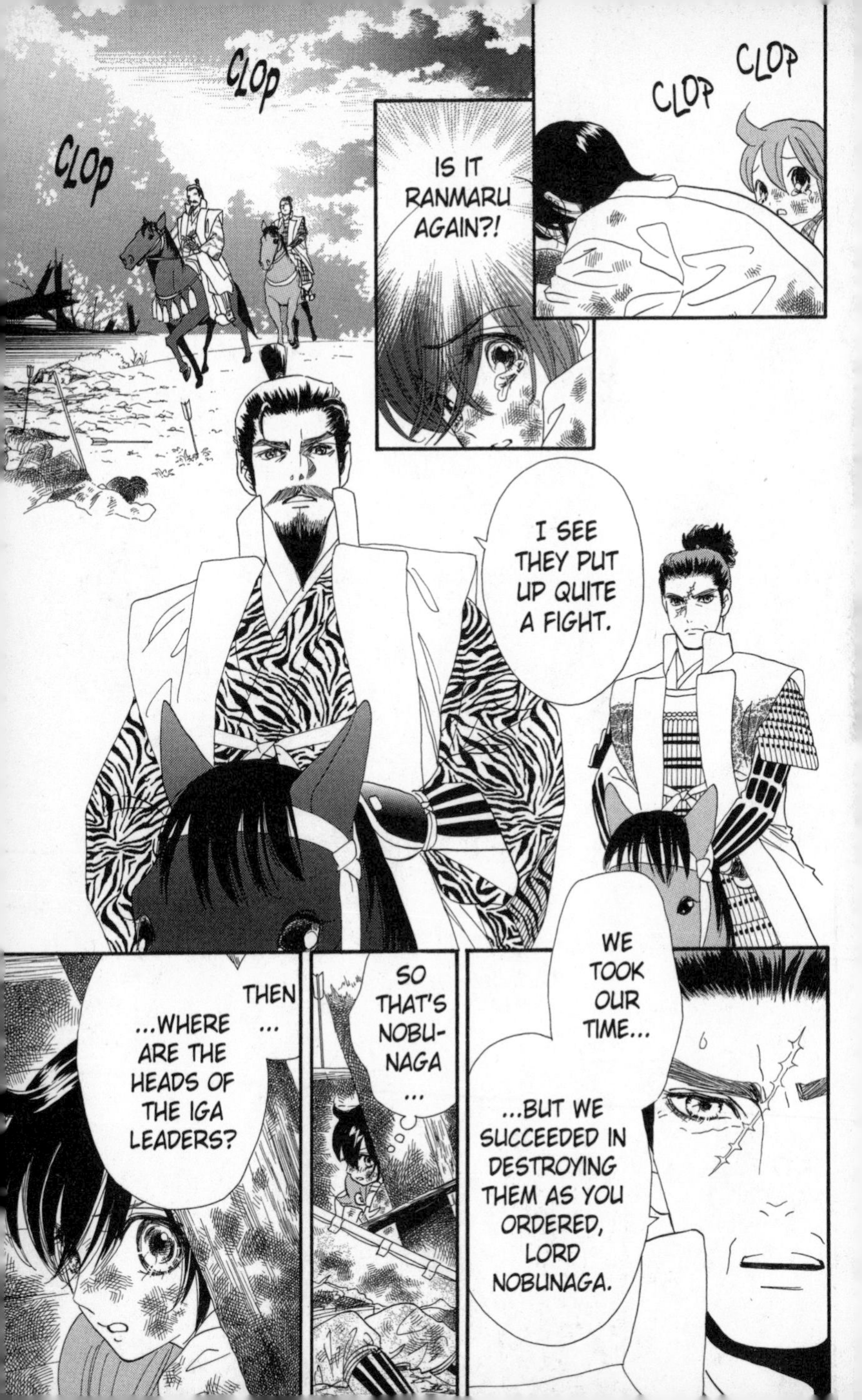
CLOP
CLOP
IS IT RANMARU AGAIN?!
CLOP
CLOP
I SEE THEY PUT UP QUITE A FIGHT.
WE TOOK OUR TIME...
...BUT WE SUCCEEDED IN DESTROYING THEM AS YOU ORDERED, LORD NOBUNAGA.
SO THAT'S NOBUNAGA...
THEN...
...WHERE ARE THE HEADS OF THE IGA LEADERS?

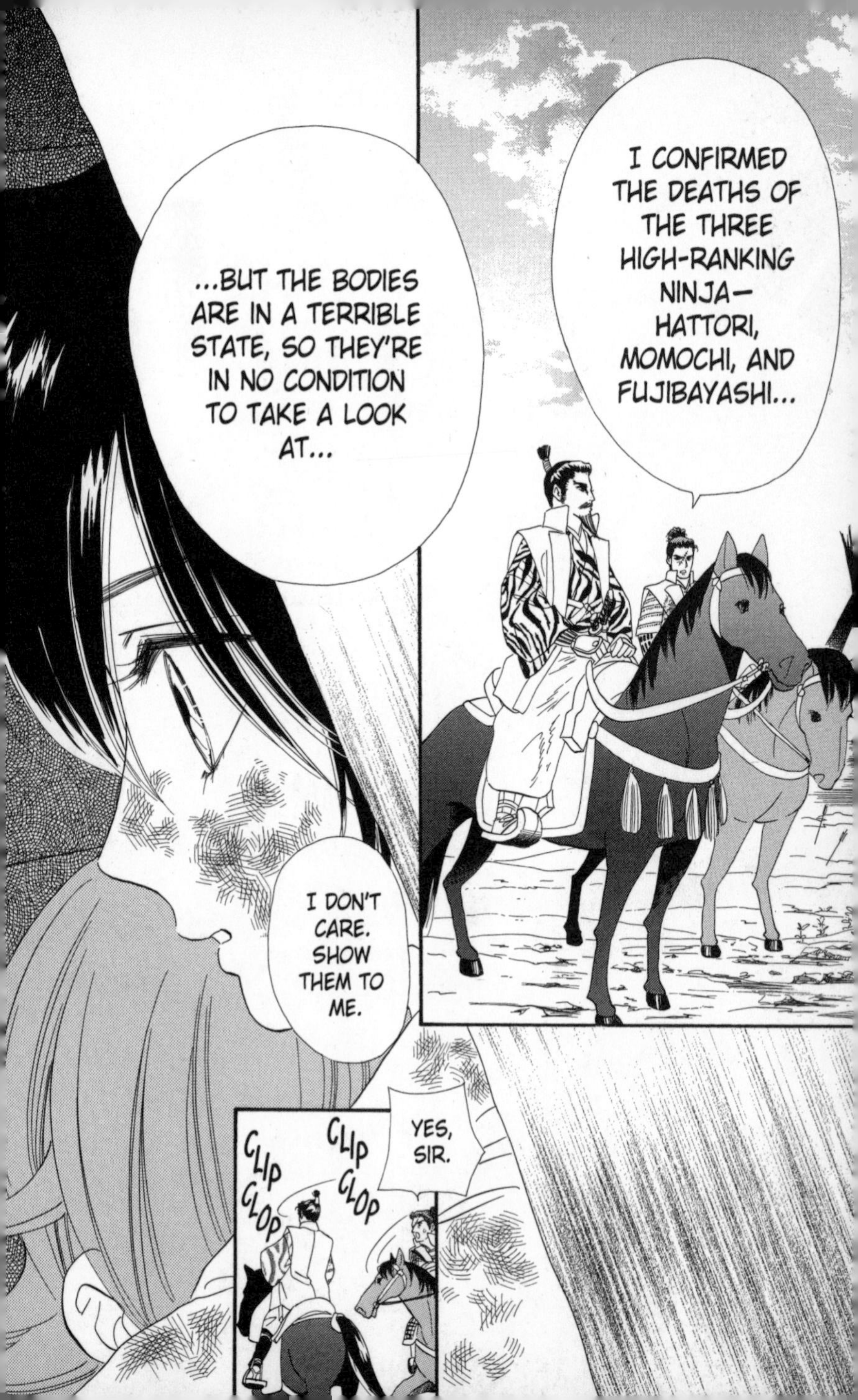
I CONFIRMED THE DEATHS OF THE THREE HIGH-RANKING NINJA—HATTORI, MOMOCHI, AND FUJIBAYASHI...
...BUT THE BODIES ARE IN A TERRIBLE STATE, SO THEY'RE IN NO CONDITION TO TAKE A LOOK AT...
I DON'T CARE. SHOW THEM TO ME.
YES, SIR.
CLIP CLOP
CLIP CLOP

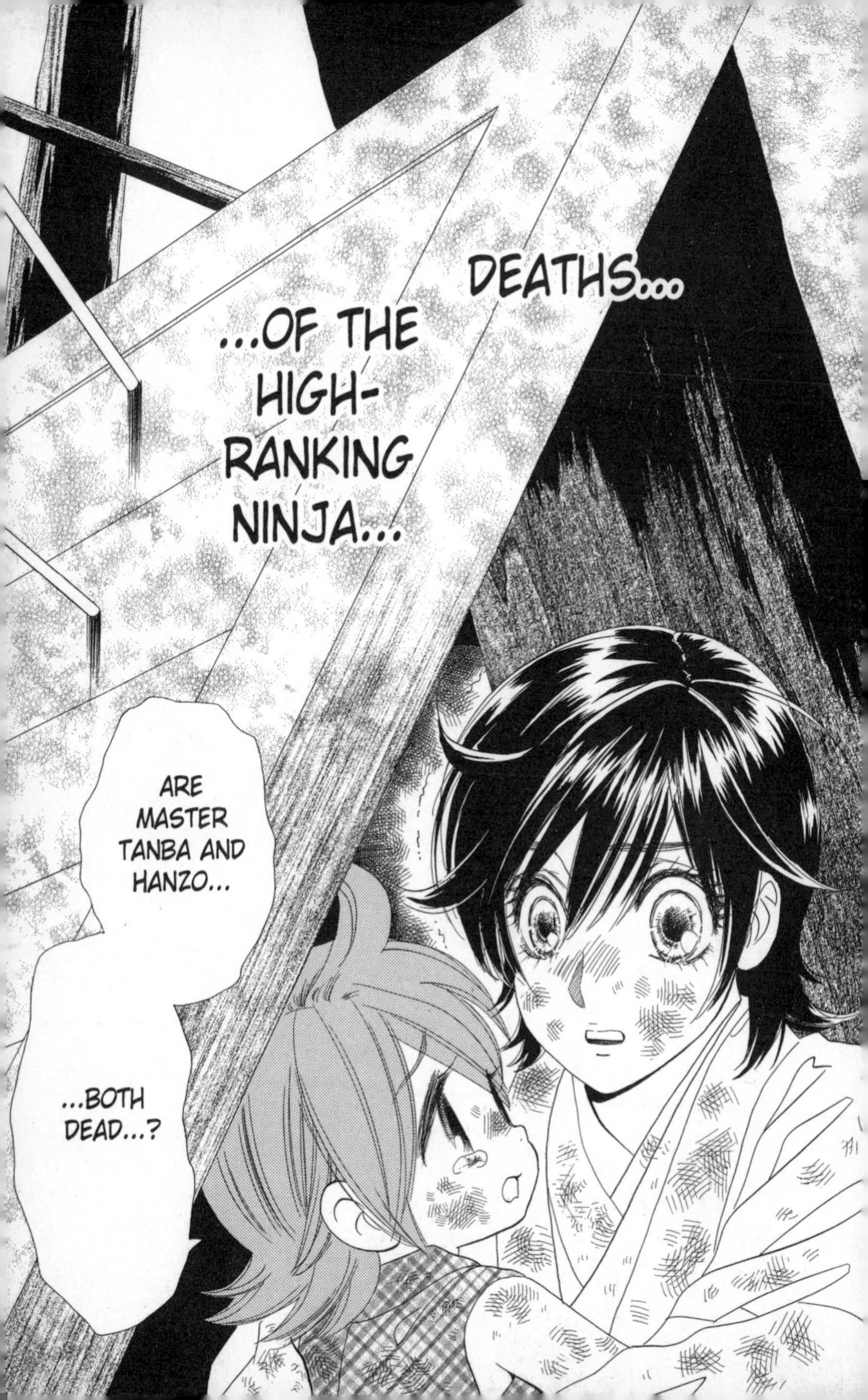
DEATHS...
...OF THE HIGH-RANKING NINJA...
ARE MASTER TANBA AND HANZO...
...BOTH DEAD...?

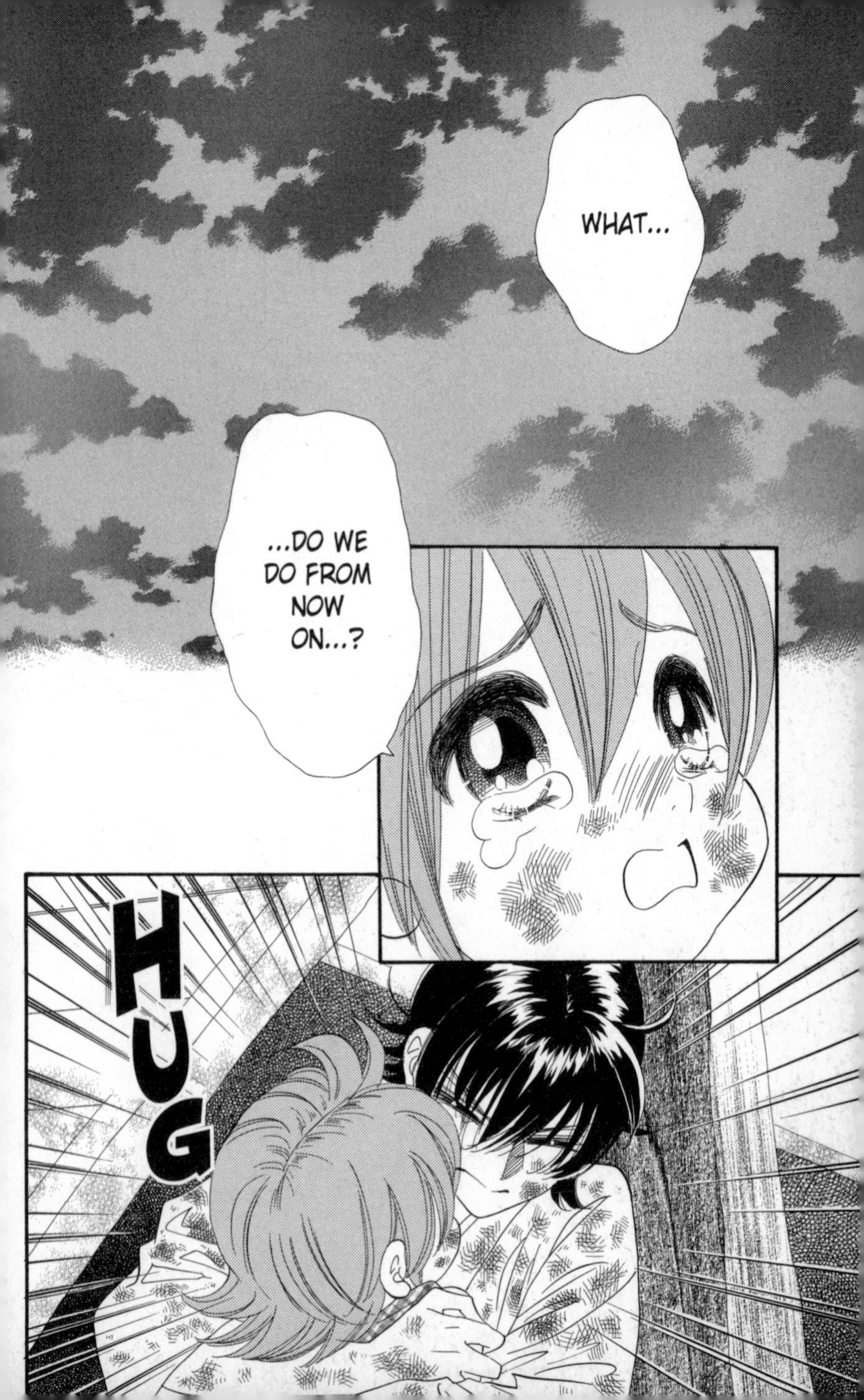
WHAT...
...DO WE DO FROM NOW ON...?
HUG

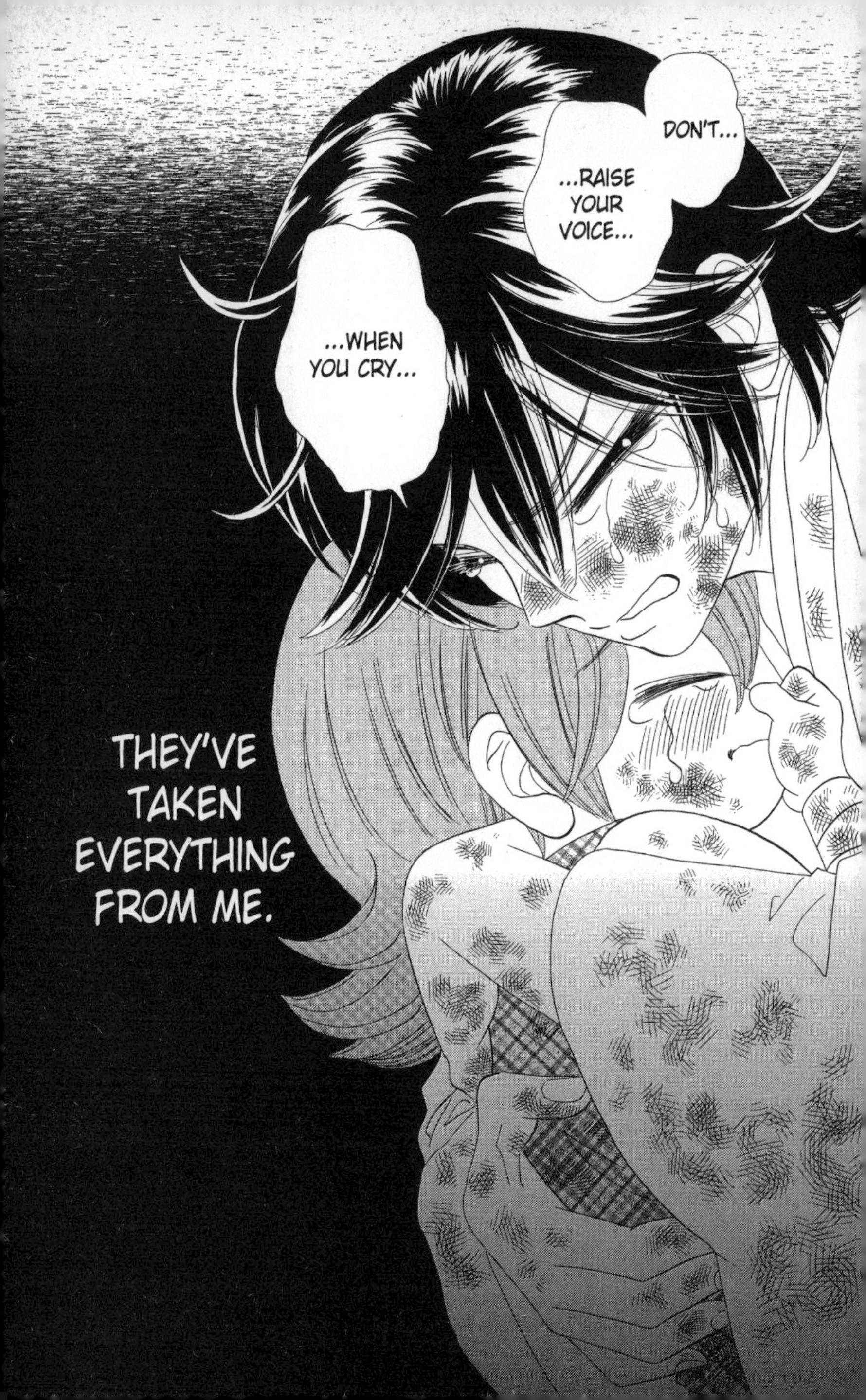
DON'T...
...RAISE YOUR VOICE...
...WHEN YOU CRY...
THEY'VE TAKEN EVERYTHING FROM ME.

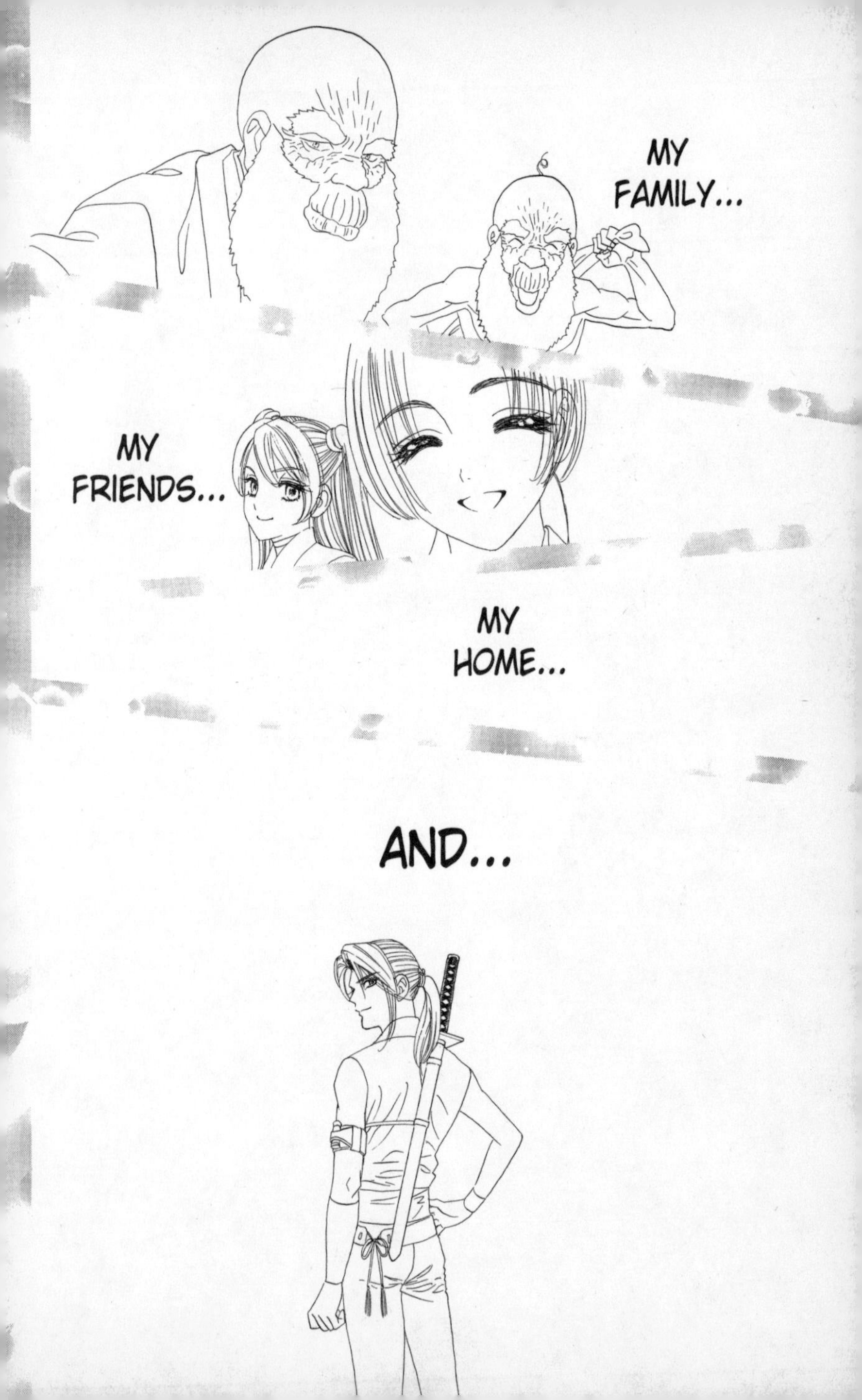
MY FAMILY...
MY FRIENDS...
MY HOME...
AND...

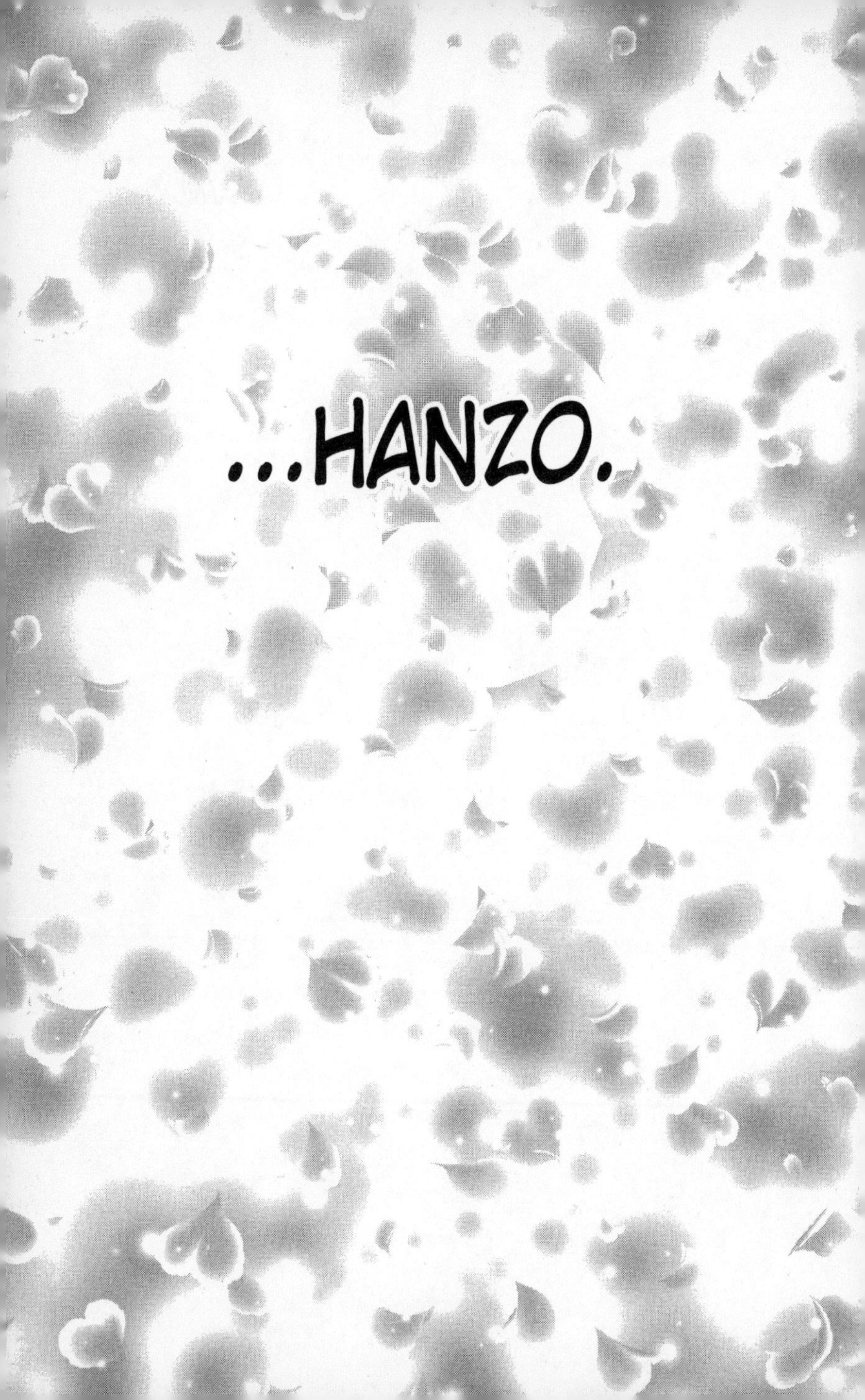
...HANZO.

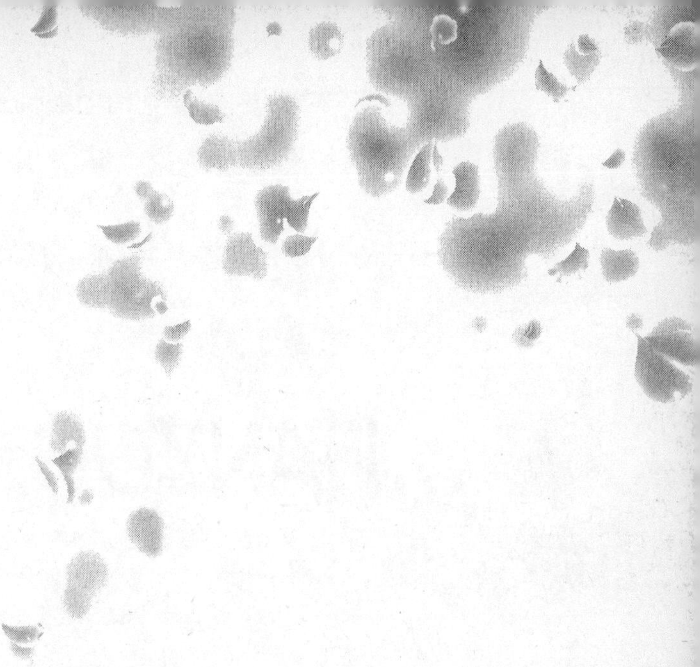

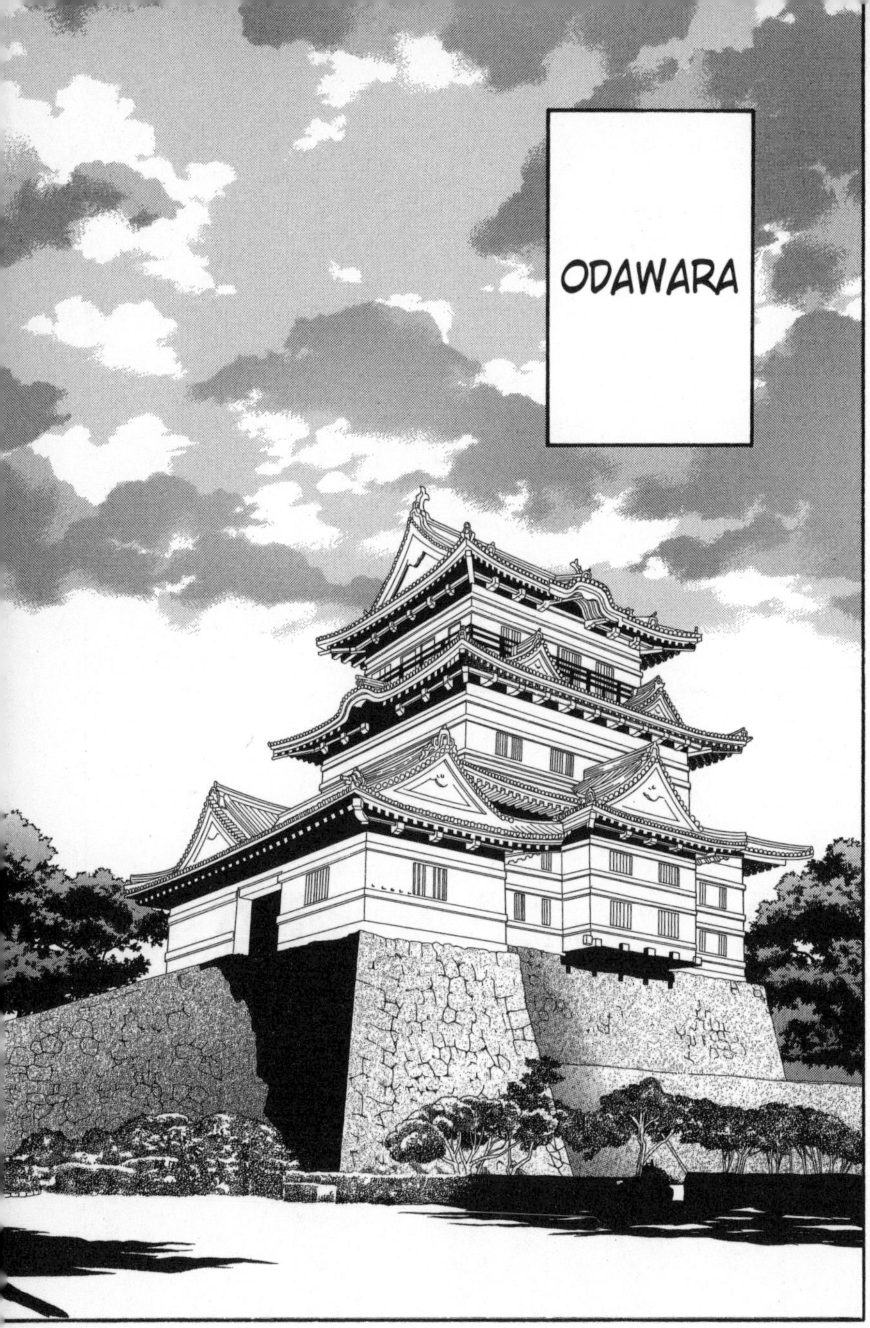
ODAWARA

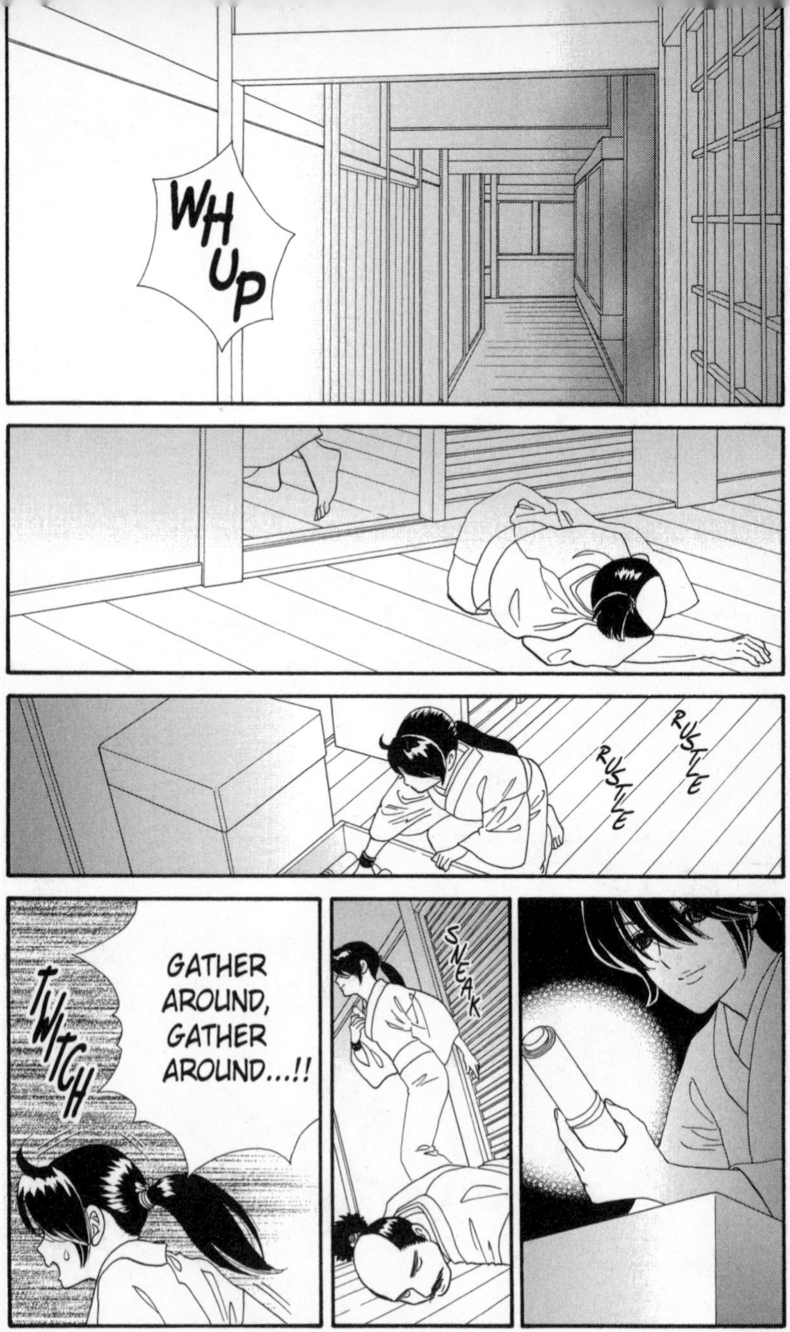
WHUP
RUSTLE
RUSTLE
SNEAK
GATHER AROUND, GATHER AROUND...!!
TWITCH

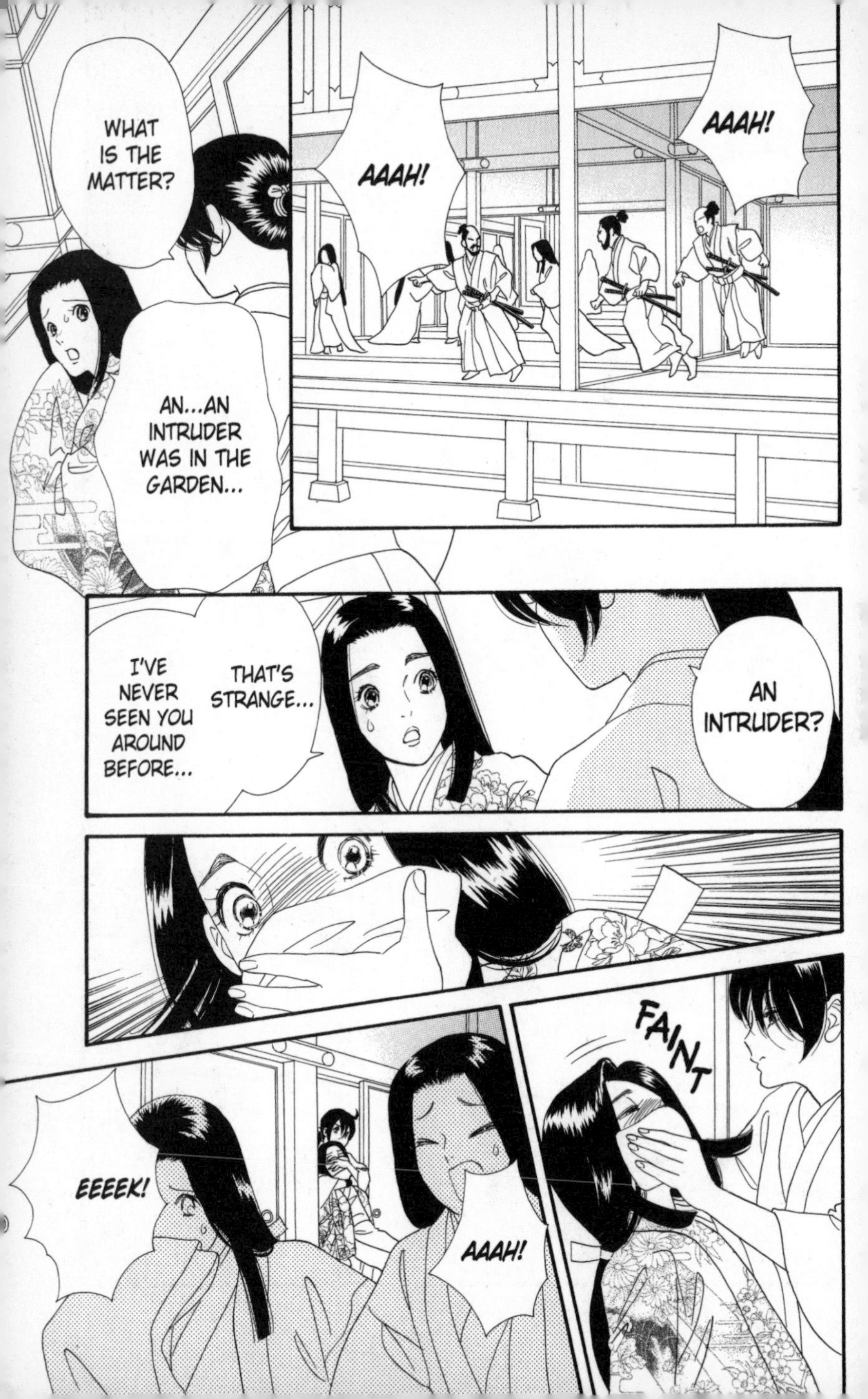
AAAH!
AAAH!
WHAT IS THE MATTER?
AN...AN INTRUDER WAS IN THE GARDEN...
AN INTRUDER?
THAT'S STRANGE...
I'VE NEVER SEEN YOU AROUND BEFORE...
FAINT
AAAH!
EEEEK!

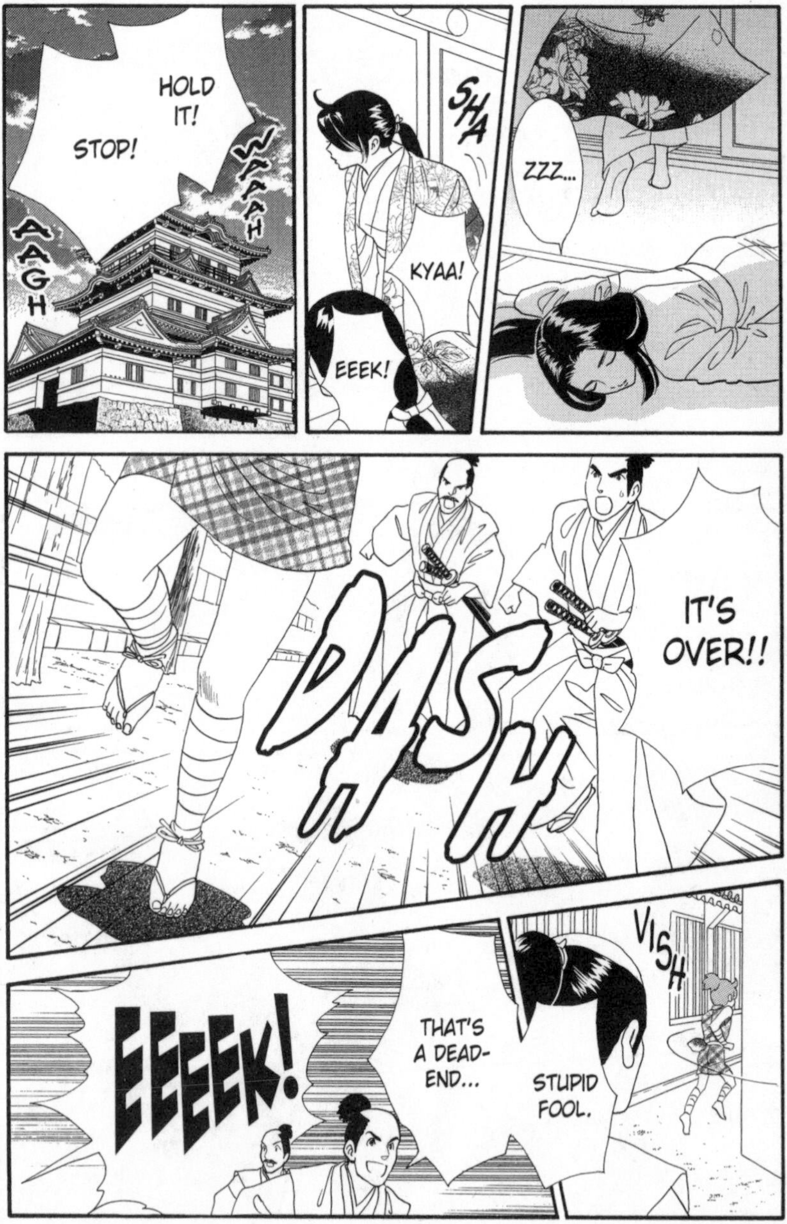
ZZZ...
SHA
KYAA!
EEEK!
WAAAH
HOLD IT!
STOP!
AAGH
IT'S OVER!!
DASH
VISH
STUPID FOOL.
THAT'S A DEAD-END...
EEEEK!

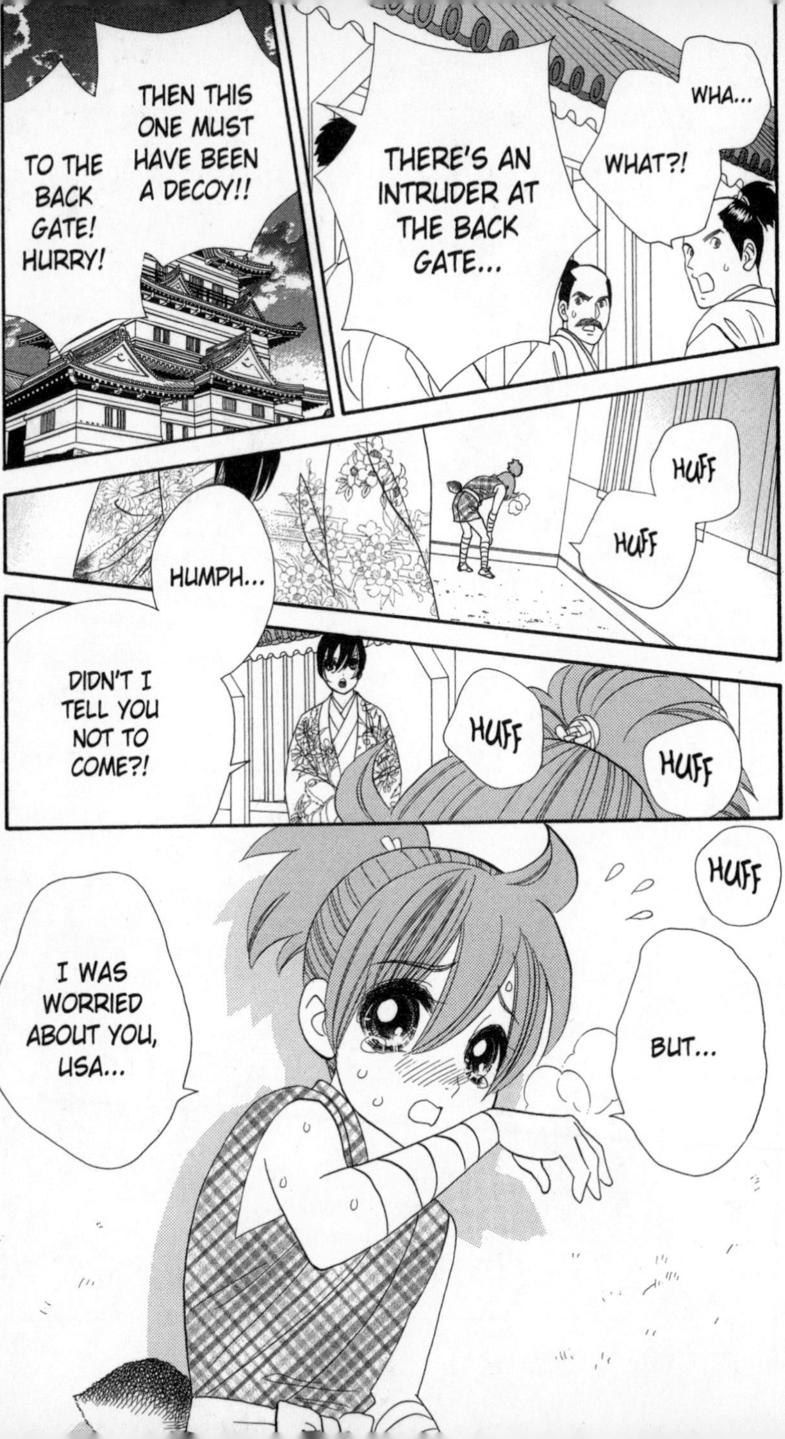
WHA...
WHAT?!
THERE'S AN INTRUDER AT THE BACK GATE...
THEN THIS ONE MUST HAVE BEEN A DECOY!!
TO THE BACK GATE! HURRY!
HUFF
HUFF
HUMPH...
HUFF
HUFF
DIDN'T I TELL YOU NOT TO COME?!
HUFF
BUT...
I WAS WORRIED ABOUT YOU, USA...

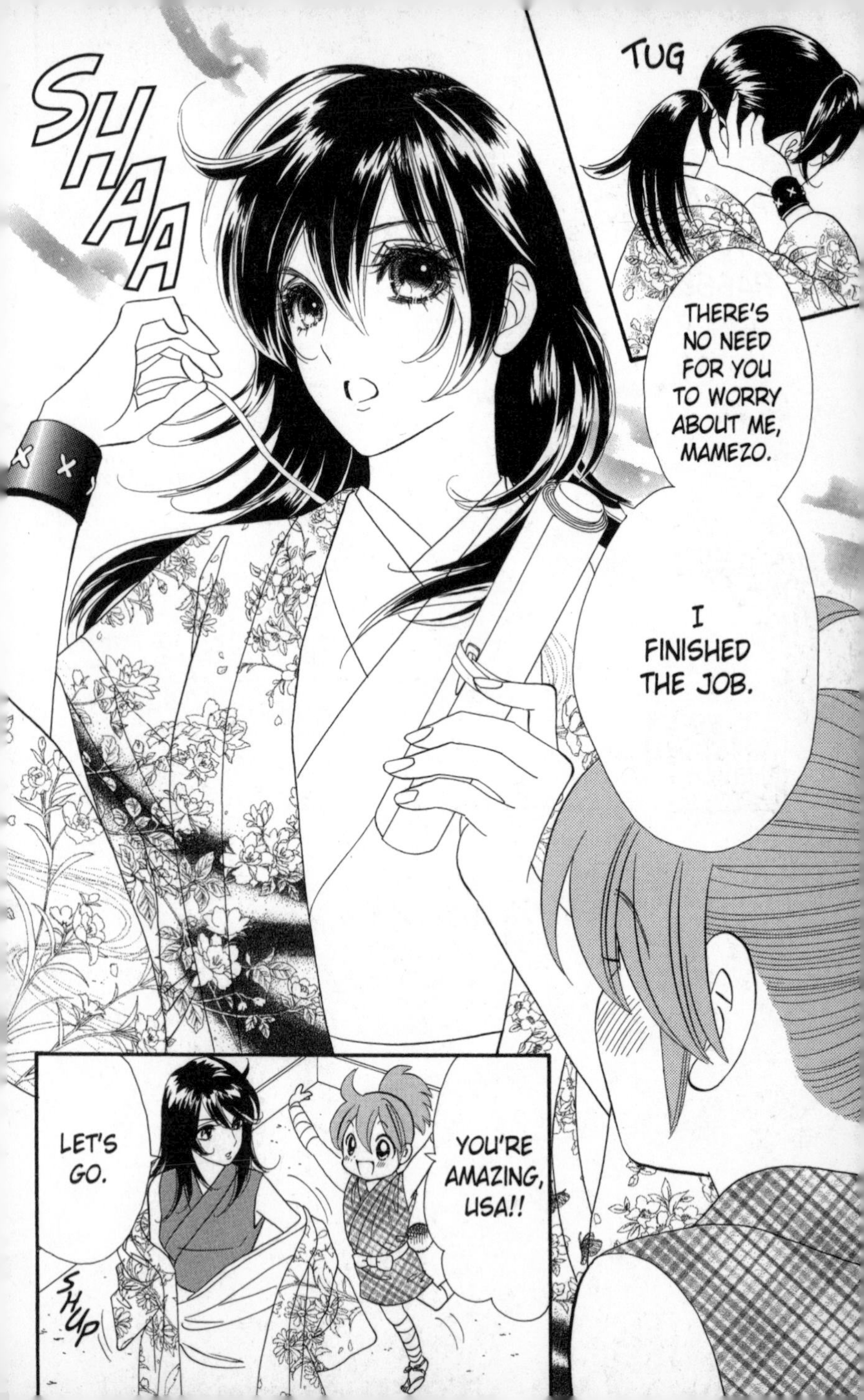
TUG
THERE'S NO NEED FOR YOU TO WORRY ABOUT ME, MAMEZO.
I FINISHED THE JOB.
SHAA
YOU'RE AMAZING, USA!!
LET'S GO.
SHUP

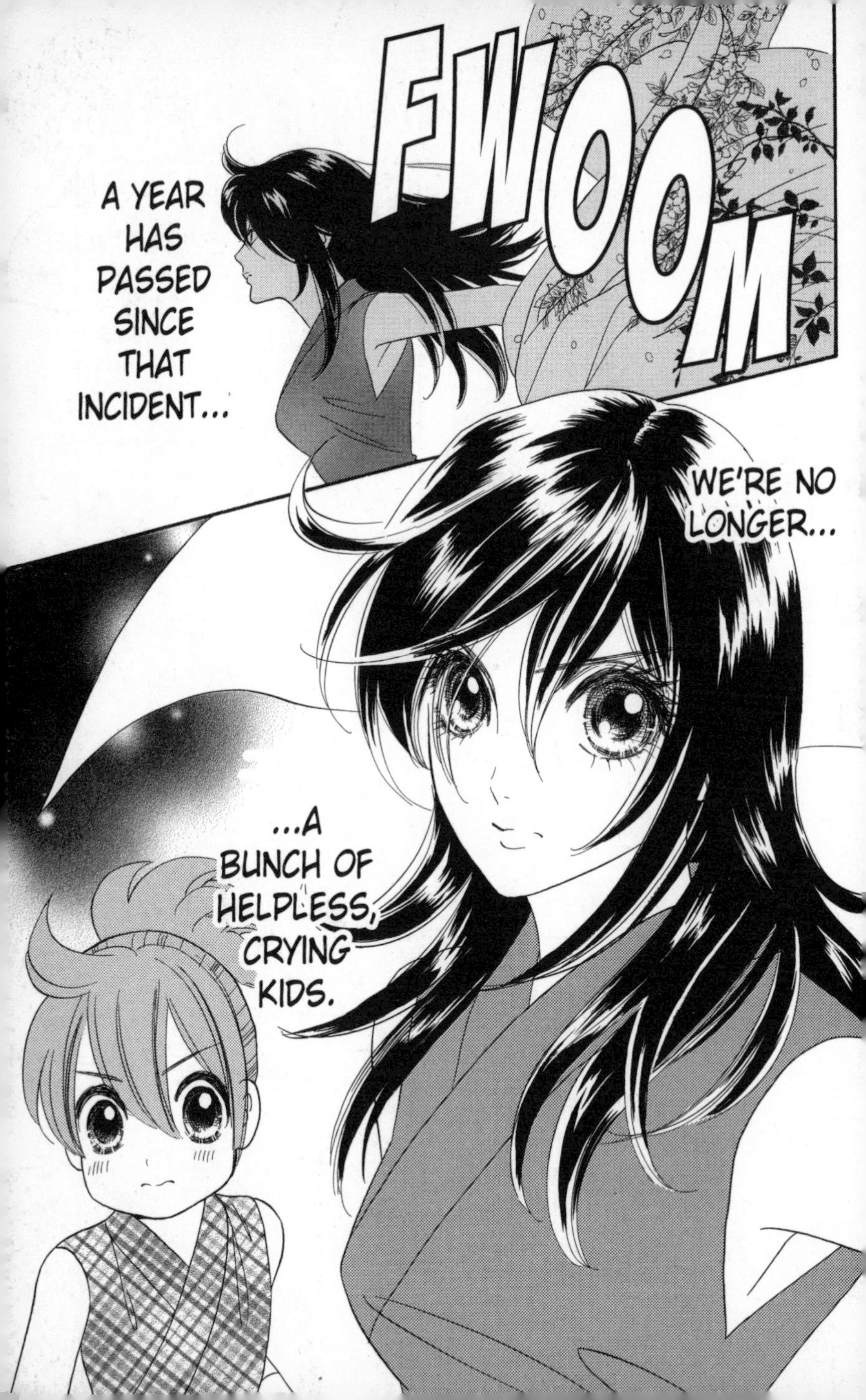
FWOOM
A YEAR HAS PASSED SINCE THAT INCIDENT...
WE'RE NO LONGER...
...A BUNCH OF HELPLESS, CRYING KIDS.

LET'S GO! LITTLE HANZO

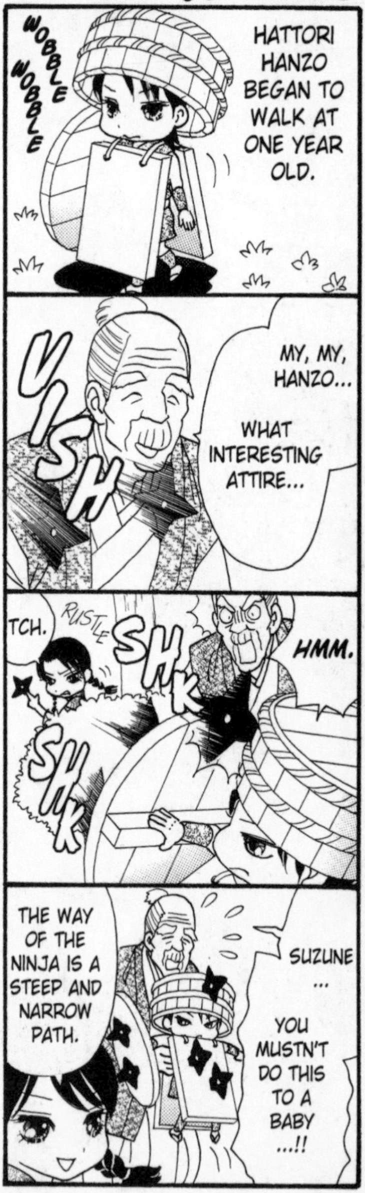
HATTORI HANZO BEGAN TO WALK AT ONE YEAR OLD.
WOBBLE WOBBLE
MY, MY, HANZO...
WHAT INTERESTING ATTIRE...
VISH
HMM.
SHK
RUSTLE
TCH.
SHK
SUZUNE ...
YOU MUSTN'T DO THIS TO A BABY ...!!
THE WAY OF THE NINJA IS A STEEP AND NARROW PATH.

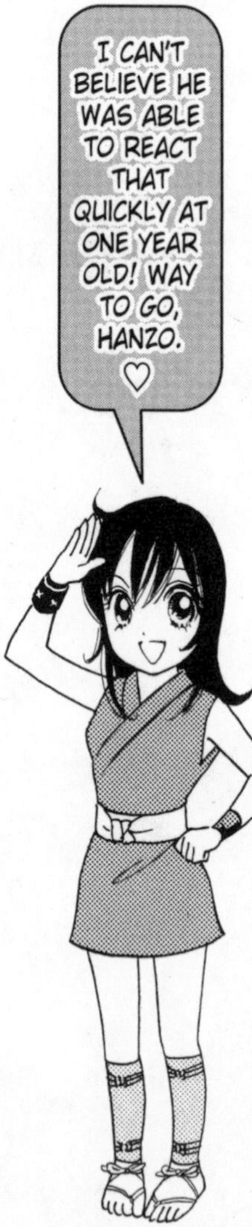
I CAN'T BELIEVE HE WAS ABLE TO REACT THAT QUICKLY AT ONE YEAR OLD! WAY TO GO, HANZO. ♡

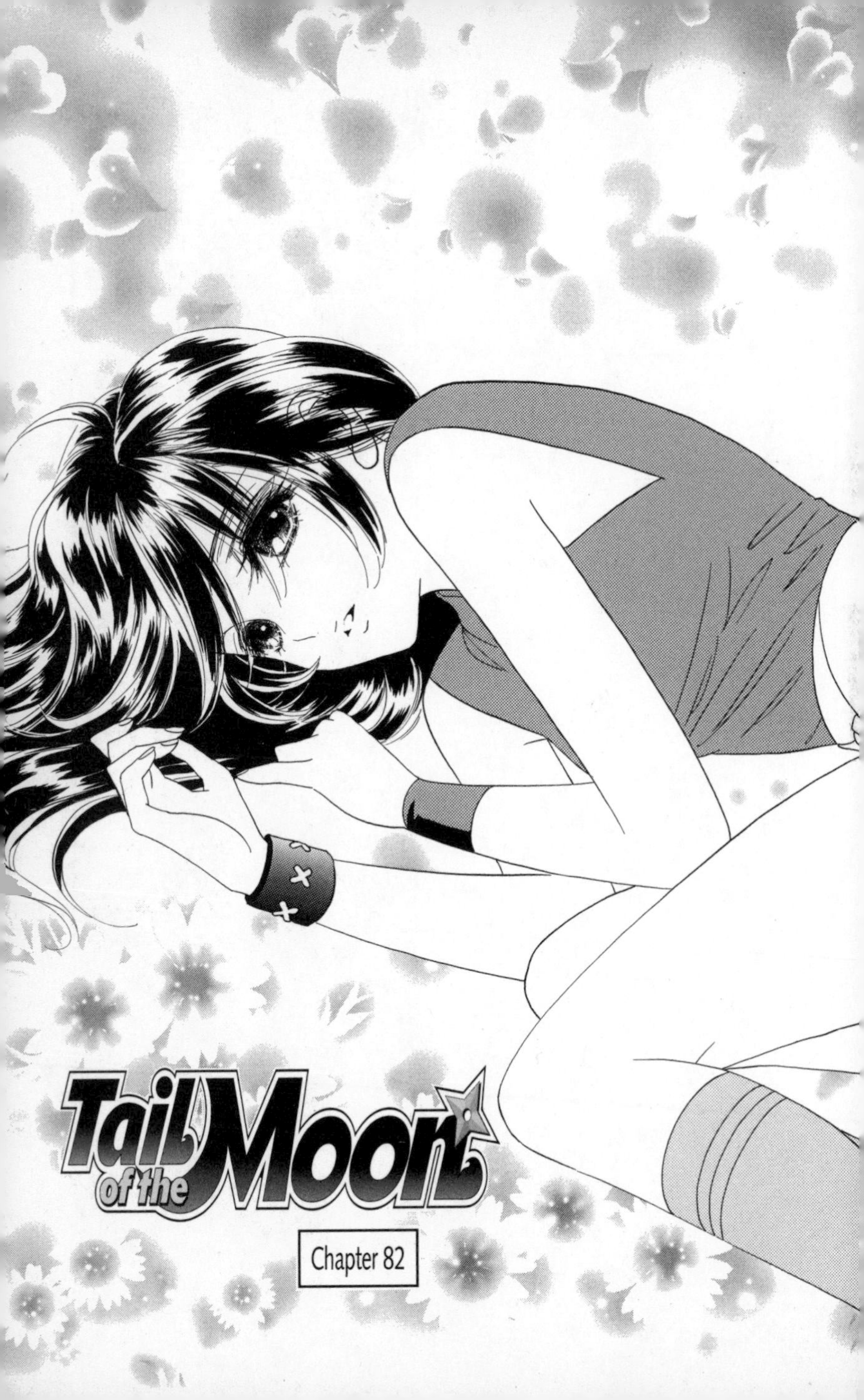
Tail of the Moon
Chapter 82

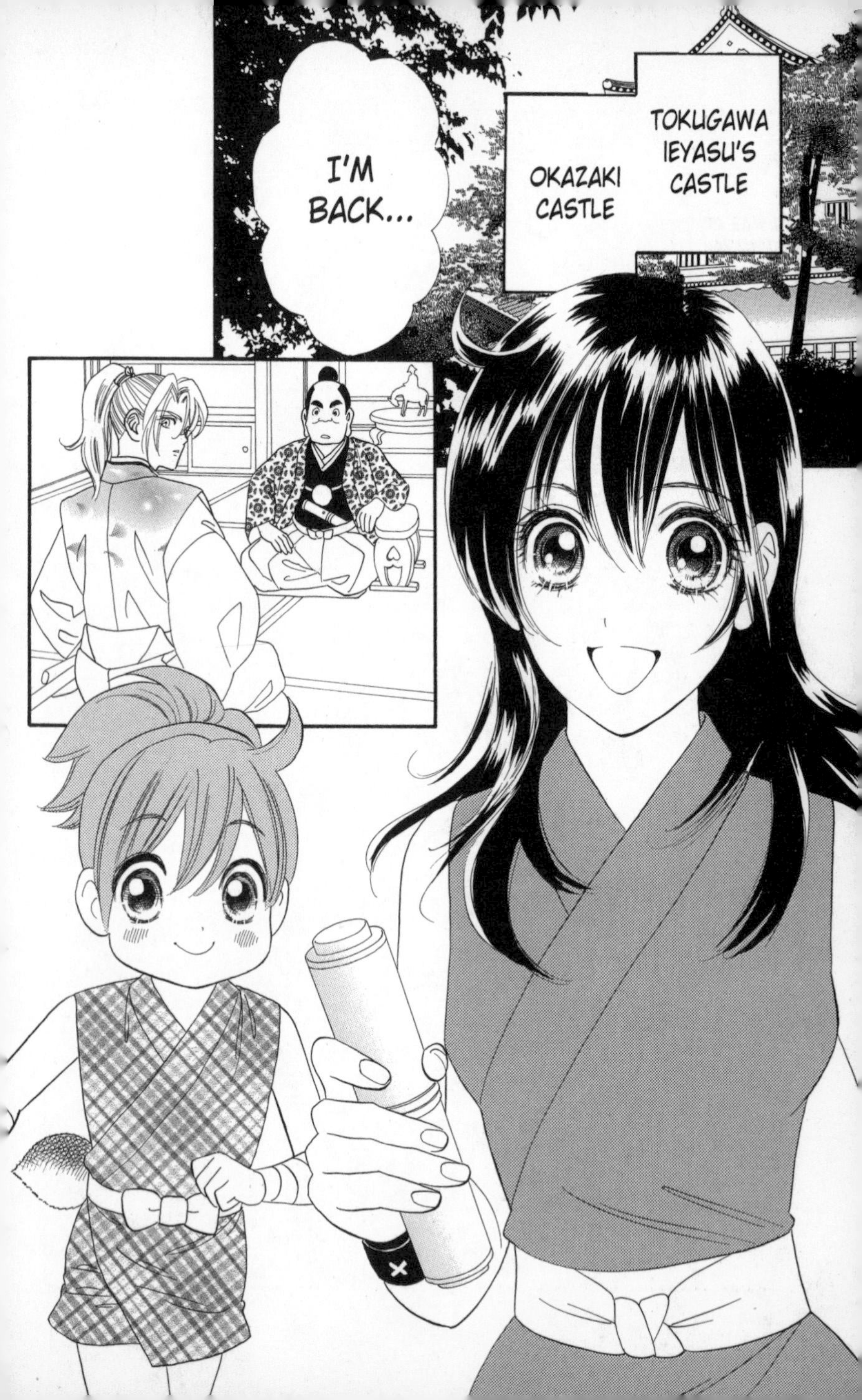
TOKUGAWA IEYASU'S CASTLE
OKAZAKI CASTLE
I'M BACK...

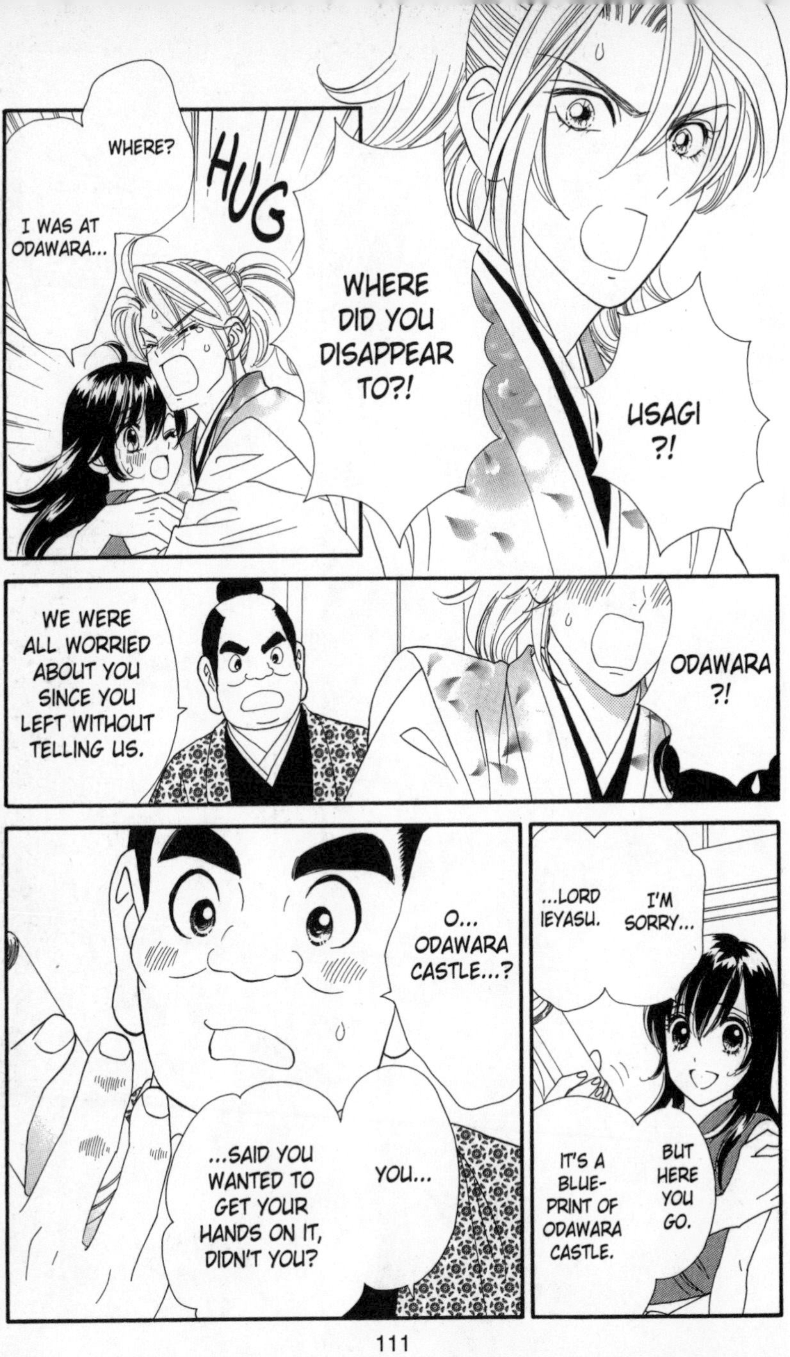
USAGI ?!
WHERE DID YOU DISAPPEAR TO?!
HUG
WHERE?
I WAS AT ODAWARA...
ODAWARA ?!
WE WERE ALL WORRIED ABOUT YOU SINCE YOU LEFT WITHOUT TELLING US.
I'M SORRY...
...LORD IEYASU.
BUT HERE YOU GO.
IT'S A BLUE-PRINT OF ODAWARA CASTLE.
O... ODAWARA CASTLE...?
YOU...
...SAID YOU WANTED TO GET YOUR HANDS ON IT, DIDN'T YOU?

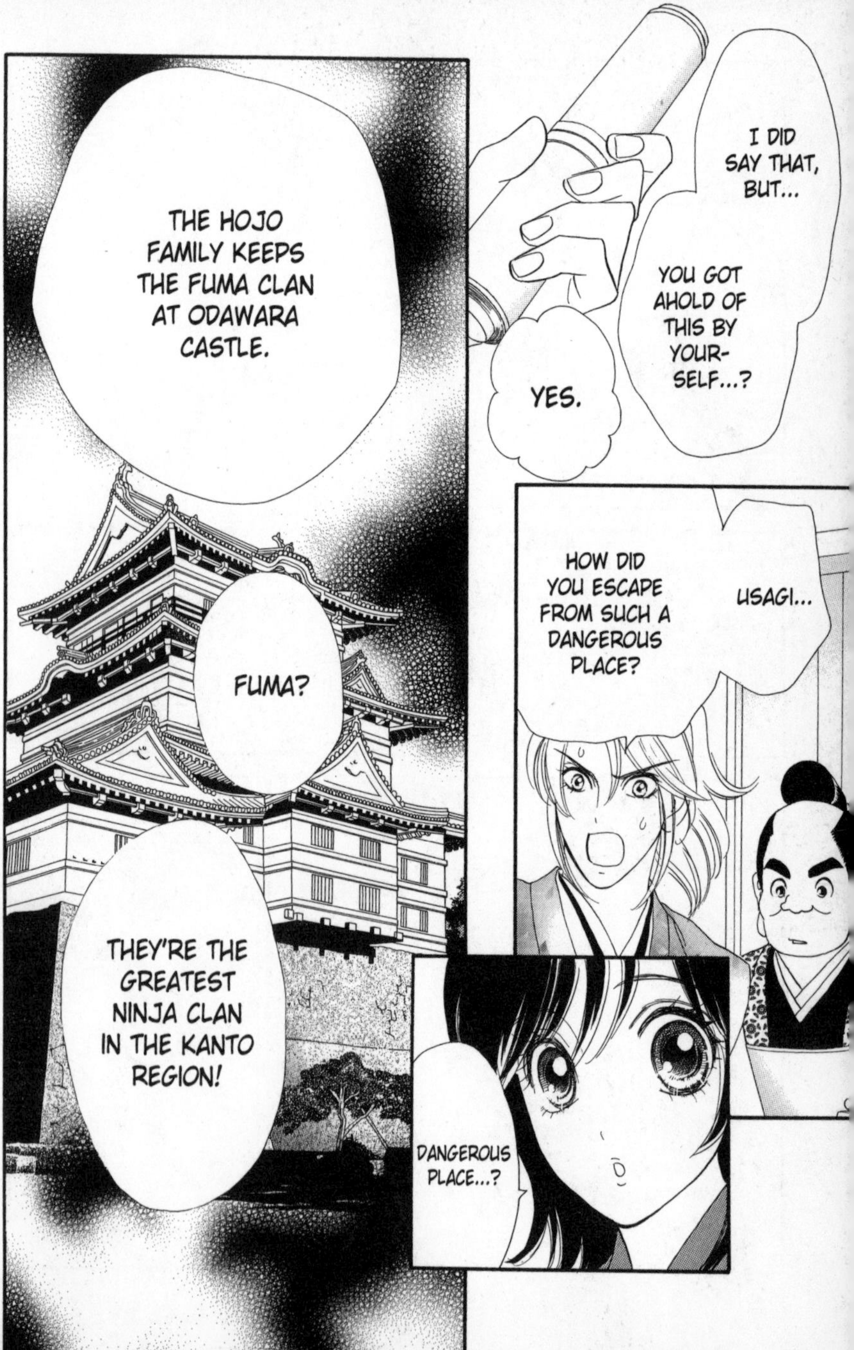
I DID SAY THAT, BUT...
YOU GOT AHOLD OF THIS BY YOUR-SELF...?
YES.
USAGI...
HOW DID YOU ESCAPE FROM SUCH A DANGEROUS PLACE?
DANGEROUS PLACE...?
THE HOJO FAMILY KEEPS THE FUMA CLAN AT ODAWARA CASTLE.
FUMA?
THEY'RE THE GREATEST NINJA CLAN IN THE KANTO REGION!

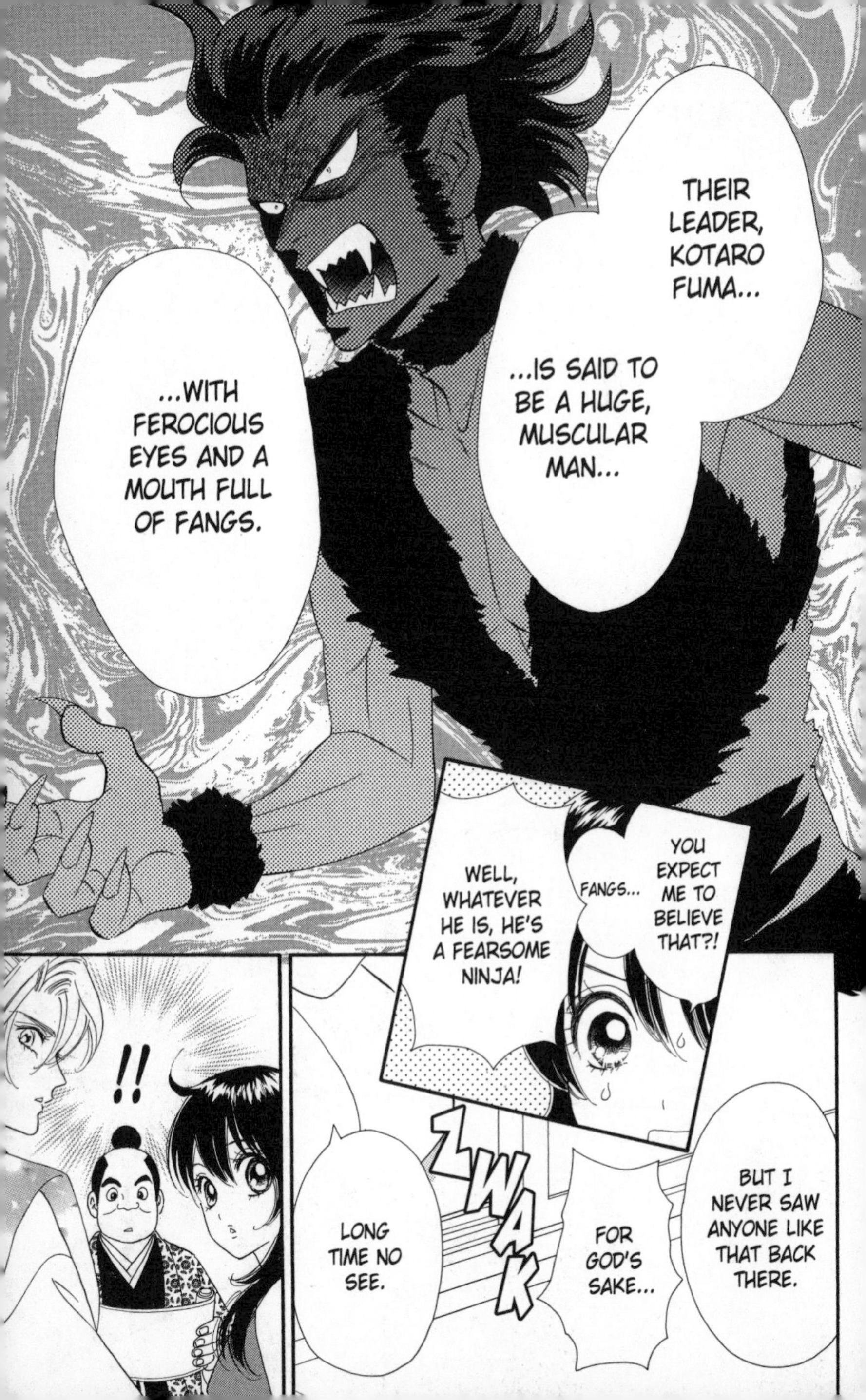
THEIR LEADER, KOTARO FUMA...
...IS SAID TO BE A HUGE, MUSCULAR MAN...
...WITH FEROCIOUS EYES AND A MOUTH FULL OF FANGS.
YOU EXPECT ME TO BELIEVE THAT?!
FANGS...
WELL, WHATEVER HE IS, HE'S A FEARSOME NINJA!
BUT I NEVER SAW ANYONE LIKE THAT BACK THERE.
FOR GOD'S SAKE...
ZWAK
LONG TIME NO SEE.
!!

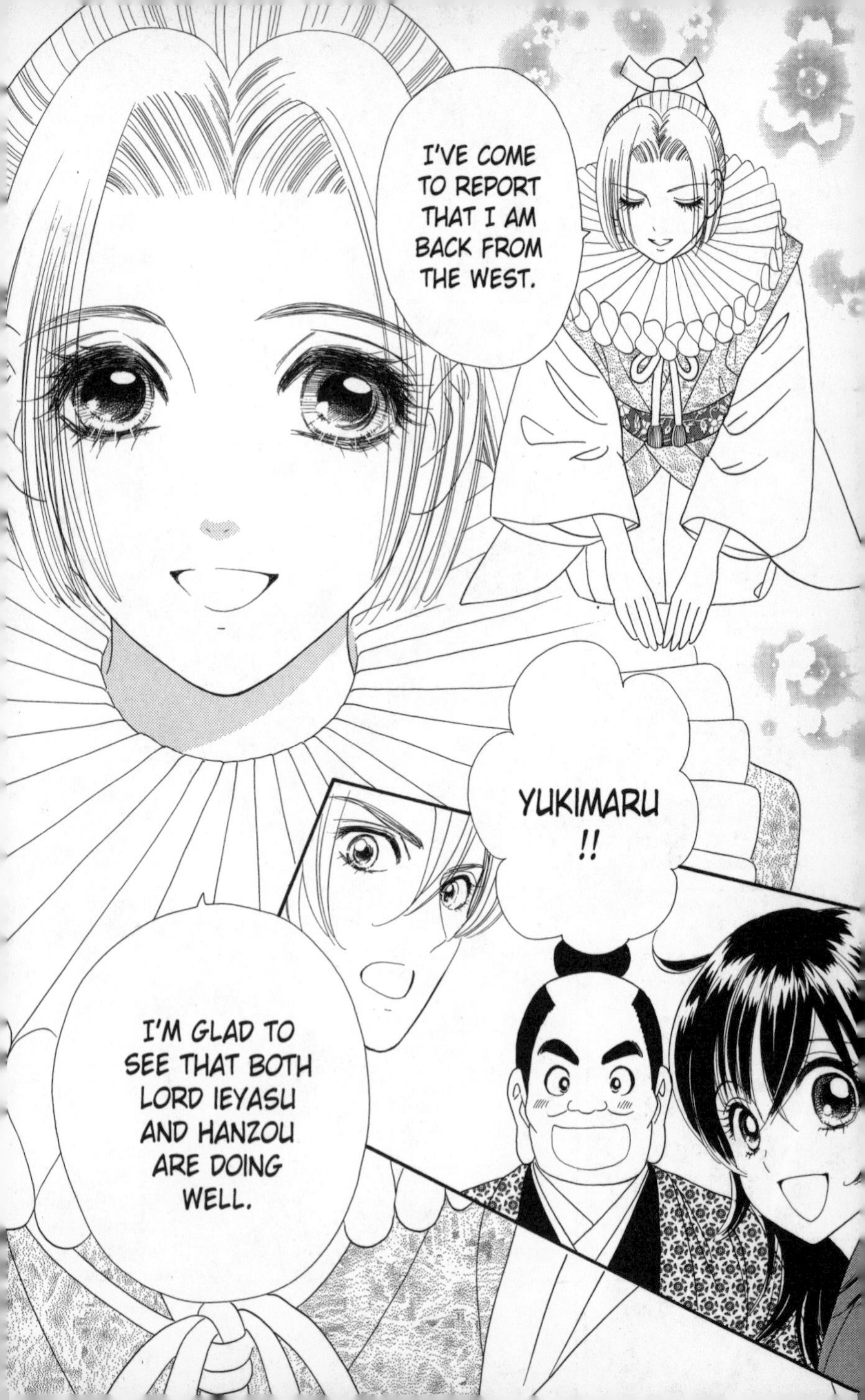
I'VE COME TO REPORT THAT I AM BACK FROM THE WEST.
YUKIMARU !!
I'M GLAD TO SEE THAT BOTH LORD IEYASU AND HANZOU ARE DOING WELL.

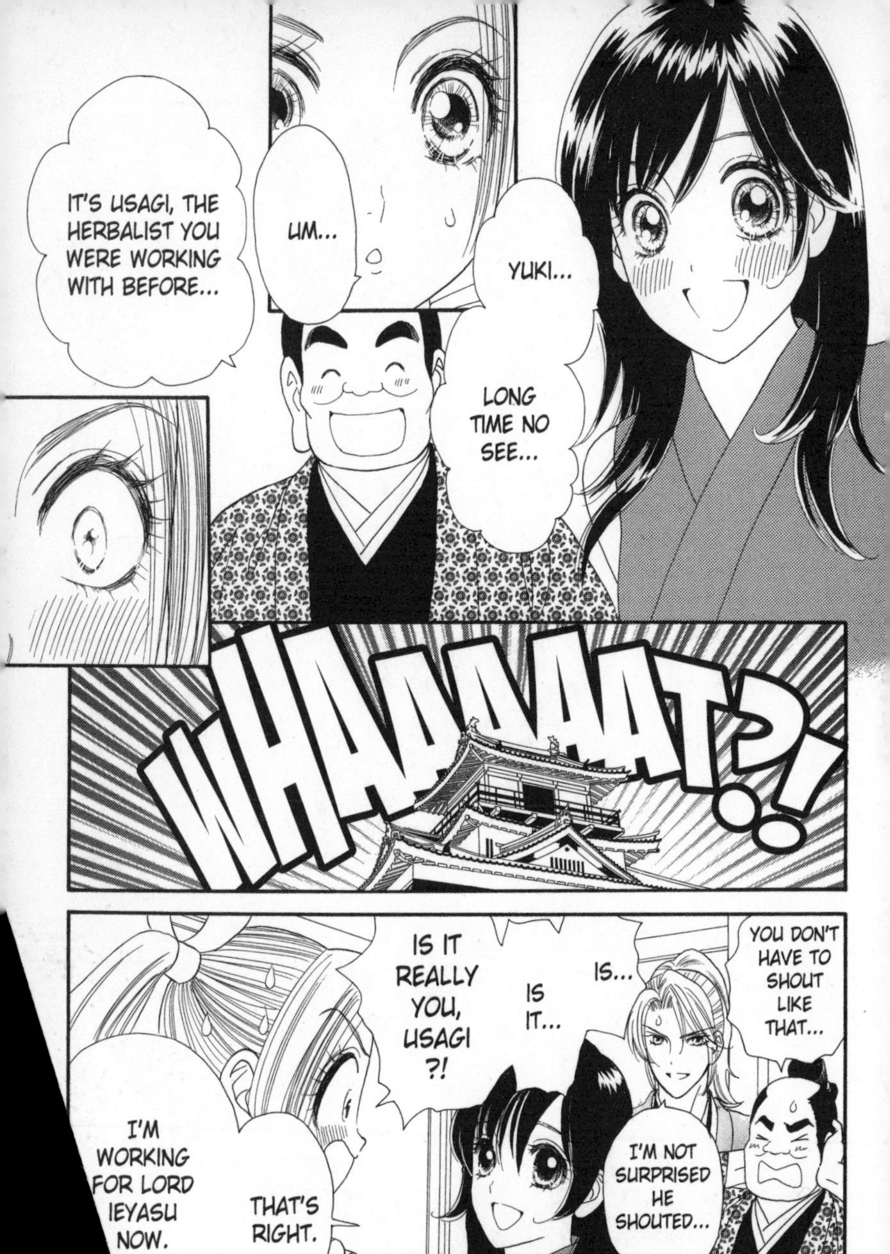
YUKI...
LONG TIME NO SEE...
UM...
IT'S USAGI, THE HERBALIST YOU WERE WORKING WITH BEFORE...
WHAAAAT?!
YOU DON'T HAVE TO SHOUT LIKE THAT...
IS...
IS IT...
IS IT REALLY YOU, USAGI ?!
I'M NOT SURPRISED HE SHOUTED...
THAT'S RIGHT.
I'M WORKING FOR LORD IEYASU NOW.

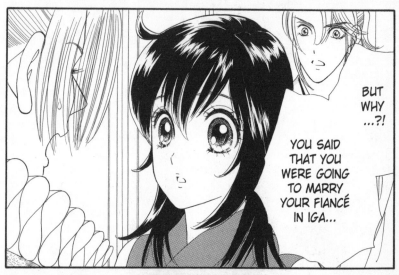

BUT WHY ...?!
YOU SAID THAT YOU WERE GOING TO MARRY YOUR FIANCÉ IN IGA...
OH...
UM... YUKIMARU...
...
WHAT IS IT?
I JUST CAME BACK FROM AN ASSIGNMENT.
...SO I'M GOING TO GET SOME REST...
REST WELL.
OH, USAGI...

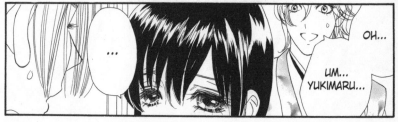

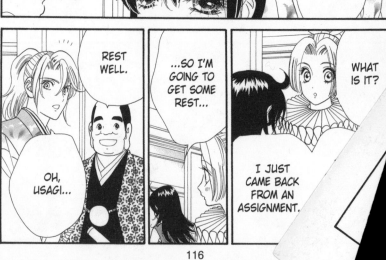

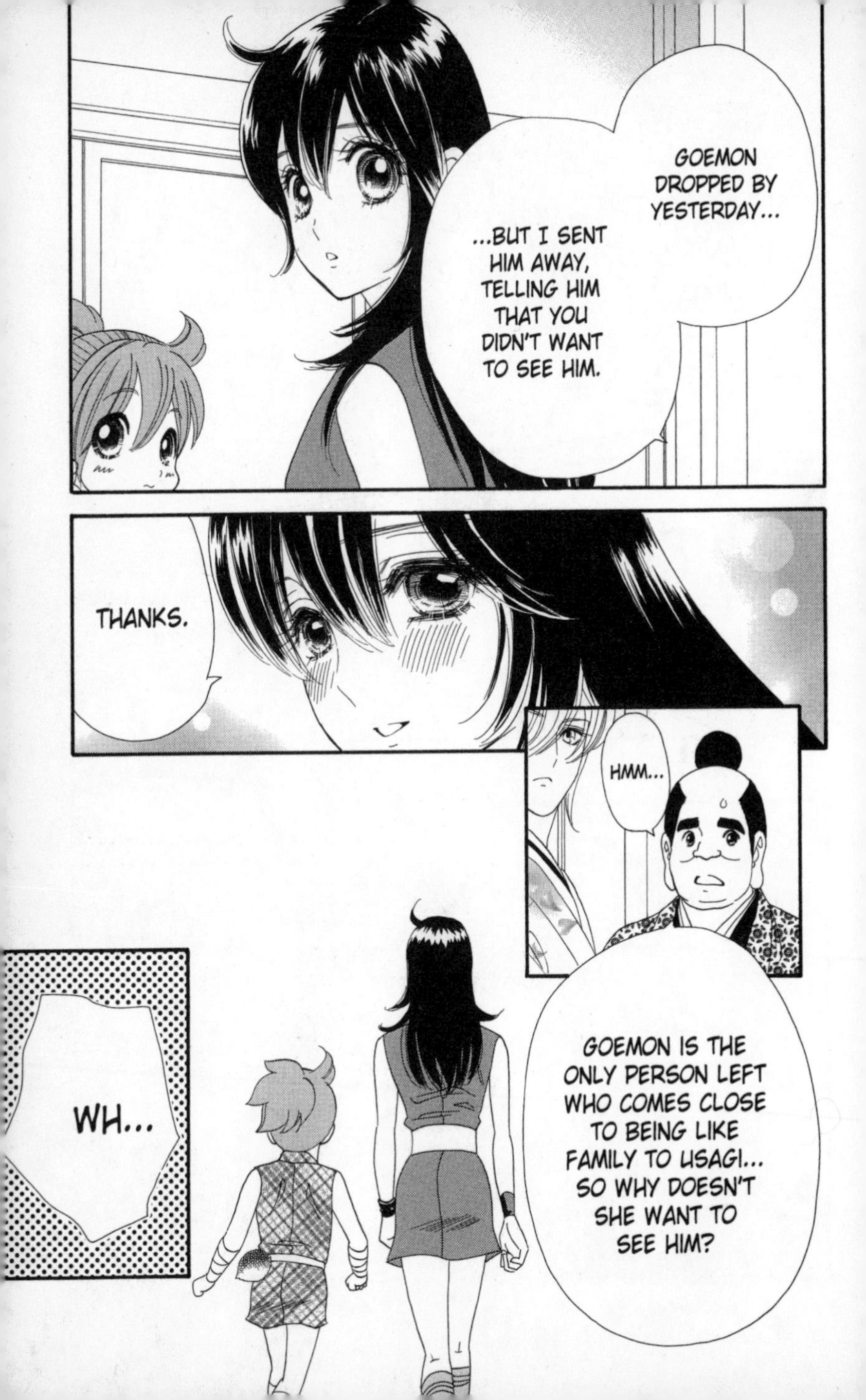
GOEMON DROPPED BY YESTERDAY...
...BUT I SENT HIM AWAY, TELLING HIM THAT YOU DIDN'T WANT TO SEE HIM.
THANKS.
HMM...
GOEMON IS THE ONLY PERSON LEFT WHO COMES CLOSE TO BEING LIKE FAMILY TO USAGI... SO WHY DOESN'T SHE WANT TO SEE HIM?
WH...

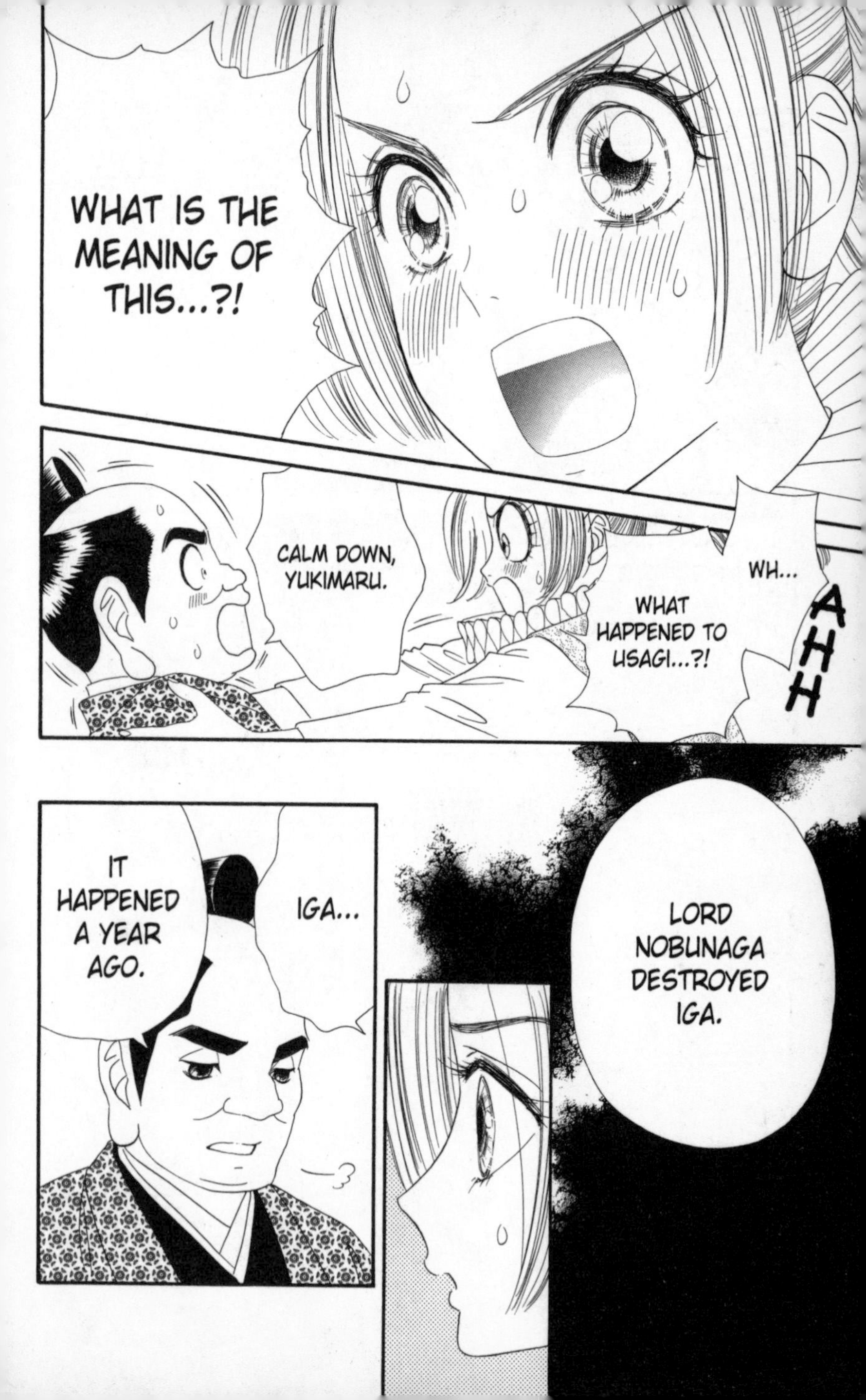
WHAT IS THE MEANING OF THIS...?!
WH...
WHAT HAPPENED TO USAGI...?!
AHH
CALM DOWN, YUKIMARU.
LORD NOBUNAGA DESTROYED IGA.
IGA...
IT HAPPENED A YEAR AGO.

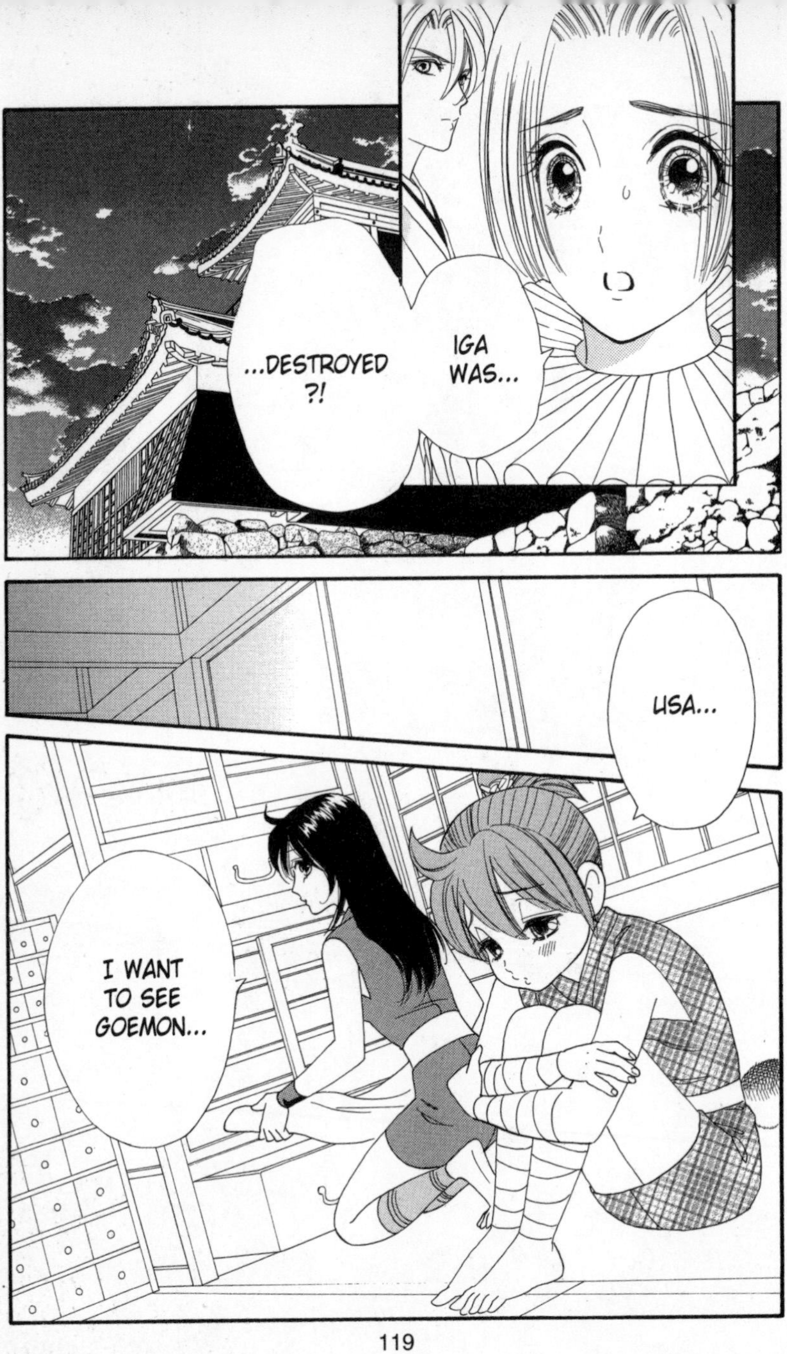
IGA WAS...
...DESTROYED?!
USA...
I WANT TO SEE GOEMON...

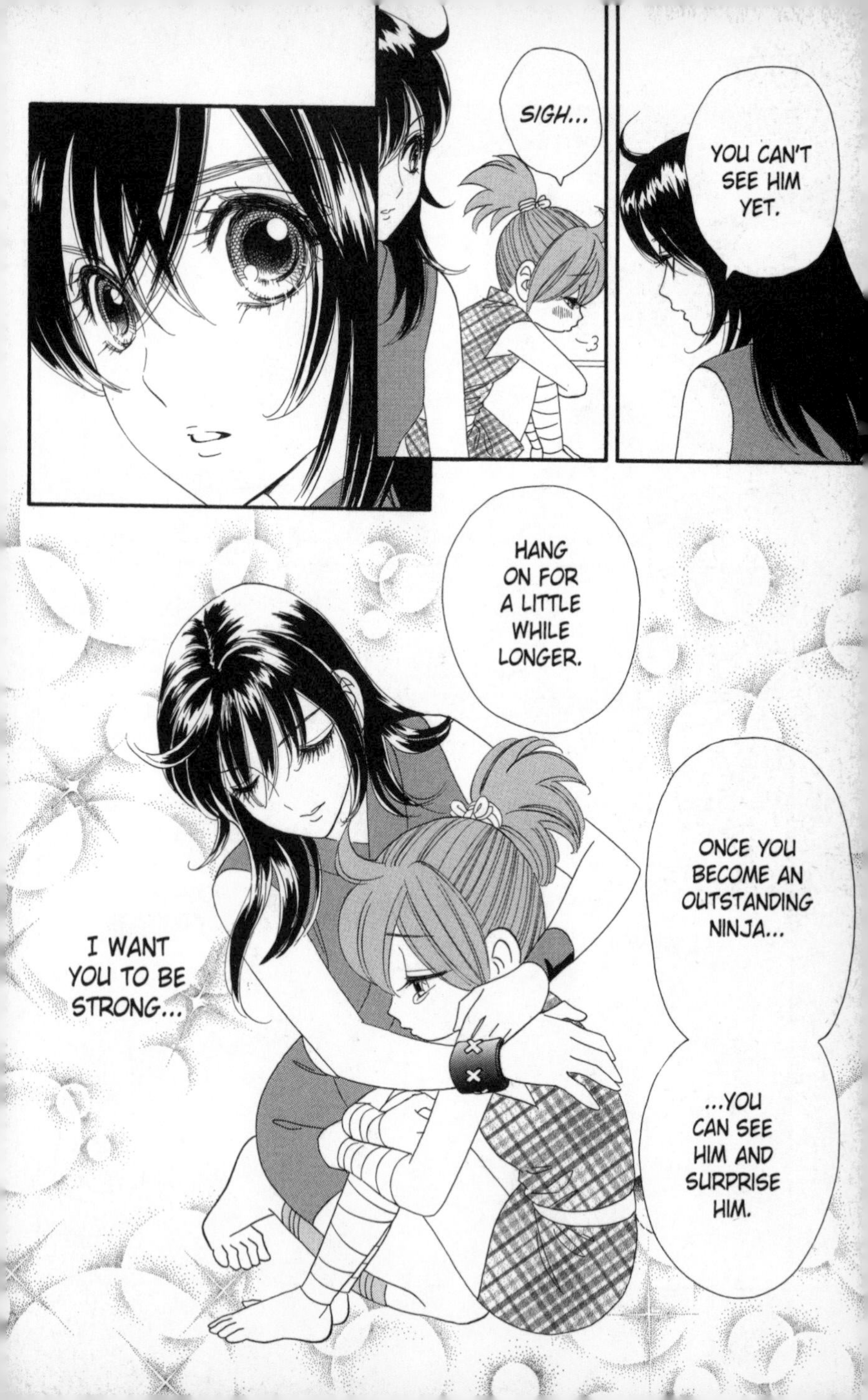
YOU CAN'T SEE HIM YET.
SIGH...
HANG ON FOR A LITTLE WHILE LONGER.
ONCE YOU BECOME AN OUTSTANDING NINJA...
...YOU CAN SEE HIM AND SURPRISE HIM.
I WANT YOU TO BE STRONG...

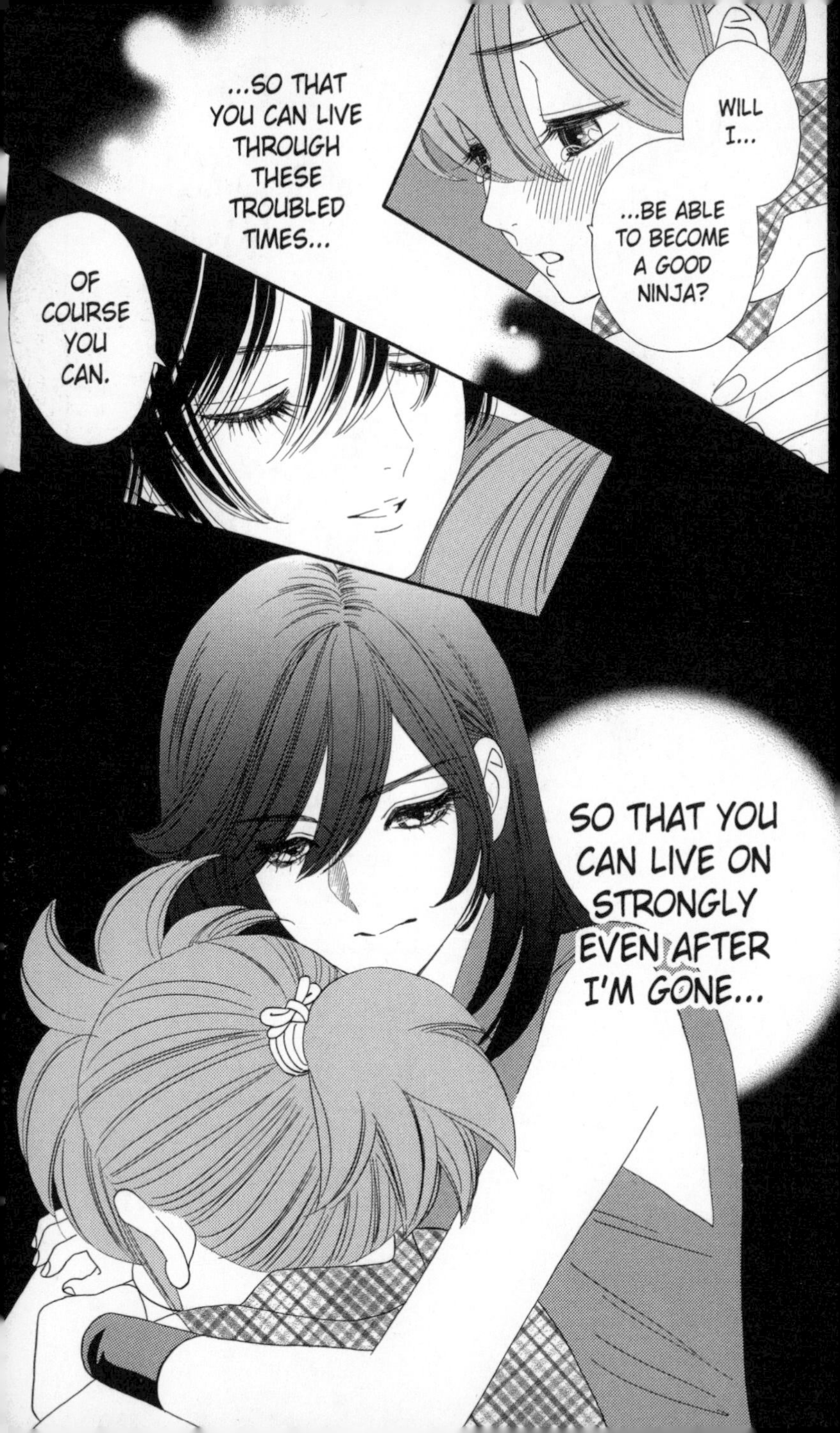
WILL I...
...BE ABLE TO BECOME A GOOD NINJA?
...SO THAT YOU CAN LIVE THROUGH THESE TROUBLED TIMES...
OF COURSE YOU CAN.
SO THAT YOU CAN LIVE ON STRONGLY EVEN AFTER I'M GONE...

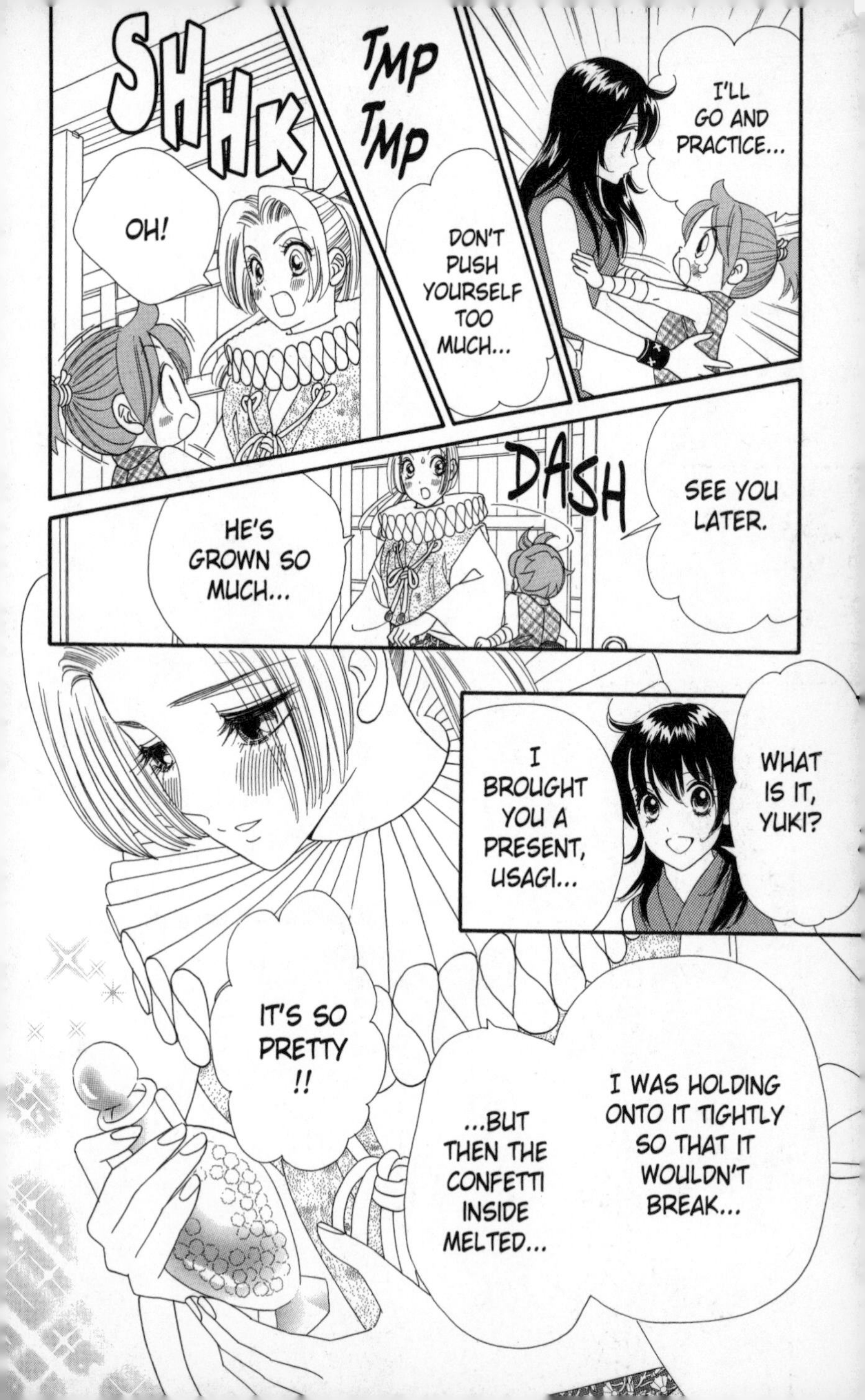
I'LL GO AND PRACTICE...
TMP TMP
DON'T PUSH YOURSELF TOO MUCH...
SHHK
OH!
SEE YOU LATER.
DASH
HE'S GROWN SO MUCH...
WHAT IS IT, YUKI?
I BROUGHT YOU A PRESENT, USAGI...
IT'S SO PRETTY !!
I WAS HOLDING ONTO IT TIGHTLY SO THAT IT WOULDN'T BREAK...
...BUT THEN THE CONFETTI INSIDE MELTED...

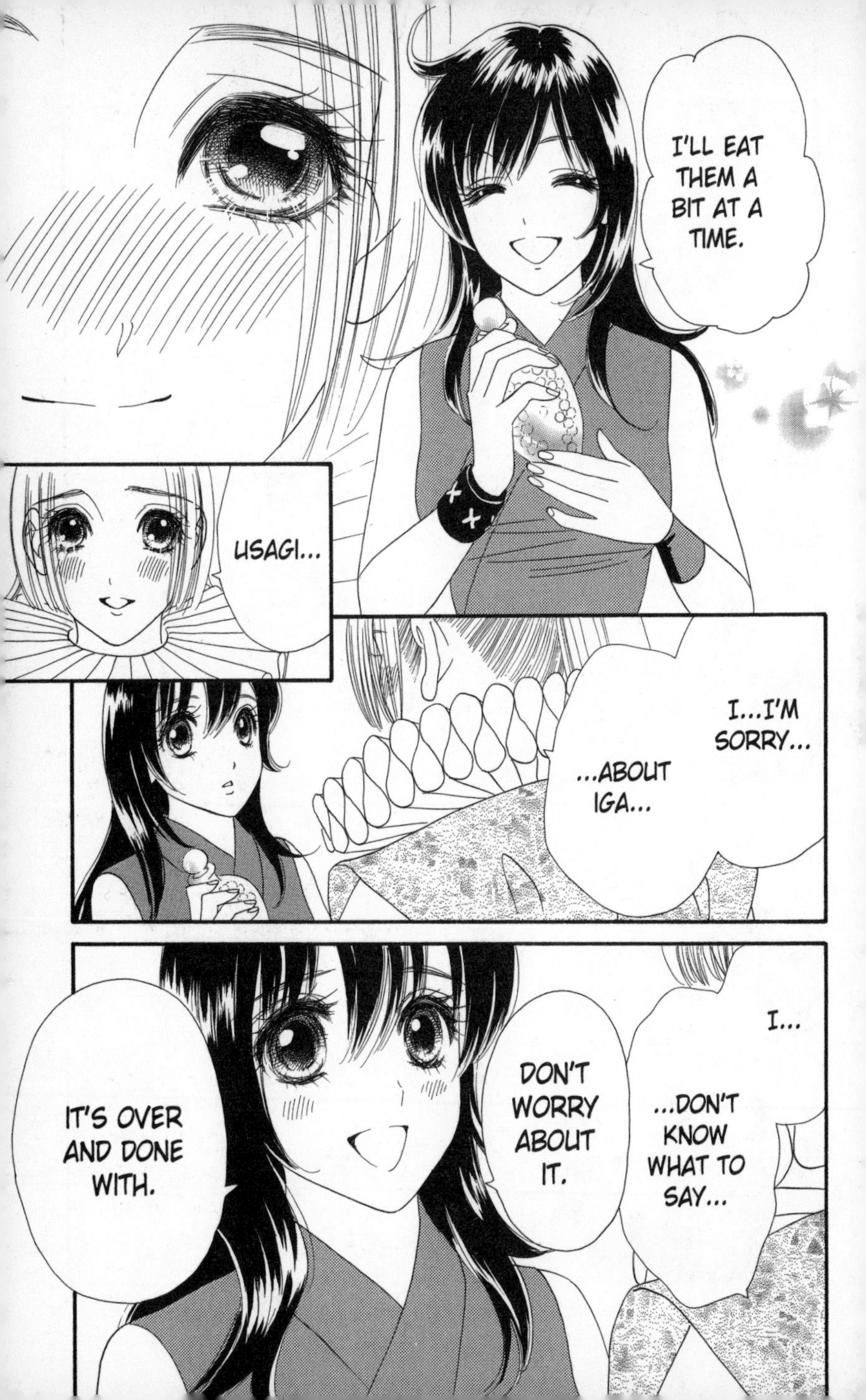
I'LL EAT THEM A BIT AT A TIME.
USAGI...
I...I'M SORRY...
...ABOUT IGA...
I...
...DON'T KNOW WHAT TO SAY...
DON'T WORRY ABOUT IT.
IT'S OVER AND DONE WITH.

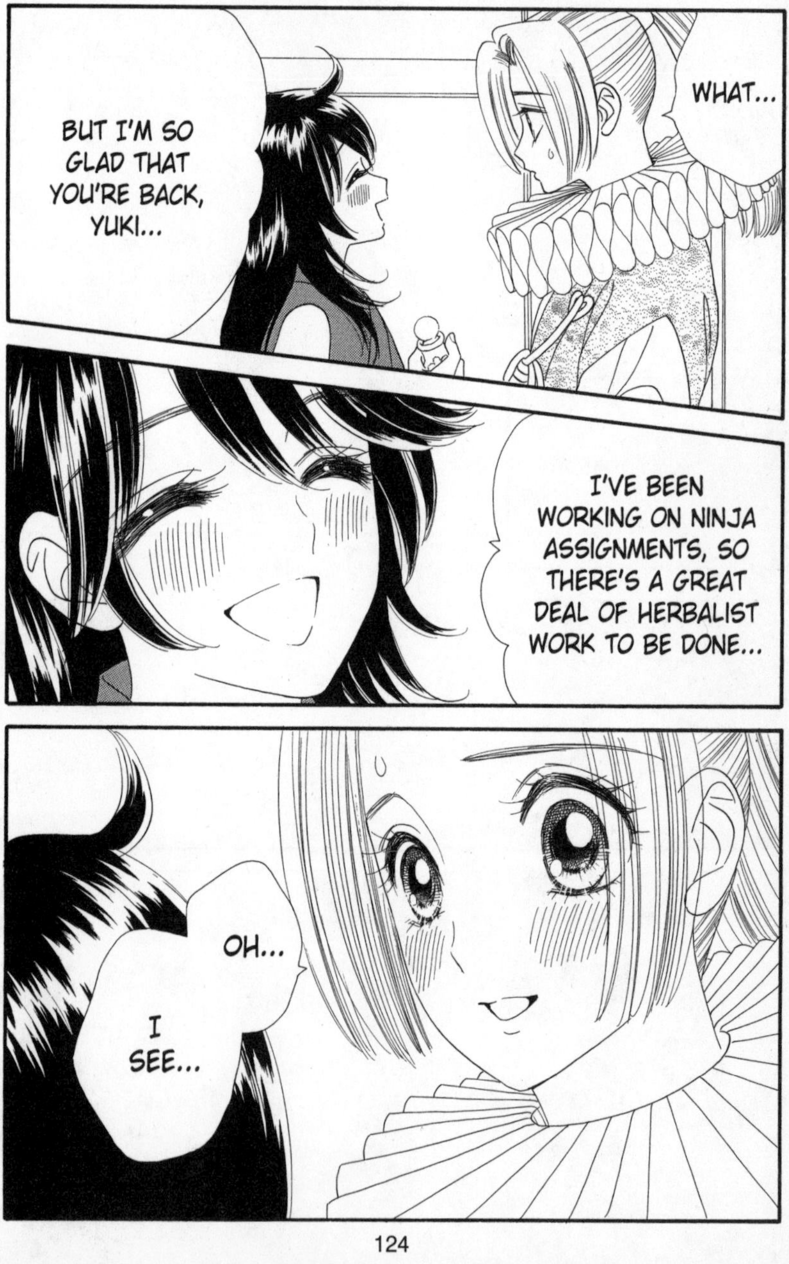
WHAT...
BUT I'M SO GLAD THAT YOU'RE BACK, YUKI...
I'VE BEEN WORKING ON NINJA ASSIGNMENTS, SO THERE'S A GREAT DEAL OF HERBALIST WORK TO BE DONE...
OH...
I SEE...

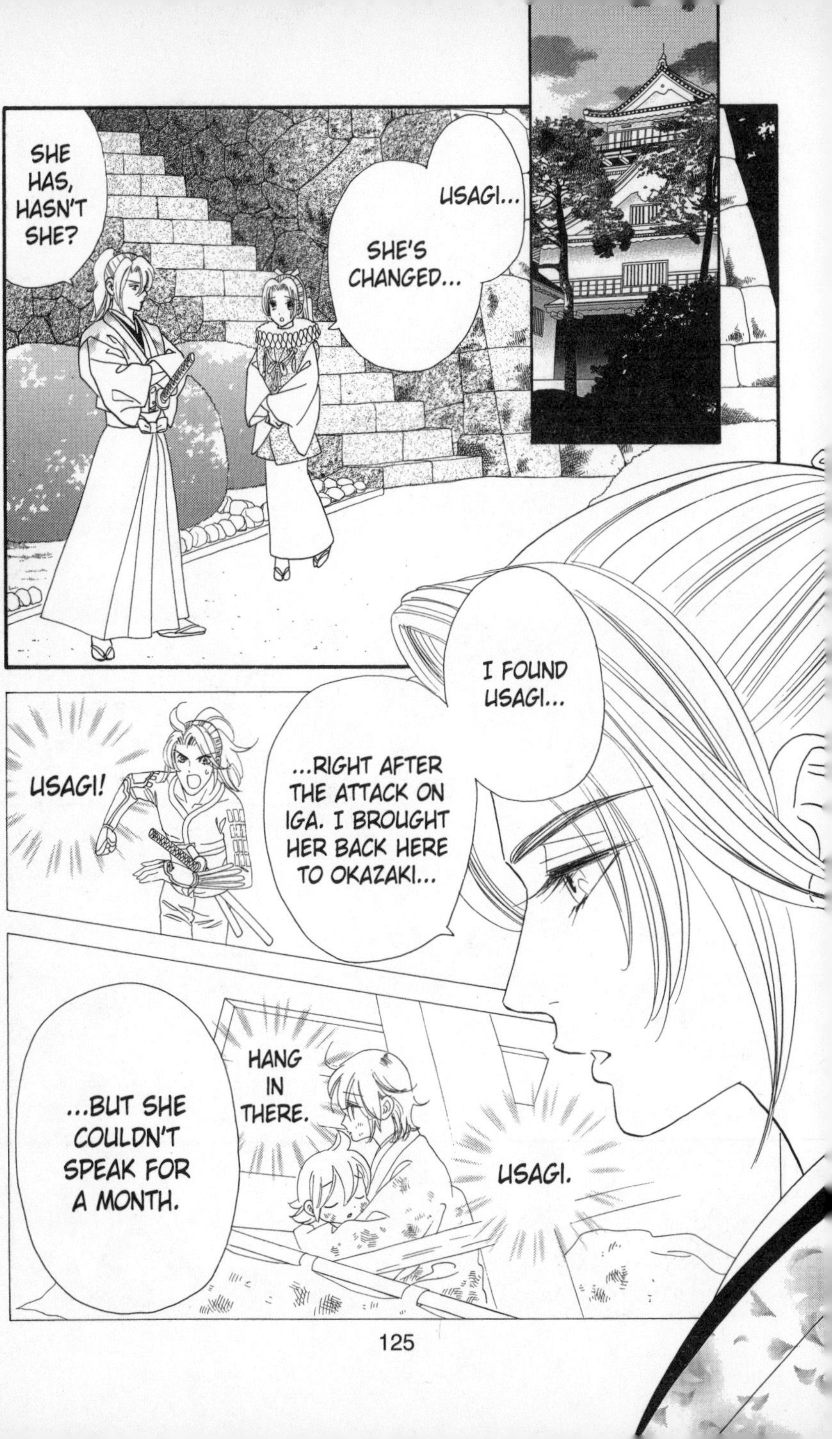
USAGI... SHE'S CHANGED...
SHE HAS, HASN'T SHE?
I FOUND USAGI...
...RIGHT AFTER THE ATTACK ON IGA. I BROUGHT HER BACK HERE TO OKAZAKI...
USAGI!
USAGI.
HANG IN THERE.
...BUT SHE COULDN'T SPEAK FOR A MONTH.

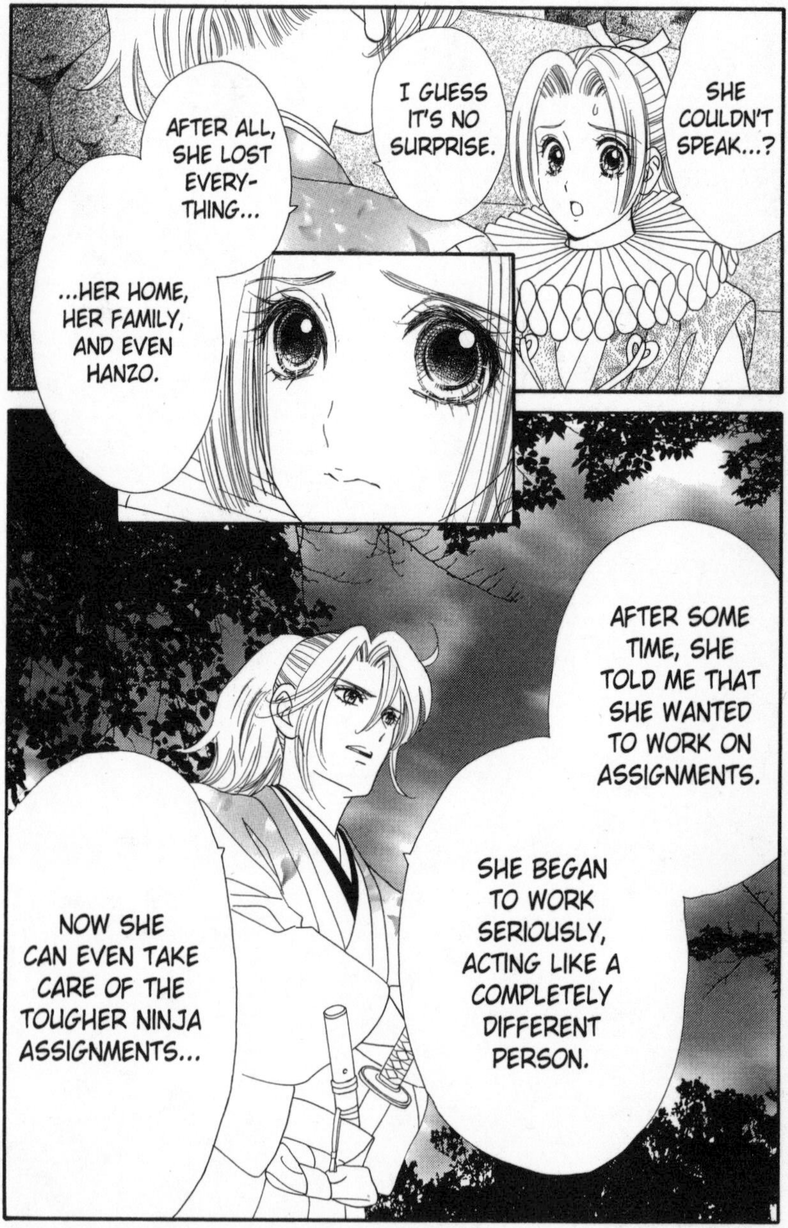
SHE COULDN'T SPEAK...?
I GUESS IT'S NO SURPRISE.
AFTER ALL, SHE LOST EVERY-THING...
...HER HOME, HER FAMILY, AND EVEN HANZO.
AFTER SOME TIME, SHE TOLD ME THAT SHE WANTED TO WORK ON ASSIGNMENTS.
SHE BEGAN TO WORK SERIOUSLY, ACTING LIKE A COMPLETELY DIFFERENT PERSON.
NOW SHE CAN EVEN TAKE CARE OF THE TOUGHER NINJA ASSIGNMENTS...

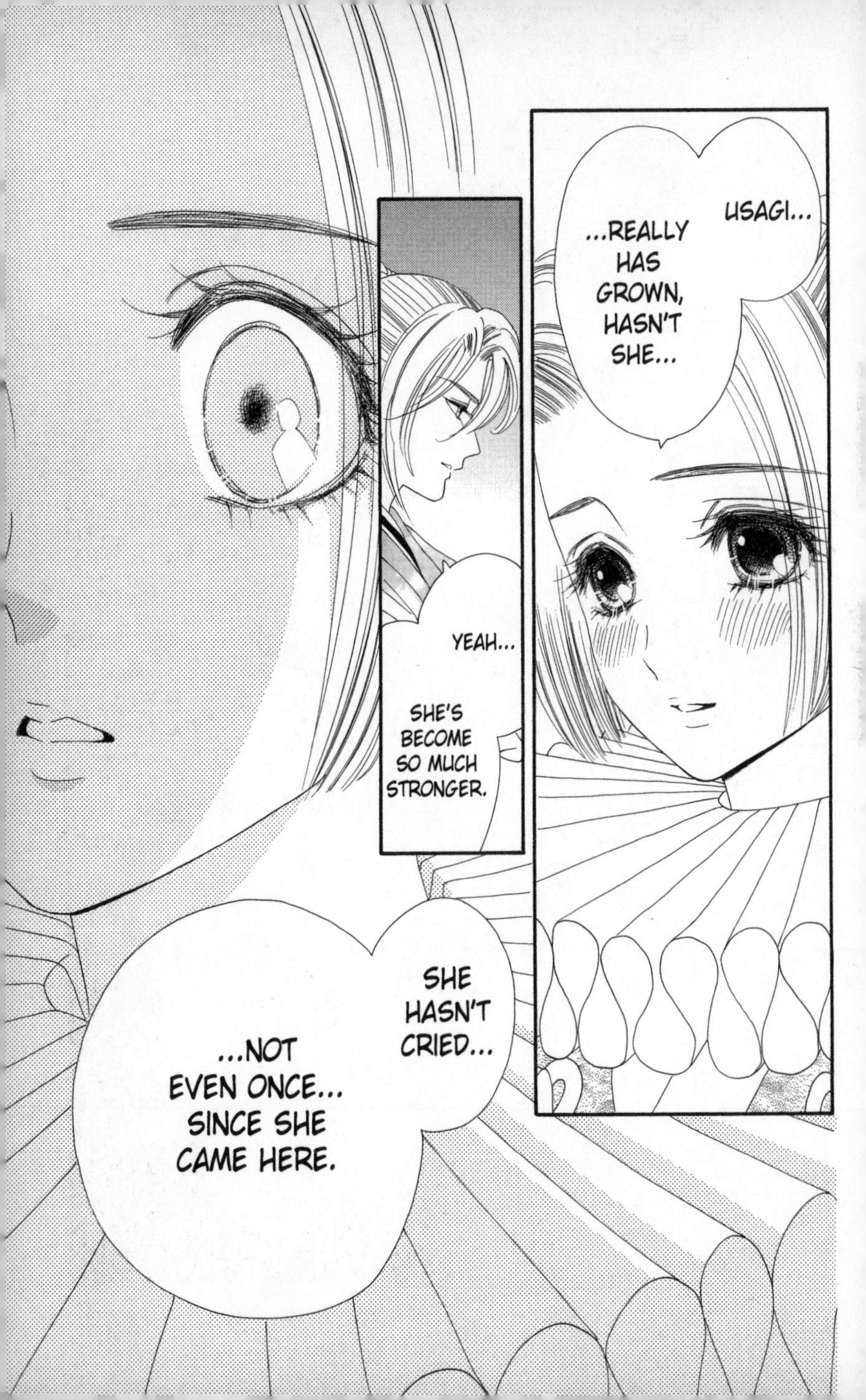
USAGI...
...REALLY HAS GROWN, HASN'T SHE...
YEAH...
SHE'S BECOME SO MUCH STRONGER.
SHE HASN'T CRIED...
...NOT EVEN ONCE... SINCE SHE CAME HERE.

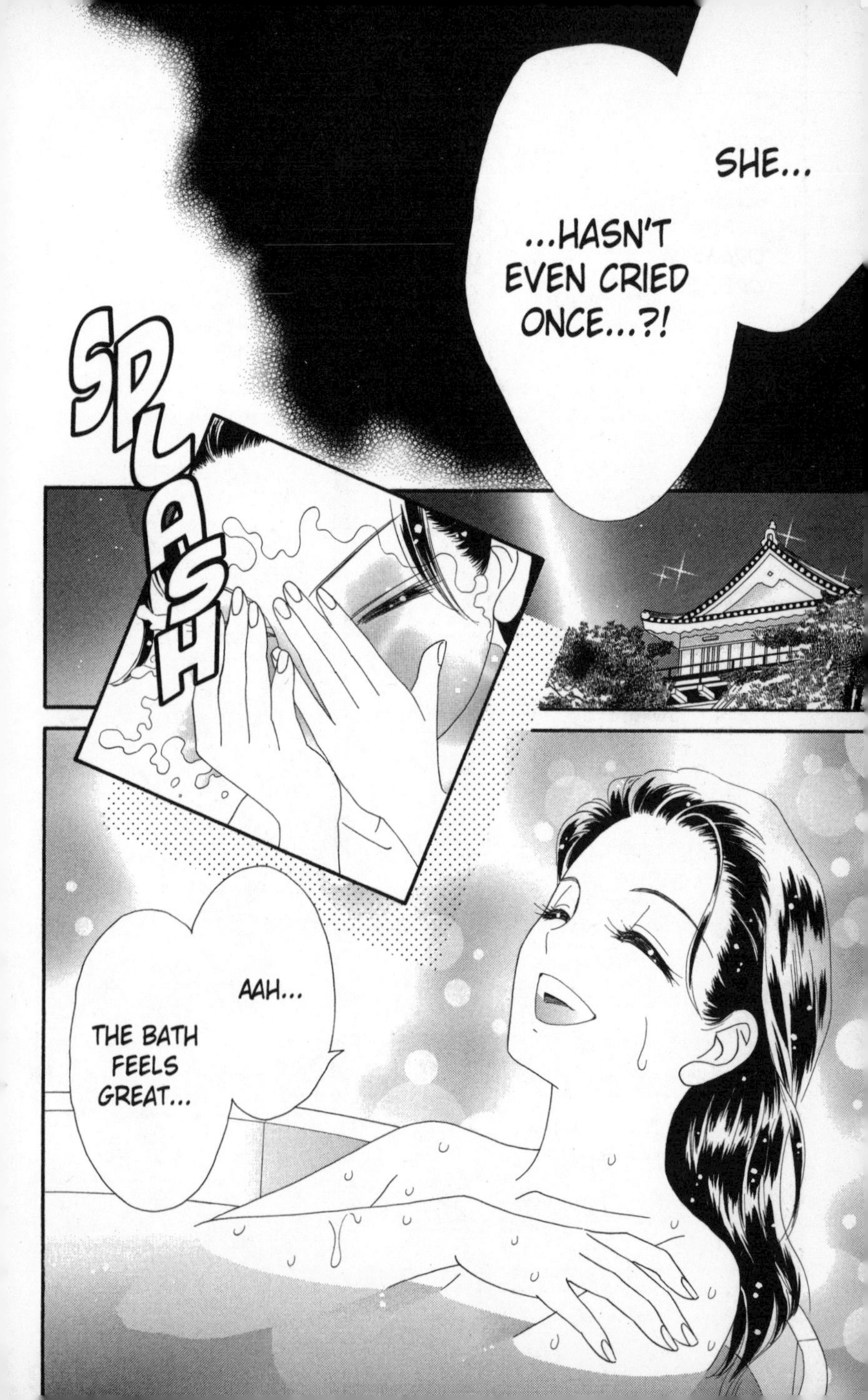
SHE...
...HASN'T EVEN CRIED ONCE...?!
SPLASH
AAH...
THE BATH FEELS GREAT...

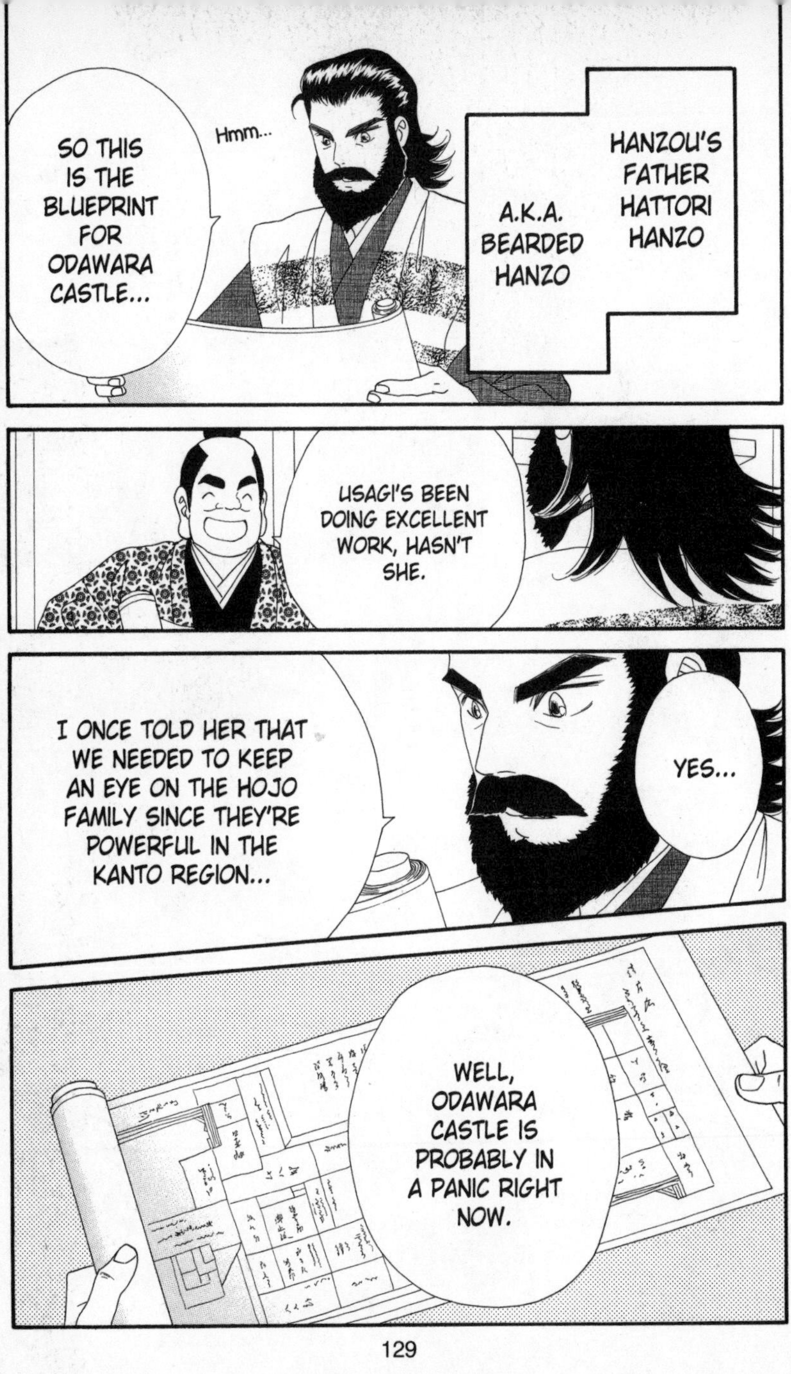
HANZOU'S FATHER HATTORI HANZO
A.K.A. BEARDED HANZO
Hmm...
SO THIS IS THE BLUEPRINT FOR ODAWARA CASTLE...
USAGI'S BEEN DOING EXCELLENT WORK, HASN'T SHE.
YES...
I ONCE TOLD HER THAT WE NEEDED TO KEEP AN EYE ON THE HOJO FAMILY SINCE THEY'RE POWERFUL IN THE KANTO REGION...
WELL, ODAWARA CASTLE IS PROBABLY IN A PANIC RIGHT NOW.

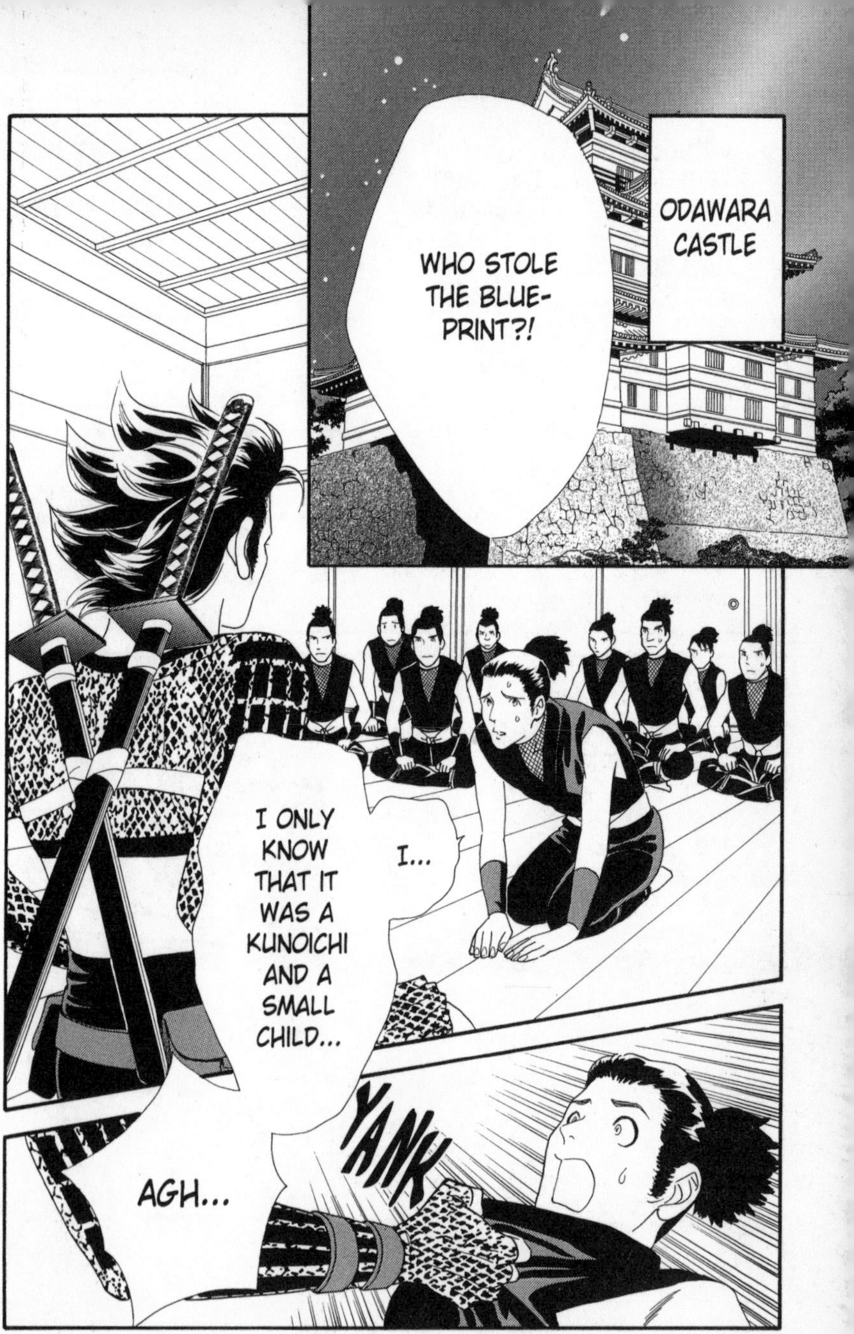
ODAWARA CASTLE
WHO STOLE THE BLUE-PRINT?!
I...
I ONLY KNOW THAT IT WAS A KUNOICHI AND A SMALL CHILD...
YANK
AGH...

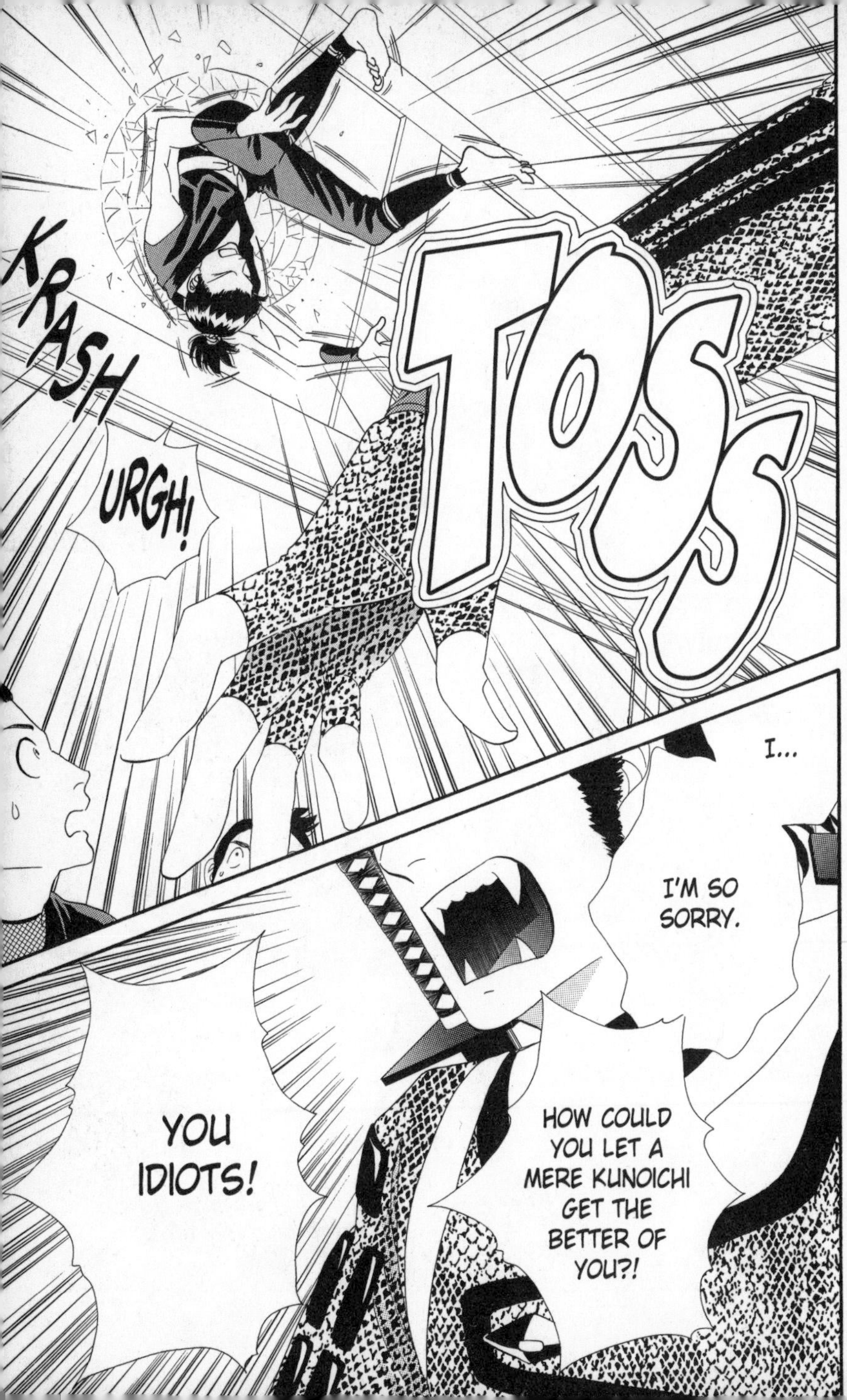
TOSS
KRASH
URGH!
I...
I'M SO SORRY.
HOW COULD YOU LET A MERE KUNOICHI GET THE BETTER OF YOU?!
YOU IDIOTS!

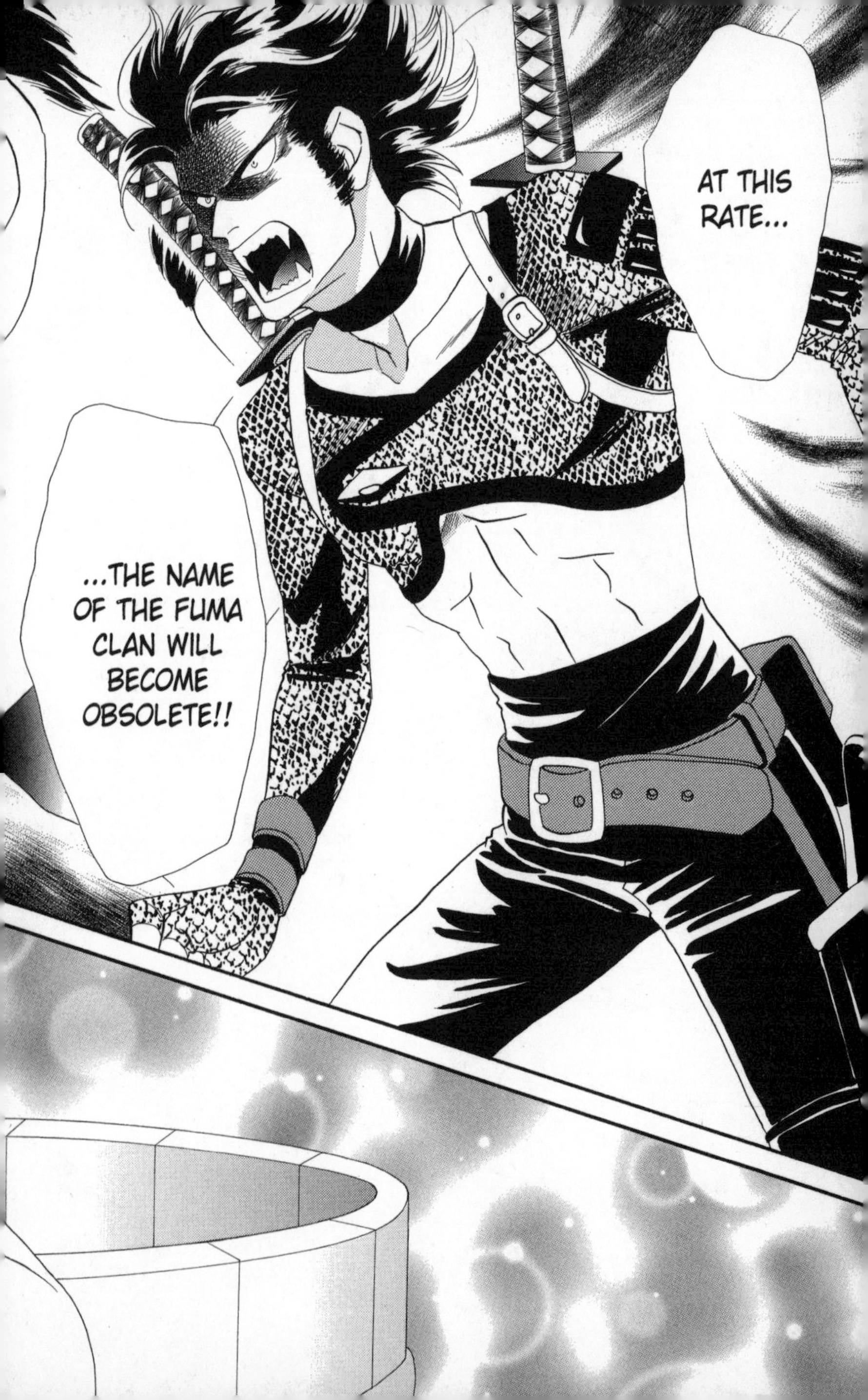
AT THIS RATE...
...THE NAME OF THE FUMA CLAN WILL BECOME OBSOLETE!!

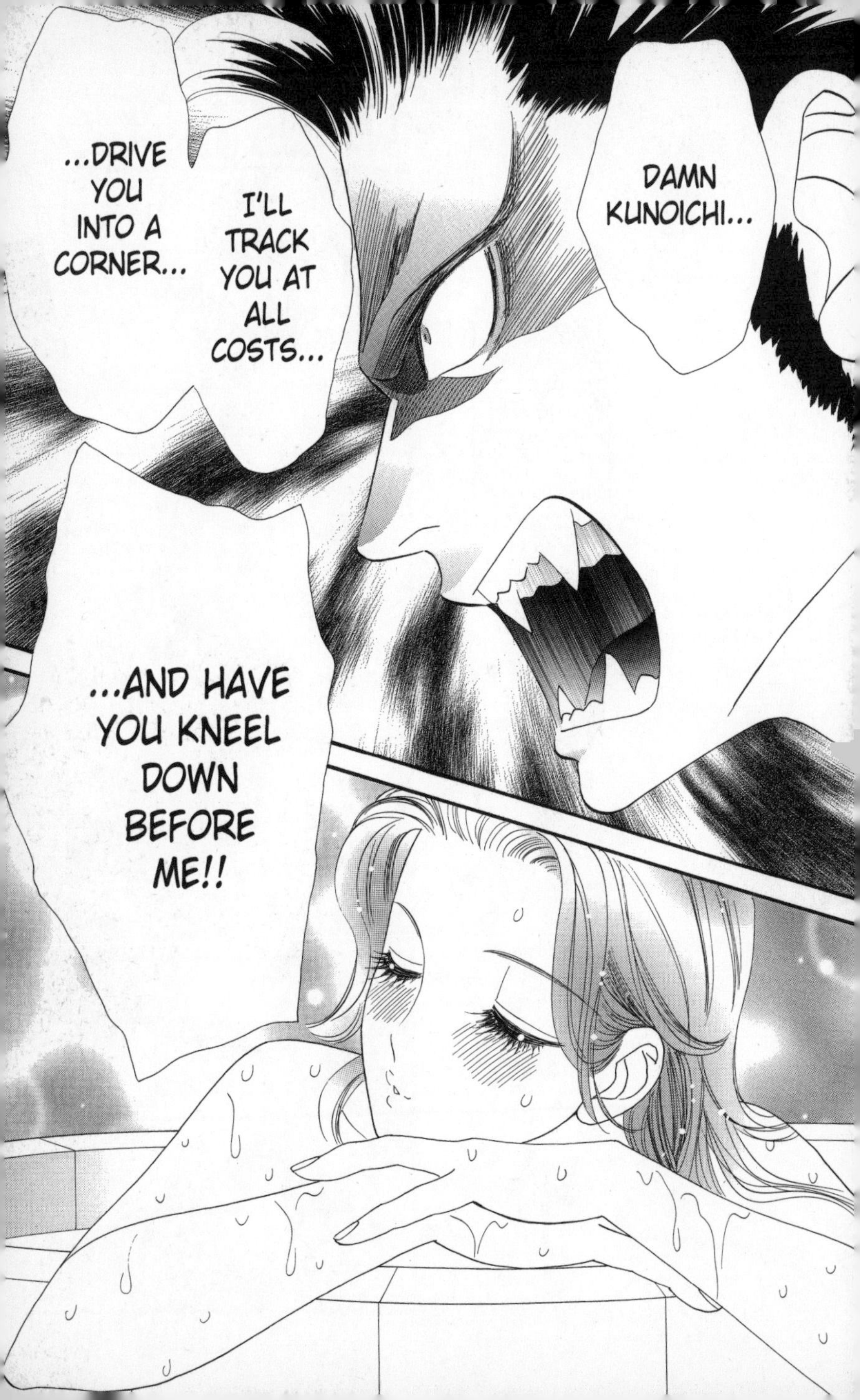
DAMN KUNOICHI...
I'LL TRACK YOU AT ALL COSTS...
...DRIVE YOU INTO A CORNER...
...AND HAVE YOU KNEEL DOWN BEFORE ME!!

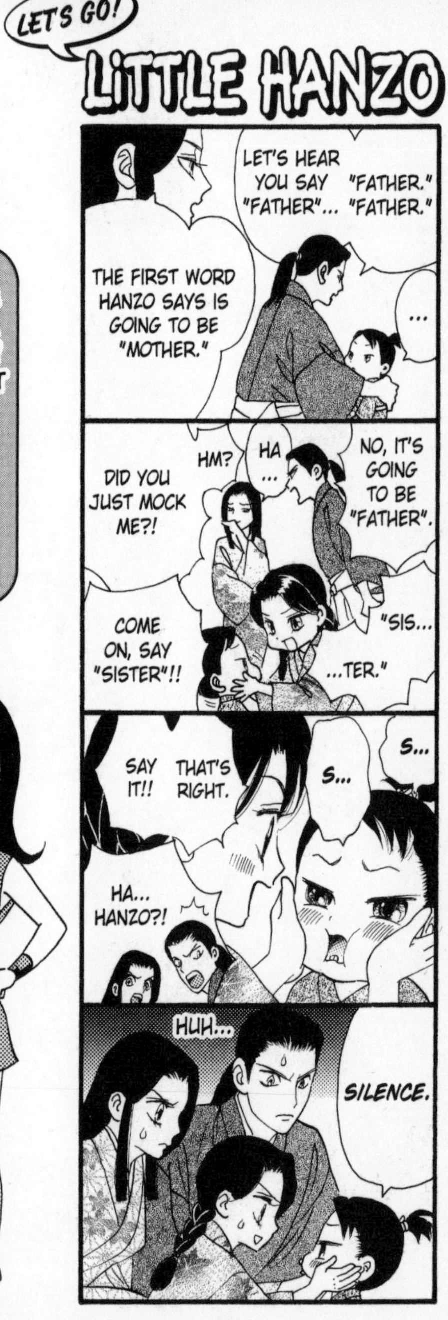
LET'S GO!
LITTLE HANZO
LET'S HEAR YOU SAY "FATHER"... "FATHER." "FATHER."
...
THE FIRST WORD HANZO SAYS IS GOING TO BE "MOTHER."
NO, IT'S GOING TO BE "FATHER".
HA...
HM?
DID YOU JUST MOCK ME?!
"SIS... ...TER."
COME ON, SAY "SISTER"!!
S...
S...
THAT'S RIGHT.
SAY IT!!
HA... HANZO?!
HUH...
SILENCE.

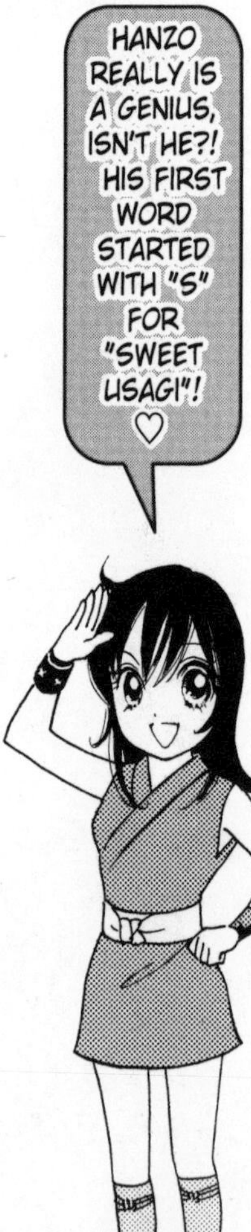
HANZO REALLY IS A GENIUS, ISN'T HE?! HIS FIRST WORD STARTED WITH "S" FOR "SWEET USAGI"! ♡

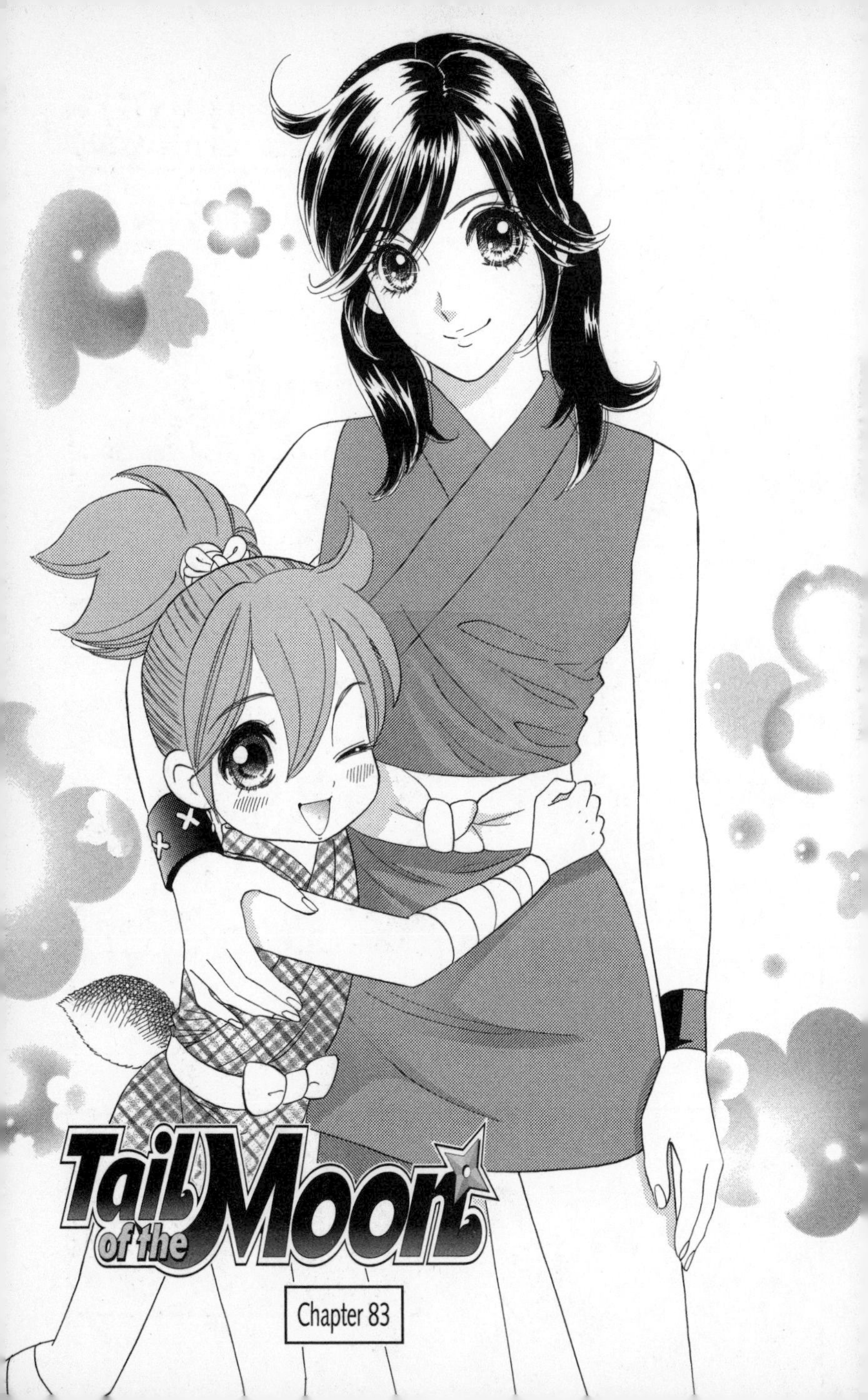
Tail of the Moon
Chapter 83

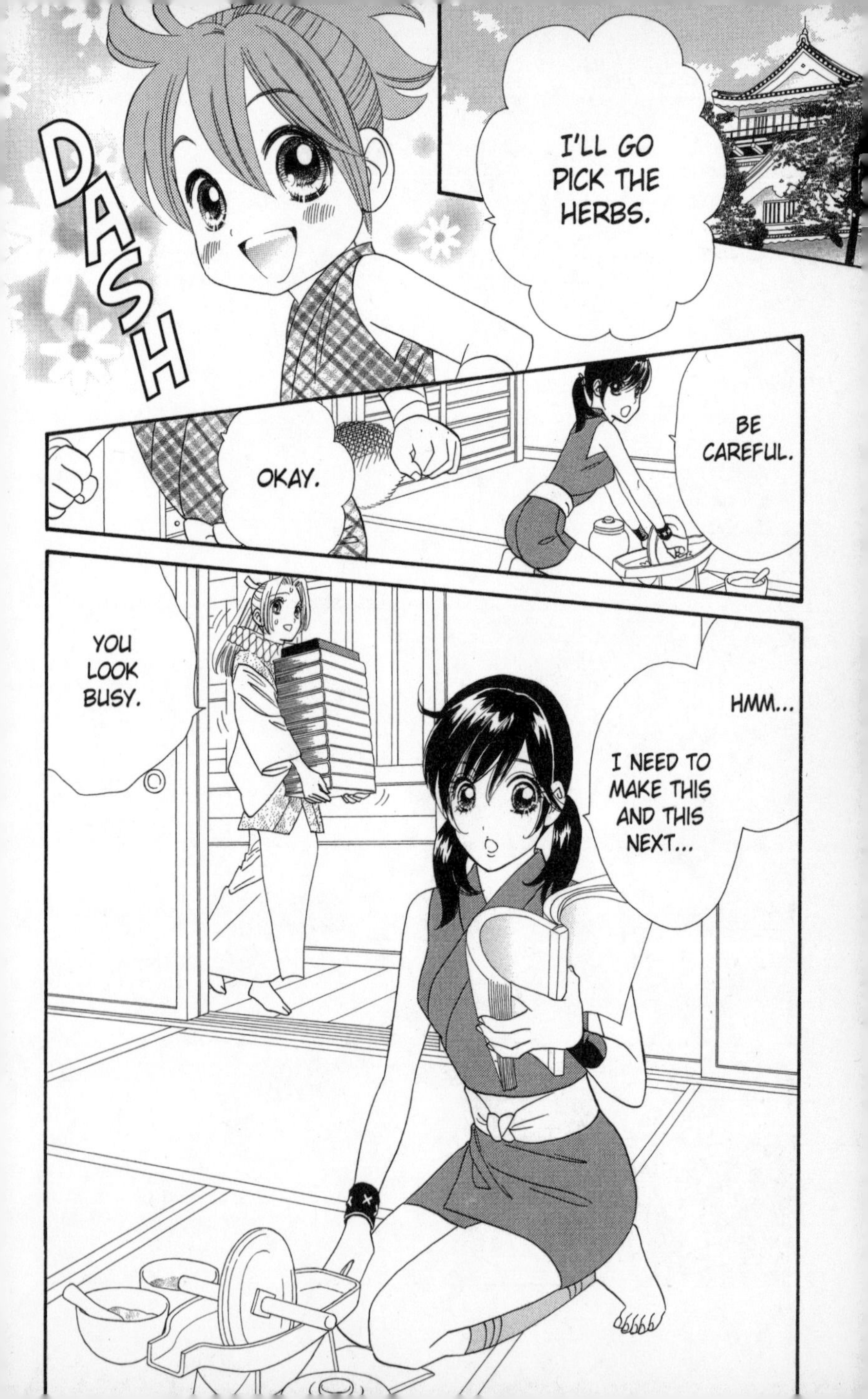
I'LL GO PICK THE HERBS.
DASH
BE CAREFUL.
OKAY.
HMM...
I NEED TO MAKE THIS AND THIS NEXT...
YOU LOOK BUSY.

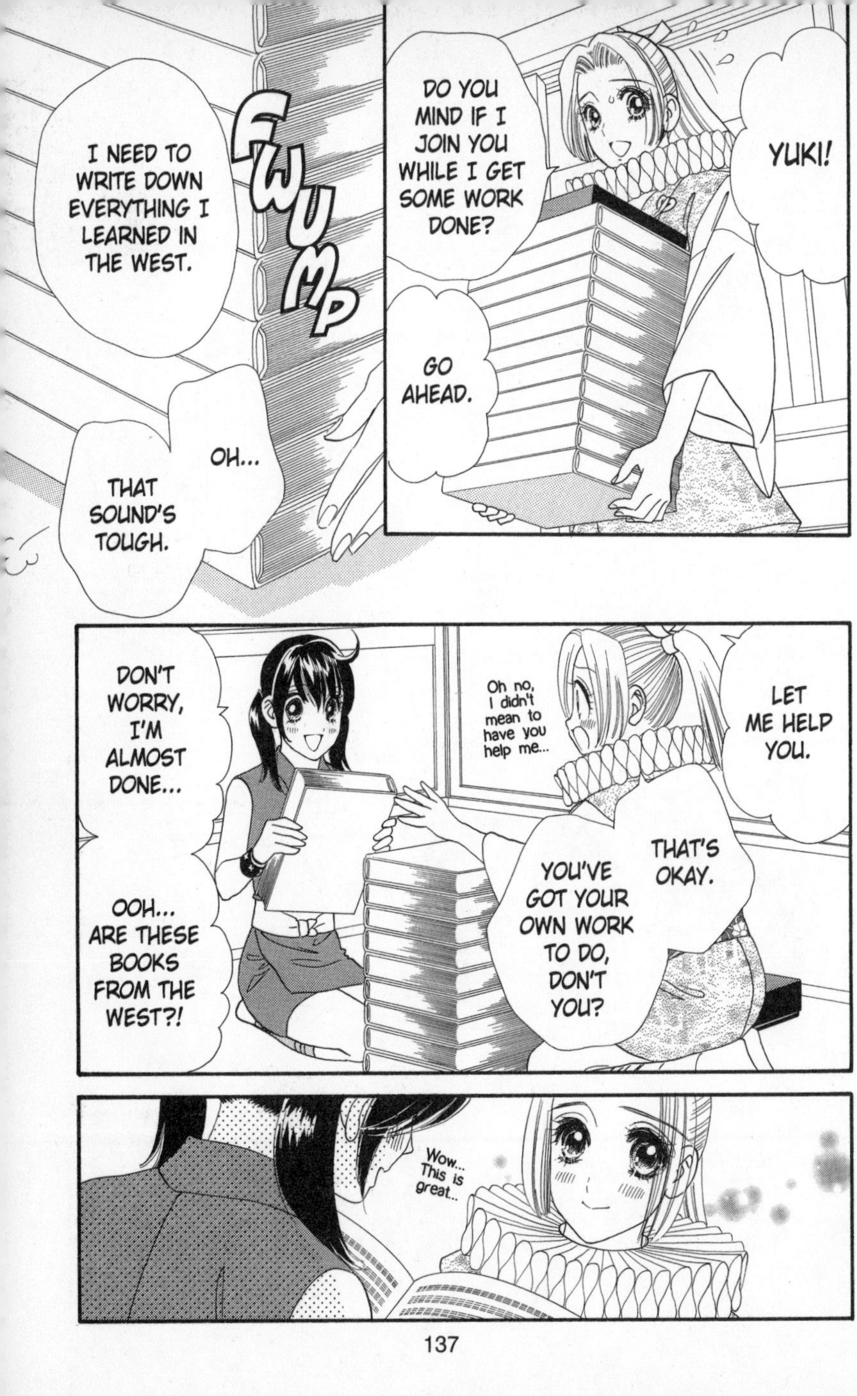
YUKI!
DO YOU MIND IF I JOIN YOU WHILE I GET SOME WORK DONE?
GO AHEAD.
FWUMP
I NEED TO WRITE DOWN EVERYTHING I LEARNED IN THE WEST.
OH...
THAT SOUND'S TOUGH.
LET ME HELP YOU.
Oh no, I didn't mean to have you help me...
DON'T WORRY, I'M ALMOST DONE...
THAT'S OKAY.
YOU'VE GOT YOUR OWN WORK TO DO, DON'T YOU?
OOH... ARE THESE BOOKS FROM THE WEST?!
Wow... This is great...

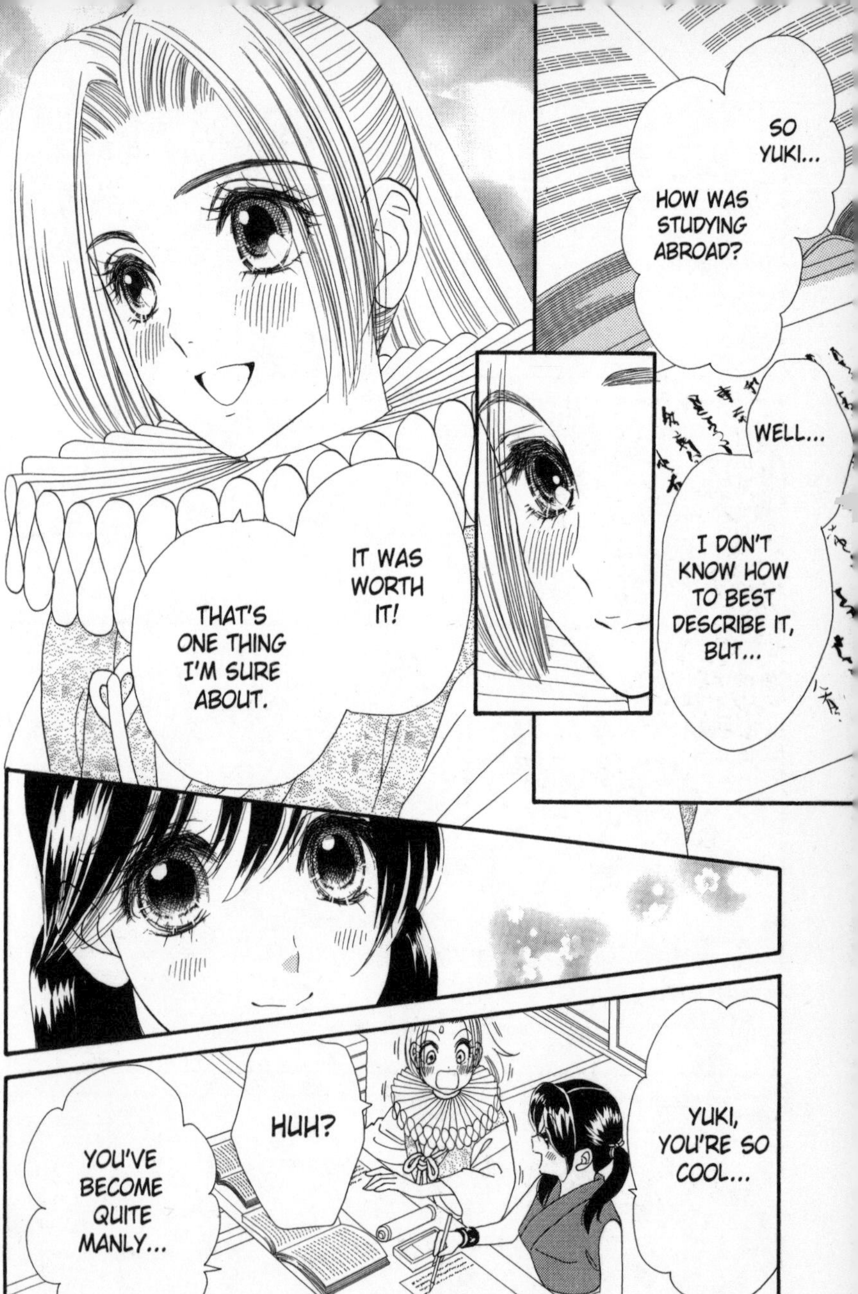
SO YUKI...
HOW WAS STUDYING ABROAD?
WELL...
I DON'T KNOW HOW TO BEST DESCRIBE IT, BUT...
IT WAS WORTH IT!
THAT'S ONE THING I'M SURE ABOUT.
YUKI, YOU'RE SO COOL...
HUH?
YOU'VE BECOME QUITE MANLY...

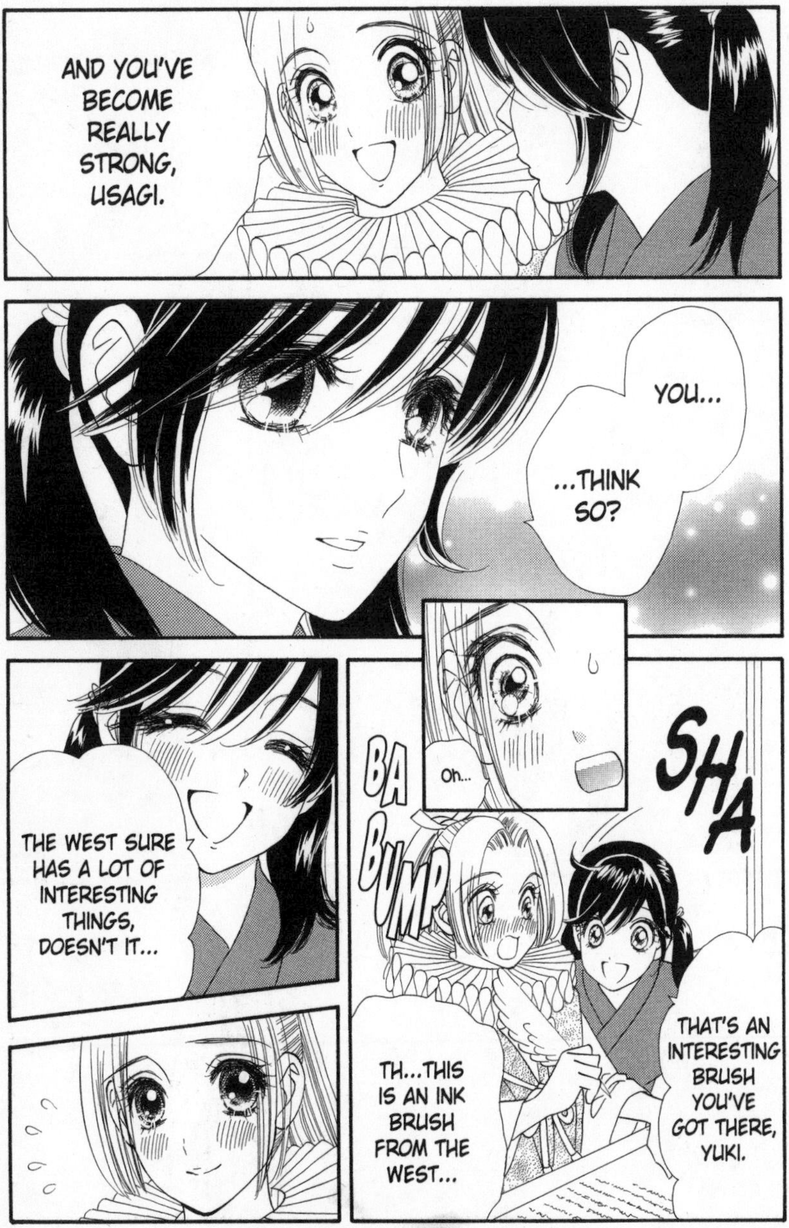
AND YOU'VE BECOME REALLY STRONG, USAGI.
YOU...
...THINK SO?
Oh...
SHA
BA BUMP
THAT'S AN INTERESTING BRUSH YOU'VE GOT THERE, YUKI.
TH...THIS IS AN INK BRUSH FROM THE WEST...
THE WEST SURE HAS A LOT OF INTERESTING THINGS, DOESN'T IT...

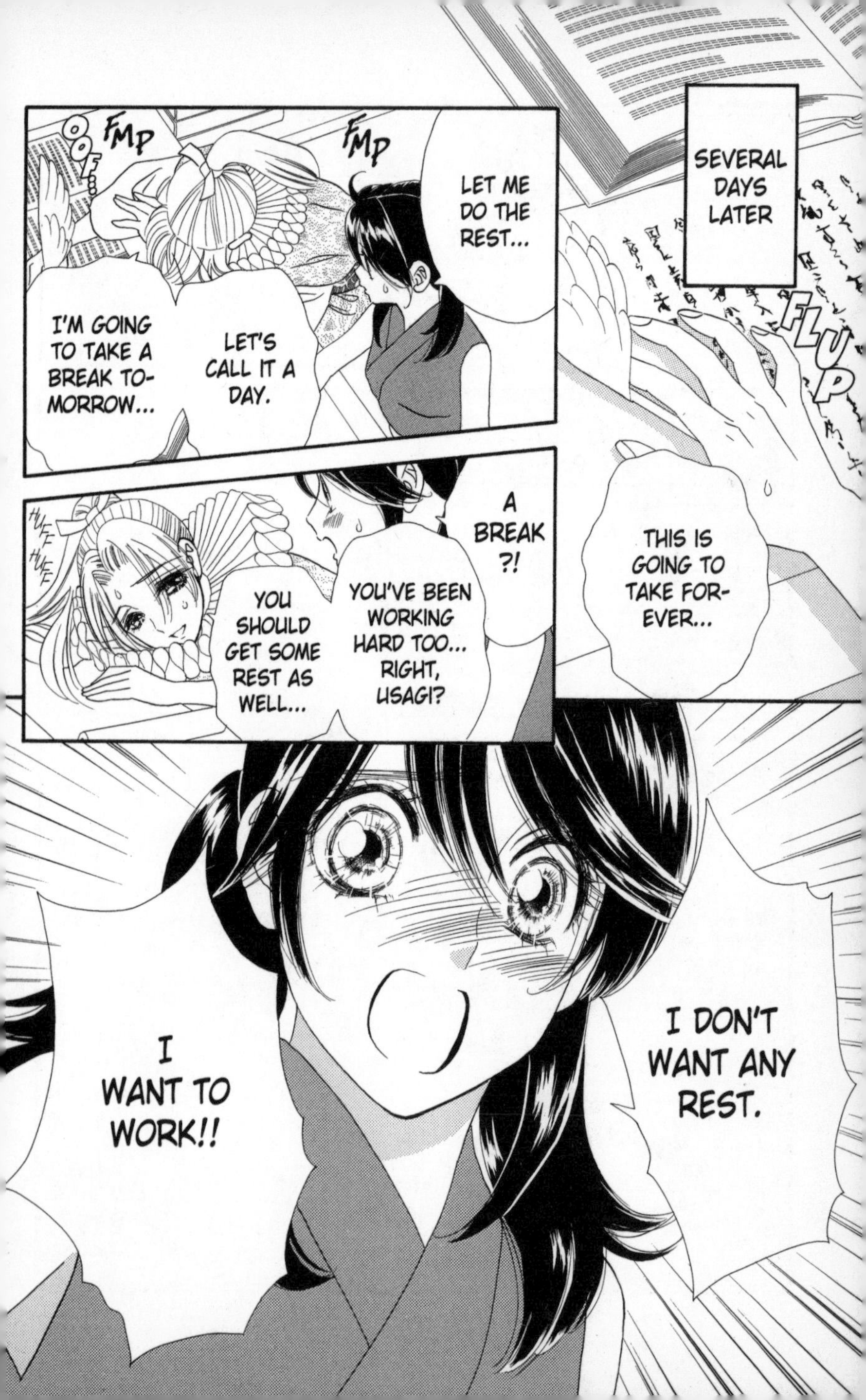
SEVERAL DAYS LATER
FLUP
THIS IS GOING TO TAKE FOR-EVER...
FMP
FMP
OOF...
LET ME DO THE REST...
LET'S CALL IT A DAY.
I'M GOING TO TAKE A BREAK TO-MORROW...
A BREAK?!
YOU'VE BEEN WORKING HARD TOO... RIGHT, USAGI?
YOU SHOULD GET SOME REST AS WELL...
HUFF HUFF
I DON'T WANT ANY REST.
I WANT TO WORK!!

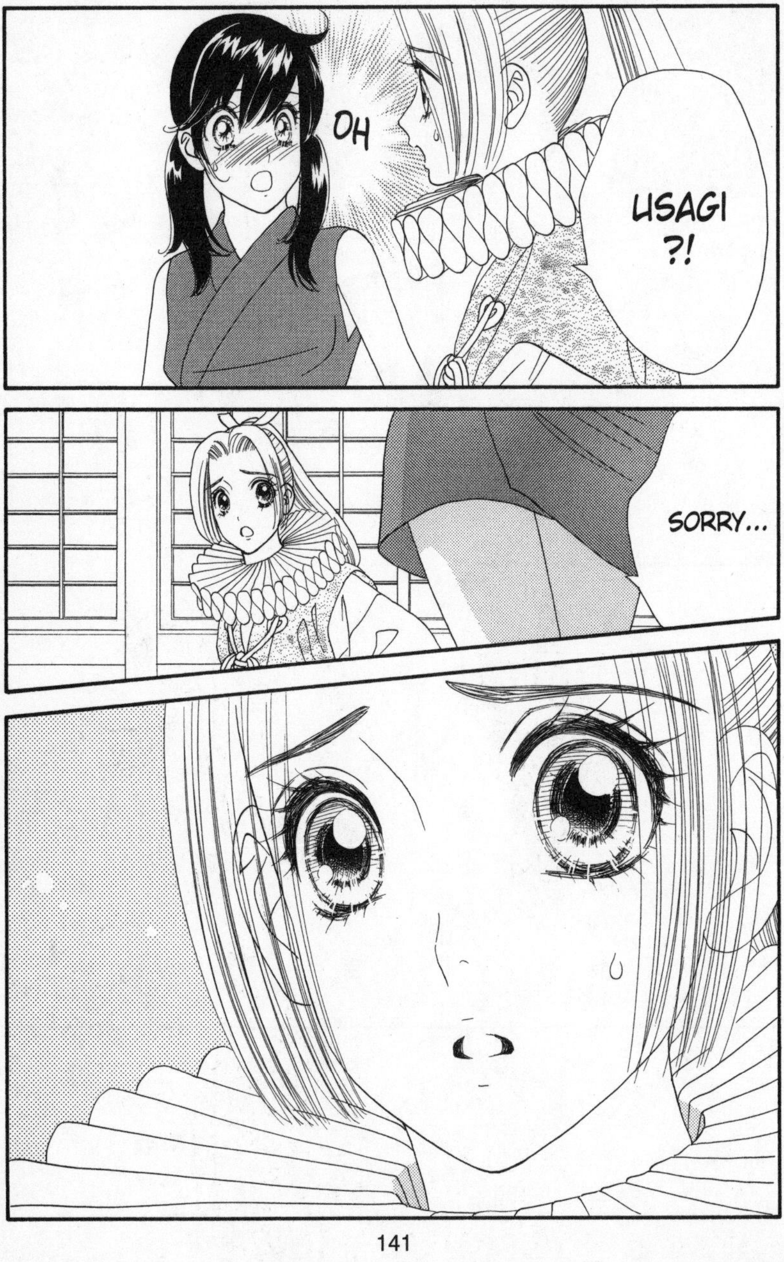
USAGI ?!
OH
SORRY...

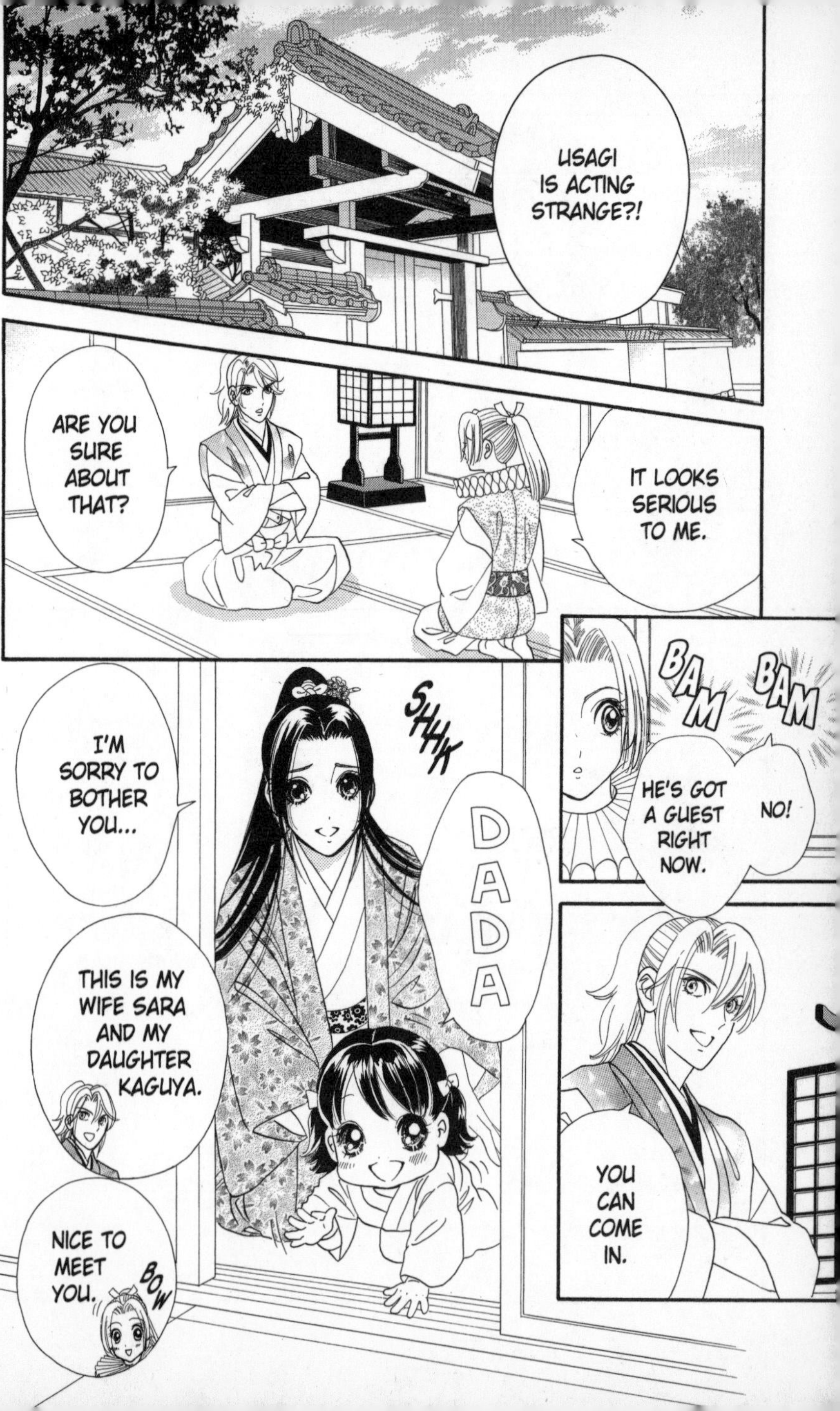
USAGI IS ACTING STRANGE?!
IT LOOKS SERIOUS TO ME.
ARE YOU SURE ABOUT THAT?
BAM BAM
NO!
HE'S GOT A GUEST RIGHT NOW.
YOU CAN COME IN.
SHHK
DADA
I'M SORRY TO BOTHER YOU...
THIS IS MY WIFE SARA AND MY DAUGHTER KAGUYA.
NICE TO MEET YOU.
BOW

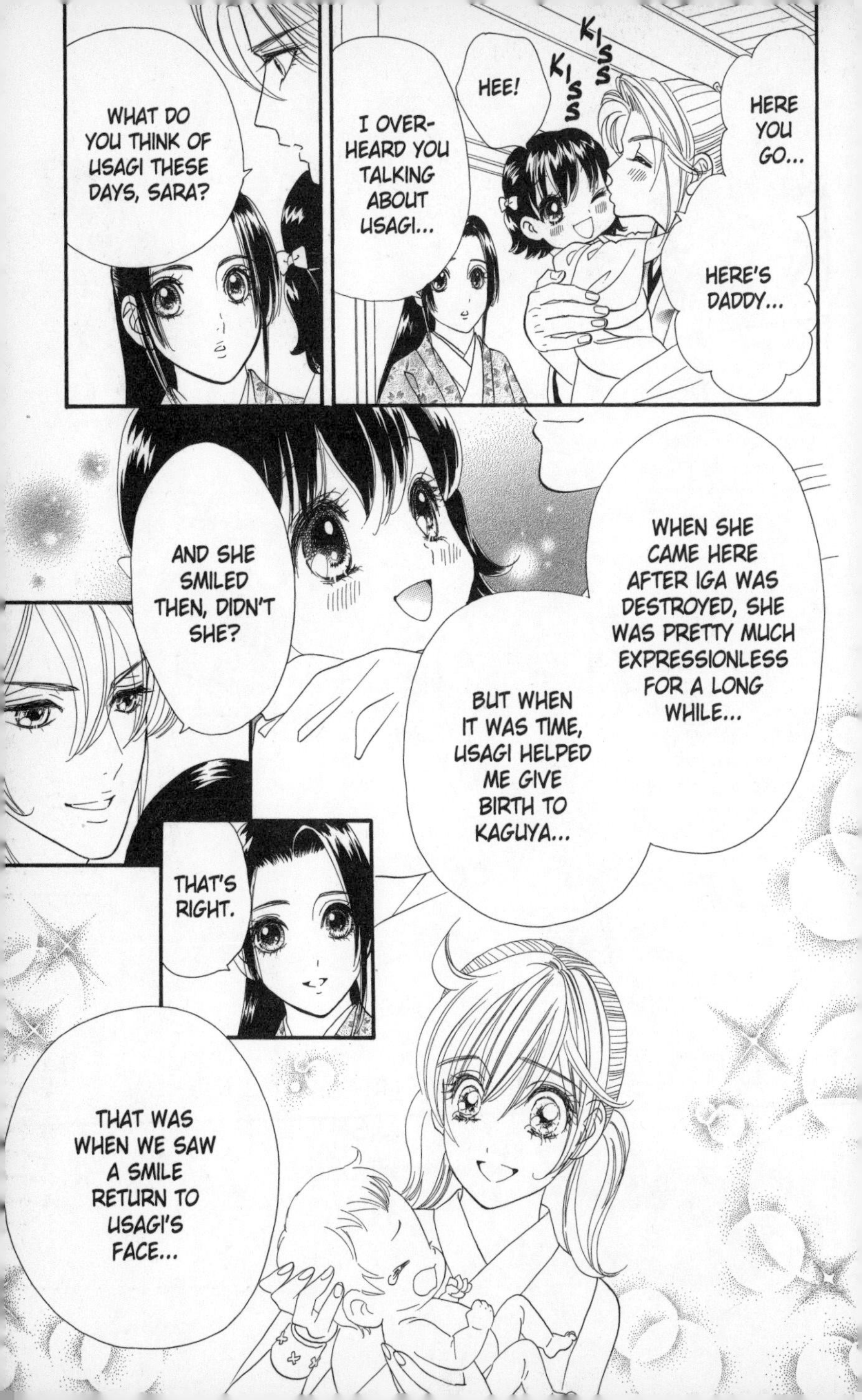
HERE YOU GO...
HERE'S DADDY...
KISS KISS
HEE!
I OVER-HEARD YOU TALKING ABOUT USAGI...
WHAT DO YOU THINK OF USAGI THESE DAYS, SARA?
WHEN SHE CAME HERE AFTER IGA WAS DESTROYED, SHE WAS PRETTY MUCH EXPRESSIONLESS FOR A LONG WHILE...
BUT WHEN IT WAS TIME, USAGI HELPED ME GIVE BIRTH TO KAGUYA...
AND SHE SMILED THEN, DIDN'T SHE?
THAT'S RIGHT.
THAT WAS WHEN WE SAW A SMILE RETURN TO USAGI'S FACE...

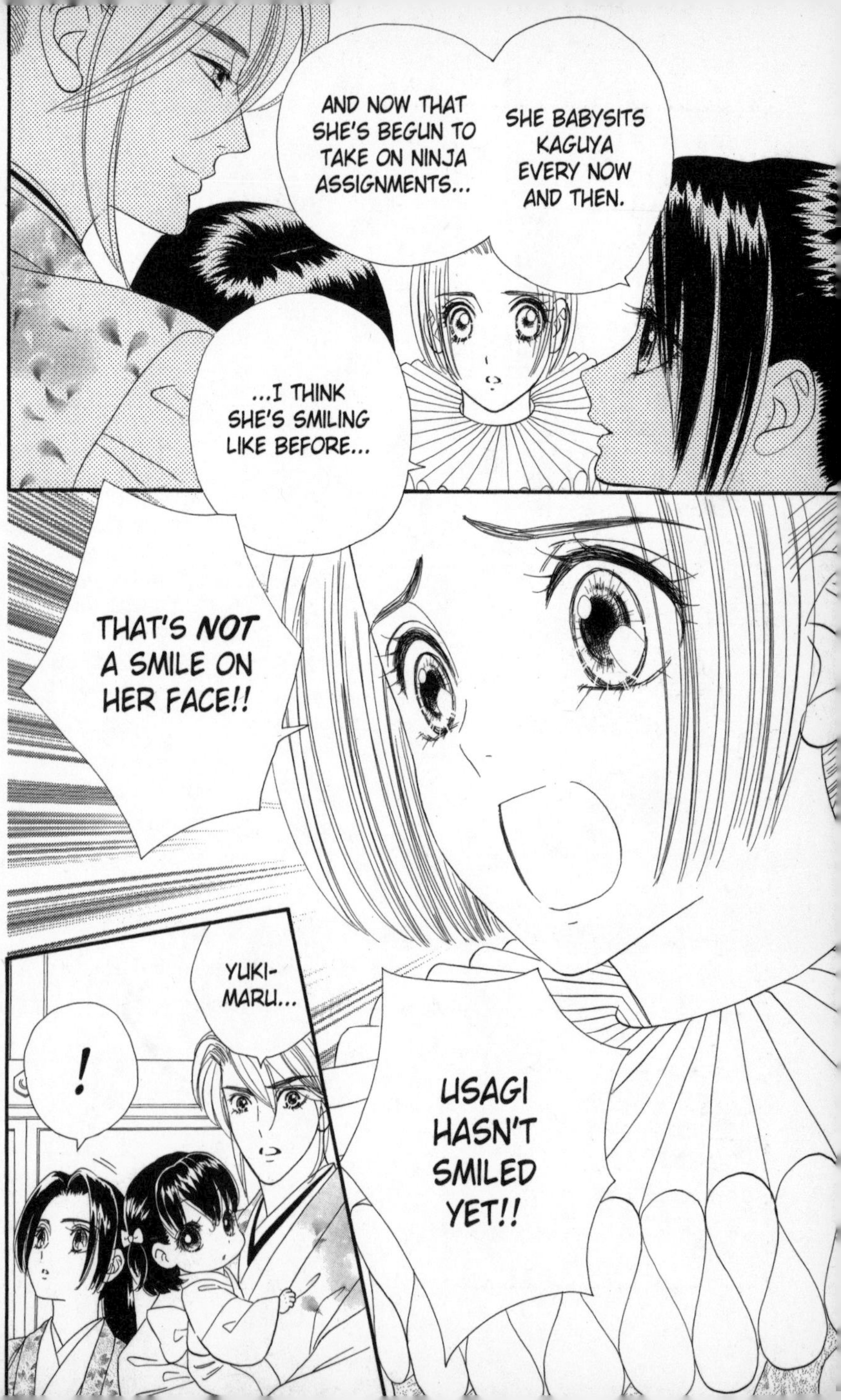
SHE BABYSITS KAGUYA EVERY NOW AND THEN.
AND NOW THAT SHE'S BEGUN TO TAKE ON NINJA ASSIGNMENTS...
...I THINK SHE'S SMILING LIKE BEFORE...
THAT'S *NOT* A SMILE ON HER FACE!!
USAGI HASN'T SMILED YET!!
YUKI-MARU...
!

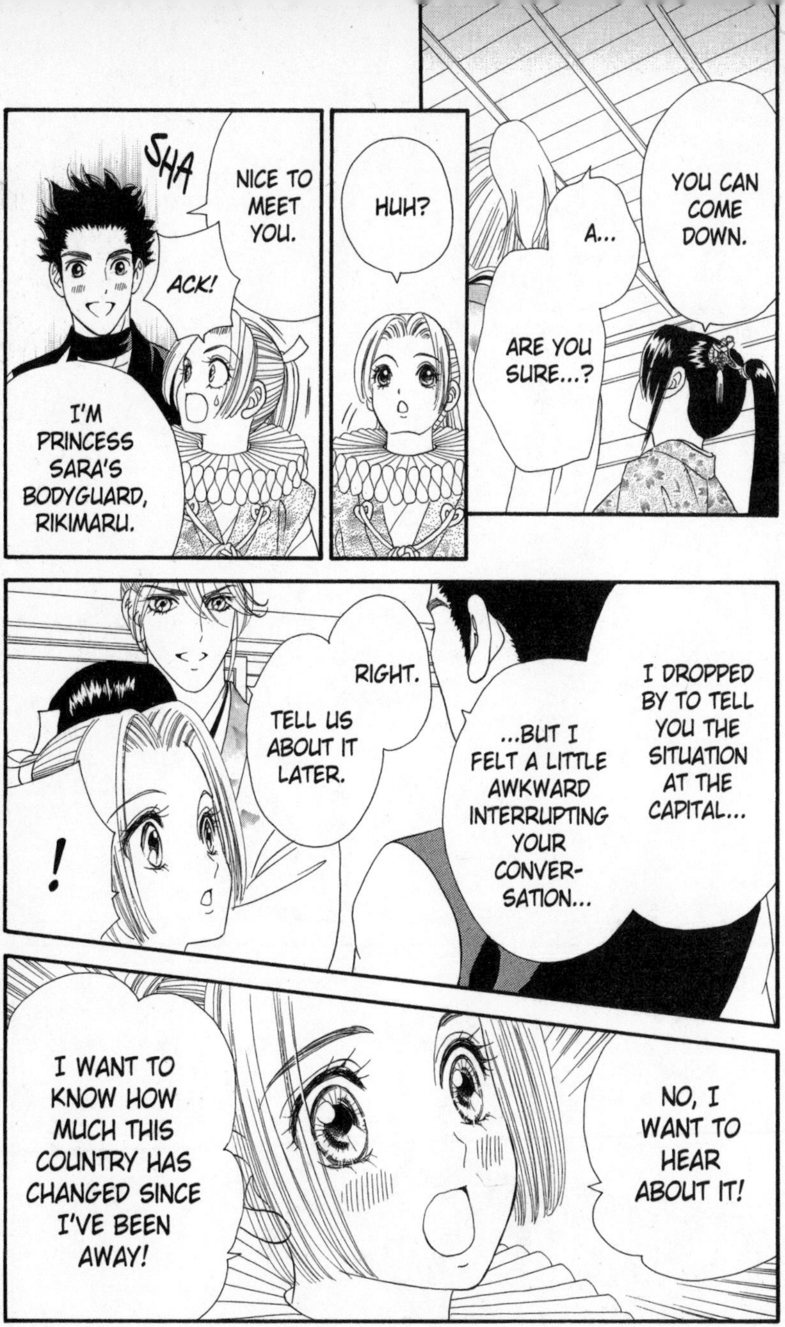
YOU CAN COME DOWN.
A...
ARE YOU SURE...?
HUH?
NICE TO MEET YOU.
SHA
ACK!
I'M PRINCESS SARA'S BODYGUARD, RIKIMARU.
I DROPPED BY TO TELL YOU THE SITUATION AT THE CAPITAL...
...BUT I FELT A LITTLE AWKWARD INTERRUPTING YOUR CONVERSATION...
RIGHT.
TELL US ABOUT IT LATER.
!
NO, I WANT TO HEAR ABOUT IT!
I WANT TO KNOW HOW MUCH THIS COUNTRY HAS CHANGED SINCE I'VE BEEN AWAY!

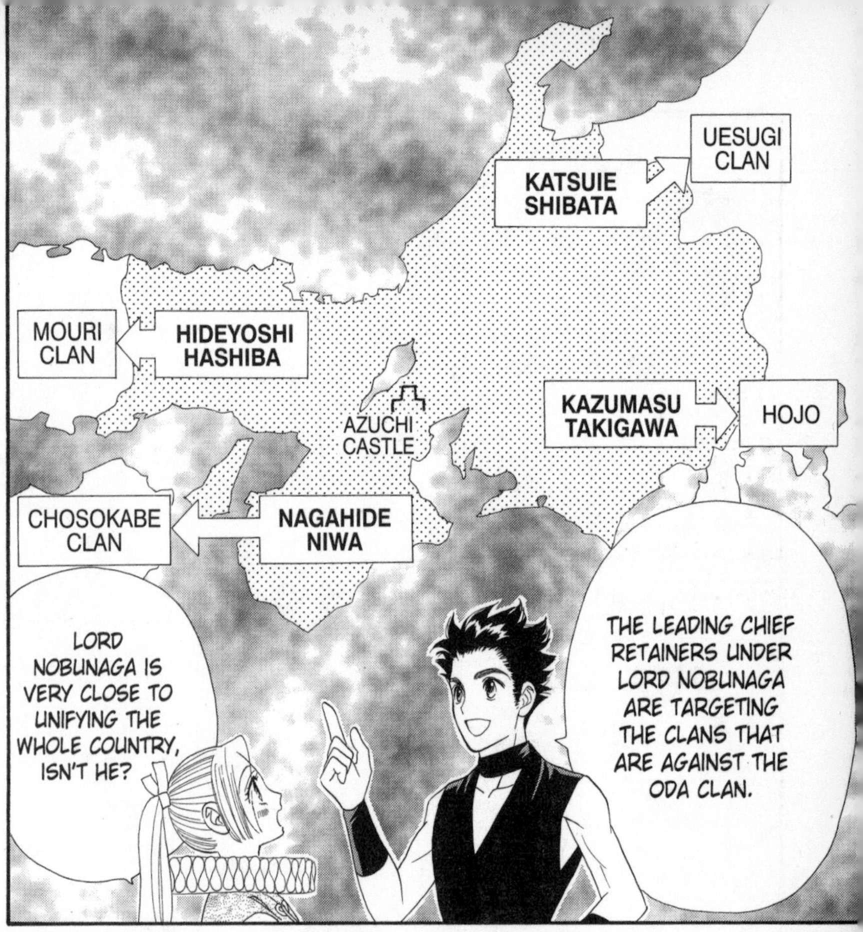
UESUGI CLAN
KATSUIE SHIBATA
HOJO
KAZUMASU TAKIGAWA
HIDEYOSHI HASHIBA
MOURI CLAN
AZUCHI CASTLE
NAGAHIDE NIWA
CHOSOKABE CLAN
THE LEADING CHIEF RETAINERS UNDER LORD NOBUNAGA ARE TARGETING THE CLANS THAT ARE AGAINST THE ODA CLAN.
LORD NOBUNAGA IS VERY CLOSE TO UNIFYING THE WHOLE COUNTRY, ISN'T HE?

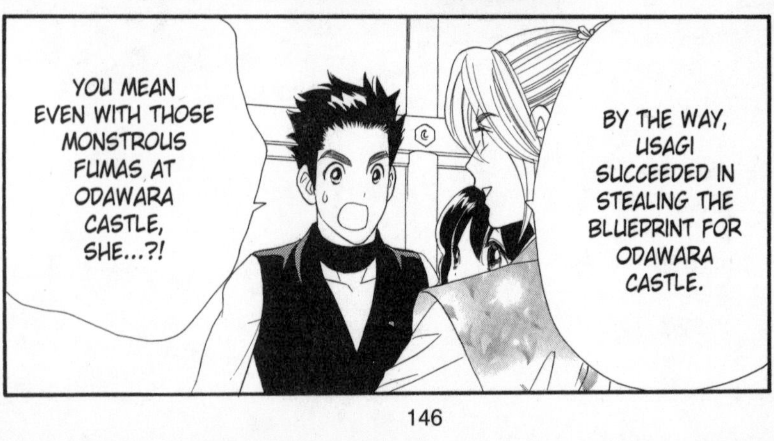
BY THE WAY, USAGI SUCCEEDED IN STEALING THE BLUEPRINT FOR ODAWARA CASTLE.
YOU MEAN EVEN WITH THOSE MONSTROUS FUMAS AT ODAWARA CASTLE, SHE...?!

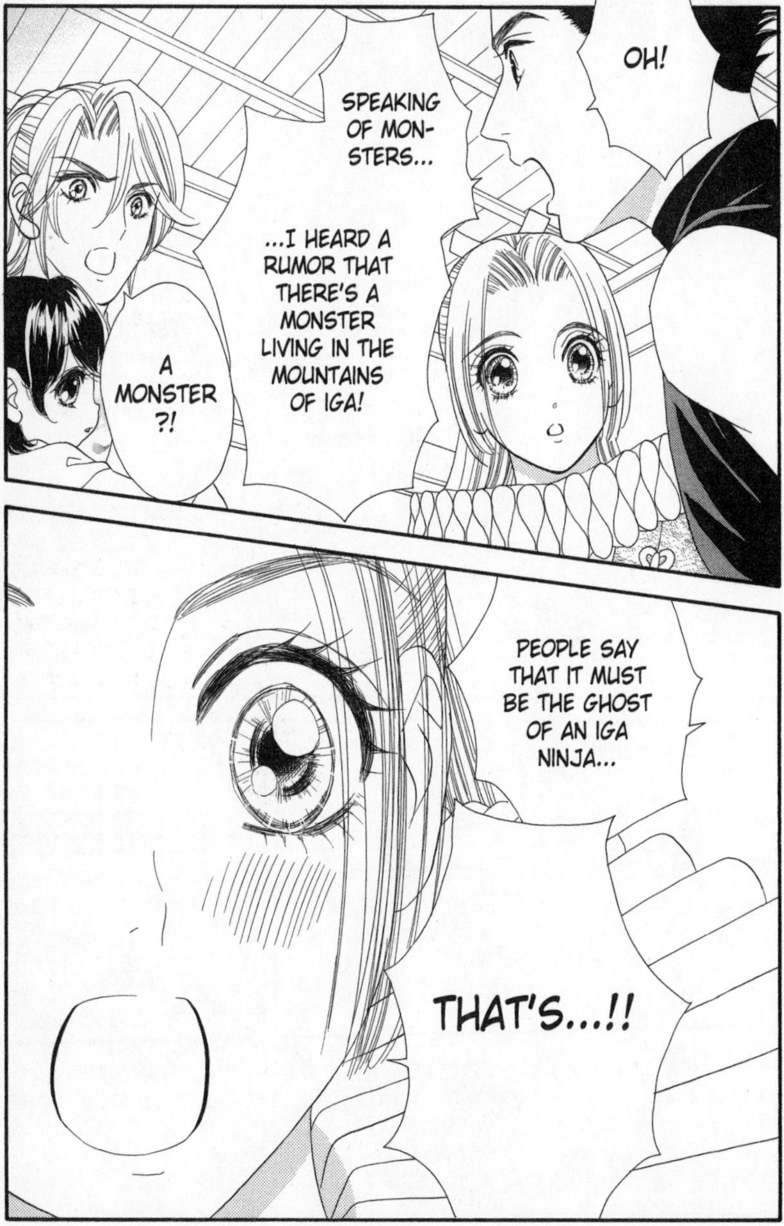
OH!
SPEAKING OF MON-STERS...
...I HEARD A RUMOR THAT THERE'S A MONSTER LIVING IN THE MOUNTAINS OF IGA!
A MONSTER ?!
PEOPLE SAY THAT IT MUST BE THE GHOST OF AN IGA NINJA...
THAT'S...!!

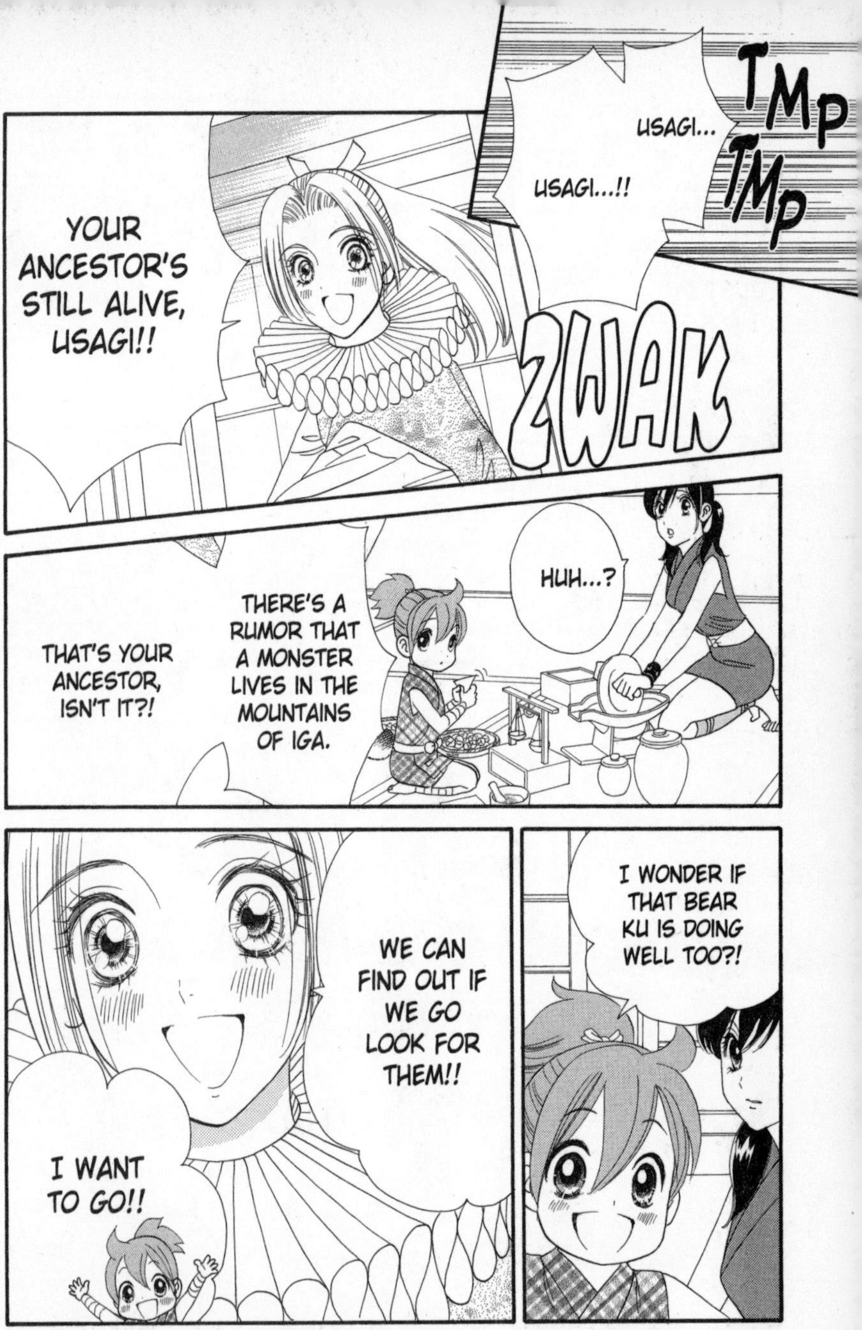
TMP TMP
USAGI...
USAGI...!!
ZWAK
YOUR ANCESTOR'S STILL ALIVE, USAGI!!
HUH...?
THERE'S A RUMOR THAT A MONSTER LIVES IN THE MOUNTAINS OF IGA.
THAT'S YOUR ANCESTOR, ISN'T IT?!
I WONDER IF THAT BEAR KU IS DOING WELL TOO?!
WE CAN FIND OUT IF WE GO LOOK FOR THEM!!
I WANT TO GO!!

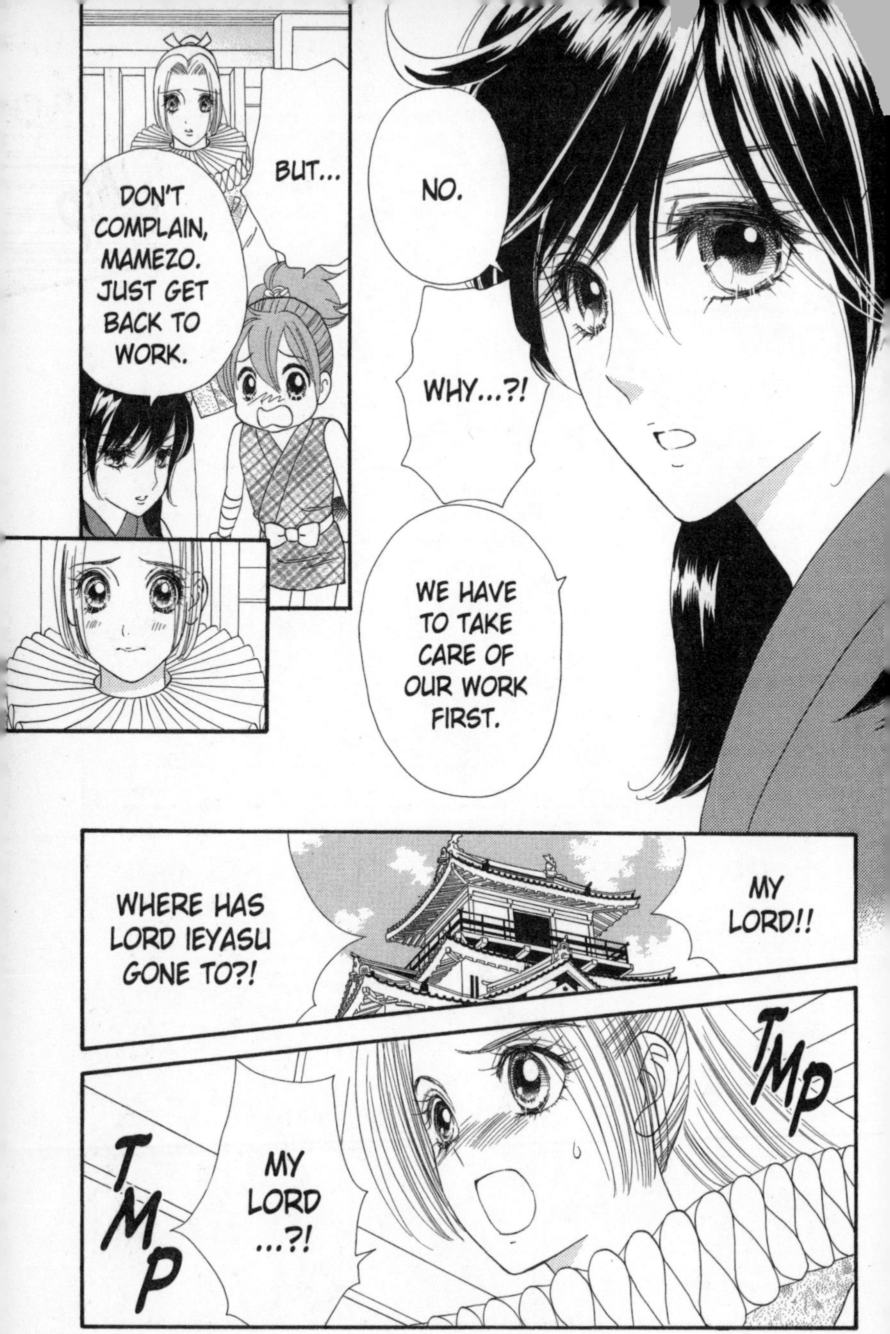
NO.
WHY...?!
WE HAVE TO TAKE CARE OF OUR WORK FIRST.
BUT...
DON'T COMPLAIN, MAMEZO. JUST GET BACK TO WORK.
MY LORD!!
WHERE HAS LORD IEYASU GONE TO?!
TMP
MY LORD ...?!
TMP

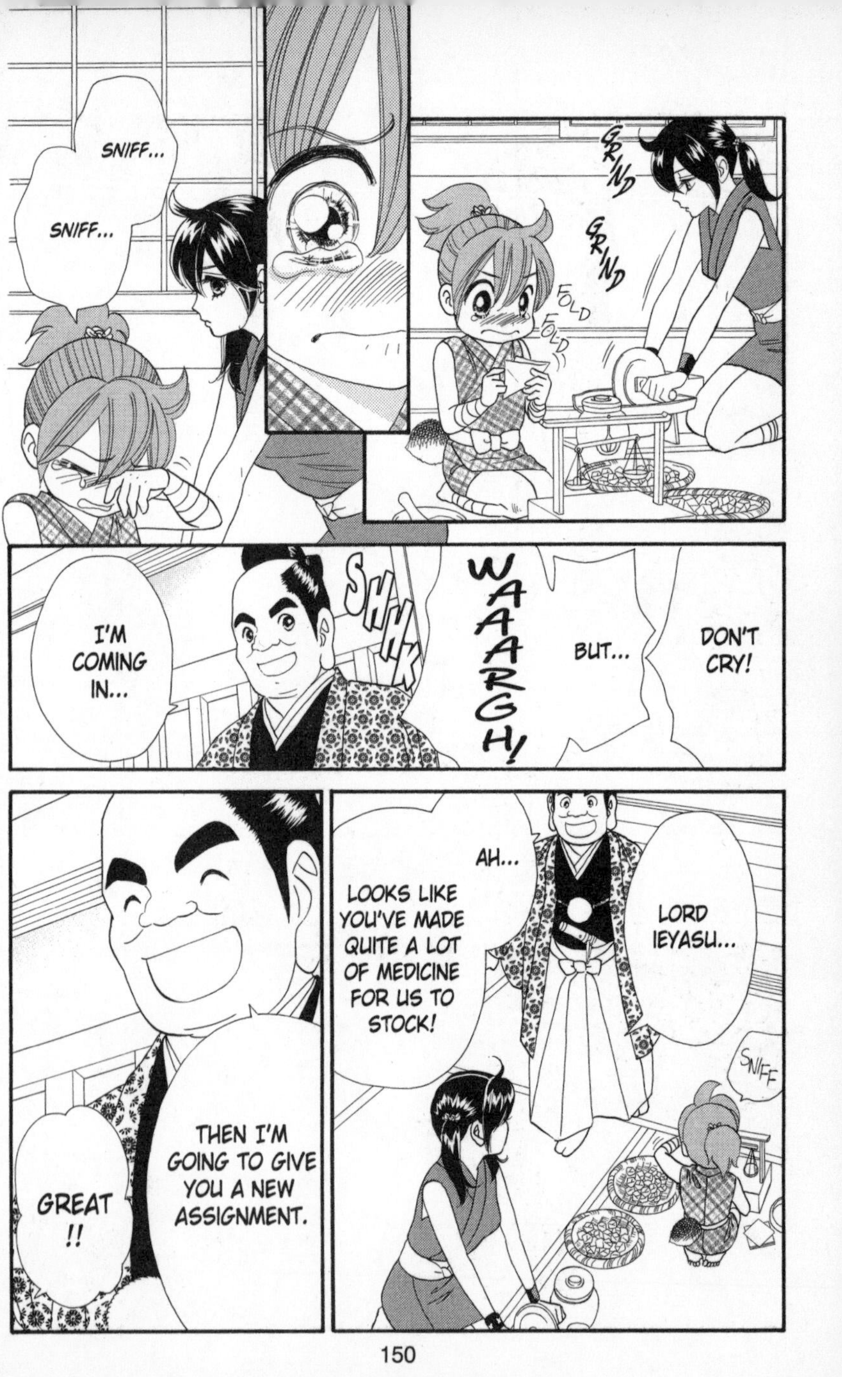
GRIND
GRIND
FOLD
FOLD
SNIFF...
SNIFF...
DON'T CRY!
BUT...
WAAARGH!
SHHK
I'M COMING IN...
LORD IEYASU...
AH...
LOOKS LIKE YOU'VE MADE QUITE A LOT OF MEDICINE FOR US TO STOCK!
SNIFF
THEN I'M GOING TO GIVE YOU A NEW ASSIGNMENT.
GREAT!!

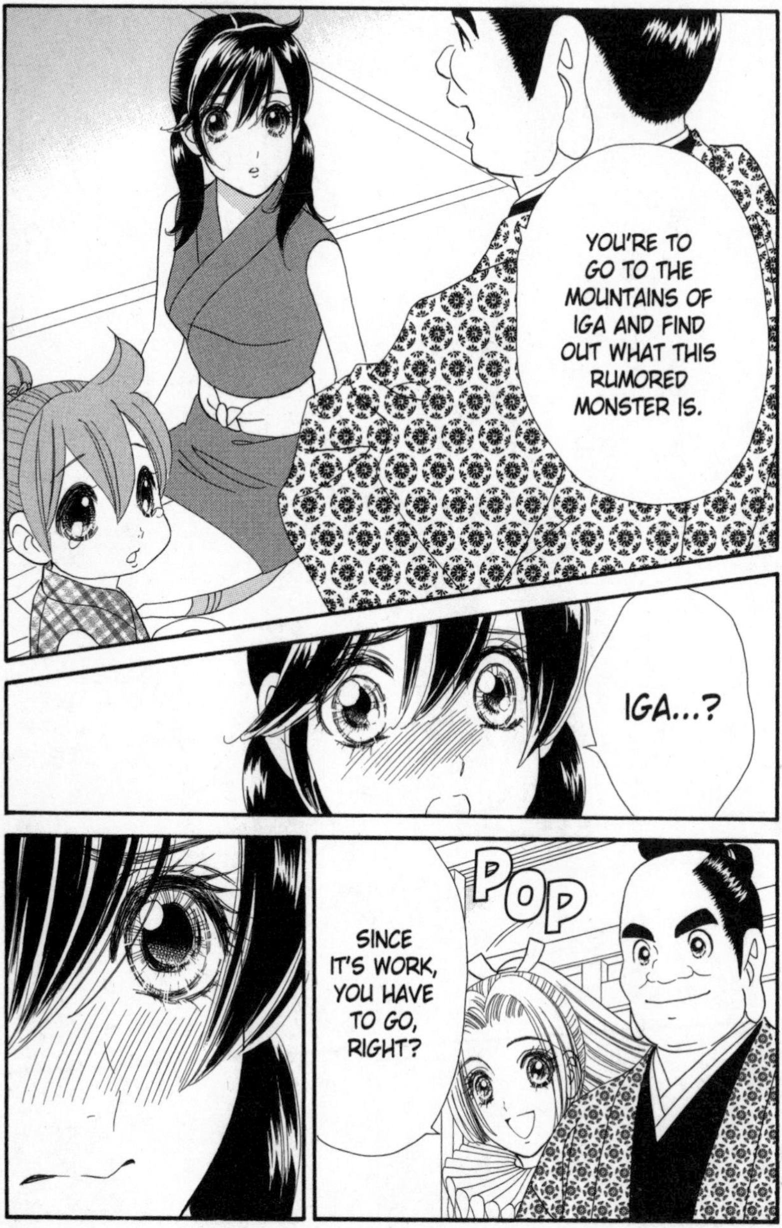
YOU'RE TO GO TO THE MOUNTAINS OF IGA AND FIND OUT WHAT THIS RUMORED MONSTER IS.
IGA...?
POP
SINCE IT'S WORK, YOU HAVE TO GO, RIGHT?

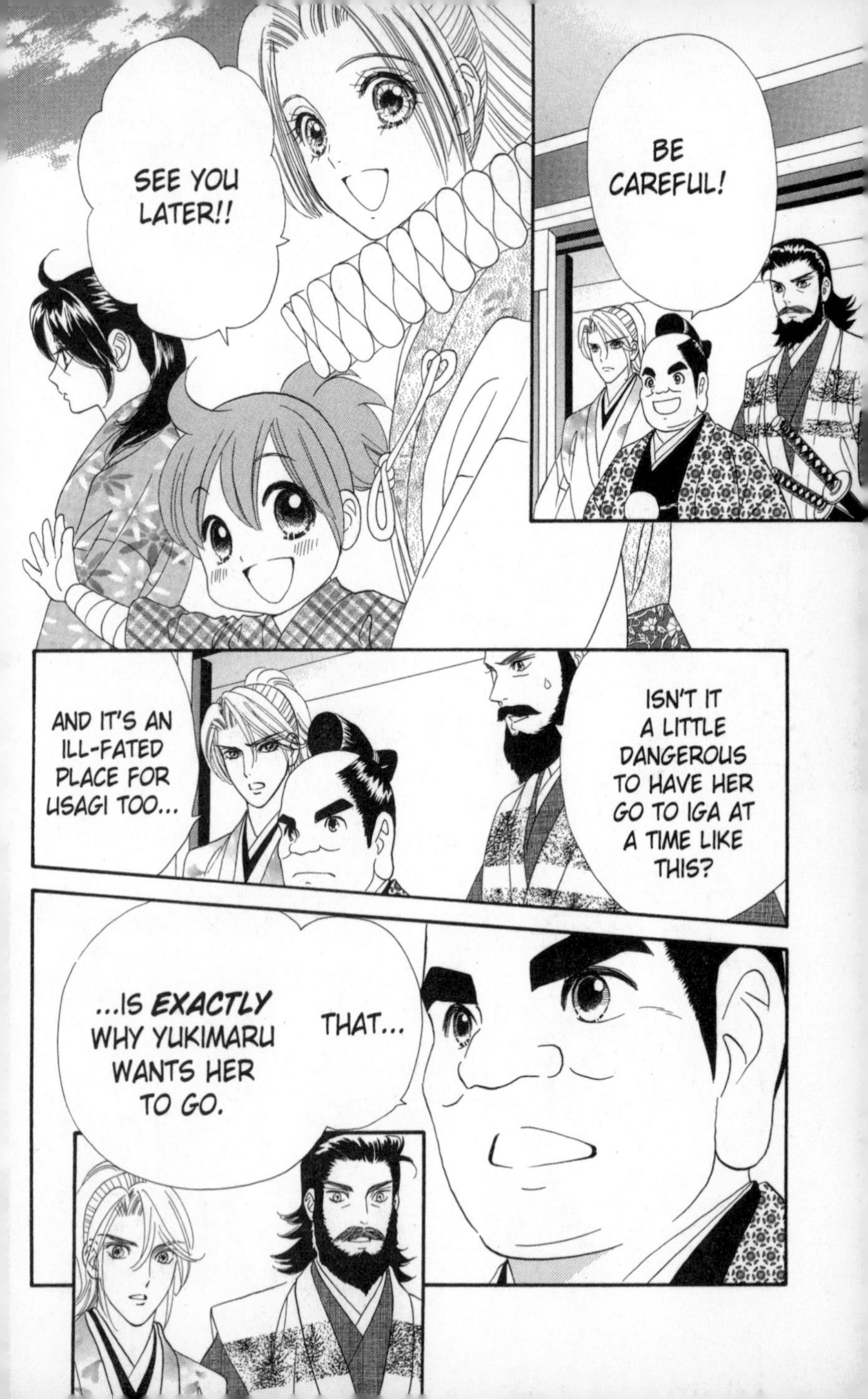
BE CAREFUL!
SEE YOU LATER!!
ISN'T IT A LITTLE DANGEROUS TO HAVE HER GO TO IGA AT A TIME LIKE THIS?
AND IT'S AN ILL-FATED PLACE FOR USAGI TOO...
THAT...
...IS *EXACTLY* WHY YUKIMARU WANTS HER TO GO.

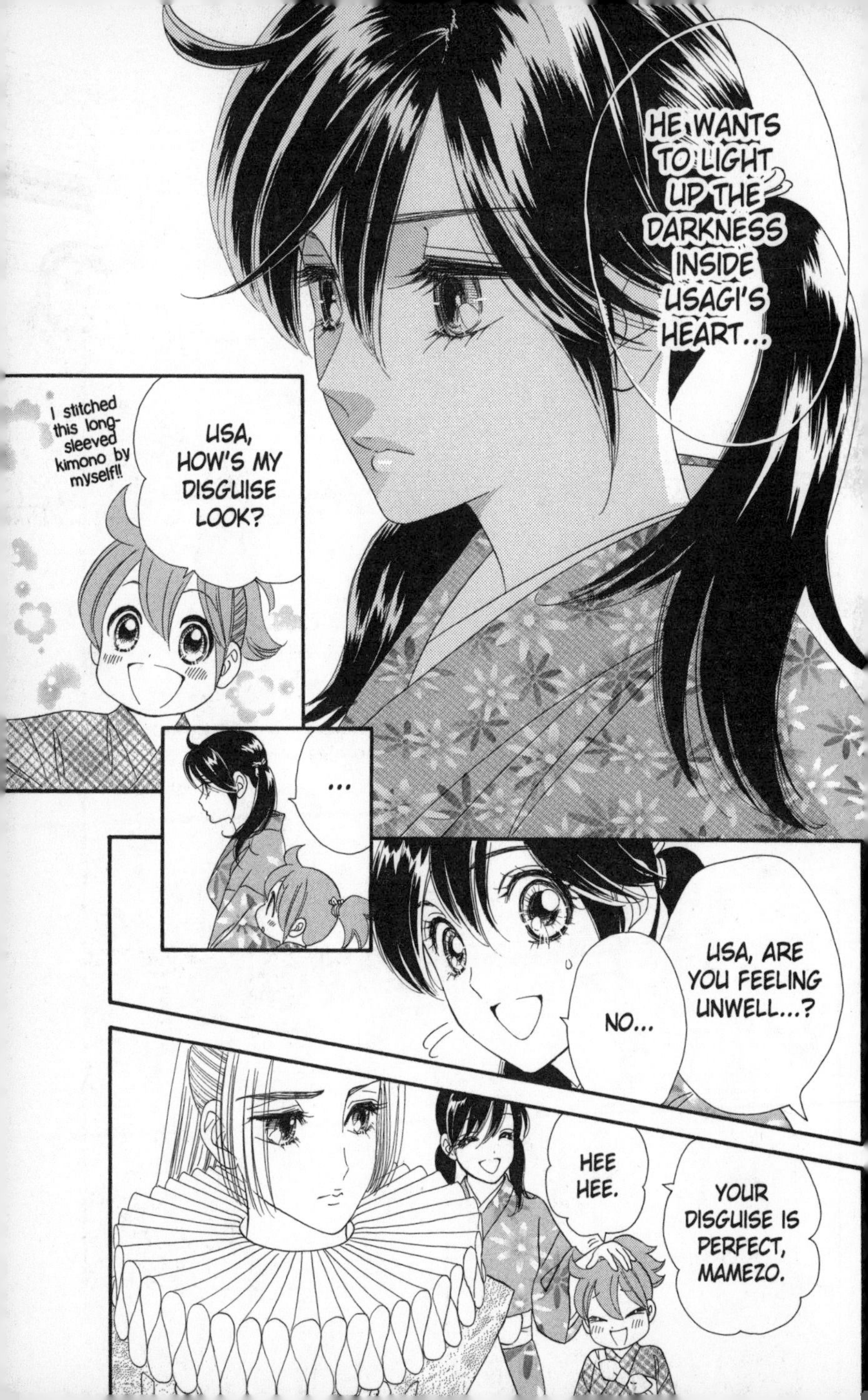
HE WANTS TO LIGHT UP THE DARKNESS INSIDE USAGI'S HEART...
USA, HOW'S MY DISGUISE LOOK?
I stitched this long-sleeved kimono by myself!!
...
USA, ARE YOU FEELING UNWELL...?
NO...
YOUR DISGUISE IS PERFECT, MAMEZO.
HEE HEE.

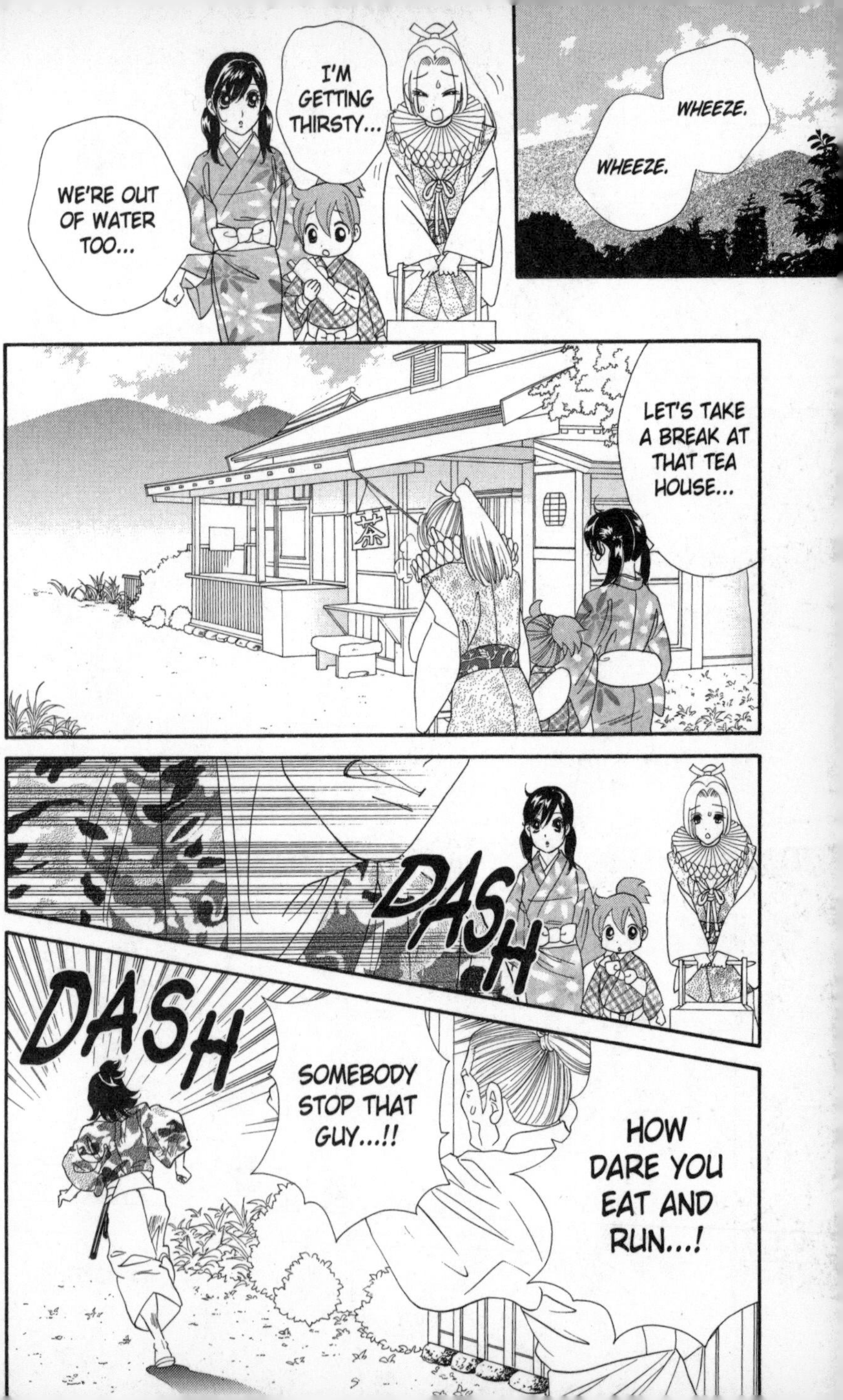
WHEEZE.
WHEEZE.
I'M GETTING THIRSTY...
WE'RE OUT OF WATER TOO...
LET'S TAKE A BREAK AT THAT TEA HOUSE...
茶
DASH
HOW DARE YOU EAT AND RUN...!
SOMEBODY STOP THAT GUY...!!
DASH

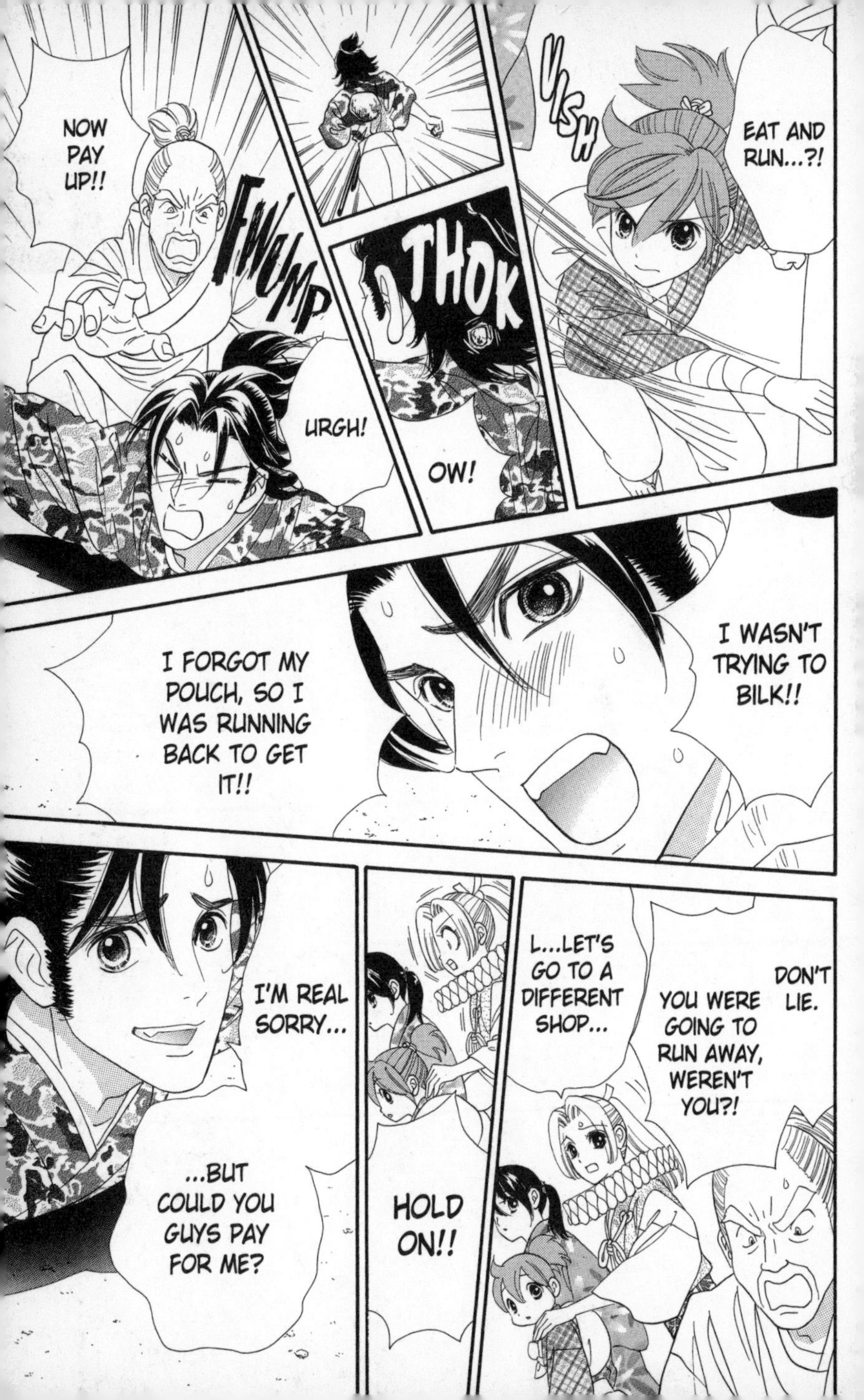
WISH
EAT AND RUN...?!
THOK
OW!
NOW PAY UP!!
FWUMP
URGH!
I WASN'T TRYING TO BILK!!
I FORGOT MY POUCH, SO I WAS RUNNING BACK TO GET IT!!
DON'T LIE.
YOU WERE GOING TO RUN AWAY, WEREN'T YOU?!
L...LET'S GO TO A DIFFERENT SHOP...
HOLD ON!!
I'M REAL SORRY...
...BUT COULD YOU GUYS PAY FOR ME?

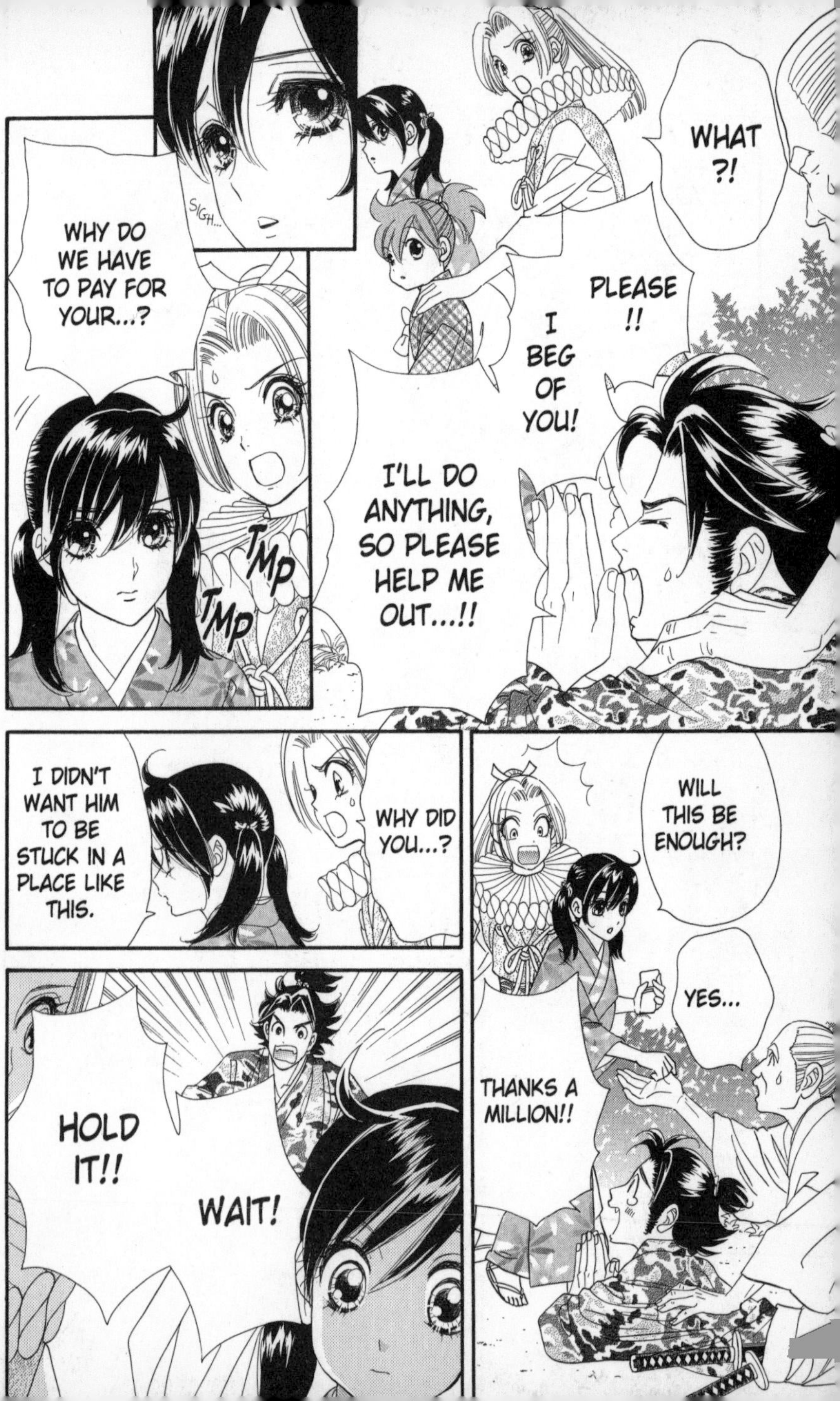
WHAT?!
PLEASE!!
I BEG OF YOU!
I'LL DO ANYTHING, SO PLEASE HELP ME OUT...!!
SIGH...
WHY DO WE HAVE TO PAY FOR YOUR...?
TMP TMP
WILL THIS BE ENOUGH?
YES...
THANKS A MILLION!!
WHY DID YOU...?
I DIDN'T WANT HIM TO BE STUCK IN A PLACE LIKE THIS.
HOLD IT!!
WAIT!

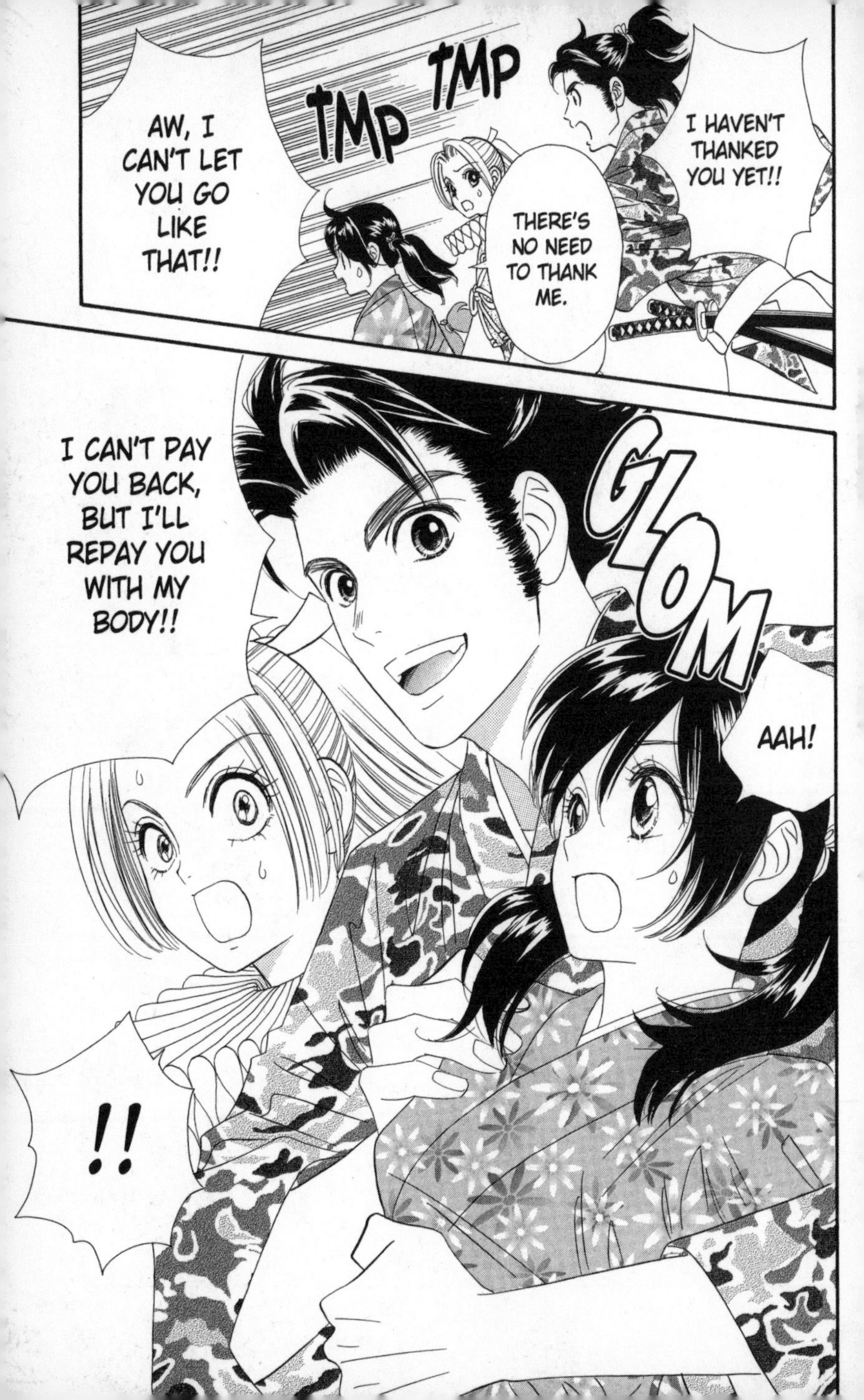
I HAVEN'T THANKED YOU YET!!
TMP TMP
TMP
THERE'S NO NEED TO THANK ME.
AW, I CAN'T LET YOU GO LIKE THAT!!
GLOM
I CAN'T PAY YOU BACK, BUT I'LL REPAY YOU WITH MY BODY!!
AAH!
!!

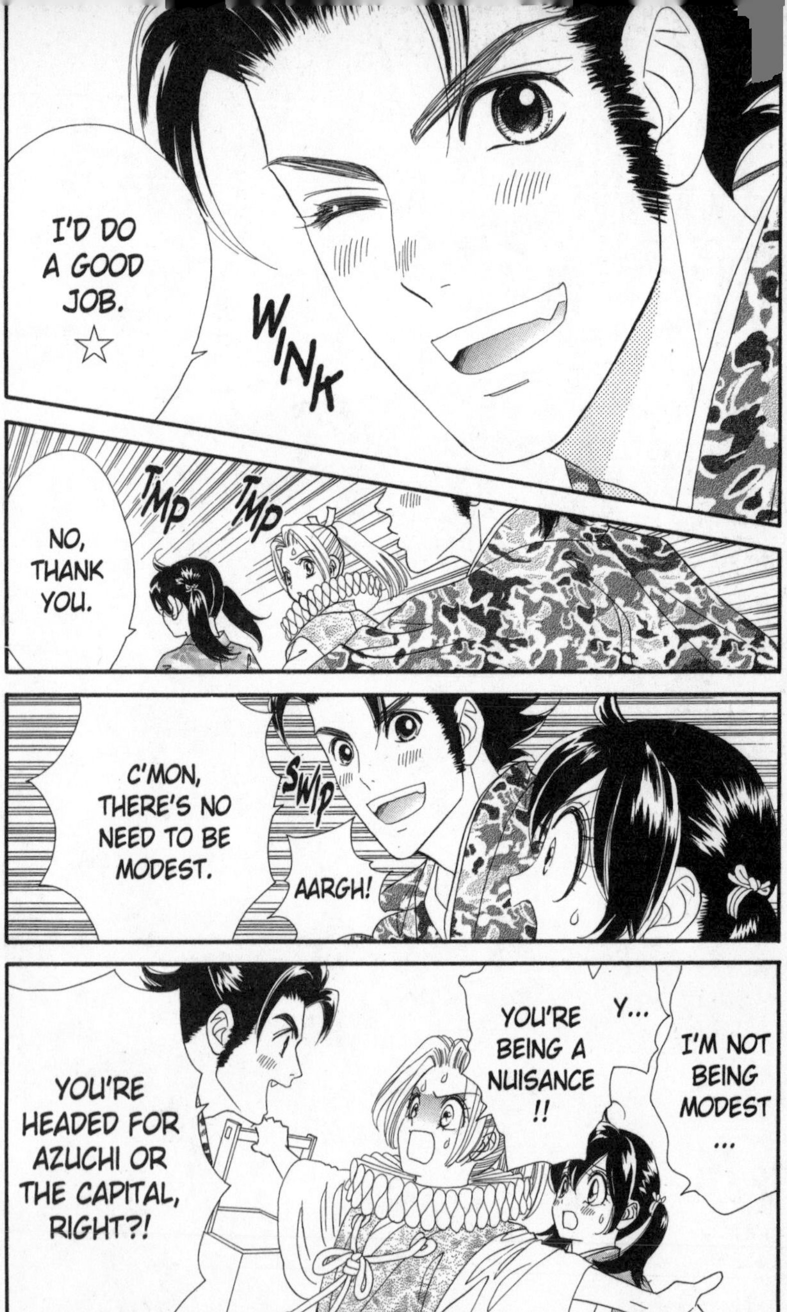
I'D DO A GOOD JOB. ☆
WINK
TMP
TMP
NO, THANK YOU.
SWIP
C'MON, THERE'S NO NEED TO BE MODEST.
AARGH!
I'M NOT BEING MODEST ...
Y...
YOU'RE BEING A NUISANCE !!
YOU'RE HEADED FOR AZUCHI OR THE CAPITAL, RIGHT?!

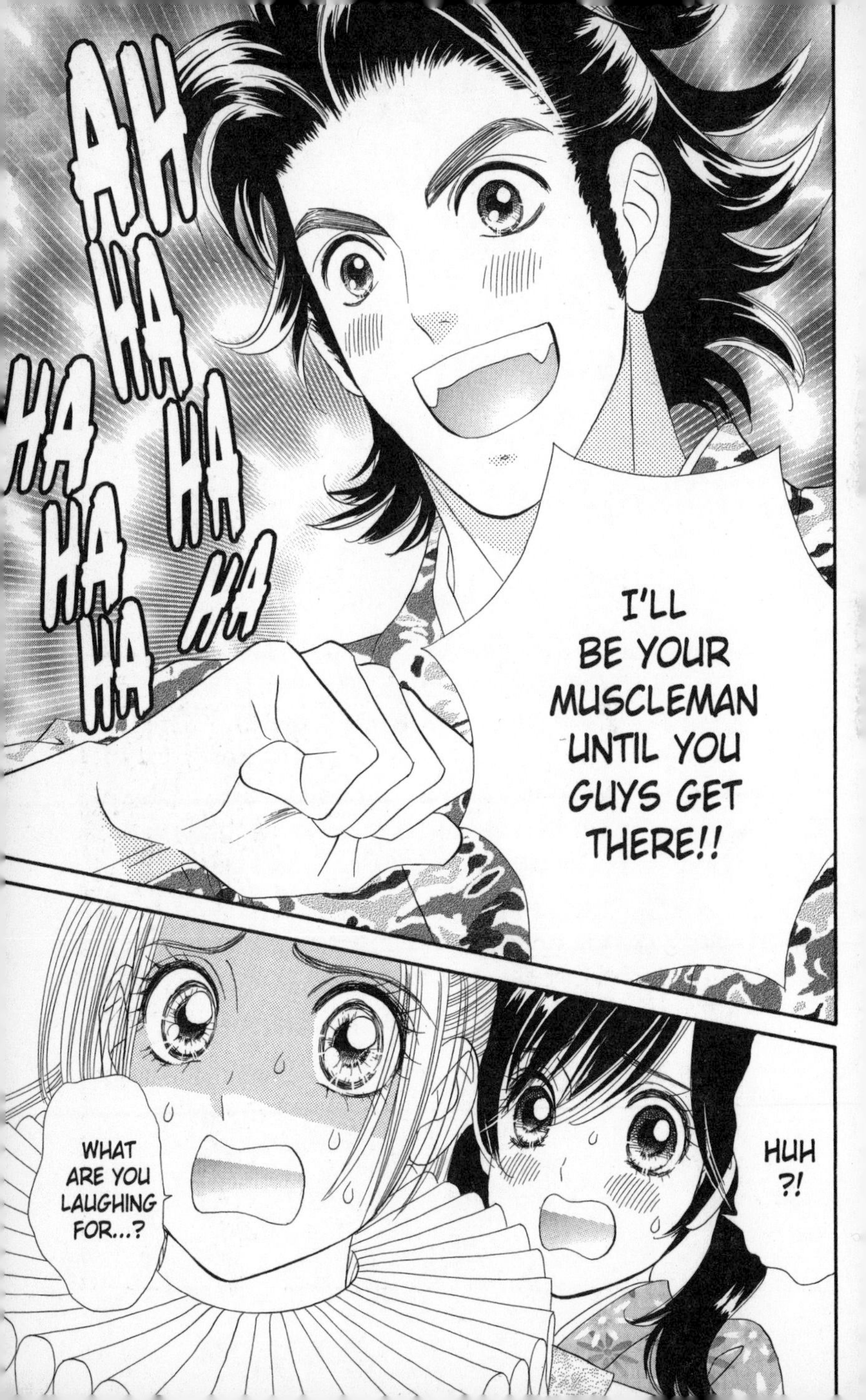
AH HA HA HA HA HA HA HA
I'LL BE YOUR MUSCLEMAN UNTIL YOU GUYS GET THERE!!
HUH ?!
WHAT ARE YOU LAUGHING FOR...?

☆ GREETiNGS ☆

Hello! It's Ue-Rin.
It's Been a while since I last wrote, so I'm
feeling a Bit excited...

Hmph.

Aaah ♡

Candy

There's a page for the fans called "Tail of the Moon
Extra" in the Japanese magazine. The image aBove is
of Little Hanzo and Little Hanzou from the comic
strips about young Hanzo and his family.
Drawing the four-panel comic strips is really tough...
I always have to think hard to come up with a new
one. But I really enjoy drawing little kids! ♡

Tail of the Moon is gradually moving to its climax. Please
continue to support Usagi and the others. And please
send your letters and messages to the following address.

Tail of the Moon Editor
Viz Media
P.O. Box 77064
San Francisco, CA 94107

See you all in volume 13... Rinko ☺ Uedd

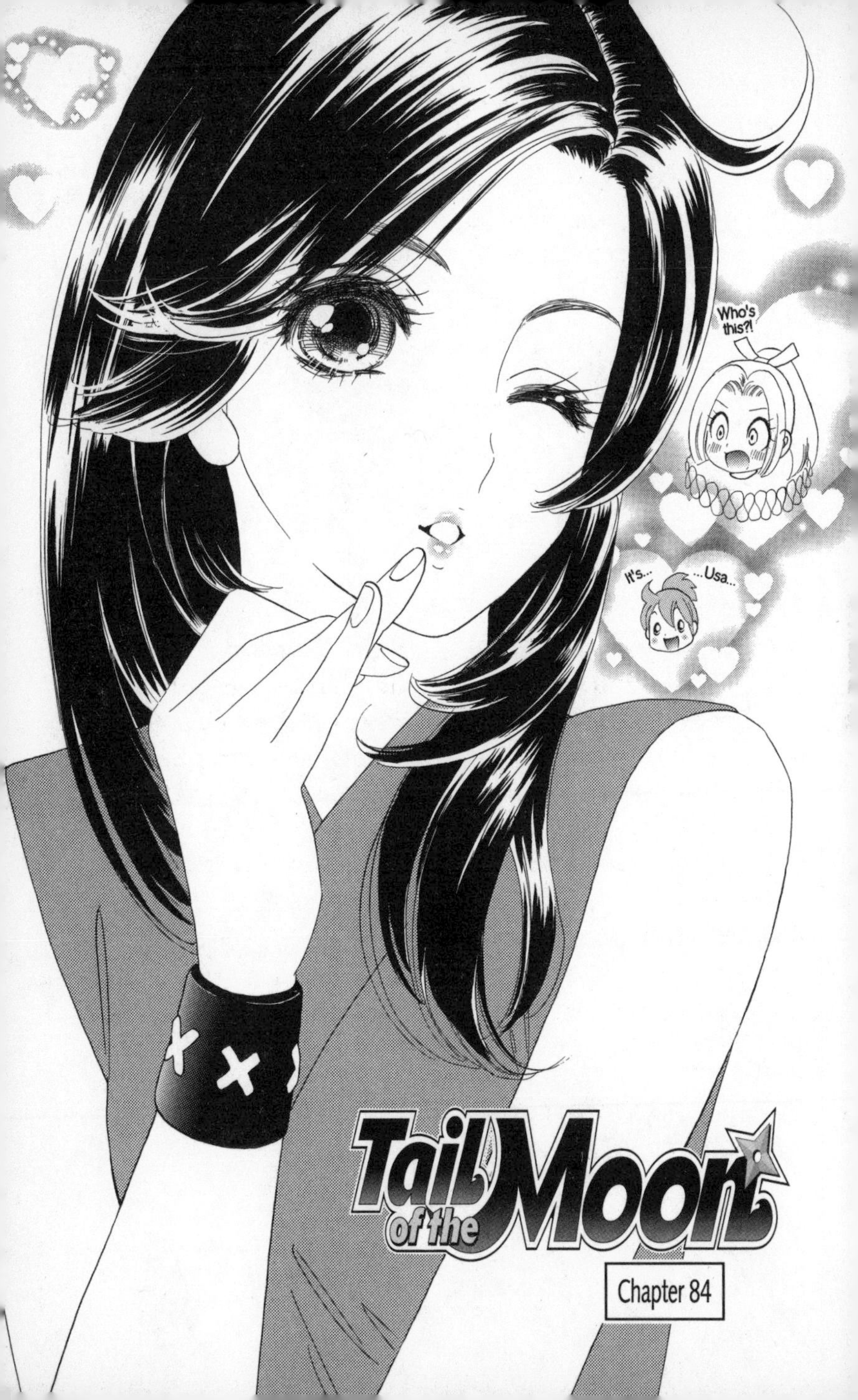

Who's this?!
It's...
...Usa...
Tail of the Moon
Chapter 84

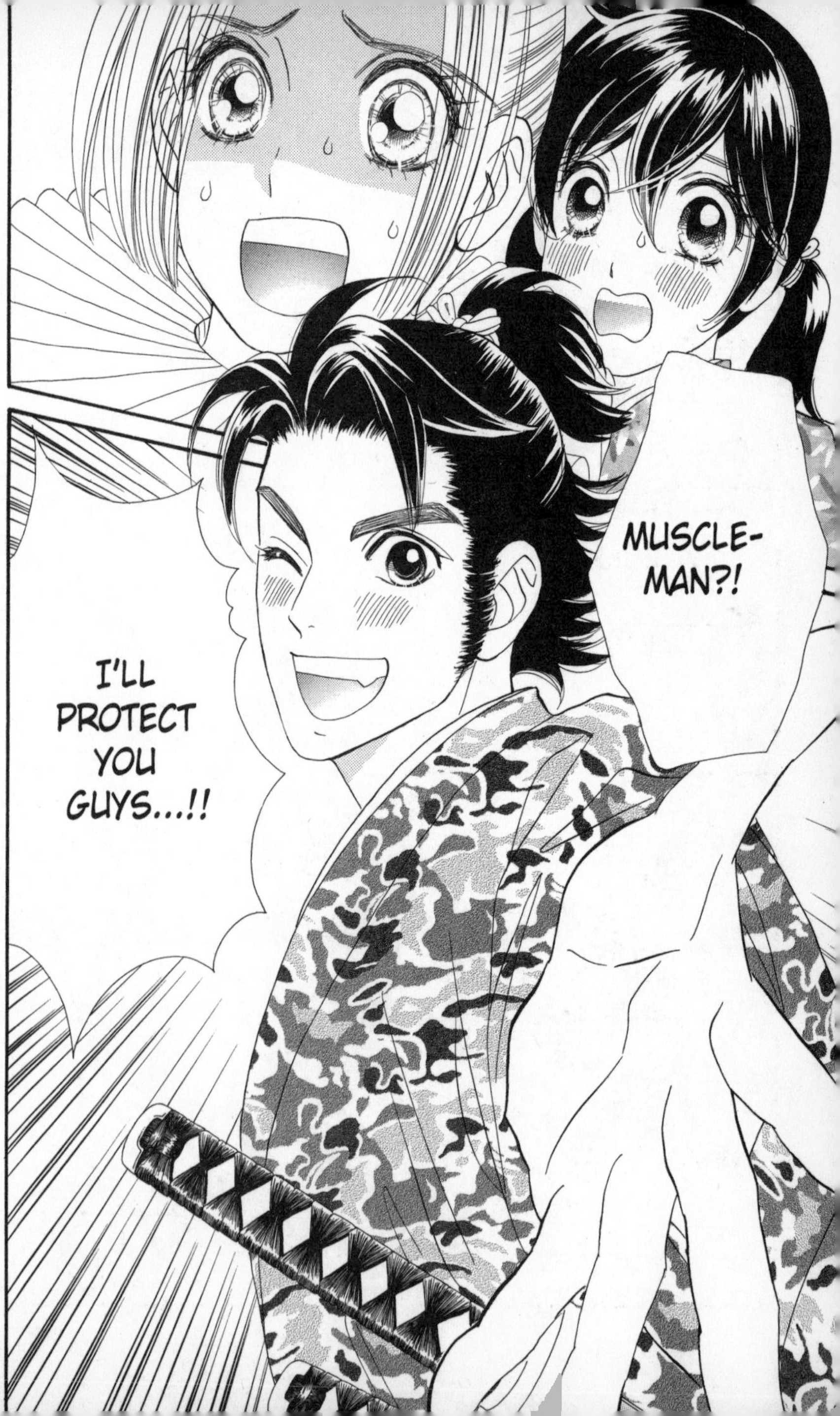
MUSCLE-MAN?!
I'LL PROTECT YOU GUYS...!!

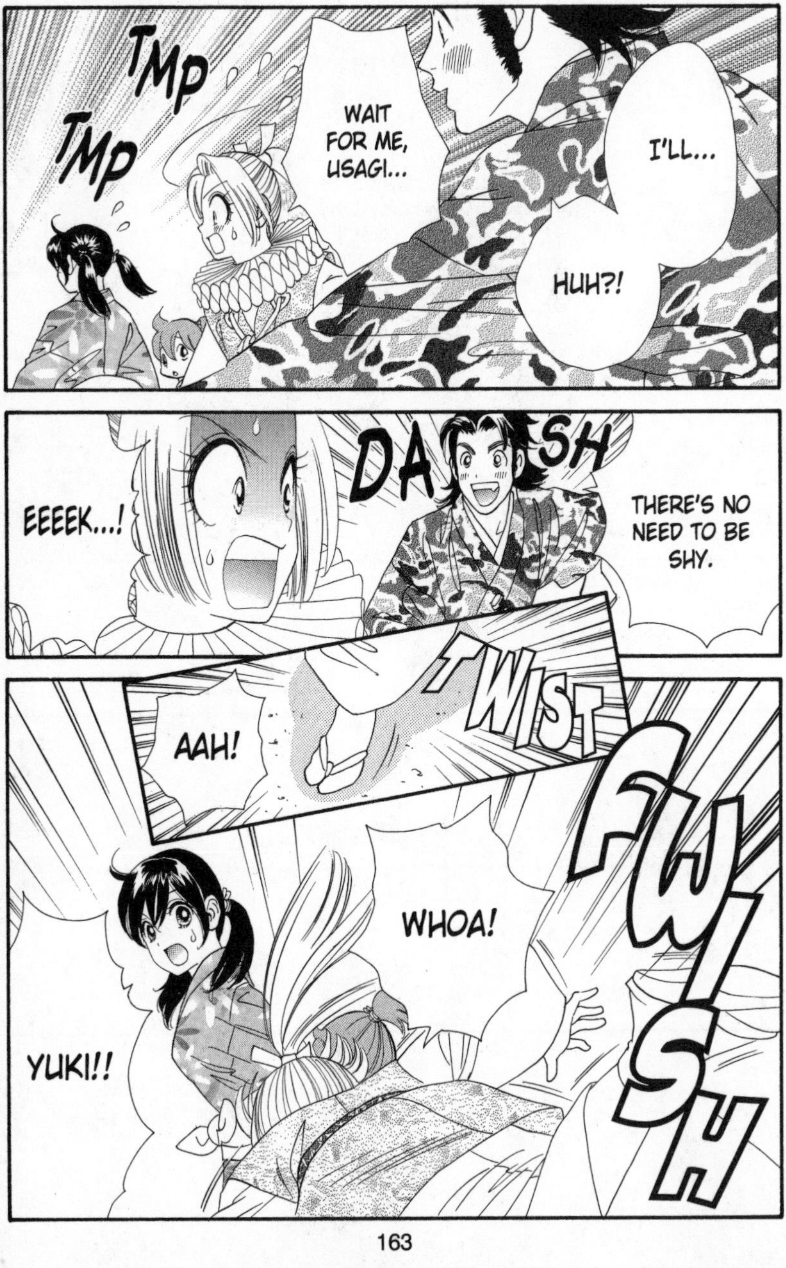
I'LL...
HUH?!
WAIT FOR ME, USAGI...
TMP
TMP
THERE'S NO NEED TO BE SHY.
DASH
EEEEK...!
TWIST
AAH!
FWISH
WHOA!
YUKI!!

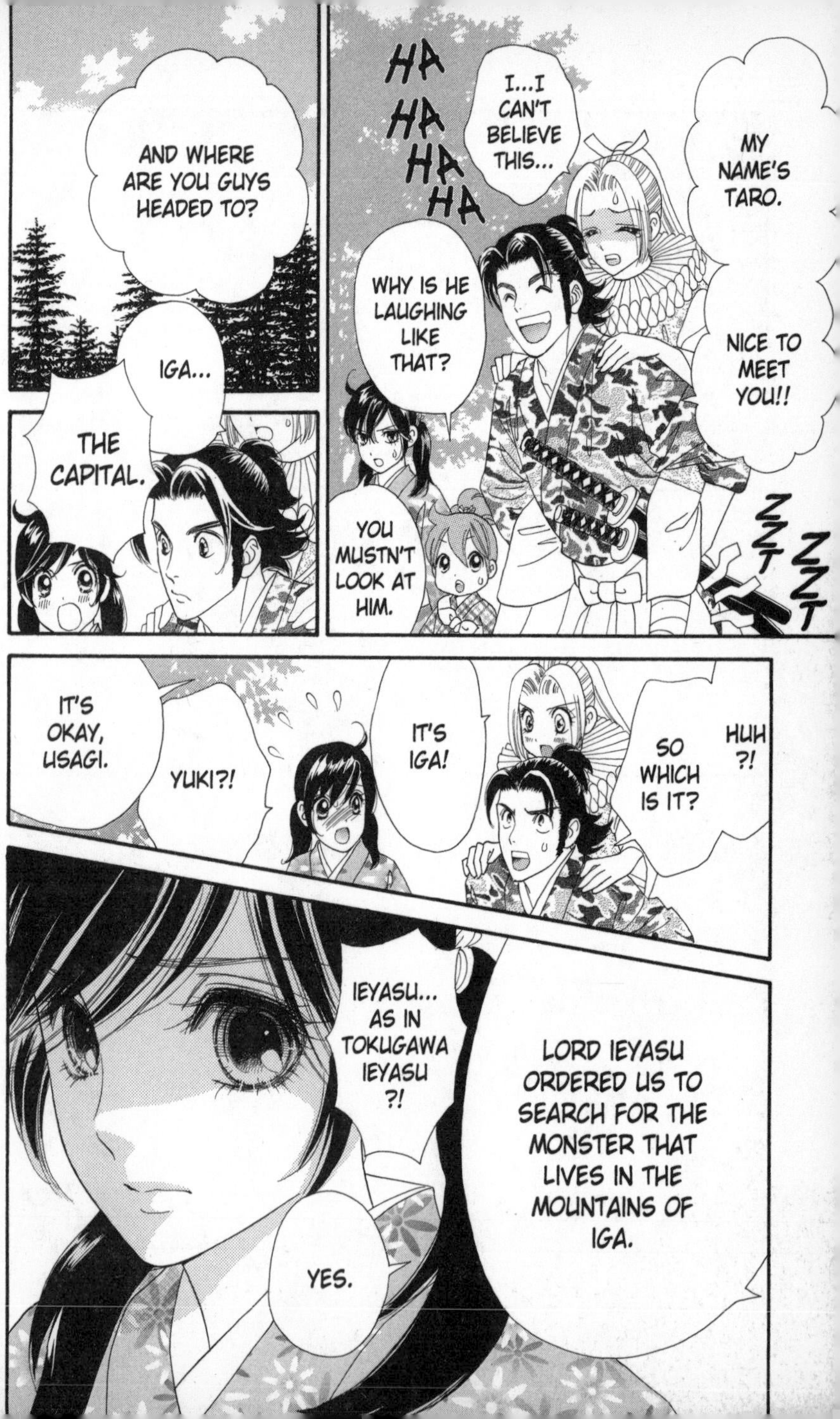
MY NAME'S TARO.
I...I CAN'T BELIEVE THIS...
HA HA HA HA
NICE TO MEET YOU!!
WHY IS HE LAUGHING LIKE THAT?
ZZT ZZT
YOU MUSTN'T LOOK AT HIM.
AND WHERE ARE YOU GUYS HEADED TO?
IGA...
THE CAPITAL.
HUH?!
SO WHICH IS IT?
IT'S IGA!
YUKI?!
IT'S OKAY, USAGI.
LORD IEYASU ORDERED US TO SEARCH FOR THE MONSTER THAT LIVES IN THE MOUNTAINS OF IGA.
IEYASU... AS IN TOKUGAWA IEYASU?!
YES.

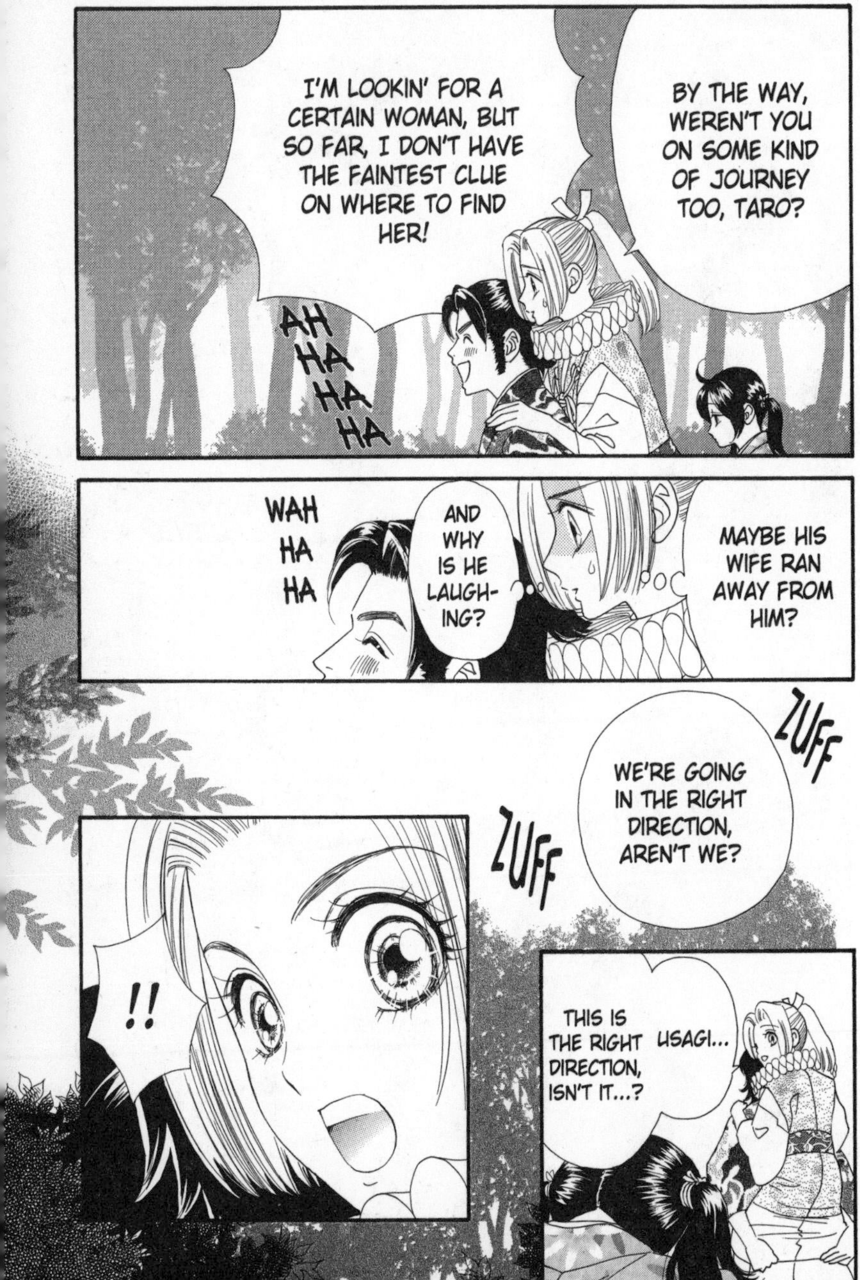
BY THE WAY, WEREN'T YOU ON SOME KIND OF JOURNEY TOO, TARO?
I'M LOOKIN' FOR A CERTAIN WOMAN, BUT SO FAR, I DON'T HAVE THE FAINTEST CLUE ON WHERE TO FIND HER!
AH HA HA HA
MAYBE HIS WIFE RAN AWAY FROM HIM?
AND WHY IS HE LAUGHING?
WAH HA HA
ZUFF
WE'RE GOING IN THE RIGHT DIRECTION, AREN'T WE?
ZUFF
USAGI...
THIS IS THE RIGHT DIRECTION, ISN'T IT...?
!!

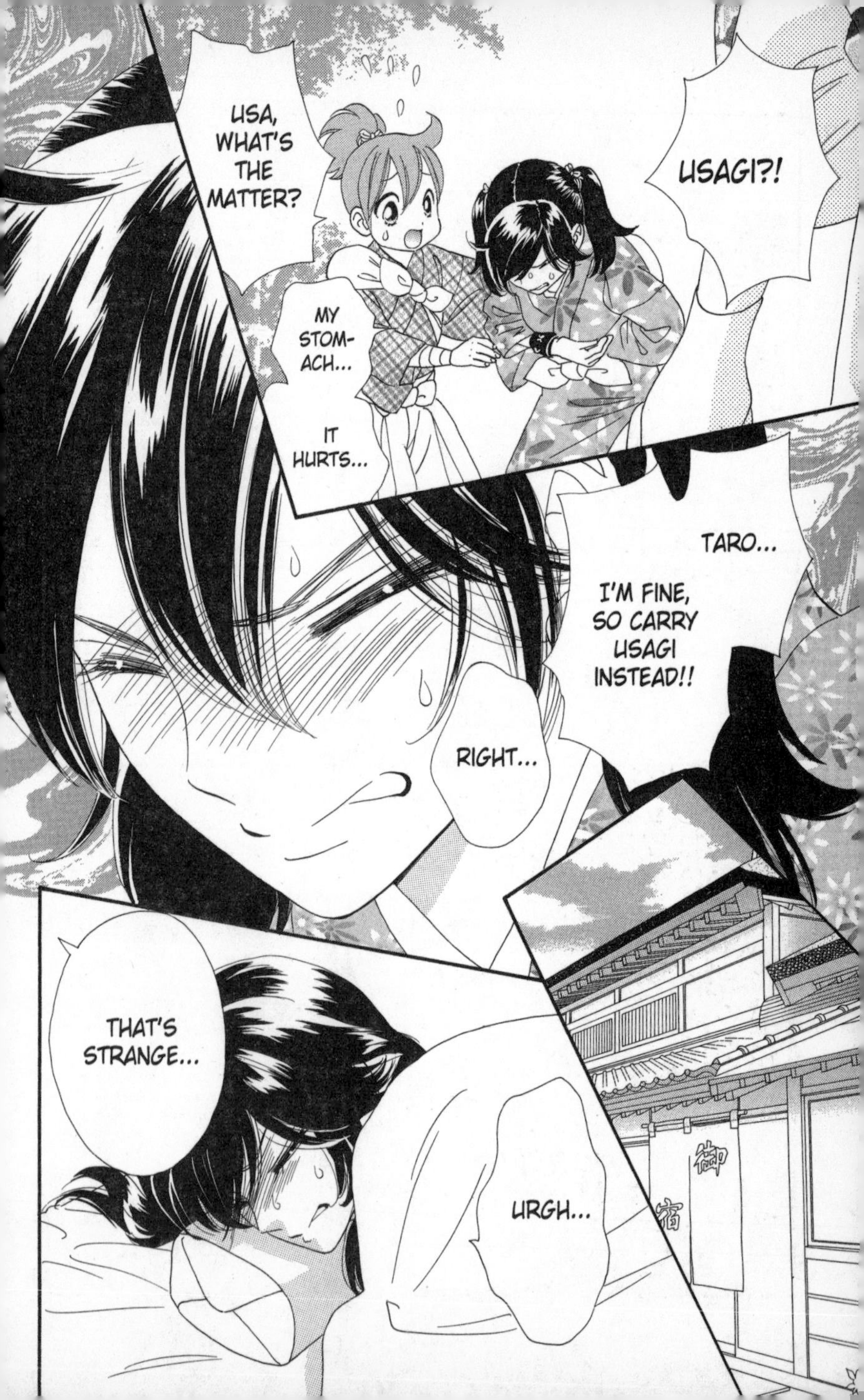
USAGI?!
USA, WHAT'S THE MATTER?
MY STOM-ACH...
IT HURTS...
TARO...
I'M FINE, SO CARRY USAGI INSTEAD!!
RIGHT...
THAT'S STRANGE...
URGH...

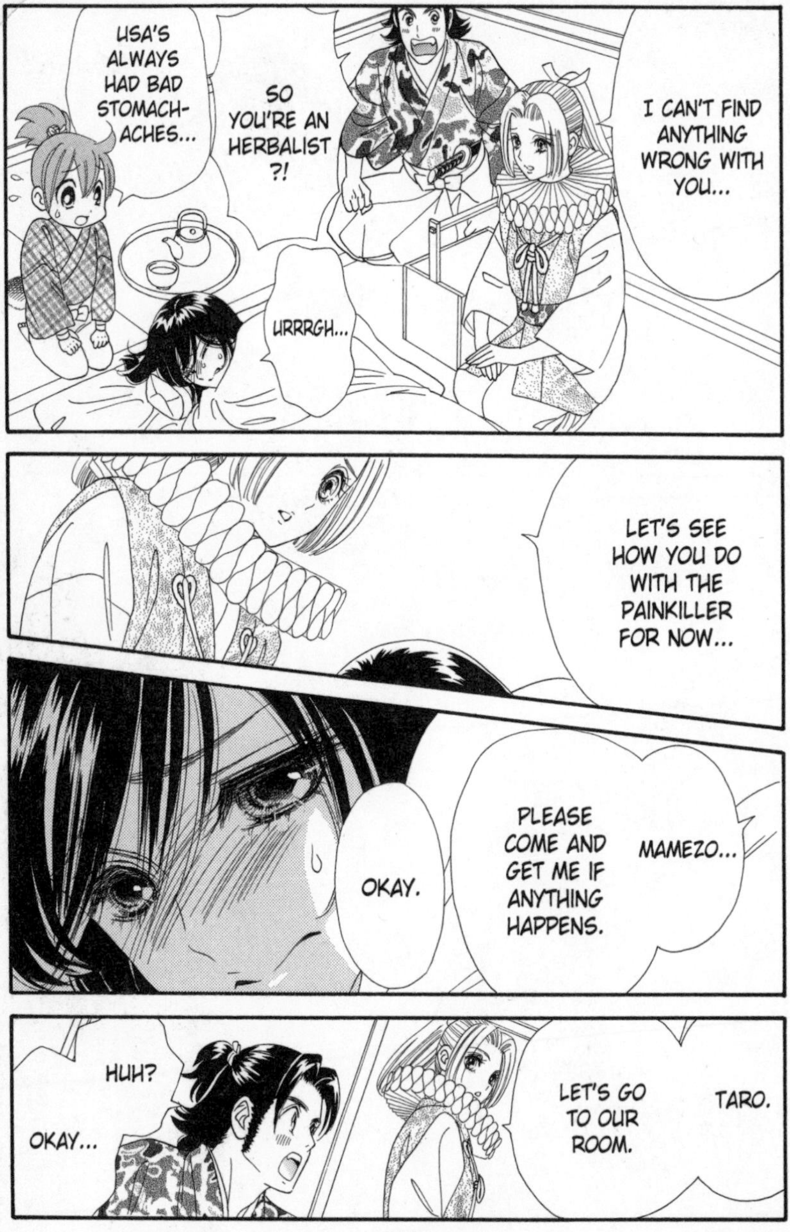
I CAN'T FIND ANYTHING WRONG WITH YOU...
SO YOU'RE AN HERBALIST ?!
USA'S ALWAYS HAD BAD STOMACH-ACHES...
URRRGH...
LET'S SEE HOW YOU DO WITH THE PAINKILLER FOR NOW...
MAMEZO...
PLEASE COME AND GET ME IF ANYTHING HAPPENS.
OKAY.
TARO.
LET'S GO TO OUR ROOM.
HUH?
OKAY...

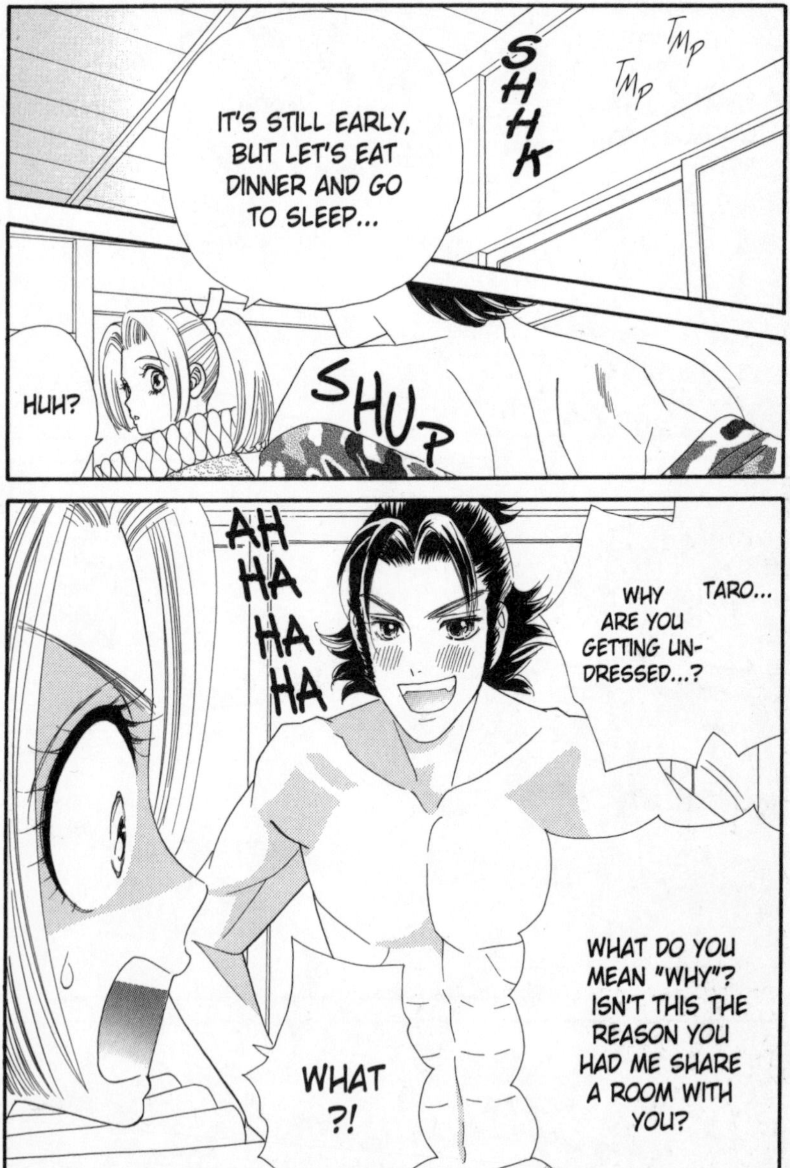
TMP
TMP
SHHK
IT'S STILL EARLY, BUT LET'S EAT DINNER AND GO TO SLEEP...
SHUP
HUH?
TARO...
WHY ARE YOU GETTING UN-DRESSED...?
AH HA HA HA
WHAT DO YOU MEAN "WHY"? ISN'T THIS THE REASON YOU HAD ME SHARE A ROOM WITH YOU?
WHAT ?!

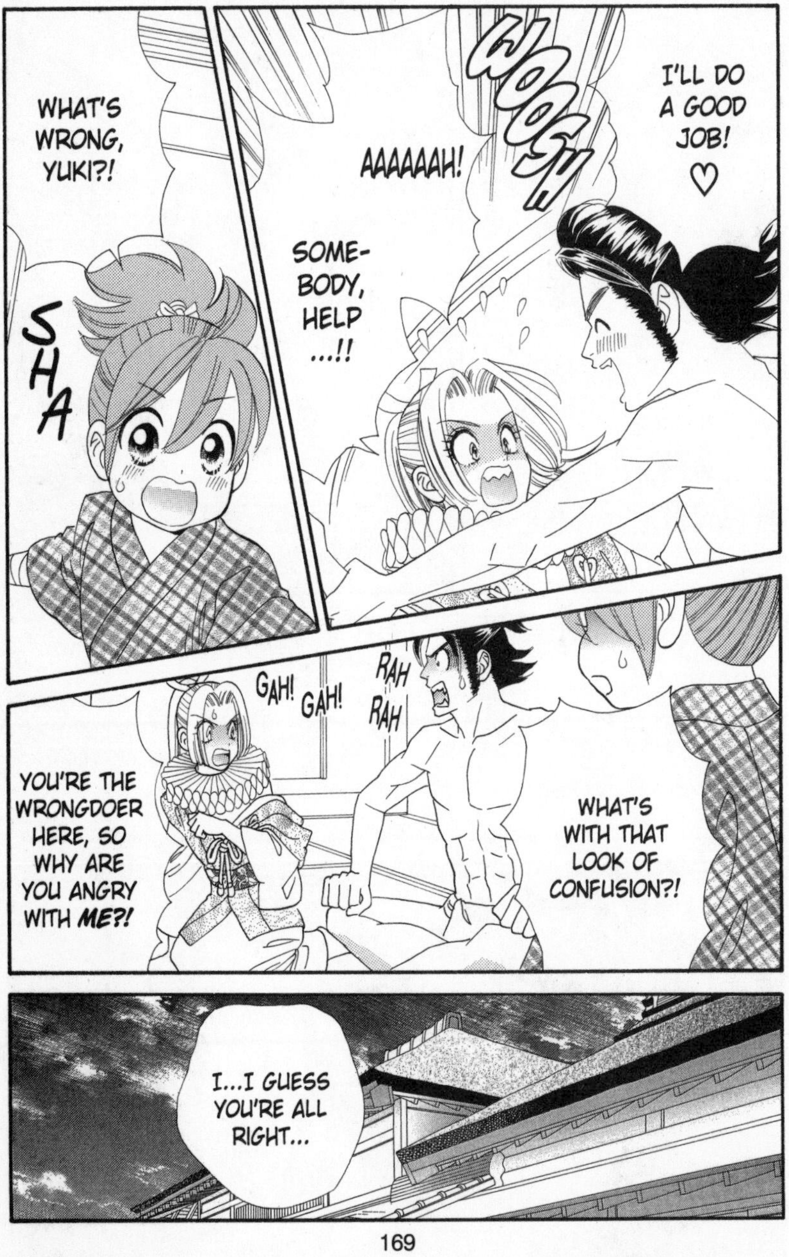
I'LL DO A GOOD JOB! ♡
WOOOSH!!
AAAAAAH!
SOME-BODY, HELP ...!!
WHAT'S WRONG, YUKI?!
SHA
WHAT'S WITH THAT LOOK OF CONFUSION?!
RAH RAH
GAH! GAH!
YOU'RE THE WRONGDOER HERE, SO WHY ARE YOU ANGRY WITH *ME*?!
I...I GUESS YOU'RE ALL RIGHT...

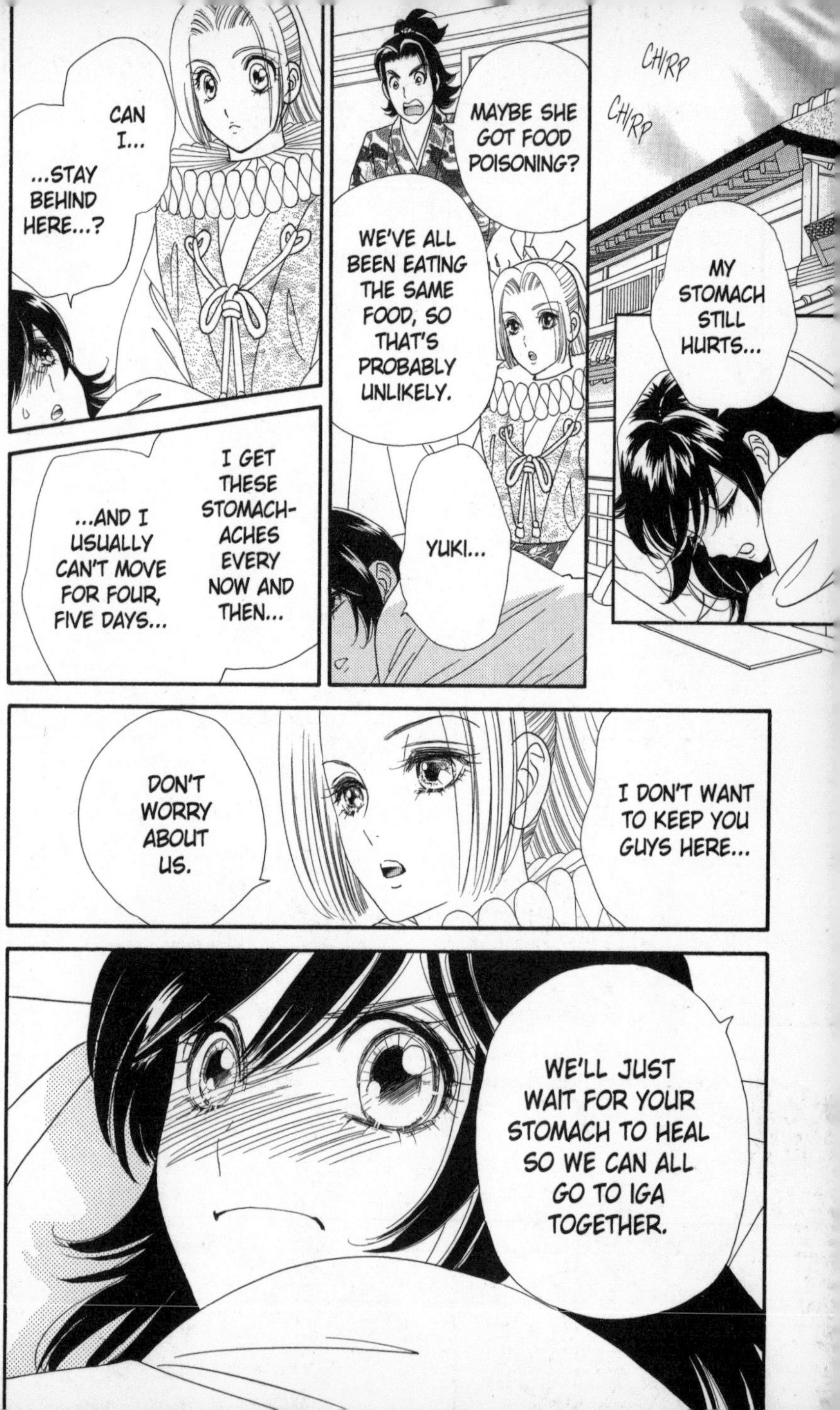
CHIRP
CHIRP
MY STOMACH STILL HURTS...
MAYBE SHE GOT FOOD POISONING?
WE'VE ALL BEEN EATING THE SAME FOOD, SO THAT'S PROBABLY UNLIKELY.
YUKI...
CAN I...
...STAY BEHIND HERE...?
I GET THESE STOMACHACHES EVERY NOW AND THEN...
...AND I USUALLY CAN'T MOVE FOR FOUR, FIVE DAYS...
I DON'T WANT TO KEEP YOU GUYS HERE...
DON'T WORRY ABOUT US.
WE'LL JUST WAIT FOR YOUR STOMACH TO HEAL SO WE CAN ALL GO TO IGA TOGETHER.

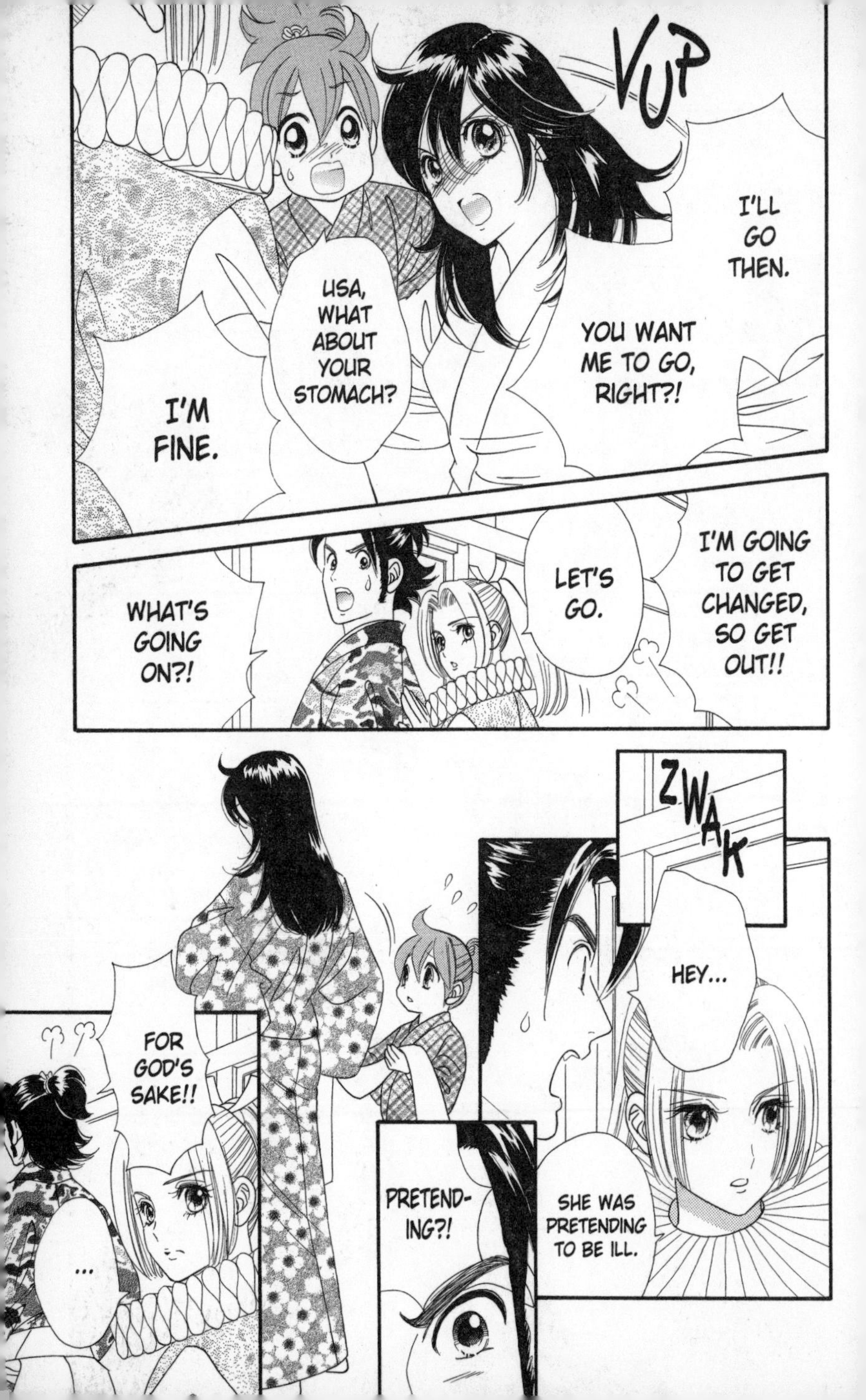
VUP
I'LL GO THEN.
YOU WANT ME TO GO, RIGHT?!
USA, WHAT ABOUT YOUR STOMACH?
I'M FINE.
I'M GOING TO GET CHANGED, SO GET OUT!!
LET'S GO.
WHAT'S GOING ON?!
ZWAK
HEY...
SHE WAS PRETENDING TO BE ILL.
PRETEND-ING?!
FOR GOD'S SAKE!!
...

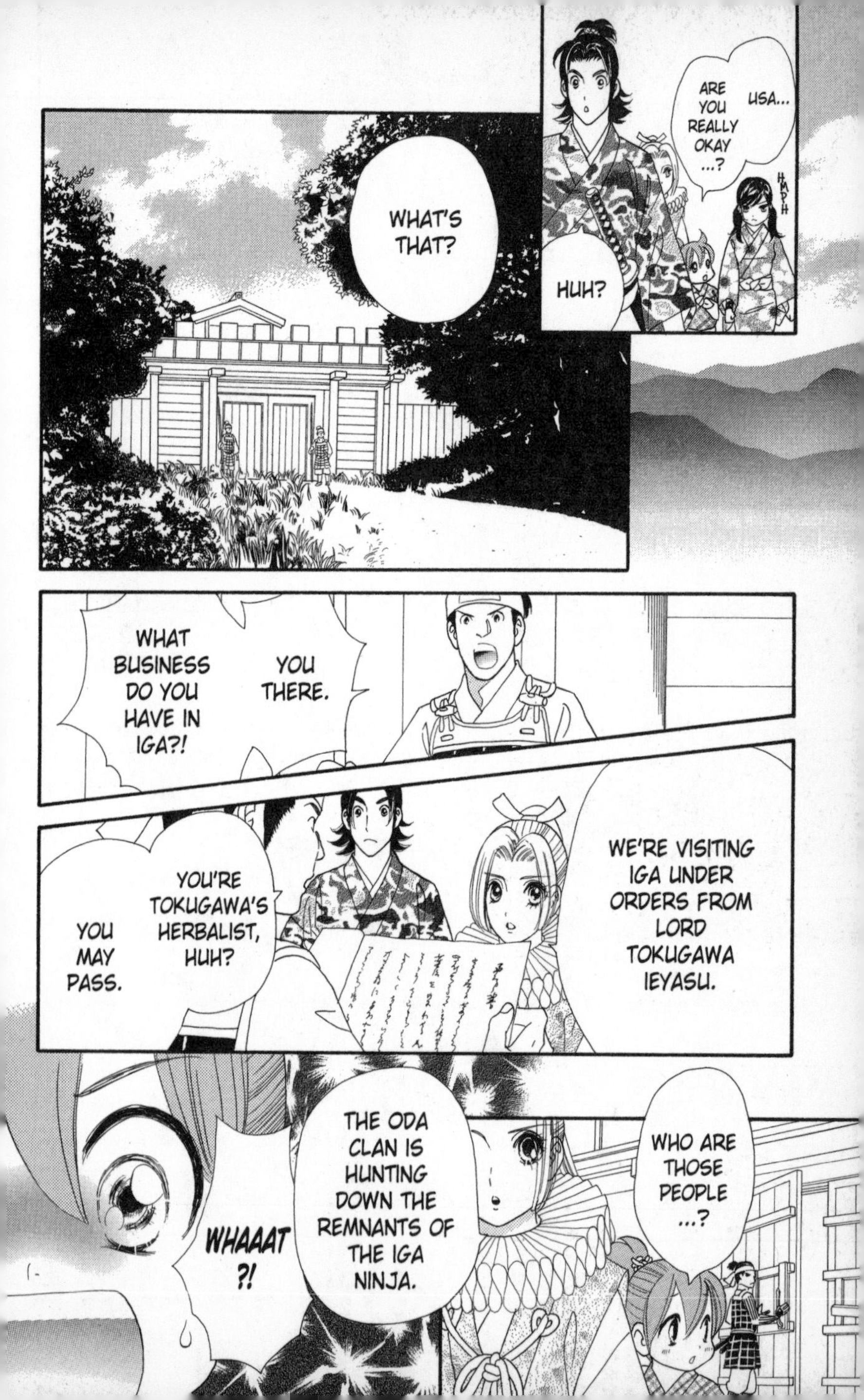
USA...
ARE YOU REALLY OKAY ...?
HMPH
HUH?
WHAT'S THAT?
YOU THERE.
WHAT BUSINESS DO YOU HAVE IN IGA?!
WE'RE VISITING IGA UNDER ORDERS FROM LORD TOKUGAWA IEYASU.
YOU'RE TOKUGAWA'S HERBALIST, HUH?
YOU MAY PASS.
WHO ARE THOSE PEOPLE ...?
THE ODA CLAN IS HUNTING DOWN THE REMNANTS OF THE IGA NINJA.
WHAAAT ?!

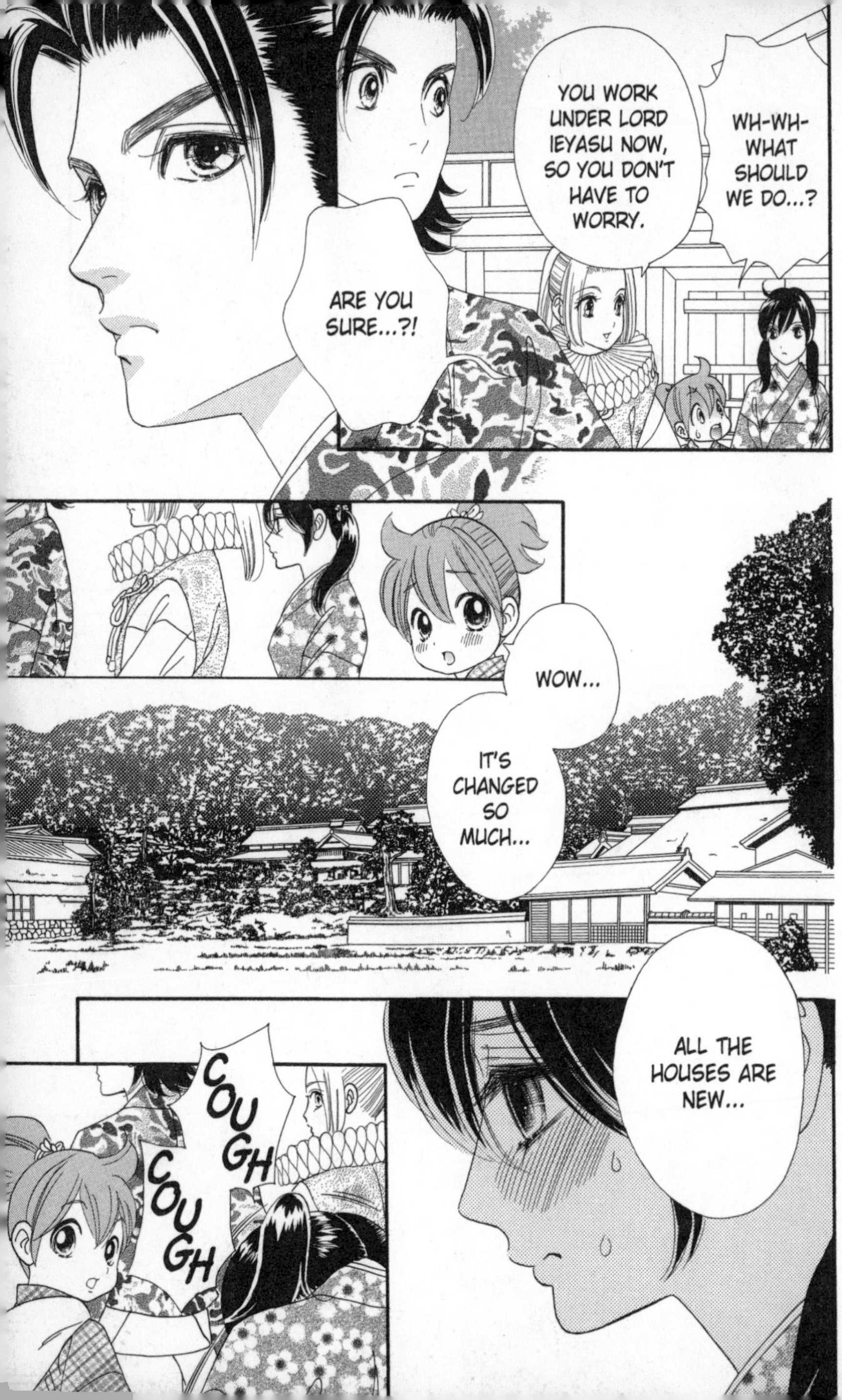
WH-WH-WHAT SHOULD WE DO...?
YOU WORK UNDER LORD IEYASU NOW, SO YOU DON'T HAVE TO WORRY.
ARE YOU SURE...?!
WOW...
IT'S CHANGED SO MUCH...
ALL THE HOUSES ARE NEW...
COUGH
COUGH

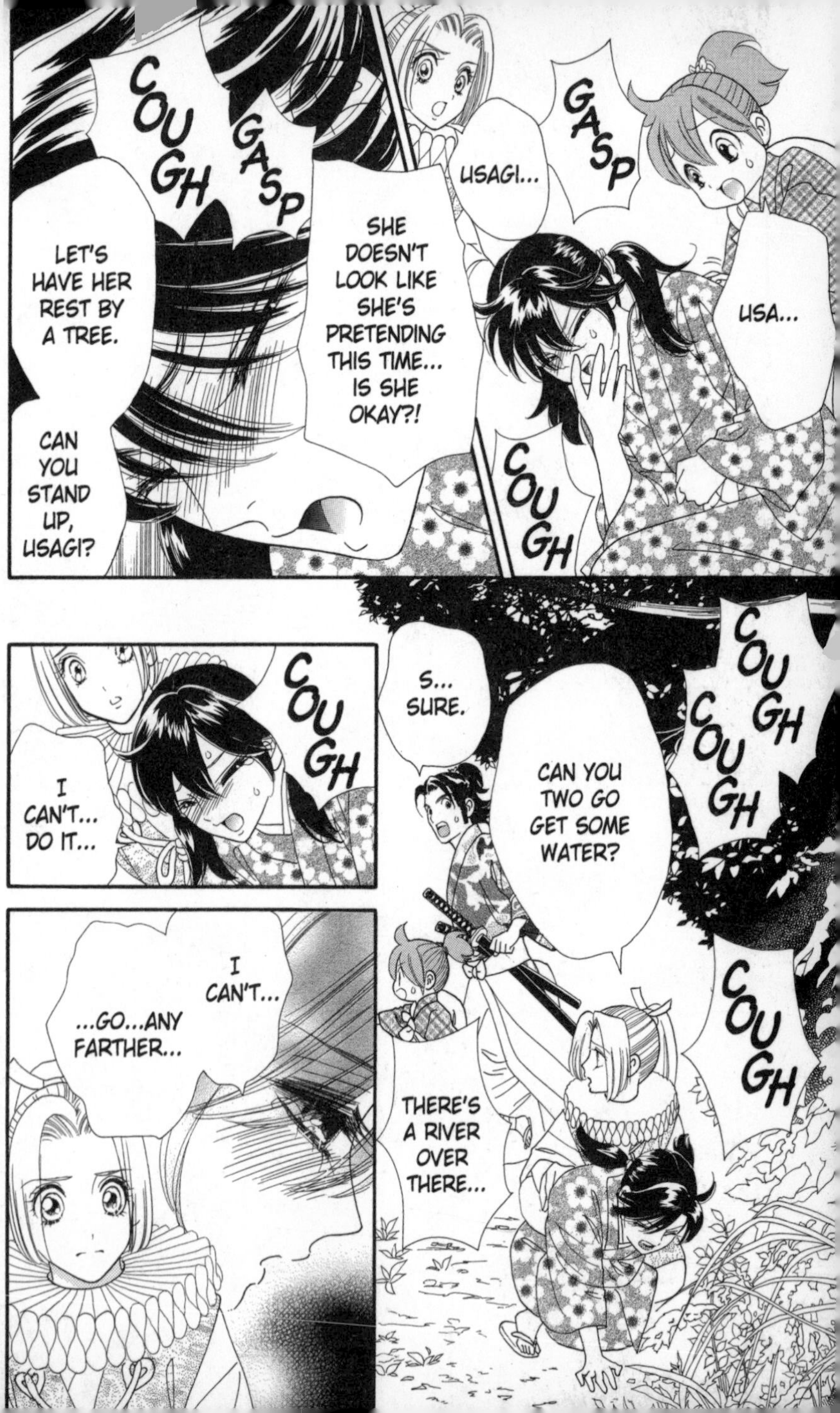
GASP
USAGI...
USA...
COUGH
SHE DOESN'T LOOK LIKE SHE'S PRETENDING THIS TIME... IS SHE OKAY?!
COUGH
GASP
LET'S HAVE HER REST BY A TREE.
CAN YOU STAND UP, USAGI?
COUGH
COUGH
CAN YOU TWO GO GET SOME WATER?
S... SURE.
COUGH
THERE'S A RIVER OVER THERE...
COUGH
I CAN'T... DO IT...
I CAN'T...
...GO...ANY FARTHER...

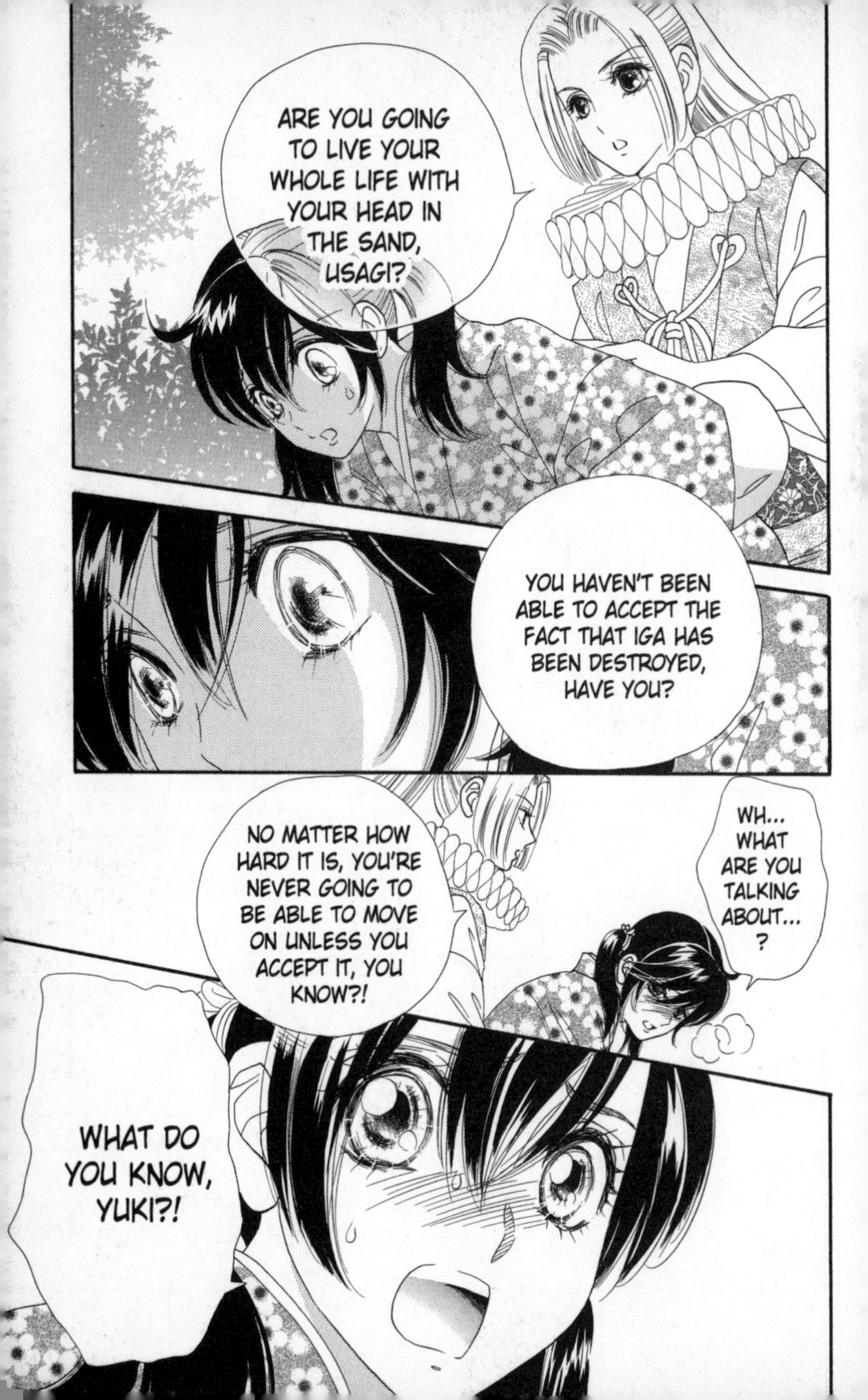
ARE YOU GOING TO LIVE YOUR WHOLE LIFE WITH YOUR HEAD IN THE SAND, USAGI?
YOU HAVEN'T BEEN ABLE TO ACCEPT THE FACT THAT IGA HAS BEEN DESTROYED, HAVE YOU?
WH... WHAT ARE YOU TALKING ABOUT...?
NO MATTER HOW HARD IT IS, YOU'RE NEVER GOING TO BE ABLE TO MOVE ON UNLESS YOU ACCEPT IT, YOU KNOW?!
WHAT DO YOU KNOW, YUKI?!

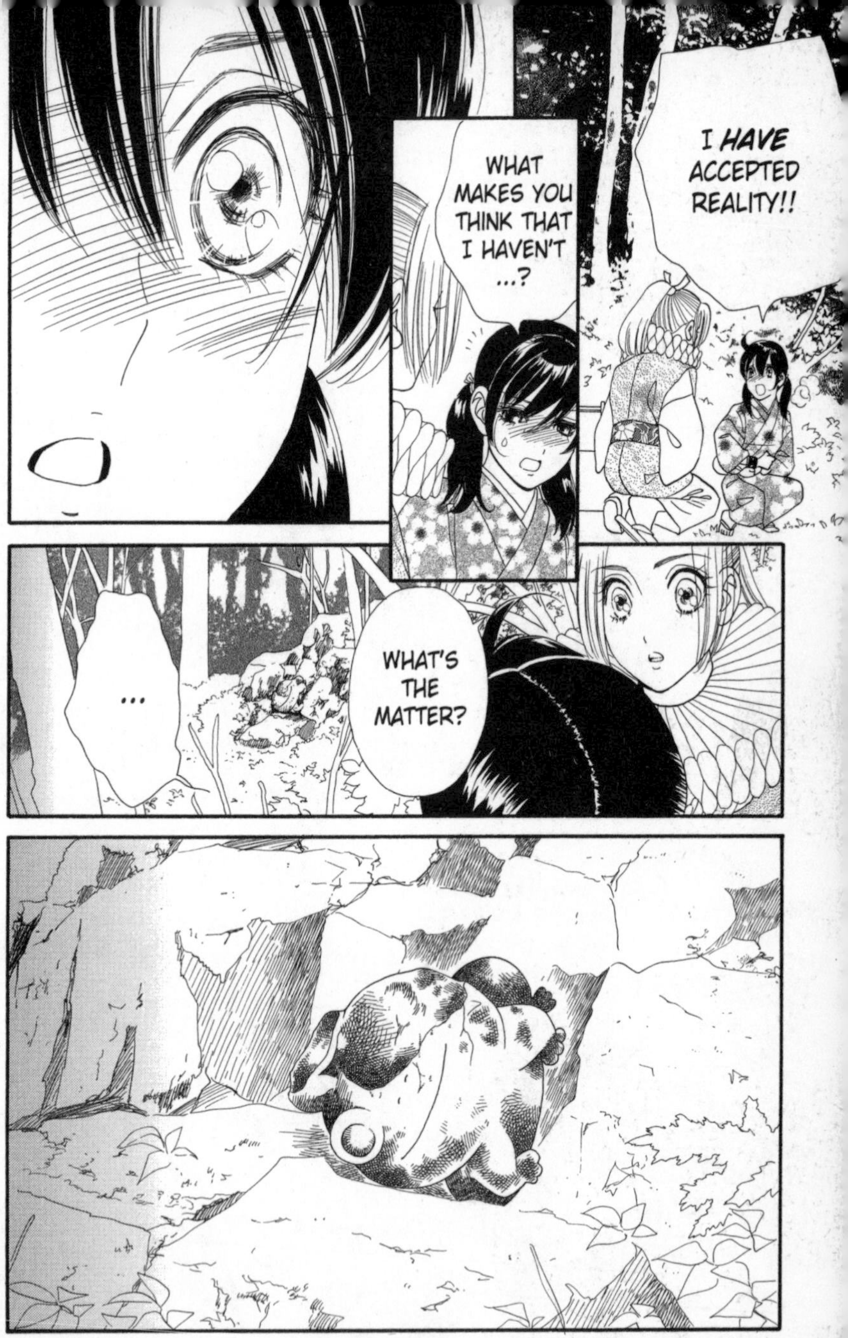
I HAVE ACCEPTED REALITY!!
WHAT MAKES YOU THINK THAT I HAVEN'T ...?
WHAT'S THE MATTER?
...

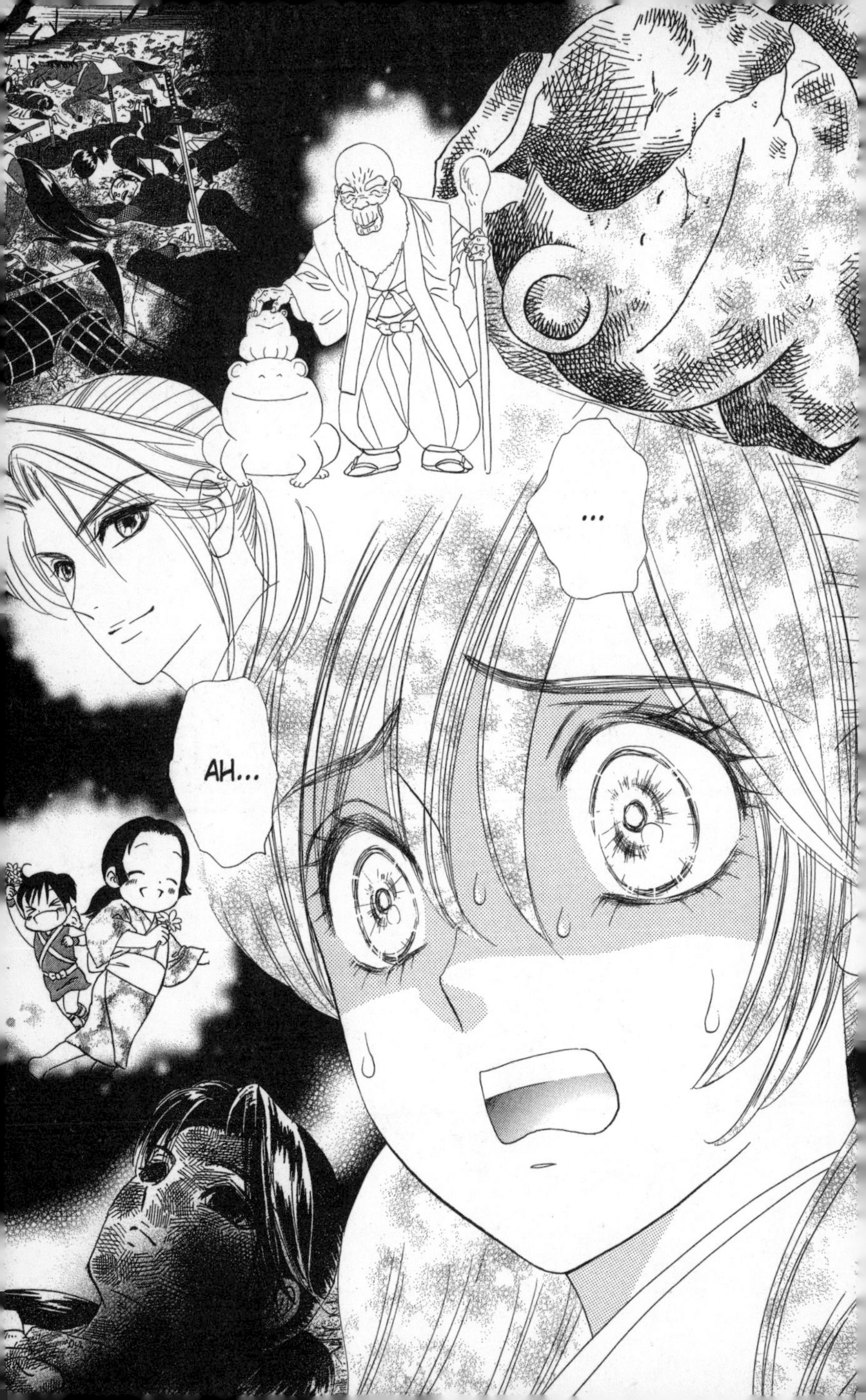
...
AH...

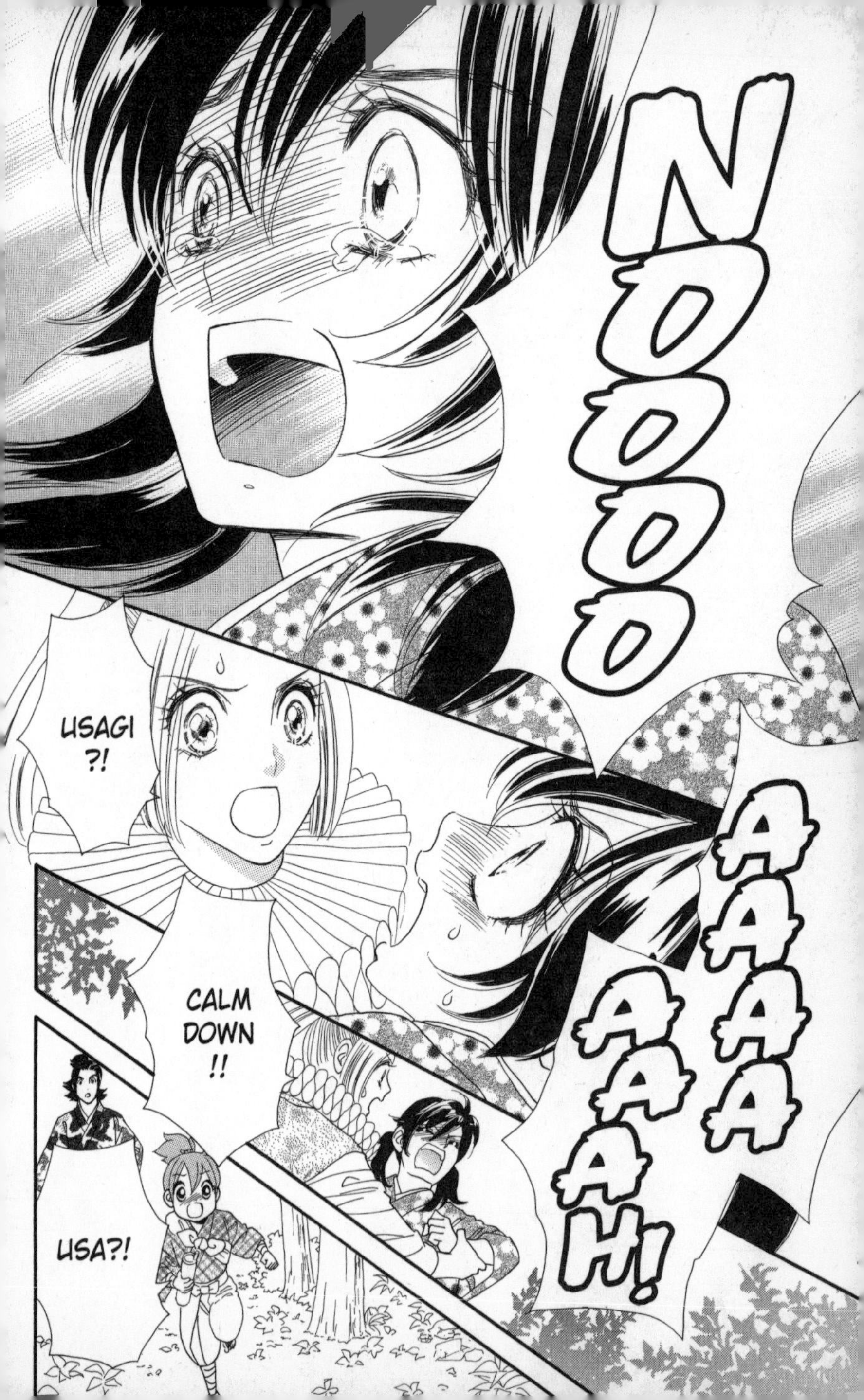
NOOOOO
AAAAAAAAAH!
USAGI ?!
CALM DOWN !!
USA?!

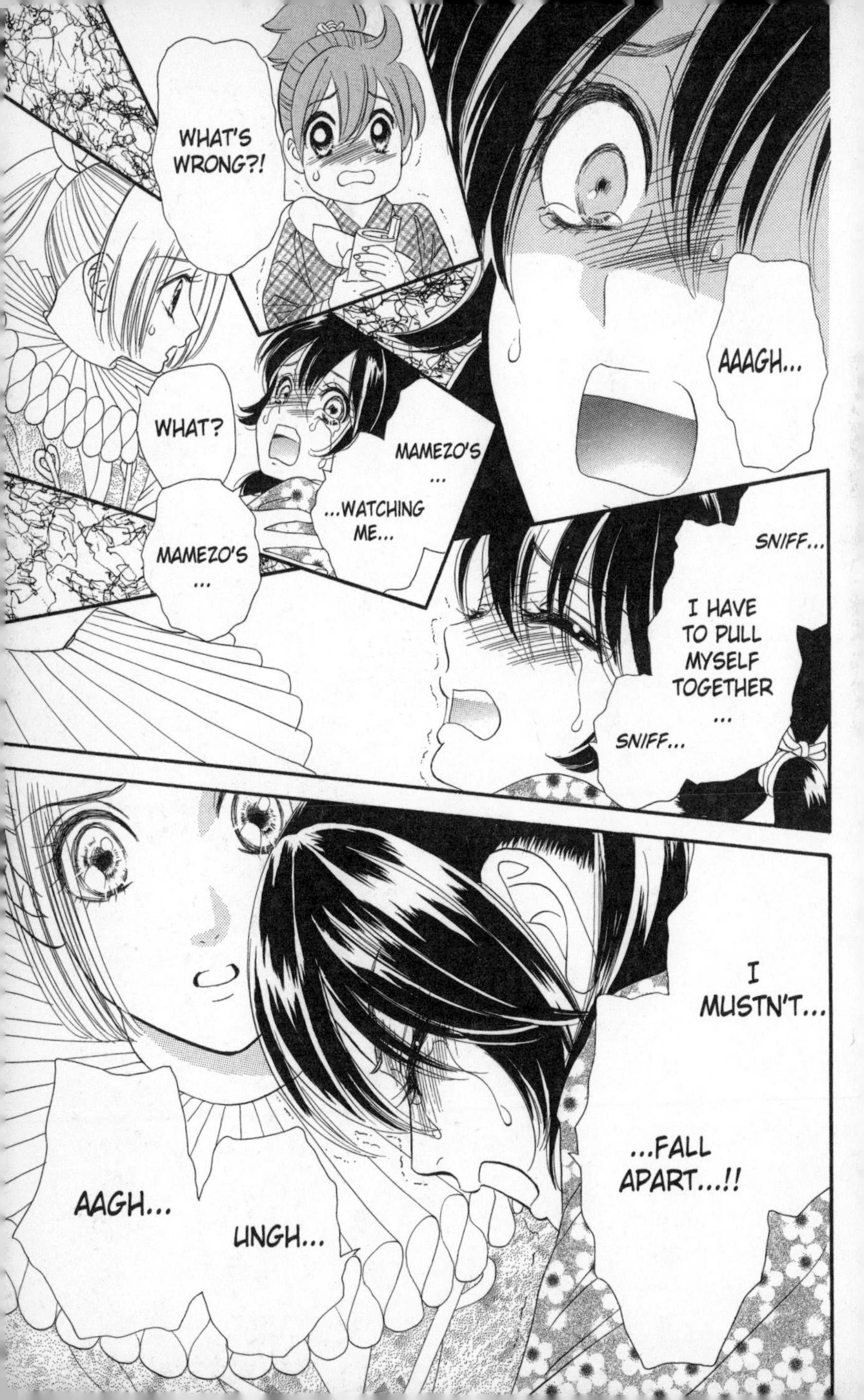
AAAGH...
WHAT'S WRONG?!
MAMEZO'S ...
WHAT?
...WATCHING ME...
MAMEZO'S ...
SNIFF...
I HAVE TO PULL MYSELF TOGETHER ...
SNIFF...
I MUSTN'T...
...FALL APART...!!
UNGH...
AAGH...

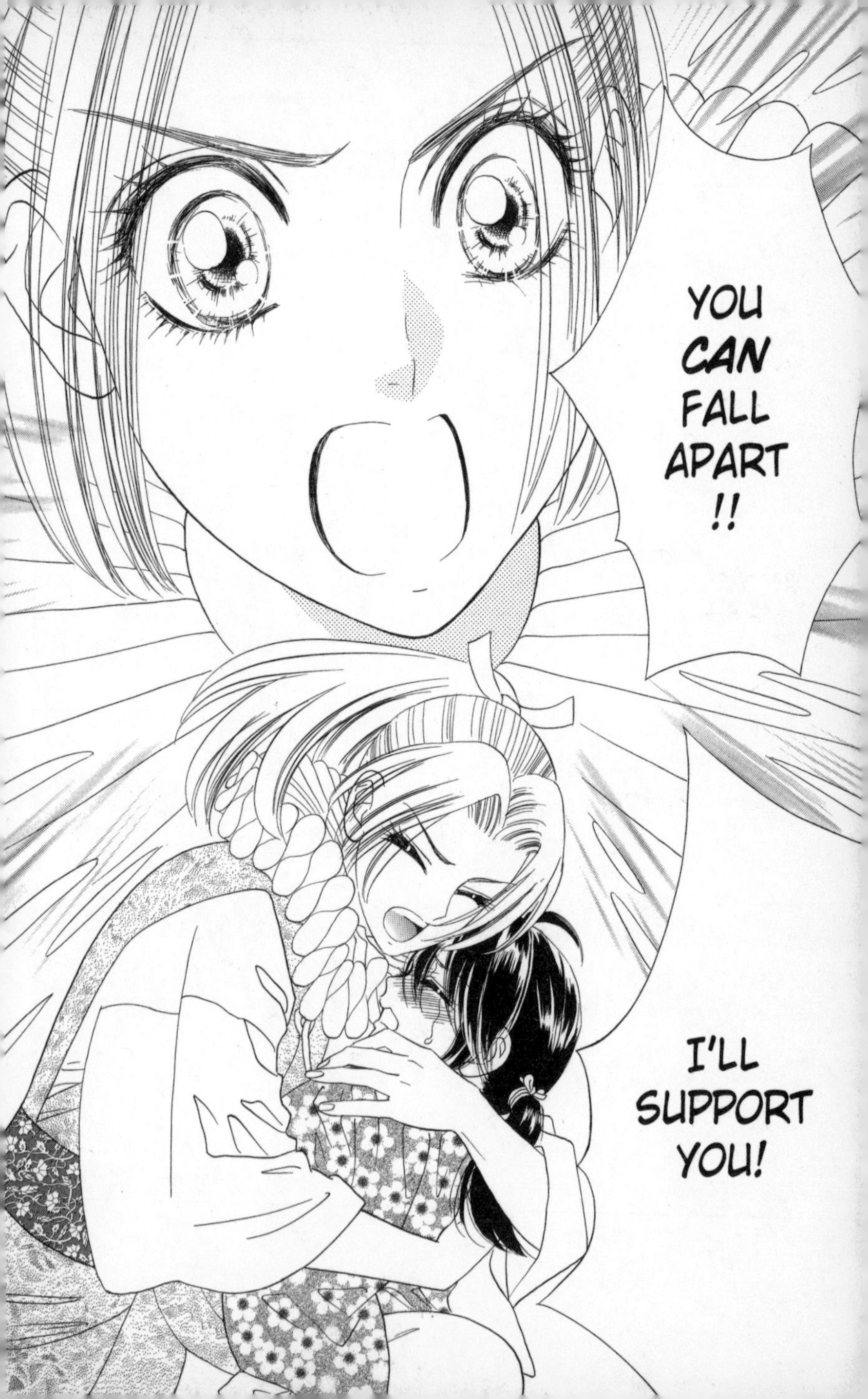
YOU CAN FALL APART !!
I'LL SUPPORT YOU!

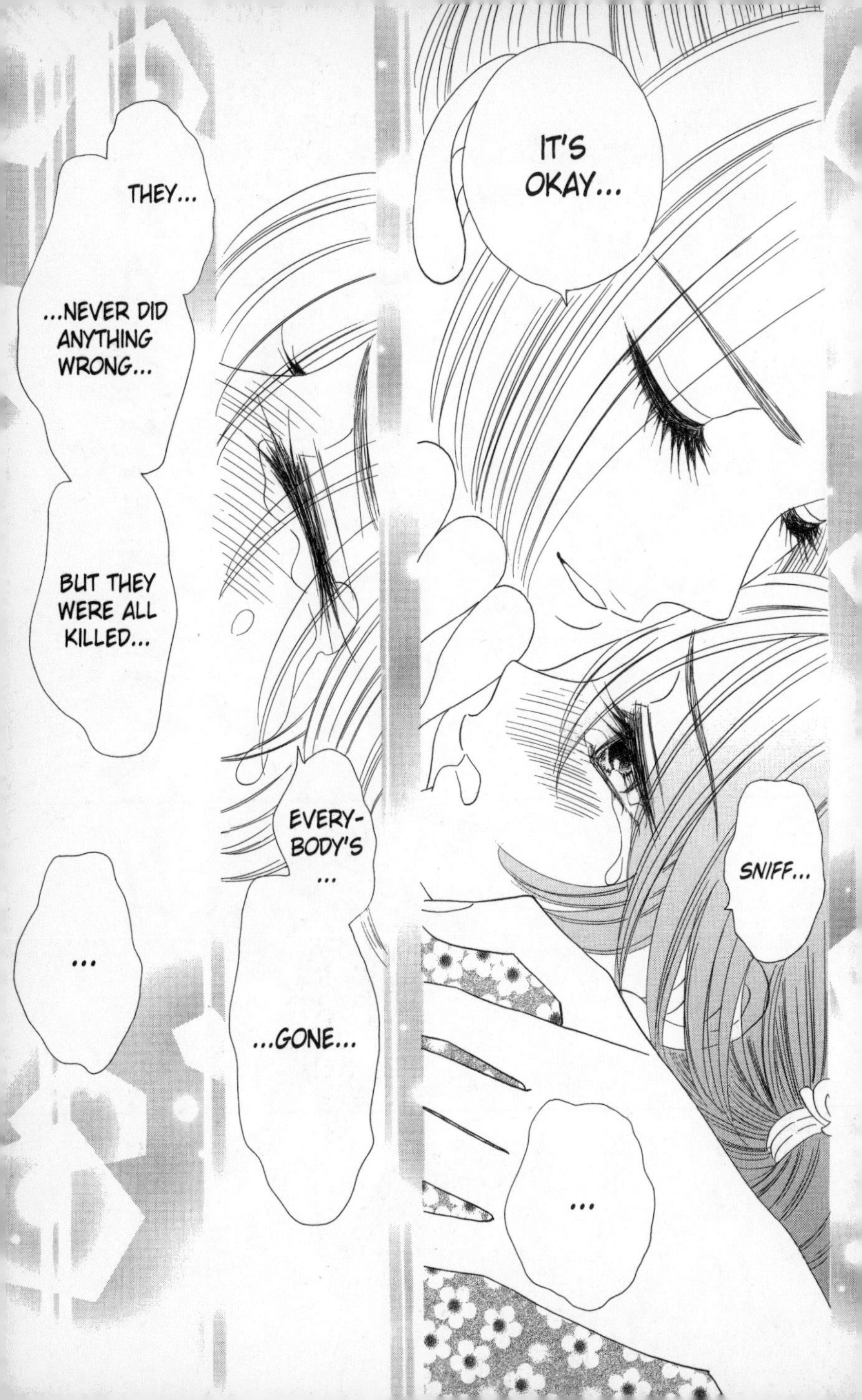
IT'S OKAY...
SNIFF...
...
EVERY-BODY'S ...
...GONE...
THEY...
...NEVER DID ANYTHING WRONG...
BUT THEY WERE ALL KILLED...
...

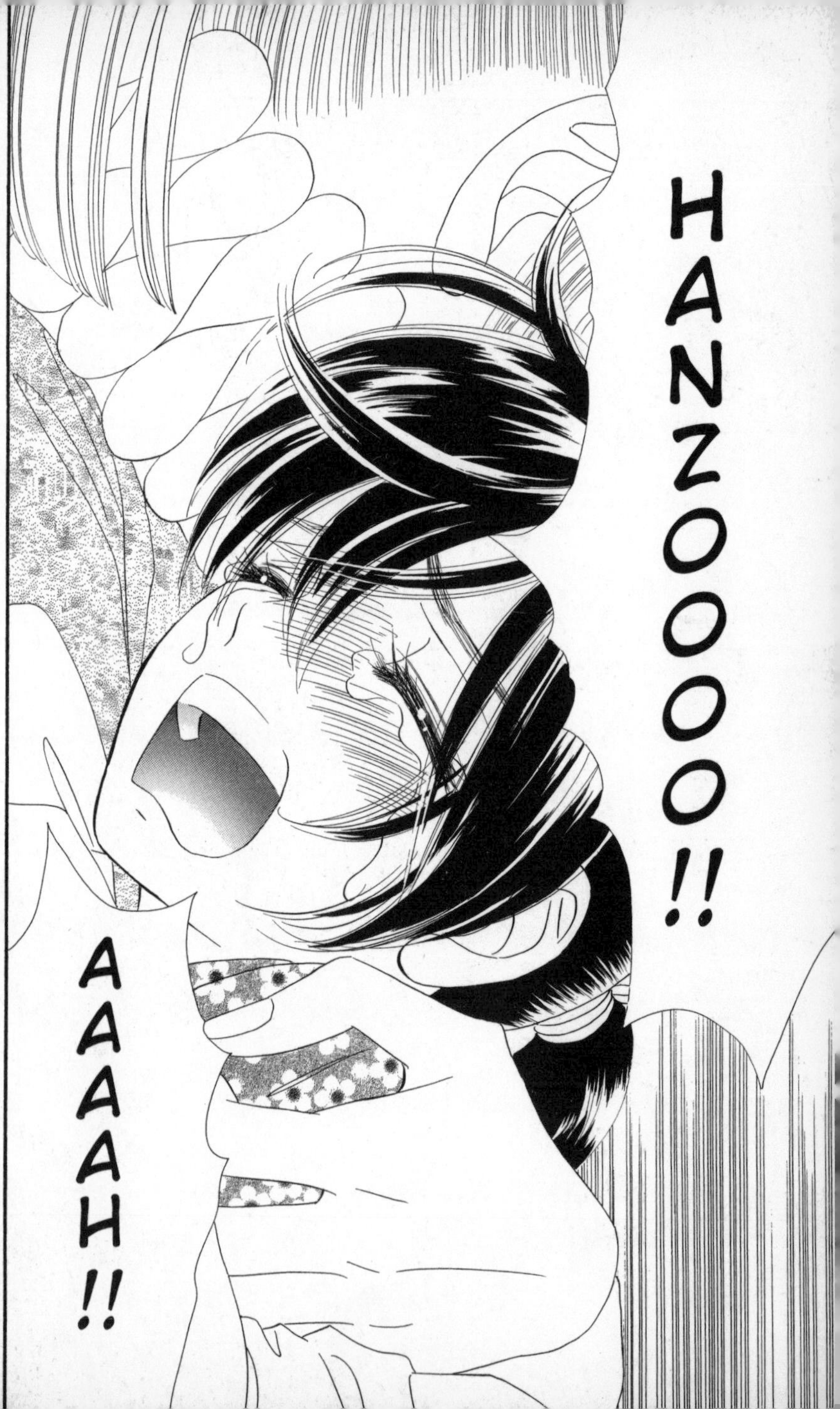
HANZOOOO!!
AAAAH!!

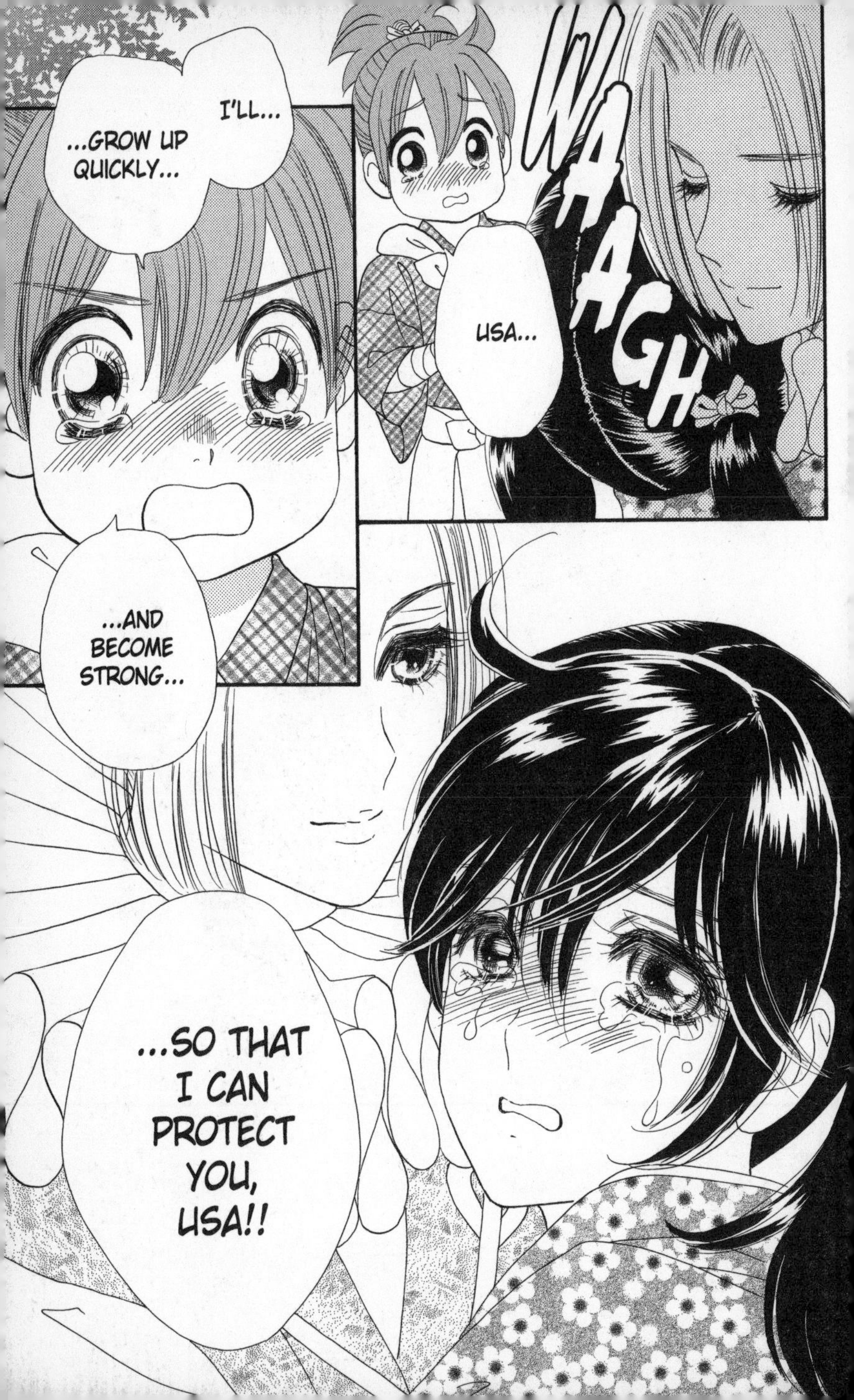
WAAGH
USA...
I'LL...
...GROW UP QUICKLY...
...AND BECOME STRONG...
...SO THAT I CAN PROTECT YOU, USA!!

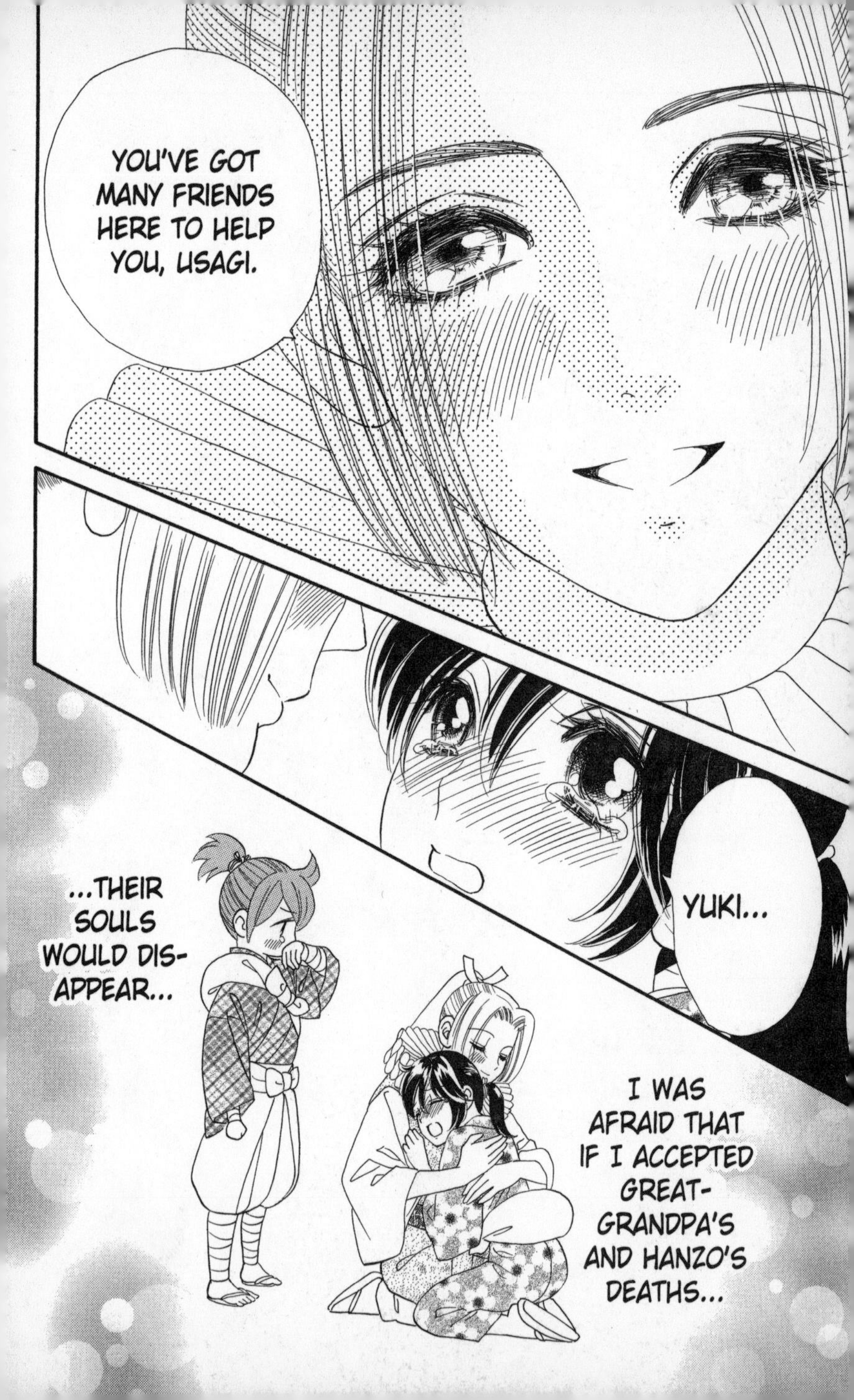
YOU'VE GOT MANY FRIENDS HERE TO HELP YOU, USAGI.
YUKI...
I WAS AFRAID THAT IF I ACCEPTED GREAT-GRANDPA'S AND HANZO'S DEATHS...
...THEIR SOULS WOULD DIS-APPEAR...

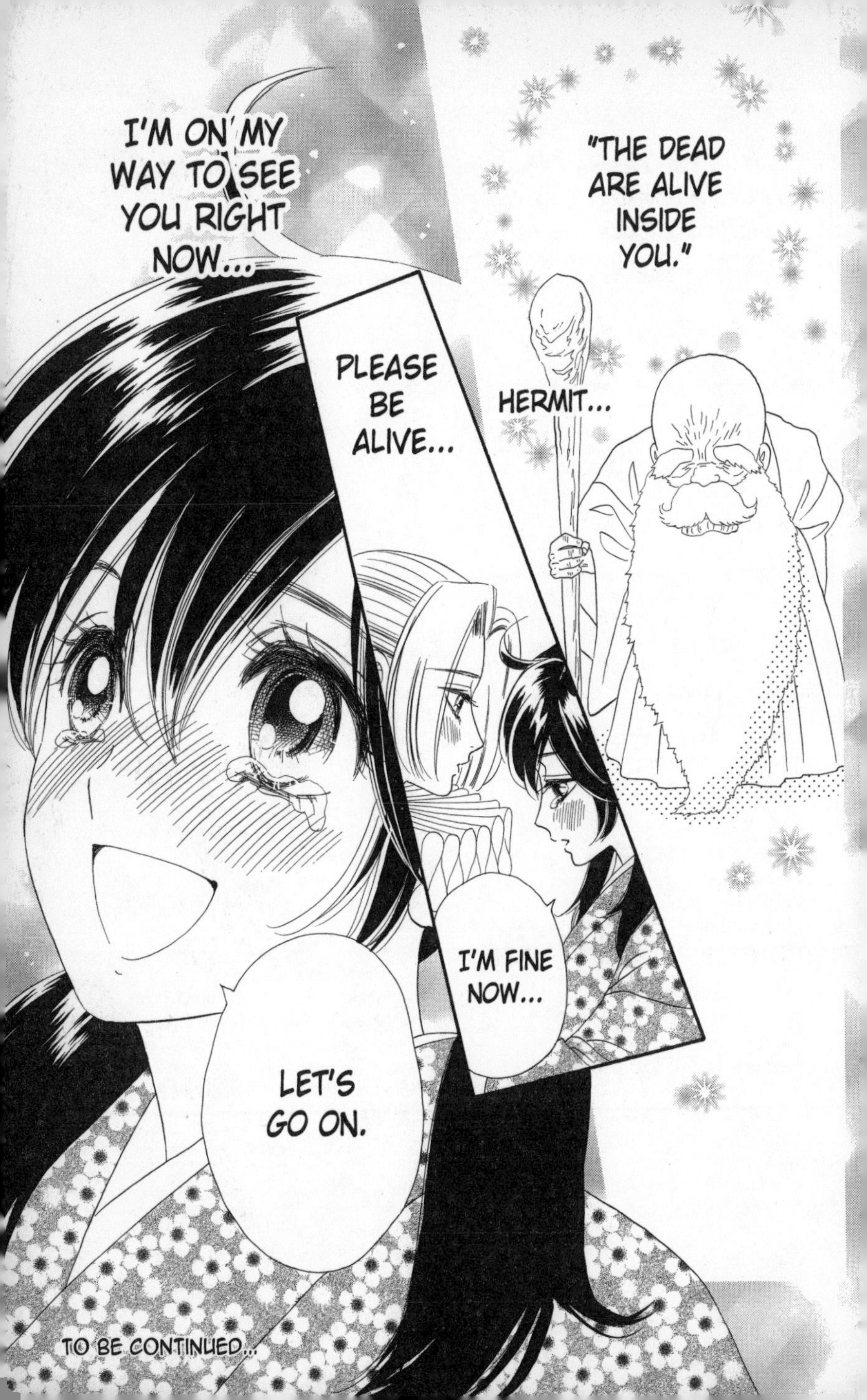

"THE DEAD ARE ALIVE INSIDE YOU."
HERMIT...
PLEASE BE ALIVE...
I'M FINE NOW...
I'M ON MY WAY TO SEE YOU RIGHT NOW...
LET'S GO ON.
TO BE CONTINUED...

The ways of the ninja are mysterious indeed, so here is a glossary of terms to help you navigate the intricacies of their world.

Page 5, panel 3: Kaeru
The phrase *Buji ni kaeru* means "Return home safely." The pun is on the word *kaeru*, which means "frog" as well as "return."

Page 10, panel 1: Sakai
Sakai is a city in Osaka prefecture that is one of the largest and most important seaports in Japan. Once known for samurai swords, Sakai is now famous for quality kitchen knives and other cutlery.

Page 56: Hanami
Hanami literally means "flower viewing," and it traditionally refers to having a picnic party while admiring the beauty of cherry blossoms.

Page 90, panel 1: Ranmaru Mori
Ranmaru Mori is one of Oda Nobunaga's most famous vassals. He became Nobunaga's attendant at a young age and was recognized for his talent and loyalty.

Page 101: Odawara
Odawara is a city in Kanagawa Prefecture, and Odawara Castle was the stronghold of various rulers in Japanese history because of its strong defenses and strategic location. The original castle was eventually destroyed by the Meiji government, but it was rebuilt in 1960.

Page 2: Shimo no Hanzo
Shimo no means "the Lower," and in this case refers to Hanzo's geographic location rather than social status.

Page 2: Iga
Iga is a region on the island of Honshu and also the name of the famous ninja clan that originated there. Another area famous for its ninja is Kouga, in the Shiga prefecture on Honshu. Many books claim that these two ninja clans were mortal enemies, but in reality inter-ninja relations were not as bad as stories might suggest.

Page 2: Oda Nobunaga
Oda Nobunaga lived from 1534 to 1582, and came close to unifying Japan. He is probably one of the most famous Japanese warlords. He was the first warlord to successfully incorporate the gun in battle and is notorious for his ruthlessness.

Page 2: Mitsuhide Akechi
Mitsuhide Akechi became one of Oda Nobunaga's retainers after Nobunaga's conquest of Mino province (now Gifu prefecture) in 1566. He is known to have been more of an intellectual and a pacifier than a warrior.

Page 3: JR
"JR" stands for "Japan Railways." About 70 percent of Japan's railway network is owned and operated by the JR Group.

Page 110, panel 1: Tokugawa Ieyasu
Tokugawa Ieyasu (1543-1616) was the first Shogun of the Tokugawa Shogunate. He made a small fishing village named Edo the center of his activities. Edo thrived and became a huge town and was later renamed Tokyo, the present capital.

Page 110, panel 1: Okazaki Castle
Okazaki Castle is in the city of Okazaki in Aichi Prefecture. This castle was home to various leaders throughout history, including Tokugawa Ieyasu. Though demolished in 1873, the castle was reconstructed in 1959.

Page 112, panel 4: Kanto
The Kanto region is to the east of Honshu and is made up of seven prefectures: Gunma, Tochigi, Ibaraki, Saitama, Tokyo, Chiba and Kanagawa.

Page 130, panel 2: Kunoichi
A term often used for female ninja. The word is spelled くノ一, and when combined, the letters form the kanji for woman, 女。

Page 146, panel 1: Azuchi Castle
Azuchi Castle was one of Oda Nobunaga's main castles. It is located on the shores of Lake Biwa in Shiga Prefecture. The castle's strategic location enabled Nobunaga to manage his foes more easily, namely the Uesugi clan to the north and the Mouri clan to the west.

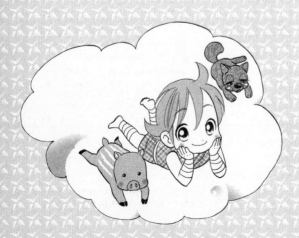

Hanzo, Age 2.

The battle of *Tensho Iga no Ran* is a historical fact, but it took a while for me to decide whether or not to include it in the story. It's going to be very sad to have the Iga Clan destroyed, and it's tough for me to draw that. But now that I've included it, I want to draw an Usagi who is unyielding to her sorrow and is making her way toward a bright future.

–Rinko Ueda

Rinko Ueda is from Nara prefecture. She enjoys listening to the radio, drama CDs, and Rakugo comedy performances. Her works include *Ryo*, a series based on the legend of Gojo Bridge, *Home*, a story about love crossing national boundaries, and *Tail of the Moon (Tsuki no Shippo)*, a romantic ninja comedy.

TAIL OF THE MOON

Vol. 12

The Shojo Beat Manga Edition

STORY & ART BY
RINKO UEDA

Translation & Adaptation/Tetsuichiro Miyaki
Touch-up Art & Lettering/Mark McMurray
Design/Izumi Hirayama
Editor/Amy Yu

Editor in Chief, Books/Alvin Lu
Editor in Chief, Magazines/Marc Weidenbaum
VP of Publishing Licensing/Rika Inouye
VP of Sales/Gonzalo Ferreyra
Sr. VP of Marketing/Liza Coppola
Publisher/Hyoe Narita

Printed in Canada

Published by VIZ Media, LLC
P.O. Box 77064
San Francisco, CA 94107

Shojo Beat Manga Edition
10 9 8 7 6 5 4 3 2 1
First printing, August 2008

www.viz.com

store.viz.com

PARENTAL ADVISORY
TAIL OF THE MOON is rated T+ for Older Teen and is recommended for ages 16 and up. This volume contains brief nudity and ninja violence.
ratings.viz.com

Save OVER 50% off the cover price!

Shojo Beat
MANGA from the HEART

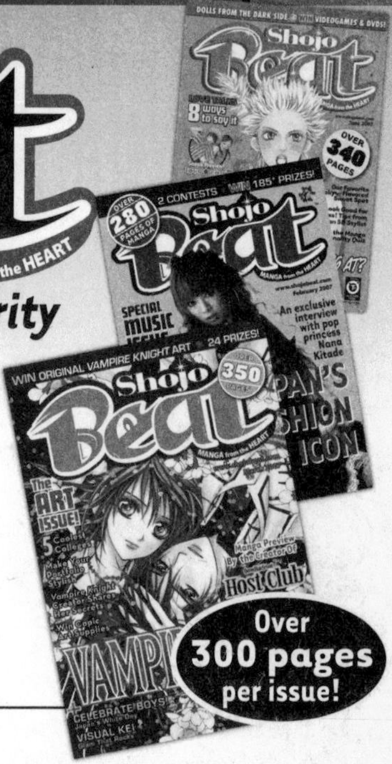
DOLLS FROM THE DARK SIDE
Shojo Beat
8 ways to say it
OVER 340 PAGES
2 CONTESTS
185* PRIZES!
OVER 280 PAGES OF MANGA
SPECIAL MUSIC
An exclusive interview with pop princess Nana Kitade
WIN ORIGINAL VAMPIRE KNIGHT ART
24 PRIZES!
OVER 350 PAGES
The ART ISSUE!
Host Club
VAMPI
CELEBRATE BOYS!
VISUAL KEI

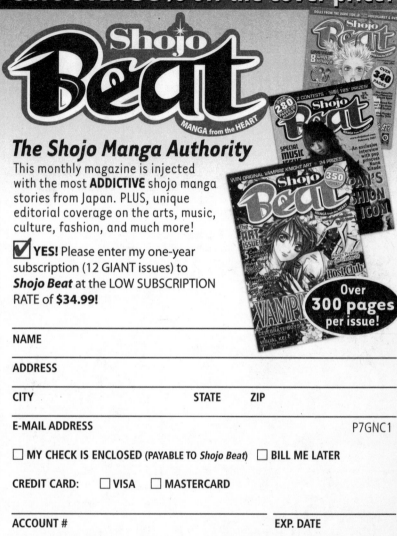

The Shojo Manga Authority

This monthly magazine is injected with the most **ADDICTIVE** shojo manga stories from Japan. PLUS, unique editorial coverage on the arts, music, culture, fashion, and much more!

Over **300 pages** per issue!

☑ **YES!** Please enter my one-year subscription (12 GIANT issues) to ***Shojo Beat*** at the LOW SUBSCRIPTION RATE of **$34.99!**

NAME

ADDRESS

CITY **STATE** **ZIP**

E-MAIL ADDRESS P7GNC1

☐ **MY CHECK IS ENCLOSED (PAYABLE TO *Shojo Beat*)** ☐ **BILL ME LATER**

CREDIT CARD: ☐ **VISA** ☐ **MASTERCARD**

ACCOUNT # **EXP. DATE**

SIGNATURE

CLIP AND MAIL TO

SHOJO BEAT
Subscriptions Service Dept.
P.O. Box 438
Mount Morris, IL 61054-0438

Canada price for 12 issues: $46.99 USD, including GST, HST and QST. US/CAN orders only. Allow 6-8 weeks for delivery. Must be 16 or older to redeem offer. By redeeming this offer I represent that I am 16 or older.

RATED T+ FOR OLDER TEEN
ratings.viz.com